Fodor's

Bed & Breakfasts, Country Inns, and Other Weekend Pleasures

MID-ATLANTIC REGION

Fodor's Travel Publications, Inc.
New York and London

First Edition

ISBN 0–679–01880–8

Fodor's Bed & Breakfasts, Country Inns,
and Other Weekend Pleasures: Mid-Atlantic Region

Editor: Conrad Little Paulus, with David Low, Denise Nolty, Carolyn Price, Linda K. Schmidt
Art Director: Fabrizio La Rocca
Cartographer: David Lindroth
Illustrators: Alida Beck, Karl Tanner
Cover Photograph: Geoffrey Clifford/Woodfin Camp
Design: Rochelle Udell and Fabrizio La Rocca

Special Sales

MANUFACTURED IN THE UNITED STATES OF AMERICA
10 9 8 7 6 5 4 3 2 1

Contributors

Susan Spano, *who lives in New York, contributed the chapters on Delaware, Maryland, Virginia, and West Virginia. She writes about travel for the* New York Times, New Woman, *and* British Heritage *and reviews books for* New York Newsday, Kirkus, *and the* Bloomsbury Review.

Alan Hines, *who wrote the chapter on Pennsylvania, is a novelist and screenwriter who lives in Bucks County, Pennsylvania. He adapted his novel* Square Dance *for the screen and has published articles in* American Artist *and the Exxon travel magazine.*

Bill Kent, *who wrote the chapter on New Jersey, lives in Philadelphia and specializes in the mid-Atlantic states. He is the author of* Fodor's Vacations on the Jersey Shore, *and has written* Under the Boardwalk *and the forthcoming* Down by the Sea, *both novels about Atlantic City.*

Deborah K. Shepherd, *author of the New York chapter, is a journalist and freelance writer who lives in upstate New York. She has been a contributor to* Reader's Digest General Books *and* Scholastic Magazine.

Contents

Foreword

While every care has been taken to ensure the accuracy of the information in this guide, the passage of time will always bring change, and, consequently, the publisher cannot accept responsibility for errors that may occur.

All prices and listings are based on information supplied to us at press time. Details may change, however, and the prudent traveler will avoid inconvenience by calling ahead.

Fodor's wants to hear about your travel experiences, both pleasant and unpleasant. When an inn or B&B fails to live up to its billing, let us know and we will investigate the complaint and revise our entries where the facts warrant it.

Send your letters to the editors of Fodor's Travel Publications, 201 E. 50th Street, New York, NY 10022.

Introduction

Fodor's Bed & Breakfasts, Country Inns, and Other Weekend Pleasures *is a complete weekend planner that tells you not just where to stay but how to enjoy yourself when you get there. We describe the B&Bs and country inns, of course, but we also help you organize trips around them, with information on everything from parks to beaches to antiques stores—as well as nightlife and memorable places to dine. We also include names and addresses of B&B reservation services, should properties we recommend be full or should you be inspired to go in search of additional places on your own. Reviews are divided by state and, within each state, by region.*

All inns are not created equal, and age in itself is no guarantee of good taste, quality, or charm. We therefore avoid the directory approach, preferring instead to discriminate—recommending the very best for travelers with different interests, budgets, and sensibilities.

It's a sad commentary on other B&B guides today that we feel obliged to tell you our reviewers visited every property in person, and that it is they, not the innkeepers, who wrote the reviews. No one paid a fee or promised to sell or promote the book, in order to be included in it. Fodor's has no stake in anything but the truth: A dark room with peeling wallpaper is not called quaint or atmospheric, it's called run-down; a gutted 18th-century barn with motel units at either end is called a gutted 18th-century barn with motel units at either end, not a historic inn.

Is there a difference between a B&B and a country inn? Not really, not any more; the public has blurred the distinction—hence our decision to include both in the title. There was a time when the B&B experience meant an extra

room in someone's home, often with paper-thin walls and
a shared bathroom full of bobby pins and used cotton balls.
But no longer; Laura Ashley has come to town with her
matching prints, and some B&Bs are as elegant as the
country's most venerable inns. The only distinction that
seems to hold is that a B&B was built as a private home
and an inn was built for paying guests. Most B&Bs, but
not all, serve breakfast, and some serve dinner, too; most
inns have full-service restaurants. B&Bs tend to be run by
their owners, creating a homey, family feeling (which can
be anathema to those who relish privacy), while inns are
often run by managers; but the reverse is true, too. B&Bs
can cost more than inns, or less. B&Bs tend to be smaller,
with fewer rooms, but not always. The truth is that many
B&Bs are called so only to circumvent local zoning laws.

What all places in this guide—B&Bs or country inns—offer
is the promise of a unique experience. Each is one of
a kind, and each exudes a sense of time and place. All are
destinations in themselves—not just places to put your
head at night, but an integral part of a weekend escape.

So trust us, the way you'd trust a knowledgeable, well-
traveled friend. And have a wonderful weekend!

***

A word about the service material in this guide:

A second address in parentheses is a mailing address that
differs from the actual address of the property. A double
room is for two people, regardless of the size or type of
beds; if you're looking for twin beds or a king- or queen-
size bed, be sure to ask.

*Rates are for two in the high season, and include breakfast;
ask about special packages and off-season discounts.
Mandatory state taxes are extra. Most places leave tipping
to the discretion of the visitor, but some add a service
charge to the bill; if the issue concerns you, inquire when
you make your reservation, not when you check out.*

*What we call a restaurant serves meals other than
breakfast and is usually open to the general public. Inns
listed as MAP (Modified American Plan) require guests to
pay for two meals, usually breakfast and dinner. The
requirement is usually enforced during the high season,
but an inn may waive it if it is otherwise unable to fill all
its rooms.*

*B&Bs don't have phones or TVs in rooms unless otherwise
noted. Pools and bicycles are free; "bike rentals" are not.
Properties are open year-round, unless otherwise noted.*

*Michael Spring
Editorial Director*

Mid-Atlantic Region

CANADA

Georgian Bay

Lake Ontario

Lake Erie

St. Lawrence River

VERMONT

Lake Champlain

Lake George

ADIRONDACK MOUNTAINS

Rutland

Saratoga Springs

Utica

Syracuse

Rochester

Niagara Falls

Buffalo

Jamestown

Warren

Bath

Binghamton

NEW YORK

CATSKILL MOUNTAINS

Hudson River

Albany

Northampton

Springfield

MASSACHUSETTS

Worcester

Hartford

CONNECTICUT

Waterbury

Bridgeport

Long Island Sound

Montauk

Southampton

LONG ISLAND

New York

Paterson

Poughkeepsie

Scranton

Stroudsburg

Williamsport

Youngstown

91

91

90

88

88

90

90

80

80

Special Features at a Glance

Name of Property	Accessible for Disabled	Antiques	On the Water	Good Value	Car Not Necessary	Full Meal Service	Historic Building	
DELAWARE								
The Addy Sea			✓				✓	
The Boulevard Bed-and-Breakfast				✓	✓			
Cantwell House		✓		✓			✓	
The Christina House	✓				✓	✓		
The Corner Cupboard Inn	✓					✓		
The David Finney Inn						✓	✓	
The Inn at Canal Square	✓		✓					
Janvier-Black House			✓				✓	
Lord and Hamilton Seaside Inn				✓				
The New Devon Inn	✓	✓						
The Pleasant Inn								
Spring Garden Bed-and-Breakfast Inn		✓		✓			✓	
The Towers		✓					✓	
MARYLAND								
The Admiral Fell Inn	✓		✓		✓	✓	✓	
The Atlantic Hotel		✓				✓	✓	
Back Creek Inn	✓		✓					
Brampton		✓					✓	
Chanceford Hall	✓	✓					✓	
Gibson's Lodgings	✓	✓					✓	
Glasgow Inn		✓	✓				✓	
The Inn at Antietam		✓						
The Inn at Buckeystown		✓					✓	

Romantic Hideaway	Luxurious	Pets Allowed	No Smoking Indoors	Good Place for Families	Near Arts Festivals	Beach Nearby	Cross-Country Ski Trail	Golf Within 5 Miles	Fitness Facilities	Good Biking Terrain	Skiing	Horseback Riding	Tennis	Swimming on Premises	Conference Facilities
				✓		✓									
				✓						✓					
	✓								✓						✓
		✓				✓				✓					
															✓
✓	✓					✓									✓
✓	✓		✓												
						✓				✓					
✓	✓					✓									✓
						✓				✓					
✓			✓							✓					
✓	✓		✓											✓	
✓	✓														✓
✓						✓				✓					
✓			✓		✓										
✓	✓							✓		✓					
✓	✓									✓				✓	
										✓					✓
✓			✓			✓		✓		✓			✓		
✓	✓						✓			✓					
✓										✓					

Name of Property	Accessible for Disabled	Antiques	On the Water	Good Value	Car Not Necessary	Full Meal Service	Historic Building
The Inn at Mitchell House		✓					✓
The Inn at Perry Cabin	✓	✓	✓			✓	✓
John S. McDaniel House				✓			✓
The Lighthouse Club at Fager's Island			✓				
The Marameade		✓					✓
The National Pike		✓					✓
Potomac View Farm			✓	✓			✓
Prince George Inn		✓					
The Robert Morris Inn		✓	✓			✓	✓
St. Michael's Manor		✓	✓	✓			✓
Shaw's Fancy		✓					
Spring Bank		✓					✓
State House Inn						✓	✓
The Strawberry Inn	✓	✓					✓
The Tavern Inn		✓	✓	✓			✓
The Turning Point		✓				✓	
Vandiver Inn		✓					✓
Victoriana		✓	✓				✓
Wades Point Inn	✓			✓			✓
The White Swan Tavern		✓					✓
The William Page Inn	✓	✓					
NEW JERSEY							
The Abbey Cape May		✓			✓		✓
Ashling Cottage		✓			✓		✓

Romantic Hideaway	Luxurious	Pets Allowed	No Smoking Indoors	Good Place for Families	Near Arts Festivals	Beach Nearby	Cross-Country Ski Trail	Golf Within 5 Miles	Fitness Facilities	Good Biking Terrain	Skiing	Horseback Riding	Tennis	Swimming on Premises	Conference Facilities
✓				✓						✓					
✓	✓									✓					
✓			✓					✓		✓					
	✓					✓			✓						✓
										✓					
										✓			✓		
✓				✓		✓				✓					
✓	✓					✓				✓			✓		
✓				✓		✓				✓					
✓		✓													
			✓							✓					
✓	✓														✓
										✓			✓		
✓										✓					
✓										✓					
✓														✓	
✓	✓							✓		✓					
✓			✓					✓		✓					
✓	✓							✓		✓					
	✓														
✓	✓		✓		✓	✓		✓		✓					
✓			✓		✓	✓		✓		✓					

	Name of Property	Accessible for Disabled	Antiques	On the Water	Good Value	Car Not Necessary	Full Meal Service	Historic Building
NJ 3	BarnaGate Bed and Breakfast		✓		✓	✓		✓
4	Barnard Good House (Cape May)		✓			✓		✓
5	Bayberry Barque		✓					✓
6	Cabbage Rose Inn		✓		✓			✓
7	Candlelight Inn		✓					✓
8	Captain Mey's Inn Cape May		✓			✓		✓
9	The Carriage House				✓	✓		
10	The Carroll Villa Cape May					✓	✓	✓
11	Cashelmara Inn		✓	✓		✓		✓
12	The Chalfonte Cape May described as "chab"		✓			✓	✓	✓
13	Charlesworth Hotel			✓				
14	The Chateau	✓				✓		
15	Chestnut Hill		✓			✓	✓	✓
16	Chimney Hill Farm		✓					✓
17	Colligan's Stockton Inn		✓				✓	
18	Columns by the Sea Cape May		✓	✓		✓		✓
19	Conover's Bay Head Inn		✓			✓		✓
20	Henry Ludlam Inn		✓	✓				✓
21	Holly House Cape May but share baths				✓			✓
22	Hollycroft		✓					✓
23	Inn at Millrace Pond		✓				✓	✓
24	Inn at the Ocean					✓		
25	Jeremiah H. Yereance House		✓			✓		✓
26	Jerica Hill		✓					✓
27	The Mainstay Inn and Cottage (Cape May)		✓			✓		✓

Romantic Hideaway	Luxurious	Pets Allowed	No Smoking Indoors	Good Place for Families	Near Arts Festivals	Beach Nearby	Cross-Country Ski Trail	Golf Within 5 Miles	Fitness Facilities	Good Biking Terrain	Skiing	Horseback Riding	Tennis	Swimming on Premises	Conference Facilities
			✓		✓	✓		✓		✓					
✓	✓		✓		✓	✓		✓		✓					
✓			✓		✓	✓				✓					
✓			✓		✓		✓	✓							
✓					✓	✓		✓		✓					
✓	✓		✓		✓	✓		✓		✓					
				✓	✓	✓		✓		✓					
			✓		✓			✓		✓					
✓			✓	✓	✓	✓		✓		✓					
			✓	✓	✓	✓		✓		✓					✓
				✓											
	✓			✓	✓	✓		✓		✓					
✓			✓		✓		✓	✓							
✓	✓		✓		✓		✓	✓							
	✓				✓		✓								✓
✓	✓		✓		✓	✓		✓		✓					
✓			✓		✓	✓		✓		✓					
			✓		✓			✓		✓				✓	
			✓		✓	✓		✓		✓					
✓			✓		✓	✓		✓		✓					
✓	✓			✓	✓		✓	✓		✓					✓
✓	✓					✓		✓		✓					✓
			✓	✓				✓		✓					
✓			✓		✓		✓	✓		✓					
✓	✓		✓		✓	✓		✓		✓					

Name of Property	Accessible for Disabled	Antiques	On the Water	Good Value	Car Not Necessary	Full Meal Service	Historic Building	
The Manor House *Cape May*		✓			✓		✓	
Normandy Inn		✓					✓	
Old Hunterdon House					✓		✓	
Peacock Inn		✓				✓	✓	
Pierrot by the Sea		✓					✓	
The Queen Victoria *Cape May*	✓	✓			✓		✓	
Sea Crest by the Sea		✓					✓	
The Seaflower		✓			✓		✓	
Springside *Cape May* *no bfast *share baths				✓	✓		✓	
Stewart Inn		✓		✓			✓	
The Studio		✓					✓	
Victoria Guest House		✓					✓	
The Victorian Rose *Cape May*		✓			✓		✓	
The Virginia Hotel *Cape May* *continental b-fast*					✓	✓	✓	
The Whistling Swan Inn		✓					✓	
Wilbraham Mansion and Inn *Cape May* *indoor pool					✓		✓	
The Wooden Rabbit *Cape May* *kids		✓			✓		✓	
NEW YORK								
The Adelphi Hotel		✓					✓	
Albergo Allegria				✓				
Anthony Dobbins Stagecoach Inn		✓		✓			✓	
The Balsam House			✓			✓		
Bassett House		✓						
Beaverkill Valley Inn	✓		✓			✓		

Handwritten page numbers in left margin: NJ 28, 29, 30, 31, 32, 33, 34, 35, 36, 37, 38, 39, 40, 41, 42, 43, 44

Romantic Hideaway	Luxurious	Pets Allowed	No Smoking Indoors	Good Place for Families	Near Arts Festivals	Beach Nearby	Cross-Country Ski Trail	Golf Within 5 Miles	Fitness Facilities	Good Biking Terrain	Skiing	Horseback Riding	Tennis	Swimming on Premises	Conference Facilities
			✓		✓	✓		✓		✓					
			✓		✓	✓		✓		✓					✓
✓	✓		✓	✓	✓		✓	✓		✓					
		✓			✓			✓		✓					✓
			✓		✓	✓		✓		✓					
	✓		✓		✓	✓		✓		✓					✓
✓			✓		✓	✓		✓		✓					
			✓		✓	✓		✓		✓					
			✓		✓	✓		✓		✓					
			✓		✓		✓	✓		✓				✓	
✓				✓	✓			✓		✓					
			✓		✓	✓				✓				✓	
✓			✓		✓	✓		✓		✓					
	✓				✓	✓		✓		✓					✓
			✓		✓		✓	✓		✓					
			✓		✓	✓		✓		✓				✓	
			✓	✓	✓	✓		✓		✓					
✓	✓				✓										
				✓	✓		✓	✓			✓			✓	
✓	✓						✓								
✓	✓			✓		✓	✓			✓				✓	
		✓			✓	✓				✓					
✓	✓			✓		✓	✓		✓	✓			✓	✓	✓

Name of Property	Accessible for Disabled	Antiques	On the Water	Good Value	Car Not Necessary	Full Meal Service	Historic Building	
The Bent Finial Manor		✓		✓			✓	
The Bird and Bottle Inn						✓	✓	
Captain Schoonmaker's Bed and Breakfast		✓	✓	✓			✓	
The Chester Inn		✓		✓			✓	
Chestnut Tree Inn		✓						
Country Road Lodge		✓		✓				
The Crary House				✓				
Crislip's Bed and Breakfast	✓			✓			✓	
Deer Mountain Inn						✓		
Donegal Manor Bed and Breakfast		✓		✓			✓	
The Eggery				✓				
Fox Manor				✓			✓	
The Friends Lake Inn			✓	✓		✓		
Greenville Arms		✓				✓	✓	
The Gregory House				✓		✓		
Hedges' Inn		✓			✓	✓		
The Hill Guest House				✓				
Hilltop Cottage Bed and Breakfast				✓				
Hudson House, A Country Inn		✓	✓		✓	✓	✓	
The Huntting Inn		✓			✓	✓	✓	
Inn at Lake Joseph			✓			✓	✓	
The Inn at Saratoga	✓	✓				✓		
The Inn at Shaker Mill				✓		✓	✓	
The Inn on Bacon Hill								
The Lamplight Inn								

Romantic Hideaway	Luxurious	Pets Allowed	No Smoking Indoors	Good Place for Families	Near Arts Festivals	Beach Nearby	Cross-Country Ski Trail	Golf Within 5 Miles	Fitness Facilities	Good Biking Terrain	Skiing	Horseback Riding	Tennis	Swimming on Premises	Conference Facilities
✓	✓														
✓	✓														
✓							✓			✓				✓	
✓				✓			✓				✓				
✓	✓		✓		✓			✓							
							✓				✓				
								✓			✓				
		✓	✓	✓											
✓	✓			✓		✓									
				✓											
				✓	✓		✓				✓	✓			
✓			✓	✓		✓				✓					
				✓			✓	✓		✓	✓			✓	✓
				✓	✓		✓			✓	✓			✓	✓
				✓		✓								✓	
✓							✓		✓	✓					
							✓			✓					
							✓								
				✓											
✓	✓						✓	✓		✓					✓
				✓			✓	✓		✓				✓	✓
				✓	✓			✓	✓						✓
✓		✓		✓	✓		✓			✓	✓			✓	✓
			✓		✓		✓			✓					
✓	✓					✓	✓			✓	✓	✓			

Name of Property	Accessible for Disabled	Antiques	On the Water	Good Value	Car Not Necessary	Full Meal Service	Historic Building	
Lanza's				✓		✓		
Le Chambord		✓				✓	✓	
The Maidstone Arms		✓			✓	✓	✓	
The Mansion		✓					✓	
Mansion Hill Inn						✓	✓	
Maple Ridge Inn		✓					✓	
The Martindale Bed and Breakfast Inn		✓		✓				
The Merrill Magee House	✓	✓		✓		✓	✓	
Mill House Inn (E. Hampton)		✓			✓		✓	
Mill House Inn (Stephentown)				✓				
The Old Post House Inn		✓				✓	✓	
Pig Hill Inn		✓			✓			
Plumbush Inn		✓				✓	✓	
Point Lookout Mountain Inn				✓		✓		
Ram's Head Inn			✓			✓		
The Redcoat's Return						✓		
Saratoga Bed and Breakfast		✓						
Saratoga Rose						✓	✓	
The Sedgwick Inn		✓		✓		✓	✓	
The 1770 House		✓			✓	✓	✓	
Simmons Way Village Inn		✓				✓	✓	
The Six Sisters		✓						
The Swiss Hutte		✓				✓		
Troutbeck		✓				✓	✓	
Village Latch Inn		✓					✓	

Romantic Hideaway	Luxurious	Pets Allowed	No Smoking Indoors	Good Place for Families	Near Arts Festivals	Beach Nearby	Cross-Country Ski Trail	Golf Within 5 Miles	Fitness Facilities	Good Biking Terrain	Skiing	Horseback Riding	Tennis	Swimming on Premises	Conference Facilities
							✓			✓					
✓	✓							✓							✓
✓	✓				✓	✓		✓		✓					
✓	✓				✓					✓				✓	
		✓													
✓	✓	✓	✓					✓		✓					
✓			✓								✓	✓			
				✓										✓	✓
✓			✓		✓	✓		✓		✓					
				✓			✓			✓	✓			✓	
✓						✓		✓		✓					
✓	✓		✓							✓					
✓	✓									✓					
		✓		✓	✓		✓			✓	✓				✓
✓	✓	✓		✓		✓				✓			✓	✓	✓
✓				✓	✓		✓			✓	✓				
				✓	✓			✓		✓					
✓							✓			✓					
✓		✓		✓			✓			✓	✓				✓
✓	✓				✓	✓		✓		✓					
✓	✓							✓		✓					✓
		✓		✓			✓	✓		✓					✓
		✓		✓	✓		✓	✓			✓	✓	✓		✓
✓	✓						✓	✓		✓			✓	✓	✓
✓	✓	✓		✓		✓		✓		✓			✓	✓	✓

Name of Property	Accessible for Disabled	Antiques	On the Water	Good Value	Car Not Necessary	Full Meal Service	Historic Building	
The Village Victorian Inn		✓						
The Westchester House		✓					✓	
PENNSYLVANIA								
Adamstown Inn		✓		✓				
Ash Mill Farm		✓		✓			✓	
The Bankhouse Bed and Breakfast				✓			✓	
Barley Sheaf Farm		✓					✓	
The Beach Lake Hotel		✓		✓		✓	✓	
The Bechtel Mansion Inn		✓		✓			✓	
Bed and Breakfast at Walnut Hill				✓				
Beechmont Inn		✓		✓				
The Brafferton Inn		✓		✓			✓	
Bridgeton House		✓	✓				✓	
Bucksville House		✓		✓			✓	
The Cameron Estate Inn	✓	✓				✓	✓	
Century Inn		✓		✓		✓	✓	
Churchtown Inn		✓		✓		✓	✓	
Clearview Farm Bed and Breakfast		✓		✓			✓	
Cliff Park Inn		✓				✓	✓	
Doneckers	✓	✓		✓		✓	✓	
The Doubleday Inn		✓		✓				
Duling-Kurtz House and Country Inn				✓		✓	✓	
Emig Mansion		✓					✓	
Evermay-on-the-Delaware		✓	✓	✓		✓	✓	

Romantic Hideaway	Luxurious	Pets Allowed	No Smoking Indoors	Good Place for Families	Near Arts Festivals	Beach Nearby	Cross-Country Ski Trail	Golf Within 5 Miles	Fitness Facilities	Good Biking Terrain	Skiing	Horseback Riding	Tennis	Swimming on Premises	Conference Facilities
✓	✓									✓					
✓	✓		✓		✓		✓	✓		✓					
					✓						✓				
✓			✓	✓	✓										
			✓	✓	✓										
✓	✓				✓									✓	✓
✓															
✓	✓		✓												
✓					✓					✓					
✓				✓	✓					✓					
✓				✓	✓		✓	✓		✓					
✓			✓	✓	✓					✓		✓			
✓	✓						✓	✓		✓	✓	✓	✓		✓
✓	✓			✓									✓		
✓	✓			✓	✓		✓			✓					
✓			✓	✓	✓		✓	✓		✓					
				✓			✓	✓		✓	✓				✓
				✓	✓					✓					
✓	✓		✓	✓	✓		✓			✓					
	✓			✓	✓			✓		✓					✓
✓	✓		✓												✓
✓	✓				✓					✓					

Name of Property	Accessible for Disabled	Antiques	On the Water	Good Value	Car Not Necessary	Full Meal Service	Historic Building	
Fairfield Inn		✓				✓	✓	
Fairville Inn		✓		✓			✓	
The French Manor						✓		
General Sutter Inn		✓		✓		✓	✓	
Glasbern						✓		
Harry Packer Mansion		✓		✓			✓	
Highland Farms		✓		✓			✓	
Highpoint Victoriana		✓		✓				
The Historic Farnsworth House Inn		✓		✓		✓	✓	
The Inn at Fordhook Farm		✓					✓	
The Inn at Meadowbrook		✓		✓		✓	✓	
Inn at Phillips Mill		✓	✓	✓		✓	✓	
The Inn at Starlight Lake			✓	✓		✓	✓	
Isaac Stover House		✓	✓				✓	
The King's Cottage		✓						
Limestone Inn		✓		✓			✓	
The Logan Inn			✓	✓	✓	✓	✓	
Longswamp Bed and Breakfast		✓		✓			✓	
Meadow Spring Farm		✓		✓				
The Mercersburg Inn		✓				✓	✓	
The Old Appleford Inn		✓		✓			✓	
The Overlook Inn						✓	✓	
Pace One						✓	✓	
Patchwork Inn		✓		✓				
Pineapple Hill		✓		✓			✓	

Romantic Hideaway	Luxurious	Pets Allowed	No Smoking Indoors	Good Place for Families	Near Arts Festivals	Beach Nearby	Cross-Country Ski Trail	Golf Within 5 Miles	Fitness Facilities	Good Biking Terrain	Skiing	Horseback Riding	Tennis	Swimming on Premises	Conference Facilities
✓				✓	✓		✓			✓	✓				
✓	✓			✓	✓					✓					
✓	✓									✓					
		✓		✓	✓										✓
✓	✓			✓				✓		✓				✓	✓
✓	✓														
✓				✓	✓			✓		✓			✓	✓	
✓				✓				✓		✓					
✓				✓	✓										
✓	✓		✓	✓				✓		✓					✓
✓				✓	✓		✓			✓	✓	✓	✓	✓	
✓	✓			✓			✓			✓					
✓				✓		✓	✓			✓	✓		✓	✓	✓
✓	✓			✓			✓			✓					
			✓		✓										
✓				✓	✓					✓					
				✓	✓										✓
✓	✓			✓				✓		✓					
				✓						✓				✓	
✓	✓		✓	✓	✓			✓	✓	✓	✓				✓
✓			✓	✓	✓			✓		✓					
✓				✓	✓			✓	✓	✓	✓			✓	✓
			✓					✓		✓	✓	✓	✓	✓	✓
			✓	✓	✓					✓					
✓			✓		✓					✓				✓	

Name of Property	Accessible for Disabled	Antiques	On the Water	Good Value	Car Not Necessary	Full Meal Service	Historic Building	
Pine Knob Inn				✓		✓		
Pinetree Farm		✓					✓	
The Settler's Inn						✓	✓	
Smithton Country Inn		✓		✓			✓	
Stottsville Inn		✓				✓	✓	
Sweetwater Farm		✓	✓			✓	✓	
Swiss Woods	✓			✓				
The Tannery Bed and Breakfast				✓	✓			
The Wedgwood Inn		✓						
The Whitehall Inn	✓	✓		✓			✓	
White Rock Farm Guest House				✓				
The Whitethorne				✓				
VIRGINIA								
Applewood		✓						
The Ashby Inn		✓					✓	
The Bailiwick Inn	✓	✓					✓	
Belle Grae Inn	✓	✓				✓	✓	
Boxwood		✓	✓	✓				
Brookside		✓					✓	
Buckhorn Inn				✓		✓	✓	
The Burton House								
Caledonia Farm		✓					✓	
The Channel Bass Inn		✓						
Chester		✓					✓	

Romantic Hideaway	Luxurious	Pets Allowed	No Smoking Indoors	Good Place for Families	Near Arts Festivals	Beach Nearby	Cross-Country Ski Trail	Golf Within 5 Miles	Fitness Facilities	Good Biking Terrain	Skiing	Horseback Riding	Tennis	Swimming on Premises	Conference Facilities
					✓		✓	✓		✓	✓		✓	✓	✓
✓	✓		✓				✓	✓		✓			✓	✓	
		✓		✓		✓	✓	✓		✓	✓				✓
✓	✓	✓	✓		✓										
✓					✓		✓	✓		✓					✓
✓	✓	✓			✓		✓	✓		✓				✓	✓
				✓	✓	✓	✓			✓	✓				
				✓	✓	✓									
✓	✓		✓	✓											
✓	✓		✓	✓			✓			✓					
			✓	✓						✓					
✓			✓	✓			✓			✓					
			✓	✓											
✓							✓			✓		✓			
✓	✓		✓	✓											
								✓	✓				✓		✓
✓			✓								✓			✓	
✓	✓		✓							✓		✓			
						✓				✓					
										✓					
✓			✓				✓			✓			✓		✓
✓	✓					✓				✓					
✓										✓					

Name of Property	Accessible for Disabled	Antiques	On the Water	Good Value	Car Not Necessary	Full Meal Service	Historic Building	
Clifton		✓					✓	
Colonial Capital		✓						
Colonial Manor Inn				✓				
The Conyers House		✓					✓	
Edgewood		✓					✓	
Fassifern		✓					✓	
Fort Lewis Lodge			✓	✓		✓		
Fountain Hall	✓	✓		✓				
The Garden and the Sea		✓					✓	
High Meadows		✓					✓	
Hotel Strasburg		✓				✓	✓	
The Inn at Gristmill Square		✓					✓	
The Inn at Little Washington		✓				✓		
The Inn at Monticello		✓					✓	
The Inn at Narrow Passage		✓	✓				✓	
Jordan Hollow Farm						✓	✓	
Joshua Wilton House		✓					✓	
L'Auberge Provençale		✓					✓	
Liberty Rose		✓						
Mayhurst		✓					✓	
Miss Molly's and the Little Traveller Inn		✓	✓	✓			✓	
The Morrison House	✓				✓	✓		
Newport House		✓						
The Norris House		✓					✓	
North Bend Plantation		✓	✓	✓			✓	

Romantic Hideaway	Luxurious	Pets Allowed	No Smoking Indoors	Good Place for Families	Near Arts Festivals	Beach Nearby	Cross-Country Ski Trail	Golf Within 5 Miles	Fitness Facilities	Good Biking Terrain	Skiing	Horseback Riding	Tennis	Swimming on Premises	Conference Facilities
✓	✓									✓			✓	✓	
				✓						✓					
✓		✓						✓		✓		✓			
✓										✓				✓	
			✓									✓			
✓				✓				✓		✓				✓	✓
✓	✓					✓									
✓	✓	✓	✓							✓					
		✓						✓				✓	✓		
✓	✓									✓		✓			
			✓							✓				✓	
✓				✓			✓				✓			✓	✓
✓				✓			✓			✓	✓	✓			
	✓										✓				
✓	✓						✓					✓			
✓			✓							✓					
✓		✓								✓					
				✓		✓									
✓	✓				✓			✓							
			✓												
✓			✓												
				✓						✓					

Name of Property	Accessible for Disabled	Antiques	On the Water	Good Value	Car Not Necessary	Full Meal Service	Historic Building	
Nottingham Ridge		✓	✓	✓				
Oak Spring Farm and Vineyard		✓		✓			✓	
Pickett's Harbor		✓	✓	✓				
The Pink House		✓					✓	
Prospect Hill		✓					✓	
The Red Fox Inn		✓				✓	✓	
The Richard Johnston Inn		✓					✓	
Sea Gate								
The Shadows		✓					✓	
The Silver Thatch Inn		✓					✓	
Sleepy Hollow Farm				✓				
Sycamore Hill								
Thornrose House		✓		✓				
Trillium House								
200 South Street		✓						
War Hill Inn		✓		✓				
Welbourne		✓		✓			✓	
Willow Grove Plantation		✓					✓	
Woodstock Hall		✓					✓	
The Year of the Horse			✓					
WEST VIRGINIA								
Aspen Hall		✓					✓	
Boydville		✓					✓	
The Cardinal Inn		✓		✓			✓	

Romantic Hideaway	Luxurious	Pets Allowed	No Smoking Indoors	Good Place for Families	Near Arts Festivals	Beach Nearby	Cross-Country Ski Trail	Golf Within 5 Miles	Fitness Facilities	Good Biking Terrain	Skiing	Horseback Riding	Tennis	Swimming on Premises	Conference Facilities
			✓	✓		✓				✓					
✓			✓												
✓			✓			✓				✓				✓	
✓					✓					✓					
✓	✓							✓						✓	✓
	✓									✓					
			✓												
						✓				✓					
✓			✓	✓						✓					
✓			✓										✓		
				✓						✓					
✓												✓			
			✓					✓					✓		
							✓	✓	✓		✓	✓	✓	✓	
	✓														
			✓	✓											
✓		✓								✓		✓			
										✓					
✓			✓							✓					
				✓		✓									
			✓							✓					
✓			✓							✓					
			✓	✓				✓		✓	✓				

Name of Property	Accessible for Disabled	Antiques	On the Water	Good Value	Car Not Necessary	Full Meal Service	Historic Building	
The Carriage Inn		✓					✓	
Cheat Mountain Club			✓	✓		✓	✓	
The Cottonwood Inn		✓					✓	
The Country Inn				✓		✓		
The Current		✓	✓	✓				
Dunn Country Inn		✓					✓	
The General Lewis Inn		✓				✓	✓	
Hampshire House 1884		✓						
Highlawn		✓					✓	
Hillbrook		✓					✓	
Hilltop House Hotel and Restaurant				✓		✓	✓	
The Inn at Elk River			✓	✓				
James Wylie House		✓					✓	
Lynn's Inn				✓				
Prospect Hill		✓					✓	
The Thomas Shepherd Inn		✓					✓	
The View								
The Wayside Inn		✓		✓			✓	

Romantic Hideaway	Luxurious	Pets Allowed	No Smoking Indoors	Good Place for Families	Near Arts Festivals	Beach Nearby	Cross-Country Ski Trail	Golf Within 5 Miles	Fitness Facilities	Good Biking Terrain	Skiing	Horseback Riding	Tennis	Swimming on Premises	Conference Facilities
										✓					
							✓			✓	✓				
				✓						✓					
							✓	✓	✓		✓	✓			✓
			✓	✓			✓			✓	✓				
				✓						✓					
		✓		✓				✓					✓		✓
				✓											
							✓	✓			✓	✓			
✓	✓									✓					
				✓											✓
				✓			✓			✓	✓				
			✓					✓					✓		
			✓					✓					✓		
				✓			✓			✓	✓				
			✓							✓					
			✓		✓		✓				✓		✓		

New York

New York

Kawartha Lakes

Ogdensburg

Kingston

Watertown

Adams

Lowvi

Lake Ontario

Oswego

Fulton

Cleveland

37

81

1

104

81

Niagara Falls

Lockport

Medina

Brockport

Rochester

Clyde

Syracuse

Or

104

104

90

Batavia

Canandaigua

Geneva

Auburn

Cazenov

Lake Erie

Buffalo

Warsaw

Finger Lakes

20

Penn Yan

Interlaken

Springfield

Genesee River

Dryden

81

90

Gowanda

390

Watkins Glen

Whitney Point

Ithaca

Franklinville

Bath

Wellsville

17

Jamestown

Olean

Corning

Elmira

Binghamton

17

Scranton

N

PENNSYLVANIA

Wilkes-Barre

0   60 miles

0   90 km

Allentow

The Lake George Region

At the gateway to a six-million-acre forest preserve known as Adirondack Park lies 32-mile-long Lake George, a four-season nirvana for those who like to vacation outdoors amid pine groves and pristine lakes. To be honest, not all of this "Queen of American Lakes" is pristine. There are plenty of ersatz Indian tepees, neon motel signs, and cheap-souvenir emporiums—in Lake George Village and at other lakeside outposts. Yet the lake itself, although not immune to 20th-century evils of acid rain and other pollutants, is probably as lovely as it was when it was discovered, in 1646. Other beautiful waterways in the area, most notably Lake Luzerne, Friends Lake, the Sacandaga River, and the northernmost reaches of the Hudson River, are worth visiting.

All this water naturally encourages water sports, including fishing for record-breaking bass and white-water rafting. Visitors also enjoy canoeing, swimming, and sunning on lakeside beaches. At times other than the peak summer season travelers come to the region for hiking, mountain climbing, and bird-watching; in winter they're drawn to the many cross-country ski trails and the excellent downhill slopes of Gore Mountain and Hickory Ski Center where skiers at all levels will find reasonable lift rates and no long lines.

The area near Lake Luzerne is, surprisingly, dude-ranch country and the home of the oldest rodeo in the United States. Horses are available for trail rides. Warrensburg, an old lumber-mill town with more than 40 antiques shops, is a mecca for those seeking the perfect Adirondack chair, twig settee, or Victorian washstand. The region also has a variety of restaurants from which to choose. You'll find everything from exceptional hamburgers (at a roadside shack in Lake Luzerne called the Brass Bucket, where

there's sometimes a two-hour wait), to haute cuisine, in
places where you might expect more modest fare.

Places to go, sights to see

Fort William Henry (Lake George Village, tel. 518/668–5471). The British
constructed the fort in 1755; it was burned by the French in 1757. The
restored complex presents visitors with a picture of life during the French
and Indian War, and history tours, with demonstrations of military skills, are
given in July and August.

Great Escape Fun Park (Lake George, tel. 518/792–6568). New York State's
largest theme park, Great Escape has 100 rides and attractions with names
like Steamin' Demon Loop Corkscrew Rollercoaster and Raging River Ride.

Hyde House (Glens Falls, tel. 518/792–1761). A 1912 Italian Renaissance–
style mansion, is filled with a collection of French 18th-century and Italian
Renaissance antiques and also houses **The Hyde Collection** of Old Masters
and American art, from the late-Gothic to the 20th century.

Lake George Steamboat Cruises (tel. 518/668–5777) and **Lake George
Shoreline Cruises** (tel. 518/668–4644) offer many lake tours, including
brunch, lunch, dinner, and moonlight cruises, some with entertainment and
some on an authentic Mississippi paddle wheeler, the *Minne-Ha-Ha*.

World's Largest Garage Sale. Each fall in Warrensburg more than 500
dealers and private sellers gather to purvey a mixed bag that might contain
anything from priceless antiques to tomorrow's collectibles (Batman
lunchboxes, anyone?). More than 150,000 visitors attend. For exact dates, call
the Warrensburg Chamber of Commerce (tel. 518/623–2161).

Tourist Information

Chestertown Chamber of Commerce (Chestertown 12817, tel. 518/494–2722).
Lake George Chamber of Commerce (Box 272, Lake George 12845, tel.
518/668–5755). **Lake Luzerne Chamber of Commerce** (Bridge St., Box 222,
Lake Luzerne 12846, tel. 518/696–3500). **Warren County Department of
Tourism** (Municipal Center, Lake George 12845, tel. 518/793–1300, 24-hour
events hot line).

Reservation Services

American Country Collection (984 Gloucester Pl., Schenectady 12309, tel.
518/370–4948). **Bed and Breakfast Association of Saratoga, Lake George
and Gore Mountain Region** (Box 99, Lake Luzerne 12846, for brochure on
member establishments).

The Balsam House

A forest preserve, mountain views, a private beach on Friends Lake, comfortable rooms, and sophisticated fare—you'll find all these at Balsam House. Built in 1845 as a farmhouse, the building became a vacation lodge in 1891; in 1982 owner Frank Ellis turned it into a year-round, full-service inn. Innkeepers Alison and Shaun Green, assisted by an able and knowledgeable staff, make sure guests lack nothing during their stay.

Guests have access to all the offerings of the Adirondacks, but they're certainly not roughing it in the wilderness. The bold Victorian decor (with a parlor painted a deep plum color and a forest-green living room enhanced by mauve rattan chairs and an Oriental rug) and the Perrier Jouet in the inn's French restaurant come as a surprise in this off-the-beaten-track location, but, delightfully, it all works.

A few Victorian antiques furnish the guest rooms, and chenille spreads cover several of the beds. There's a bilevel suite with a narrow spiral staircase, and a downstairs suite offers a wet bar and a pull-out sofa. Upstairs is a chamber with a king-size canopy bed. Room 30 features a skylight and a view of nearby Gore Mountain.

The inn's beach on Friends Lake has its own dock, canoes, paddleboat, and screened bungalow. Bikes are available for rental, and hiking trails abound. Winter sports fans will find nearby cross-country ski trails, and they can also go ice fishing on Friends Lake. The inn's two restaurants offer cosmopolitan cuisine. Escargots, ceviche, and duck *framboise* may be accompanied by a selection from Le Papillon's extensive wine list. Open-grill specialties are served in the pine-panel 1891 Room.

The actress Mary Frann, from TV's "Newhart," stayed at the inn to soak up atmosphere and pick up pointers from Alison and Shaun before assuming the role of innkeeper on that long-running show. Rumor has it that the three backwoods brothers on the show—Larry, Darryl, and Darryl—were inspired by a couple of colorful locals who stop in here from time to time. Larry, Darryl, and Darryl—and vintage champagne? Somehow nothing seems incongruous here. It all adds up to a delightful, and memorable, stay.

Address: *Friends Lake, Chestertown, NY 12817, tel. 518/494-2828, fax 518/494-4431.*
Accommodations: *19 double rooms with baths, 1 suite.*
Amenities: *Restaurants, air-conditioning in some rooms, TV in parlor.*
Rates: *$75–$110; full breakfast; MAP available. AE, DC, MC, V.*
Restrictions: *No pets, 2-night minimum on weekends, closed 3 weeks in Nov. and 3 weeks in spring.*

The Bent Finial Manor

The Bent Finial, definitely among the most elegant, is certainly one of the most opulent of the bed-and-breakfasts in the area. The stunning, 1904 Queen Anne Victorian mansion opened in 1989. Owner Patricia Scully, a former vice president for an oil-and-gas company, searched for three years from Maine to South Carolina before she found her dream house, which was built by cattle baron Lewis Thomson.

During the Civil War Thomson made his fortune supplying beef to Union troops. Like many of the nouveaux riches of his era, he wanted his home to duplicate the opulent excesses of the European nobility—and he succeeded. Twenty-three kinds of wood—including oak, birch, hemlock, pine, and several varieties of cherry—make up the floors, moldings, wainscoting, and the impressive staircase. You enter the front parlor between Corinthian columns; all the rooms have their original beveled, etched, or stained-glass windows.

It's to Pat's credit that the furnishings do justice to this magnificent house. The parlor contains a Victorian game table (for chess, cards, or backgammon). Breakfast is served on a Victorian dining table set with antique linens and fine china. The color scheme in the upstairs Master Chamber complements the plum hues of its stained-glass windows. The Eastlake Chamber, furnished in eponymous style, has an antique dressmaker's dummy clothed in a Victorian frock—"My first guest," jokes Pat.

Pat's sense of whimsy is reflected in the antique Teddy bear (dressed like Theodore Roosevelt, complete with wire-rim glasses) perched on the stairway landing—and Teddy also reflects her sense of history. When President William McKinley died, Roosevelt was on an Adirondack camping trip. He was sworn in as president in the railroad station of the neighboring town of North Creek. Roosevelt brought the rich and famous to the Adirondacks. Fortunately, today's guests needn't be wealthy or well known to enjoy the Bent Finial's architectural legacy.

Address: *194 Main St., Warrensburg, NY 12885, tel. 518/623–3308.*
Accommodations: *4 double rooms with baths.*
Amenities: *1 room with fireplace and private porch.*
Rates: *$65–$85; full breakfast. No credit cards.*
Restrictions: *No smoking in bedrooms, no pets.*

The Lamplight Inn

In 1890 the Lamplight Inn, a grand Victorian Gothic in the village of Lake Luzerne, was built by a wealthy bachelor lumberman as his summer playhouse. One can only guess at the romantic trysts of this 19th-century playboy, but adjoining doors (no longer used) to two other bedrooms from the master bedroom hint at the possibilities.

Today, the Lamplight is a romantic bed-and-breakfast for 20th-century guests, thanks to innkeepers Gene and Linda Merlino. The couple were still dating when they bought this mansion on a whim. Within a year they were husband and wife; they spent their honeymoon painting the front porch. Honeymooning guests and couples who may or may not be considering a wedding in the future love the Lamplight, as room-diary accolades attest: "Our privacy was respected and our newness as a couple treated with gentleness and humor," one newlywed wrote, and there have been quite a few proposals uttered on bended knee under this romantic roof.

The decor helps considerably. The downstairs sitting room has its original chestnut molding, wainscoting, and unusual keyhole staircase. On cool evenings the room is lit by two fireplaces. Wicker chairs beckon visitors to the comfortable front porch, and the airy dining room provides the perfect backdrop for Linda's granola and muffins and Gene's peach crepes and three-egg omelets.

Guest rooms are Victorian in the romantic sense of the word—they are flowery and lacy. One of the nicest places to stay is the Canopy Room, with an original carved-oak mantel, hearth tiles, and a gas fireplace. In a newly constructed wing is a unique room that perfectly matches the rest of the house: The Skylight Room has a carved-oak, high-back Victorian bed covered in an antique patchwork quilt, with a skylight overhead. It's hard to choose a room here, because so much love and attention to detail have gone into each one.

A guest entry in the Canopy Room diary probably sums up the Lamplight experience best: "Your rocking chairs, soft quilts, and warm hospitality have transformed us back into human beings."

And isn't that the purpose of getting away from it all?

Address: *2129 Lake Ave., Box 70, Lake Luzerne, NY 12846, tel. 518/696-5294.*
Accommodations: *10 double rooms with baths.*
Amenities: *Air-conditioning, 5 rooms with fireplaces; beach across street.*
Rates: *$65–$125; full breakfast. AE.*
Restrictions: *No smoking in bedrooms, no pipes or cigars, no pets, 2-night minimum on weekends.*

The Chester Inn

Since it was built, in 1837, only three families have occupied the Greek Revival mansion that now houses The Chester Inn Bed and Breakfast. The inn, on Chestertown's Main Street, was the home of Charles Fowler, a wealthy merchant. His son-in-law commanded the 118th Adirondack Regiment during the Civil War.

A love of history and fond memories of European B&B stays persuaded Bruce and Suzanne Robbins to open an inn. Bruce, who had worked in construction, and Sue, who was in retail sales, carefully researched the house's past and attended to every detail in its restoration (they even had an original shade of paint reproduced by computer). Guests are pampered with candlelit breakfasts served on Syracuse Federal-style china. Three guest rooms are furnished with Victorian antiques; and a fourth, the Library Suite, is decorated in a spare, Shaker-like manner. While in Chestertown, don't miss the Robbinses' restored, turn-of-the-century ice-cream parlor, one block from the inn.

Address: *Box 163, Main St., Chestertown NY 12817, tel. 518/494-4148.*
Accommodations: *2 double rooms with baths, 2 suites.*
Amenities: *Dinner available, cross-country ski trails.*
Rates: *$85–$100; full breakfast. MC, V.*
Restrictions: *No smoking, no pets, 2-night minimum on holiday weekends.*

Country Road Lodge

You'll find nothing fancy at the Country Road Lodge: This was once a small, rustic camp cottage at the end of a long, winding dirt road, and, with some additions and improvements, it still is. The real draw here is the location. The lodge sits on the bank of what seems to be a captivating country creek; on closer inspection it turns out to be the Hudson River. You are also offered a terrific mountain vista. An abandoned logging road runs from the river into the woods—it becomes a primitive cross-country ski trail in winter and is perfect for hiking the rest of the year.

Innkeepers Steve and Sandi Parisi keep the small guest rooms clean and comfortable; the unpretentious decor is "early garage sale," with some nice patchwork quilts. Steve worked on Madison Avenue before opening the lodge to skiers in 1974 (the Hickory Ski Center—Mogul Madness—is just down the way). Hearty breakfasts are provided for hikers, skiers, and those who wish to just sit on the riverbank and commune with nature. Good conversation abounds: The meal sometimes lasts for hours.

Address: *HCR 1, No. 227 Hickory Hill Rd., Warrensburg, NY 12885, tel. 518/623-2207.*
Accommodations: *4 double rooms share 2 baths.*
Amenities: *Lunch and dinner served on winter weekends.*
Rates: *$52; full breakfast. No credit cards.*
Restrictions: *No pets.*

Crislip's Bed and Breakfast

You can see the Green Mountains of Vermont from the Italianate veranda of the Crislip's Bed and Breakfast. The Federal house, built around 1813 and remodeled in 1848 in the popular Greek Revival style, was owned by Queensbury's first doctor, who later became town supervisor. Queensbury is about halfway between Saratoga Springs and Lake George—near, but just far enough off the beaten track.

Joyce Crislip is a former teacher, and her husband, Ned, teaches music. The hosts' musical interests are in evidence throughout the house: A Steinway grand piano is the focal point of the living room; the framed, 15th-century score of a Gregorian chant hangs on the wall of the studio; and a rare 1830 E. N.

Sheer Philadelphia pianoforte, one of five in the country, graces a hallway. The Blue Room, with its canopied, carved mahogany bed and mahogany highboy, is favored by honeymooners; and the first-floor studio (with a kitchenette) is often the choice of older couples. The Green Room has a king-size four-poster bed.

Address: *R.D. 1, Box 57, Ridge Rd., Queensbury, NY 12804, tel. 518/793-6869.*
Accommodations: *3 double rooms with baths.*
Amenities: *TV in two rooms and in common room.*
Rates: *$45–$75; full breakfast. MC, V.*
Restrictions: *No smoking, small pets permitted with prior arrangement.*

Donegal Manor Bed and Breakfast

Irish hospitality characterizes Donegal Manor, a bed-and-breakfast housed in an 1820 building with Italianate Victorian additions in the middle of Warrensburg. Owner Dorothy Dill Wright hails from Donegal, Ireland. She worked downstate as a nurse before opening this B&B and its accompanying antiques shop. An Irish-pine dresser in the dining room displays her collection of Blue Willow and Flow Blue china, and an old Irish churn stands nearby. A 1776 cradle in one of the guest rooms is a family heirloom.

James Fenimore Cooper was a guest here while he did research for *The Last of the Mohicans;* and the Cooper Room, with a double-spindle bed covered in velvet patchwork, is named after him. The Tara Room

(named for Mrs. Wright's daughter) features a 1910 oak Stickley rocker and a carved Victorian bed.

Address: *117 Main St., Warrensburg, NY 12885, tel. 518/623-3549.*
Accommodations: *1 double room with bath, 2 doubles share a bath, 1 suite.*
Amenities: *Air-conditioning, cable TV in suite and parlor.*
Rates: *$65–$85; full breakfast. MC, V.*
Restrictions: *Smoking in parlor and on porch only, no pets.*

The Friends Lake Inn

The New York State record small-mouth bass was caught in Friends Lake, but you don't have to be an angler to enjoy the Friends Lake Inn and all it has to offer. This traditional Adirondack lodge was built in stages. The original building was a farmhouse constructed around 1850; a later addition served as a boardinghouse for workers in local tanneries. Innkeepers Greg and Sharon Taylor are avid skiers, and at the inn they have established a cross-country ski touring center with trails; they also offer special packages for Alpine skiing.

After a day spent skiing (or fishing, rafting, canoeing, or hiking), guests gather at the inn's restaurant, which has received culinary accolades. With its pressed-tin ceiling and original chestnut woodwork, it is a romantic spot for lingering. Guest rooms are small, simple, and cozy and are furnished with antique beds and oak dressers. Ask for one of the lakeview rooms, which are most popular.

Address: *Friends Lake Rd., Chestertown, NY 12817, tel. 518/494–4751.*
Accommodations: *10 double rooms with baths, some with hot tubs.*
Amenities: *Restaurant, wine bar; beach.*
Rates: *$65–$125; full breakfast; MAP available. AE, MC, V.*
Restrictions: *Smoking in common rooms only, no pets, 2-night minimum on weekends, 3-night minimum on holiday weekends.*

Hilltop Cottage Bed and Breakfast

Once the caretaker's house on a Lake George estate, Hilltop Cottage is now an easygoing, reasonably priced alternative to the ersatz log cabins and tacky motels that proliferate in this popular resort area. Running a bed-and-breakfast comes naturally to retired educators Anita and Charlie Richards. Anita's parents lived in the 11-room house, and her mother rented rooms to tourists. During the 1920s and early '30s the building housed students of legendary Metropolitan Opera diva Marcella Sembrich, who had a summer home nearby.

The moldings, floors, and banister in this vine-covered house are made of Adirondack fir, and all the antique beds are covered with printed quilts from the 1940s and '50s. A former toolshed on the estate has been converted into a cottage for two and is paneled in knotty pine.

Address: *Box 186, Rte. 9N, Bolton Landing, NY 12814, tel. 518/644–2492.*
Accommodations: *3 double rooms share 1 bath, 1 cottage.*
Amenities: *Cable TV and refrigerator in cottage.*
Rates: *$40–$55; full breakfast. No credit cards.*
Restrictions: *No smoking in bedrooms, no pets, 2-night minimum on holiday weekends.*

The Merrill Magee House

In a grove of trees adjacent to a 19th-century bandstand sits the Merrill McGee House, a Greek Revival mansion built around 1840. The great-grandfather of Grace Merrill Magee, for whom the inn is named, fought in the American Revolution. Innkeepers Florence and Ken Carrington owned housekeeping cottages on Lake George for 30 years. A brief, unhappy retirement led to a new career as proprietors of this irresistible country inn.

The house overlooks gardens where weddings are often held, and a field of wildflowers lies in back. Most of the guest rooms are located in a new (but architecturally compatible) building behind the inn. All the new rooms have fireplaces and are decorated country style, with antique beds, patchwork quilts, and folk art. The inn features what may be the oldest (circa 1928) private swimming pool in New York State—it's a beauty. In summer guests can also enjoy evening concerts performed at the bandstand.

Address: *2 Hudson St., Warrensburg, NY 12885, tel. 518/623-2449.*
Accommodations: *10 double rooms with baths, 3 doubles share 1 bath.*
Amenities: *Restaurant, tavern, air-conditioning, pool, whirlpool.*
Rates: *$65–$100; full breakfast. AE, MC, V.*
Restrictions: *No smoking in dining room, no pets, 2-night minimum on summer and holiday weekends, closed mid-Mar.–mid-Apr.*

Saratoga Rose

The Victorian mansion now housing this bed-and-breakfast inn was built in 1885 as a wedding gift for the daughter of one of the founding fathers of Hadley, a tiny Adirondack village between the Sacandaga and Hudson rivers. "I guess that's why it works so well for us," says innkeeper Nancy Merlino. "We're on an extended honeymoon here."

Nancy and her husband and co-owner, Anthony (he's also the chef for the inn's restaurant), married and soon after found the inn, a few years ago. The couple are proud of the acclaimed restaurant, which serves American regional and Italian cuisine. Candlelit dinners are served in the romantic, Victorian dining room with burgundy curtains and a fireplace, or on what is probably the only bright-pink veranda in the Adirondacks. The guest rooms have Victorian furnishings and decor; two rooms have oak high-back beds, and one has a fireplace. The Victorian Room even has a pink fainting couch, and the Garden Room has a private deck with a 20th-century conceit: a whirlpool bath.

Address: *Box 238, Rockwell St., Hadley, NY 12835, tel. 518/696-2861.*
Accommodations: *4 double rooms with baths, 1 suite.*
Amenities: *Restaurant, bar.*
Rates: *$60–$125; full breakfast. AE, MC, V.*
Restrictions: *Smoking downstairs only, no pets, 2-night minimum Aug. and on holiday weekends.*

The Capital and Saratoga Region

Reminders of America's past—political, commercial, and social—abound in New York's Capital and Saratoga region. A favorite of visitors seeking both history and 20th-century diversions, the area encompasses the city of Albany, the nation's sixth largest port, at the northernmost point of the navigable Hudson. Once on the decline—as described in Ironweed *and other works of William Kennedy, a local favorite son—Albany is currently enjoying the revitalization of its downtown area. The latest addition to the city, the Nelson A. Rockefeller Empire State Plaza (completed in 1978), and the Knickerbocker Arena (Frank Sinatra was the opening headliner) have inspired the restoration of surrounding neighborhoods. A tour of the city often includes the governor's mansion and the State Capitol—one of the few such buildings without a dome. You won't want to miss the Performing Arts Center, nicknamed "The Egg" for obvious reasons. It makes the Albany skyline unlike any other in the world.*

Landlocked though Saratoga is, it boasts a natural asset, a prehistoric sea, trapped under limestone and capped with a layer of shale. The mineral waters that bubble through the cracks in the shale have made Saratoga Springs and the neighboring Ballston Spa a noted resort for two centuries. Here visitors still "take the cure," sampling mineral waters from various fountains strategically located around town. Bring a drinking cup, and don't expect the water to taste like Evian or Perrier. Each spring reputedly possesses different elements conducive to health. The cure may include a trip to one of the area's mineral baths (several of which are located in Saratoga Spa State Park) and a massage.

"The August Place to Be," as Saratoga Springs advertises itself, attracts crowds each August, when the month-long thoroughbred-racing season is the centerpiece of a series of

*festive events. Lodging and seats at the city's excellent
restaurants are hard to come by during this time; and
hotel, inn, and bed-and-breakfast rates often shoot up to
nearly twice the normal prices. To really enjoy this lovely
city we recommend a visit at other times of the year.*

*Saratoga is a great place for strolling, with its superb
Victorian architecture, especially along Union Avenue,
North Broadway, Lake Avenue, and Circular Street. And
don't miss the scene of the 1777 Battle of Saratoga, the
"turning point of the Revolution," now a historic park
between the nearby towns of Stillwater and Schuylerville.*

Places to go, sights to see

Historic Cherry Hill (Albany, tel. 518/434–4791). This Georgian home, built
in 1787 by Philip Van Rensselaer, was inhabited by five generations of his
family, until 1963. The furnishings range from 18th-century artifacts of the
China trade to early-20th-century kitchen appliances. First floor wheelchair
accessible.

New York State Capitol (Albany, tel. 518/474–2418). Built between 1867 and
1899 at a cost of $25 million, the seat of New York State government
incorporates several styles of architecture. The interior features elaborate
carvings and an impressive staircase. Wheelchair accessible.

New York State Museum (Albany, tel. 518/474–5843). Lifelike dioramas of
New York State's past (including some depicting immigrant life in New York
City in the late 19th and early 20th centuries) and a walk through the
Adirondack wilderness make this museum one of Albany's most popular
attractions. Also featured are changing art exhibits, films, lectures,
demonstrations, and hands-on displays. The museum is an absorbing
adventure for children. Wheelchair accessible.

Saratoga Race Course (Saratoga Springs, tel. 518/584–6200). The nation's
oldest thoroughbred track, in operation since 1863, is the focus of Saratoga's
August social scene. Post time is 1:30 PM. Early risers may breakfast at the
trackside café (tel. 518/584–6200) and watch morning workouts. The National
Museum of Racing and Thoroughbred Hall of Fame (tel. 518/584–0400), right
by the track, touches on every aspect of the sport and includes
a reconstructed training barn and portraits of such champions as Man o' War
and Secretariat.

Saratoga Spa State Park (between Rtes. 9 and 50, tel. 518/584–2000). The
land that now makes up this 2,000-acre park was reserved in 1909 to protect
the area's unique mineral springs. Mineral baths (some of which still operate)

were opened in the 1920s, and in the '30s the Works Progress Administration completed the spa buildings. The park has an Olympic-size swimming pool, golf courses, tennis courts, and ice-skating rinks. It is also the home of the Saratoga Performing Arts Center (tel. 518/584–9330), summer host of the New York City Opera, the New York City Ballet, the Philadelphia Orchestra, and Jazz Festival–Saratoga.

Yaddo (Saratoga Springs, tel. 518/584–0746). This 19th-century estate was the summer home of Katrina and Spencer Trask, wealthy patrons of the arts. Yaddo is their permanent legacy to creative work, an enclave where artists, writers, and musicians may work without disruption. Since 1926 more than 3,000 artists have resided here, including John Cheever, Langston Hughes, Katherine Anne Porter, Aaron Copland, and Milton Avery. Yaddo's gardens, modeled on turn-of-the-century Italian designs, complete with statuary, are open to the public.

Tourist Information

Albany County Convention and Visitors Bureau (52 S. Pearl St., Albany 12207, tel. 518/434–1217 or 800/622–8464). **Rensselaer County Regional Chamber of Commerce** (251 River St., Troy 12180, tel. 518/274–7020). **Saratoga Springs Chamber of Commerce** (494 Broadway, Saratoga Springs 12866, tel. 518/584–3255).

Reservation Services

The American Country Collection (984 Gloucester Pl., Schenectady 12309, tel. 518/370–4948). **Bed and Breakfast Association of Saratoga, Lake George and Gore Mountain Region** (Box 99, Lake Luzerne 12846, for brochure on member establishments). **Bed and Breakfast USA, Ltd.** (Box 606, Croton-on-Hudson 10520).

The Adelphi Hotel

If Kublai Khan had decreed that his "stately pleasure dome" be built in late-19th-century Saratoga instead of in Xanadu, he might have come up with the Adelphi Hotel. This lodging is nothing like home, unless home is an Italian palazzo with the requisite piazza and ornamented by a maze of Victorian fretwork. The opulent lobby is done in a style so reminiscent of La Belle Epoque that one could picture the Divine Sarah Bernhardt holding court amid its splendor. It's hard to believe that not too long ago the Adelphi stood empty, evidence of fortune gone sour. Saratogans shook their heads and laughed at what they took to be the foolhardiness of Gregg Siefker and Sheila Parkert when they bought the place in 1988, but no one's laughing anymore: the hotel is one of Saratoga's showplaces, its lobby bar and café a gathering place of natives and visitors alike (in July it's a favorite hangout of members of the New York City Ballet).

No two rooms are the same: all the furnishings are eclectic—and recherché. If you seek accommodations that hark back to the Adirondack camps enjoyed by some of America's wealthiest families ask for Room 16, the Adirondack Suite, with Mission-style furniture manufactured in upstate New York, a twig settee, Papago Indian baskets on the wall, and a wood-panel bathroom. If you yearn for the south of France but can't afford to go there, the Riviera Suite (Room 12) may lessen the pangs somewhat. Its sitting area, furnished with rattan, is graced with a Mediterranean mural; an amusing Casbah painting hangs on the bedroom wall; and the bathroom is decorated in apricot tones. Other rooms are furnished with Tiffany lampshades, brass-and-iron beds with crocheted bedspreads, wicker settees, and Victoriana.

The Adelphi was built when Saratoga was known as the Queen of the Spas. Today the city is still the center of a lively and elegant social scene, especially in August, when the raceway is open—but keep in mind that Saratoga has a lot to offer during the other eleven months of the year, when hotel reservations are easier to come by.

Address: *365 Broadway, Saratoga Springs, NY 12866, tel. 518/587-4688.*
Accommodations: *17 double rooms with baths, 17 suites.*
Amenities: *Restaurant (open July and Aug.), bar, air-conditioning, cable TV, and phones in bedrooms, room service.*
Rates: *$70–$280; Continental breakfast. AE, MC, V.*
Restrictions: *No pets, 2-day minimum on weekends July–Aug., closed Nov.–Apr.*

The Mansion

Rock City Falls, a 19th-century mill town 7 miles west of Saratoga Springs, seems an unlikely destination for travelers. The Kayaderosseras Creek still flows, but the mills and factories are quiet. Aside from a few antiques shops, there doesn't seem to be much that would draw visitors to this sleepy village . . . not much, that is, until one spots the Mansion, one of the most elegant and romantic bed-and-breakfasts you'll encounter anywhere. The Venetian villa–style residence, soon to be listed on the National Register of Historic Places, was built in 1866 as a summer home for George West, a prominent industrialist and inventor of the folding paper bag. No expense was spared in the construction of the 23-room mansion; it has etched-glass doors; marble fireplaces with inlaid mantels; copper and brass lighting fixtures and Tiffany chandeliers.

It is a credit to proprietor Tom Clark and innkeeper Alan Churchill, who restored the mansion, that this bed-and-breakfast is both sumptuous and friendly. The art books stacked invitingly in the library are for browsing, perhaps while sipping iced tea or Saratoga water on the side porch on a lazy summer afternoon. Classical music—anything from Bach to Berlioz—wafts through the house. The artwork, which Tom collects on his travels, invites close inspection. The antique parlor organ is there for the playing. All the guest rooms are enticing, but the Four-poster Room, with its queen-size carved bed, and the Queen Room, with garden views, are particularly handsome.

And there are the flowers. Baskets of fuchsia hang from the porches (if you're quiet—and lucky—you might spot a hummingbird or two); roses, peonies, and delphiniums fill the gardens; and bouquets of fragrant Casablanca lilies and foxglove may greet you in the front hall or parlors. Alan of the green thumb even grows orchids: In one guest room the mauve of an orchid plant picks up the colors of the bedspread.

Alan nurtures his guests the way he nurtures his flowers—you are made to feel like a treasured friend in this hospitable house. Everything here—from the Victorian furnishings to the homemade fruit breads served with breakfast—is in excellent taste. As Alan says, "The house demands it. It's so special."

Address: *Rte. 29, Box 77, Rock City Falls, NY 12863, tel. 518/885–1607.*
Accommodations: *4 double rooms with baths, 1 suite.*
Amenities: *Air-conditioning; swimming pool.*
Rates: *$85–$150; full breakfast. No credit cards.*
Restrictions: *No smoking in dining room, no pets, 2-night minimum in Aug. and on holiday weekends, closed Thanksgiving and Christmas.*

Maple Ridge Inn

I n Cambridge, right in the middle of "Grandma Moses Country" near the New York–Vermont border, is a distinctive Victorian mansion with a Texas accent. The Dallas connection is owner Ken Riney, a purveyor of fine antique jewelry and silver, who by his own admission spent "a fortune" restoring and furnishing the 1869 estate and turned it into a bed-and-breakfast both opulent and relaxed. The antique silver coffee service, the 1840s silver urn, and the silver fruit baskets are not just for display—they're used every morning for breakfast in the main dining room. The same goes for the Tiffany china.

Guest rooms show off gems from Ken's collection: a Victorian carved-walnut bed in a downstairs bedroom, a European carved settee and a leather wing chair in one upstairs room, and a dresser from Saratoga's old Grand Union Hotel in another. Most bedrooms have Tiffany lamps, Persian carpets, and silver dresser sets.

Because his guests' ease is paramount, Ken favors comfortable, contemporary, white-leather couches rather than Victorian chairs in the parlor, where in the afternoons visitors often gather for tea or brandy. It doesn't matter that the couches are not antiques: They blend in perfectly because Ken's taste is impeccable.

He is no less knowledgeable when it comes to food. Only the freshest, mostly homegrown ingredients go into the breakfasts he serves: the eggs come from Maple Ridge hens and preserves are made from fruit grown on the property. On summer afternoons guests relishing the view from the porch might be treated to homemade cakes or pies along with their iced tea.

The Cambridge area offers abundant antiques shops and auctions. In the fall, tours to view the foliage are popular; summer draws guests to the attractions of nearby Saratoga. But most visitors to Maple Ridge like to "set and stay awhile." It's that kind of place, run by that kind of host. Ken calls innkeeping "one of the most pleasant things you'd want to do."

Address: *Rte. 372 (RD 1, Box 391C, Cambridge, NY 12816), tel. 518/677–3674.*
Accommodations: *4 double rooms with baths, 1 double suite, 1 double housekeeping suite.*
Amenities: *Air-conditioning, cable TV and phones in rooms; antiques shop in Carriage House, airport and New York City limousine service arranged.*
Rates: *$175–$250; Continental breakfast. No credit cards.*
Restrictions: *No smoking indoors, pets permitted with prior arrangement, 2-night minimum in Aug. and Oct.*

The Sedgwick Inn

The Sedgwick Inn, a rambling New England farmhouse with Victorian additions, was built in 1791 as a stagecoach stop. It sits on 12 verdant acres at the foot of the Berkshires, in Berlin; it was once a favorite getaway of New York politicos and their cronies and later became a popular tavern. It is said that Cole Porter once performed here. Today the inn combines all three of its earlier incarnations: It's a way station, where vacationers and second-home owners stop to refresh themselves on their journeys to points north; New York City residents come to get away from it all; and the inn's renowned restaurant (with live piano music on Friday and Saturday nights) draws visitors and locals alike.

Innkeepers Bob and Edie Evans abandoned their previous careers— he as the administrator of a psychiatric hospital and she as a psychiatric social worker—when they found the inn, 11 years ago. It took a year to restore the building (it had been out of operation for 15 years) and to furnish the delightful Victorian guest rooms and public areas.

If the bedrooms could talk they might say "Lincoln could have slept here." Of course there's no record that the 16th president ever did pass through Berlin, but if he had he might have felt right at home in Room 9, with its four-poster bed and Oriental rug; and he probably would have been delighted with the king-size bed in Room 7 and the book-lined shelves in Room 11.

The Evanses pride themselves on their restaurant. It's not just the food and drink that soothe the soul here but also the innkeepers' attitude: "We only have one sitting a night for each table," notes Bob. "We don't want our guests to feel rushed."

In fact, it's doubtful whether Bob and Edie ever really left the "helping professions." To quote one of the inn's most popular ads: ". . . frozen chocolate mousse pie with two forks . . . a shared snifter of Calvados while Charlie plays 'As Time Goes By' . . . then up to bed. . . . Blueberry muffins, scrambled eggs and the morning paper. . . . If that doesn't fix it, it probably cannot be fixed."

Address: *Rte. 22, Berlin, NY 12022, tel. 518/658–2334.*
Accommodations: *9 double rooms with baths, single room with bath, suite.*
Amenities: *Restaurant, TV/VCR in some rooms, room service; gift and gourmet shops.*
Rates: *$60–$100; full breakfast. AE, MC, V.*
Restrictions: *Smoking in motel only, pets in motel with advance arrangements, 2-night minimum on holiday weekends.*

Chestnut Tree Inn

This 1860 Empire-style bed-and-breakfast on a side street near the center of Saratoga Springs has a somewhat colorful history: It was a notorious flophouse. Bruce DeLuke, a retired firefighter, and his wife, Cathleen, both antiques dealers, have turned the place into an alluring, romantic retreat. Wicker furnishings, cabbage roses, and old-lace decor prevail, and the exterior color scheme of pink, mauve, and gray is repeated in the bedrooms and common areas.

The inn offers a first-floor double room, with an antique brass-and-iron bed and pink Victorian lamp (which imparts an appropriate rosy glow). There is a tiny but charming Tree House in the back yard (it's not actually in a tree, but it does have a loft bed for the children). The atmosphere here is easy and undemanding. Guests are free to mingle or not, and breakfast is laid out on a leisurely basis; you can serve yourself any time of the morning.

Address: *9 Whitney Pl., Saratoga Springs, NY 12866, tel. 518/587–8681.*
Accommodations: *5 double rooms with baths, 5 double rooms with showers and sinks share 2 men's and women's rest rooms.*
Amenities: *Cable TV in parlor; off-street parking.*
Rates: *$65–$200; Continental breakfast. MC, V.*
Restrictions: *No smoking, no pets, 3-night minimum in Aug. and on special-event weekends, closed Nov.–mid-Apr.*

Fox Manor

For those of us who are not "to the manor born," a stay at this bed-and-breakfast in Sand Lake could be the fulfillment of a fantasy. Here it's not hard to imagine living in the mid-19th century, presiding over this stately Greek Revival mansion: Hosts Barbara and Ken Brady have turned most of the house—including the living room, library, entertainment room, and airy porches—over to their guests. The couple are on hand for breakfast and at night, but she's a nurse and he's a probation officer, so guests are literally given the keys to the manor. "We tell them to lock up when they leave. I trust my guests," laughs Ken.

The mansion was built in 1840; according to local lore it was once a stop on the Underground Railroad. Bedrooms are furnished in period style, with refinished chairs, desks, and dressers. Common rooms hark back to a more gracious era, and the rocking chairs on the Ionic-column front porch invite guests to view the passing scene.

Address: *Rte. 66/43, Box 178, Sand Lake, NY 12153, tel. 518/674–8220.*
Accommodations: *3 double rooms share 1 bath.*
Amenities: *Air-conditioning, cable TV in common room.*
Rates: *$40–$50; full breakfast on weekends, Continental breakfast on weekdays. No credit cards.*
Restrictions: *No smoking, no pets.*

The Gregory House

Guests at this inn set in the center of the small village of Averill Park in Rensselaer County have been known to come down to breakfast in their bathrobes—it's that kind of place. Innkeepers Bette and Bob Jewell have lived in the 1830s house for 25 years. Fourteen years ago they opened a restaurant on the premises and, eight years later, added the inn ("I think it's every man's desire to own a restaurant or a bar," says Bette of her husband, a former personnel director). This is a family operation: Bob and daughter Sue preside over the kitchen, and Bette tends to the rest. The inn's common room, with a beamed cathedral ceiling and fireplace, is furnished with country-style reproductions. Bedroom decor tends to four-posters, rocking chairs, and Oriental rugs.

Averill Park, a once-bustling resort area, is today a quiet Albany suburb. Seasonal pleasures include sports afforded by the nearby lakes and two major ski areas, Brodie Mountain and Jiminy Peak.

Address: *Rte. 43, Box 401, Averill Park, NY 12018, tel. 518/674–3774.*
Accommodations: *12 double rooms with baths.*
Amenities: *Restaurant, air-conditioning, cable TV in common room; swimming pool.*
Rates: *$60–$75; Continental breakfast. AE, DC, MC, V.*
Restrictions: *No pets.*

The Inn on Bacon Hill

The Inn on Bacon Hill is on Wall Street, just a few minutes' drive from downtown Saratoga Springs. But the street bears no resemblance whatsoever to the *other* Wall Street—this one runs through some of the state's lushest farmland. The Italianate Victorian farmhouse, built about 1865, retains its original garden, carefully restored (along with the house) by Andrea Collins-Breslin and her mother, Millie.

Andrea, a former specialist in employee relations and education, left the corporate world to spend more time with Millie and to get involved in a more "people-oriented" job. She likes to get to know her guests, so she serves them drinks and chats with them on their arrival. A golden retriever, Vicki, serves as greeter.

The congenial and homey inn has rooms furnished with antique cannonball, four-poster, or Jenny Lind beds. The rooms are named Morning Glory, Poppy, Queen Anne's Lace, and Tulip (this last was named after the flower in the original wallpaper frieze along the top of the room's walls—which on closer inspection turned out to be a crocus—but the original name stuck).

Address: *200 Wall St., Schuylerville, NY 12871, tel. 518/695–3693.*
Accommodations: *2 double rooms with baths, 2 doubles share 1 bath.*
Amenities: *Air-conditioning.*
Rates: *$60–$125; full breakfast. MC, V.*
Restrictions: *No smoking, no pets, 2-night minimum on Aug. weekends.*

The Inn at Saratoga

Although the Inn at Saratoga, built about 1880, lacks Victorian charm (in a city that is chock-full of Victoriana), its midtown location is convenient. It also offers amenities not found in the city's small inns and bed-and-breakfasts. Guests who are reluctant to give up such creature comforts as room service and whirlpool baths can be quite comfortable in the inn's ersatz Victorian bedrooms. And they can have their whirlpool baths courtesy of the inn's arrangement with the local YMCA.

All the bedrooms are similarly furnished; the differences lie only in size or color scheme. They feature Victorian-style antiques, stuffed chairs, four-poster beds, and brass lamps. The two honeymoon suites and two minisuites have comfortable seating areas. The inn's most attractive features are its Earl Grey dining room and the English garden in the rear of the building, where guests may have breakfast or afternoon tea.

Address: *231 Broadway, Saratoga Springs, NY 12866, tel. 518/583–1890.*
Accommodations: *23 double rooms with baths, 9 single rooms with baths, 6 suites.*
Amenities: *Restaurant, banquet facilities, air-conditioning, cable TV in rooms; use of nearby YMCA pool and whirlpool.*
Rates: *$60–$320. AE, MC, V.*
Restrictions: *No pets, 2-night minimum in Aug., 3-night minimum on the Traver's Stakes weekend.*

Mansion Hill Inn

Albany's only downtown inn, Mansion Hill, is located around the corner from the governor's mansion and occupies several adjacent, restored Victorian-era buildings, one of which was once the neighborhood saloon. Owners Maryellen and Steve Stofelano, Jr. (she's a bank vice president and he once taught high school), bought the buildings in 1984 and finished their first renovation project the following year. The inn's attractive restaurant soon became the neighborhood's hub—and Steve its unofficial mayor.

Accommodations range from double rooms with queen-size beds to two huge suites—each with a living room, den, full kitchen, bedroom, bath, and balcony. Furnishings are undistinguished but comfortable, and the carpeted halls and stairways are cozy underfoot. Those who wish to explore Albany will find the State Capitol, the Empire State Plaza, and numerous historic sights easily accessible.

Address: *115 Philip St., Albany, NY 12202, tel. 518/465-2038.*
Accommodations: *9 double rooms with baths, 3 suites.*
Amenities: *Restaurant, air-conditioning, cable TV in rooms, one room accessible to the handicapped by elevator.*
Rates: *$95–$145; full breakfast. AE, DC, MC, V.*

Mill House Inn

Twenty years ago Frank and Romana Tallet bought an "old, falling-down" sawmill in Stephentown that was considered so hazardous it was about to be torn down. After a year of extensive renovation it was reincarnated as Mill House Inn, a place as warm and inviting as a mug of hot cider on a brisk fall day. The Tallets, who moved to the country for a simpler life, pride themselves on the number of guests who return year after year to enjoy the inn's hospitality.

Rough-hewn paneling and heavy beams are found throughout the inn. The piano and crackling fire in the common room are comforting during ski season, the time when the inn is probably at its best (Jiminy Peak and Brodie Mountain ski areas are just 2 and 3 miles away), and two of the suites have fireplaces. In summer, the swimming pool becomes a gathering place. This friendly, relaxed inn is also whimsical—how can you not be charmed by an establishment that has a Red Suite, named not because of its color scheme but because it was once occupied by Lucille Ball?

Address: *Rte. 43, Stephentown, NY 12168, tel. 518/733-5606.*
Accommodations: *7 double rooms with baths, 5 suites.*
Amenities: *Air-conditioning; swimming pool.*
Rates: *$80–$145; Continental breakfast. AE, MC, V.*
Restrictions: *No smoking, no pets, 2-night minimum in July and on Aug. weekends.*

Saratoga Bed and Breakfast

Amid the new wave of bed-and-breakfasts in the town, Saratoga Bed and Breakfast is a pioneer—it's been seven years since Kathleen and Noel Smith opened their 1860 Victorian home to guests. The operation is a family affair—even Bates, the dog, gets into the act: He's the official welcoming committee. The rooms are charming, more farmhouse-country than high Victorian, as befits a house on the outskirts of the city that boasts "the very last address" in Saratoga proper. They are named for the city's gracious old hotels. Handmade, signed quilts adorn the antique beds. The largest room, Union Hall, offers a carved-oak bed, wicker furnishings, and a view of pine trees from every window.

Noel is a former restaurateur, and his full Irish breakfasts are the high point of a stay here. If you can move after breakfast, Kathleen, an amiable ambassador for her native city, will set up an itinerary.

Address: *Out Church St., Saratoga Springs, NY 12866, tel. 518/584-0920.*
Accommodations: *3 double rooms with baths, 2 doubles share 1½ baths.*
Amenities: *Air-conditioning, cable TV in common room.*
Rates: *$55–$125; full breakfast. MC, V.*
Restrictions: *Smoking only in sitting room, no pets, 2-night minimum on Aug. weekends.*

The Six Sisters

Just across the street from Saratoga's thoroughbred racetrack stands this unique Victorian home with a scallop-edge roof and basket-weave porches. Owned by Kate Benton and Steve Ramirez, the inn is named in honor of Kate and her five sisters. Kate, a former high-school guidance counselor, hails from a native Saratoga family of 12, but the name Six Sisters and Six Brothers was a bit unwieldy. She attended college in Hawaii ("If you had 11 siblings, wouldn't you want to get as far away as possible?"), where she met Steve.

One of the most inviting of the guest rooms is furnished in tropical style, with wicker chairs, a king-size brass-and-iron bed, and some of Steve's evocative photos of Hawaii on the wall. Steve is a terrific cook, so breakfast—which includes what may be the best corn bread north of the Mason-Dixon Line and delightful conversation with the hosts—is a real drawing card.

Address: *149 Union Ave., Saratoga Springs, NY 12866, tel. 518/583–1173.*
Accommodations: *2 double rooms with baths, 2 suites.*
Amenities: *Air-conditioning, refrigerators in some rooms, TV in parlor.*
Rates: *$55–$195; full breakfast. No credit cards.*
Restrictions: *No smoking, no pets, 2-night minimum on weekends Apr.–Nov., 5-night minimum in Aug.*

The Westchester House

This Queen Anne Victorian structure was built in 1885 by a master carpenter in Saratoga, to house his own family. The elaborately carved fireplaces, fluted columns, artful, handcrafted chestnut moldings, and other details make this bed-and-breakfast especially impressive. Innkeepers Stephanie and Bob Melvin furnished the house with antiques and works of art, but there is no air of the museum here. The Melvins—he worked in government and she sang opera in Washington, DC—are outgoing and are happy to converse on subjects ranging from the Eastlake influence on their house to the culture and history of their adopted city.

The guest rooms are tastefully furnished with such antique treasures as Louis XVI bedroom sets, Thonet chairs, oak washstands, Empire chests, and an art-nouveau cheval glass. The hosts point out that the Victorians were the most eclectic of collectors and believe that they and the Westchester House "embody the true Victorian spirit."

Address: *102 Lincoln Ave., Box 944, Saratoga Springs, NY 12866, tel. 518/587–7613.*
Accommodations: *5 double rooms with baths, 2 doubles share bath.*
Amenities: *Air-conditioning.*
Rates: *$60–$175; Continental breakfast. MC, V.*
Restrictions: *Smoking on porch only, no pets, 4-night minimum in Aug., closed Jan.*

The Catskills

The Catskills are the stuff of legends both old and new. Several hundred years ago, Washington Irving's Rip Van Winkle took a 20-year nap in these mountains. In more modern times, popular performers such as Milton Berle, Eddie Fisher, Sid Caesar, and Jackie Mason got their starts at Catskills resorts.

The region's tradition of hospitality and fine dining dates back about 100 years. Originally the area attracted a number of wealthy New Yorkers who built their summer residences here, but it wasn't until such resorts as Grossinger's and the Nevele arrived on the scene, during the 1920s, that the Catskills became known across the country. Especially famous for the prodigious amounts of food they served, these establishments once catered to a primarily Jewish clientele, but today the major resorts attract a more diverse group of vacationers.

The Catskills still has its ethnic enclaves—East Durham and Leeds draw a great number of Irish-Americans, Round Top and Purling reflect a German influence, Haines Falls and Tannersville promote a number of Italian attractions, and a Ukrainian festival is held each year near Lexington and Jewett. The mountains everywhere, however, are the main lure for those who want a country vacation just a few hours' drive from Manhattan.

The area offers a variety of outdoor and seasonal pleasures, not the least of which is the region's natural beauty, which can be enjoyed whether you're fishing from one of the many Catskills lakes or streams or sitting on a front porch with a mountain view. Golfers have a choice of more than 40 courses. Alpine skiers can schuss down various slopes, including Belleayre Mountain, Big Vanilla at Davos, Bobcat, Cortina Valley, Deer Run, Holiday Mountain, Hunter Mountain, and Ski Windham. Miles of pristine cross-country ski trails are also accessible, both at a number of the larger resorts and at Eldred Preserve, Frost Valley, Hyer Meadows, and White Birches.

The Catskills attracts a good number of anglers because the waters here teem with fish. One of the most famous trout-fishing streams in the United States—The Beaverkill—lies in the southern part of the area. Mountain-climbing enthusiasts find some of the East Coast's most challenging treks among the Catskills peaks. In addition biking and hiking trails are plentiful.

Antiques, art, and craft aficionados continue to find treasures in small towns and along back roads. The Woodstock Art Colony is noted for its galleries, boutiques, and restaurants. It was not, however, the location of the major celebration of the 1960s peace-and-love generation— that landmark cultural event occurred in a field on Max Yasgur's farm, in Bethel, about 45 minutes from Woodstock.

Places to go, sights to see

Bronck Museum (Coxsackie, tel. 518/731–8862). Listed on the National Register of Historic Places, this complex of Dutch Colonial houses and 19th-century barns has been a working farm for nine generations of the Bronck family. Exhibits include 18th- and 19th-century furnishings and art.

Catskill Game Farm (Catskill, tel. 518/678–5518). Rare and exotic animals from around the world can be seen here, and children will be well entertained at the petting zoo. Kids (the two-legged kind) bottle-feeding kids (the four-legged kind) makes for interesting photos.

Hunter Mountain Festivals (Hunter Mountain, tel. 518/263–3800). Each summer this ski area hosts major ethnic and music festivals, attracting visitors from all over the country. Events include the Italian Festival, with headliners such as Tony Bennett and Vic Damone; the German Alps Festival, with oompah bands and a Hummel-figurine look-alike contest; two country music festivals; the National Polka Festival; the Celtic Festival; the American Music Festival, featuring everything from big bands to Motown; and the Mountain Eagle Indian Festival, which draws 400 tribes from throughout North America.

Irish American Heritage Museum (East Durham, tel. 518/634–7497).
Located in the heart of the Irish Catskills, this recently opened museum
plans to house changing exhibits on Ireland and the role of Irish-Americans
in the cultural, political, and social history of the United States. There is also
a library of books on Irish culture.

Opus 40 and **Quarryman's Museum** (Saugerties, tel. 914/246–3400). This
environmental sculpture garden built in an abandoned quarry offers sunset
concerts in summer. The site is popular for outdoor weddings.

Tubing the Esopus (Phoenicia). A 5-mile stretch of the Esopus Creek,
between Shandaken and Mt. Pleasant, is the place to be on hot summer days
in the Catskills. Visitors enjoy taking an inner tube to drift with the current
and ride the rapids. The **Town Tinker** (Bridge St., tel. 914/688–5553) rents
tubes and will show you how and where to tube.

Tourist Information

Delaware County Chamber of Commerce (56 Main St., Delhi 13753, tel.
607/746–2281; outside NY, 800/642–4444). **Greene County Promotion
Department** (Box 527, Catskill 12414, tel. 518/943–3223; outside NY,
800/542–2414). **Sullivan County Office of Public Information** (County
Government Center, Monticello 12701, tel. 914/794–3000, ext. 5010; outside
NY, 800/343–INFO; in NY, 800/882–2287). **Ulster County Public
Information Office** (Box 1800 CR, Kingston 12401, tel. 914/331–9300;
outside NY, 800/342–5826).

Beaverkill Valley Inn

I have laid aside business, and gone a-fishing," wrote Izaak Walton in *The Compleat Angler;* Walton would probably have loved the Beaverkill, America's most famous fly-fishing stream. Although the Beaverkill Valley Inn, built in 1893 as a boardinghouse at Lew Beach, never played host to Walton, President Jimmy Carter, Robert Redford, Sigourney Weaver, Gary Trudeau, Jane Pauley, and assorted Kennedys have all been guests here. Owned and developed by Laurance Rockefeller and managed by able innkeeper Christine Dennis, the inn caters to those who cherish privacy. Its surrounding forests and nearby fields, preserved as "forever wild," are protected from development.

This is not to say that accommodations are rustic—not by a long shot. A comfortable, old-money look enhances the place. White-painted rocking chairs line the wide porch, a welcoming fire warms the living room on frosty days, and the bay-window dining room affords a view of the grounds. The card and billiard rooms, with their green-shade lamps, have a clubby, masculine atmosphere; they call to mind an era when men took leave of their female companions to enjoy their after-dinner brandy and cigars.

The fare that precedes that post-prandial brandy is sumptuous, with such offerings as poached Norwegian salmon with watercress sauce, and fillet of beef with blue-cheese sauce. All baked goods are made on the premises, and the inn uses home-grown herbs and salad greens.

Guest rooms are simply furnished with brass-and-iron beds, comfortable chairs, handmade quilts, and good reading lamps. Many of the rooms have twin beds.

Although fishing is the main draw here (the inn has a package arrangement with the Joan & Lee Wulff Fishing School nearby), it's certainly not the only attraction. A converted barn with a cathedral ceiling houses a heated swimming pool, a help-yourself ice-cream parlor, a theater, and a children's playroom. Sports enthusiasts also have access to tennis courts, hiking and cross-country ski trails, hunting in fall, and skating in winter.

Address: *Lew Beach, NY 12753, tel. 914/439-4844.*
Accommodations: *11 double rooms with baths, 9 doubles share 5 baths.*
Amenities: *Restaurant, bar, conference facilities, game rooms, 1 room equipped for the disabled; stocked pond; Beaverkill fishing.*
Rates: *$300–$470; breakfast, lunch, afternoon tea, dinner. AE, MC, V.*
Restrictions: *Smoking in card room and on porch only, no pets, 2-night minimum stay on weekends, 3-night minimum on holiday weekends.*

Captain Schoonmaker's Bed-and-Breakfast

You'll find it easy to lose yourself in the past at this meticulously restored 1760 Hudson Valley stone house. Americana is everywhere. The place at High Falls even claims its own early American ghost, Captain Fred. The hosts, Sam and Julia Krieg, also very friendly, are quite knowledgeable about local history. Julia teaches third grade and Sam is a biology professor at the State University of New York (the stuffed golden eagle on the landing once presided over his classroom).

Captain Schoonmaker's is, actually, four different places: the stone house, with four bedrooms (one with a fireplace), a living room, dining room, library, solarium, and canopied decks; the Towpath House, a half mile from the main house; Krum House, an 1840 Victorian in town; and the 1820 Carriage House, in front of the main house.

In the days when mules towed barges through New York State's canals, the Towpath House was the home of the lock tender for the Delaware and Hudson Canal. Guest rooms here (one with a fireplace) have four-poster, cannonball, or Victorian beds; pine cupboards; blanket chests; and wing chairs.

The Krum House has two large rooms with private baths. The upstairs room has a small kitchenette. The Carriage House rooms, the most sought-after and romantic, overlook a trout stream with a private waterfall. The two upstairs were once a hayloft, and the original beams have been left exposed. One downstairs room has a brass bed and a tree growing through the middle of a private deck. A Lone Star quilt covers the canopy bed in the other.

Probably only the Kriegs's famous breakfasts could tear guests away from their waterfall rooms—it's hard to ignore seven courses of such culinary delights as lemon poppy-seed cake, cheese soufflé, and blueberry strudel. Guests breakfast at an antique black-walnut table by the dining-room fireplace. Against the wall stands an antique printer's cabinet. The living room has another fireplace and an early American cupboard used to display quilts and coverlets. Nearby is the De Puy Canal House, a highly touted restaurant with an international menu.

Address: *Rte. 213 W, (RD 2, Box 37), High Falls, NY 12440, tel. 914/687-7946.*
Accommodations: *2 double rooms with baths, 10 doubles share 5 baths.*
Amenities: *TV in common room; swimming and trout fishing in stream.*
Rates: *$75–$85; full breakfast. No credit cards.*
Restrictions: *No pets, 2-night minimum on weekends mid-Sept.–Thanksgiving, closed Christmas week.*

The Redcoat's Return

Up a twisting mountain road in the Catskill Game Preserve, you'll encounter a little bit of the spirit of England at the Redcoat's Return. Once the center of a potato-and-dairy farm, the 1860 home at Elka Park was later a summer boardinghouse. Now this lodging is known in the area for its Saturday-night prime rib and Yorkshire pudding and for its English country hospitality.

Tom (the Redcoat) and Peg Wright have owned the inn for 19 years; he was once a chef on the *Queen Mary,* and she was an actress. The inn features extensive art and antiques collections that bring together mementos of trips abroad—and there's a moose head, named Basil, over the fireplace. Tom, who has a quirky sense of humor, says that he plays golf in his spare time and that "Peg is interested in metaphysics." Both are practiced conversationalists. Tom is full of stories about his objets d'art, which include a cricket bat and a framed antique scarf commemorating the first boxing match between an Englishman and an American, in 1860. Winston, the Wrights' Bernese mountain dog, can also be a charming host.

The Wrights have chosen to preserve the atmosphere of the old boardinghouse, so rooms are small but pleasantly cozy. All the mattresses are new, but the antique iron beds and oak dressers are part of the original decor. Third-floor bedrooms have eaved ceilings, and one large room offers two double beds. The eight guest rooms that share four baths are all supplied with bathrobes for guests.

Hikers should enjoy the numerous trails that lead from the inn onto nearby Overlook, Indian Head, Twin, and Hunter mountains. The Tour de Trump bicycle race goes right by the property. There are cross-country trails and three Alpine ski areas close by. Spring anglers have access to a trout stream on the property, and golfers will find several fine courses a short drive away.

Antiques shops and galleries are available for the less athletic, and for those who really want to sit and do nothing it's hard to beat the view from the inn's porch. It's also hard not to gain weight after sampling Tom's chocolate mousse, English-sherry trifle, and apple pie à la mode.

Address: *Platte Cove (Dale La.), Elka Park, NY 12427, tel. 518/589–6379 or 518/589–9895.*
Accommodations: *6 double rooms with baths, 8 doubles share 4 baths.*
Amenities: *Restaurant.*
Rates: *$70–$95; full breakfast. AE, MC, V.*
Restrictions: *No pets, 2-night minimum on Feb. and Oct. weekends; 3-night minimum on holiday weekends, closed Apr. 1–Memorial Day.*

Albergo Allegria

This gingerbread Victorian mansion in the northern Catskills—midway between Ski Windham and the White Birches cross-country trails—was originally two cottages that were part of a 19th-century summer boardinghouse colony. Owners Lenore and Vito Radelich had the two structures joined seven years ago: The new middle section is indistinguishable from those sections built in 1867.

The bed-and-breakfast is noted for its stunning oak floors, original chestnut moldings, and keyhole windows. Guest rooms take their names from the seasons and months of the year: June has a stained-glass window, a cathedral ceiling, and a terrific view of Ski Windham; and Summer, the honeymoon suite, offers a king-size bed, a skylight, and a double whirlpool bath.

The Radeliches spent 25 years in the restaurant business before becoming innkeepers. Albergo's kitchen not only turns out such breakfast specialties as Belgian waffles and polenta, but it is also frequently used for Italian cooking classes.

Address: *Rte. 296, Windham, NY 12496, tel. 518/734-5560.*
Accommodations: *15 double rooms with baths, 1 suite.*
Amenities: *TV in rooms; swimming hole.*
Rates: *$45-$175; full breakfast. MC, V.*
Restrictions: *No smoking in public areas, no pets, 2-night minimum on weekends.*

Deer Mountain Inn

If Deer Mountain Inn in Tannersville resembles a lodge designed for European nobility, it's no accident. Owner Danielle Gortel and her husband come from the mountains of Poland: it was only natural that these two avid skiers settle in Catskills ski country and that they keep an inn that resembles Spala, the ancient hunting seat of Polish kings.

Built as a private residence, the circa 1900 mansion stands in a 15-acre wooded enclave. It is said that the house was once owned by the notorious gangster Legs Diamond. Danielle knows for sure that it once contained a casino, but by 1964, when the property became a Catholic camp for city children, no traces of Prohibition-era gangsters remained.

Today the focus of the gracious cherry-paneled living room is a huge stone fireplace. In winter an après-ski snack of cheese, sausages, and wine is served by a bone-warming fire. The inn has a bright, airy breakfast room, and glass doors lead to the deck, a romantic spot for a summer evening. Some guest rooms have fireplaces, pine wainscoting, and diamond-pane windows.

Address: *Rte. 25, Box 443, Tannersville, NY 12485, tel. 518/589-6268.*
Accommodations: *7 double rooms with baths or showers.*
Amenities: *Restaurant.*
Rates: *$70-$120; full breakfast. MC, V.*
Restrictions: *Smoking in public areas only, no pets.*

The Eggery

In this 18th-century farmhouse a chess set sits on an antique game table standing by a picture window that overlooks a leafy bower. A player piano waits nearby, and in winter a cheery fire welcomes guests to the relaxed bed-and-breakfast, at a 2,200-foot elevation near the small town of Tannersville. The Dutch Colonial farmstead became a tourist house in 1935 and continued as such until the late 1970s. In 1979 Abe and Julie Abramczyk—a former hospital administrator and a registered nurse, both avid skiers—opened the Eggery, so named because of the property's earlier incarnation.

Oak predominates in the common areas—there are Mission Oak chairs in the living room, a handcrafted bar in the dining room, and a stunning balustrade leading upstairs. Guest rooms are simply furnished, with antique beds, many of them made of brass or painted iron. The wrap-around porch is a peaceful spot for contemplating the seasonal pleasures of the Catskills rising 4,100 feet.

Address: *County Rd. 16, Tannersville, NY 12485, tel. 518/589-5363.*
Accommodations: *13 double rooms with baths, 1 suite.*
Amenities: *Cable TV in rooms.*
Rates: *$55–$95, suite price on request; full breakfast. AE, MC, V.*
Restrictions: *No pets, 3-night minimum on holiday weekends, 2-night minimum on other weekends.*

Greenville Arms

Start with a turreted 1889 Queen Anne Victorian (built by William Vanderbilt as a private residence) on a tree-lined street in the center of the small town of Greenville. Add columned porches with the obligatory wicker rockers and gliders, croquet on the lawn, a brook, carriage house, an intimate restaurant, and admirable antiques, and you have the Greenville Arms.

This delightful property features a swimming pool, a lit shuffleboard court, two playgrounds on 6 acres, and nearby golf and tennis. It's an activity-filled retreat for families and groups. The inn also offers 14 yearly painting workshops, with distinguished artist-instructors, in the heart of Thomas Cole and Frederick Church country.

Eliot and Letitia Dalton are the inn's newest owners. Eliot may be the only innkeeper in the state who was once a river pilot and tugboat captain. Letitia's background in the graphic arts has stood her in good stead here, both in setting up the painting workshops and in decorating the inn.

Address: *RD 1, Box 2, Greenville, NY 12083, tel. 518/966-5219.*
Accommodations: *13 double rooms with baths, 5 doubles share 3 baths.*
Amenities: *Restaurant, 1 room with air-conditioning; swimming pool.*
Rates: *$55–$120; full breakfast. MC, V.*
Restrictions: *Smoking restricted to bedrooms, no pets, 2-night minimum on holiday weekends.*

Inn at Lake Joseph

T his circa 1870 Victorian mansion, once the vacation estate of Cardinals Hayes, Spellman, and Cook, sits on 20 acres of lawn and woods. Surrounded by a 2,000-acre wildlife preserve, it's an ideal country place in which to relax, which is exactly why innkeeper Ivan Weinger bought the property.

Ivan, an artist and communications consultant, is in his element presiding over elegant dinners (such as pheasant stuffed with pheasant mousse) either on the screened porch or in the Victorian dining room. After dinner, guests may play a game of billiards or choose from a collection of 80 videotapes.

Guest rooms have Victorian-style wallpaper and antique furnishings; three rooms have fireplaces. The carriage house, with a beamed ceiling, kitchen, and two bedrooms, is suitable for a family. The private lake here is said to have the best pickerel fishing in the state. Miles of cross-country ski trails span the property, and equipment is available for rent.

Address: *Box 81, Forestburg, NY 12777, tel. 914/791-9506.*
Accommodations: *9 double rooms with baths.*
Amenities: *Restaurant; lake.*
Rates: *$118–$218; breakfast, afternoon tea, dinner. AE, MC, V.*
Restrictions: *No smoking in dining room, no pets, 2-night minimum on weekends.*

Lanza's

W hen asked what a retired Navy man is doing running an inn in the landlocked southern Catskills, Dick Lanza counters with the story of the boatswain who carried an anchor on his shoulders. When asked why, he dropped the anchor and stated: "This is where I'll stay." The 1905 farmhouse in Livingston Manor has been a boardinghouse, a hotel, and even a bowling alley.

Lanza's sits in the heart of Sullivan County's trout haven, and anglers fly-fish on the nearby Beaverkill and Willowmec rivers. The property consists of 7 acres, complete with a beaver pond and herb and flower gardens. Guests may breakfast in the greenhouse dining room, surrounded by native pine and a variety of plants. A downstairs tap room has a fireplace, TV, and game machines, and pizza is served there.

Guest rooms are furnished with antiques from various periods. Room 6 features an art deco–style bedroom set, and Room 5 has a high-back Victorian oak bed and an oak dresser (the same one advertised for $5.95 from the 1905 Sears Roebuck catalogue).

Address: *RD 2, Box 446, Livingston Manor, NY 12758, tel. 914/439-5070.*
Accommodations: *8 double rooms with baths.*
Amenities: *Restaurants, tap room.*
Rates: *$72–$84; full breakfast. AE, MC, V.*
Restrictions: *No pets, 2-night minimum on holiday weekends.*

Point Lookout Mountain Inn

On a clear day, you can see forever—almost—from Point Lookout Mountain Inn. The Victorian-style bed-and-breakfast lies on the Mohican Trail at a stagecoach stop. The first Point Lookout tower, built as a tourist attraction, was used during World War II for spotting enemy aircraft. It was destroyed by fire in 1965, when the present structure was built.

In 1980 schoolteachers Rosemary Jensen, Mariana Di Toro, and her brother Lucio Di Toro bought what was then an abandoned discothèque, and the inn is once again a travelers' haven. The quiet rooms are tastefully decorated in low-key mountain style in desert tones. The best colors, however, are provided by spectacular sunrises, sunsets, fall foliage, and rainbows, which come free at Point Lookout.

The inn's health-oriented restaurant combines a variety of cuisines, including Italian and Mexican. Guests can raid the refrigerator and choose from breakfast goodies left on the table.

Address: *Rte. 23, Box 33, East Windham, NY 12439, tel. 518/734–3381.*
Accommodations: *12 double rooms and 1 single with baths.*
Amenities: *Restaurant, TV in rooms, pets permitted with deposit.*
Rates: *$60–$115; Continental breakfast. AE, D, DC, MC, V.*
Restrictions: *2-night minimum on weekends, 3-night minimum on holiday weekends.*

The Hudson River Valley

Of all America's waterways, few can compete with the Hudson River's combination of majestic grace and history. From the earliest explorations of the continent, in the 17th century, through the Revolutionary War, this 315-mile-long river has played an important part in the development of the nation.

Long a major thoroughfare of commerce, the Hudson was home to the first commercial steam-power boat, Fulton's Clermont; several years later the opening of the Erie Canal clinched the river's claim as the nation's most important waterway; and in the mid-1800s the river port of Hudson even became a center of the whaling industry.

The natural beauty of the river has attracted many prominent artists and writers. In the 19th century the Hudson River School of painters was formed, inspired by the noble river and by the works of Washington Irving, one of the first American writers to be recognized abroad. As we retreat up the Hudson from where it empties into the Atlantic Ocean of Manhattan, we behold the same beautiful vistas—the majestic hills and splendid palisades—that inspired those 19th-century artists. Many old river towns, such as Tarrytown, Cold Spring, and Hudson, retain the atmosphere of the distant past, and some have even been restored to their 19th-century glory.

The valley merits careful exploration by the traveler. The largely unspoiled countryside includes prosperous farms and splendid estates once inhabited by some of America's most distinguished families: the Roosevelts, Vanderbilts, Harrimans, and Rockefellers. In addition to such palatial estates, visitors can explore numerous historical sites, such as Philipsburg Manor (the residence of a 17th-century Dutch shipping magnate), Sunnyside (home of Washington Irving), Stony Point Battlefield, and Washington's

*Headquarters in Newburgh. Also, the valley is home to
some of the nation's most prestigious institutes of higher
learning: the U.S. Military Academy at West Point, Vassar
College, Sarah Lawrence College, and Bard College. The
Culinary Institute of America, which has schooled many
prominent chefs, is in the area.*

*Travelers can reach the Hudson and its valley both on
Hudson River cruises and on Amtrak. Driving through the
valley, however, gives explorers more freedom to visit
historic places and pursue antiquing, hiking, fishing,
sailing, and hot-air ballooning as the mood strikes.*

*The valley's seasonal pleasures include cross-country skiing
in state parks in winter, strolls through historic gardens in
spring, summer picnics on river bluffs, and leaf peeping
and apple picking in fall. The many valley orchards make
the region one of the country's chief apple producers:
A perfect excursion could include a picnic in one of the
area's pick-your-own orchards—with dessert right off the
tree, of course. The Hudson Valley's vineyards are also
starting to build a worldwide reputation, and many can be
visited.*

Places to go, sights to see

The Culinary Institute of America (Hyde Park, tel. 914/471–6608). Many of
this country's leading chefs received their training at CIA, which was
founded in New Haven in 1946. In 1972 the school moved to its present site,
a former Jesuit seminary at Hyde Park, overlooking the Hudson River. Over
4,000 meals are prepared here every day, and visitors may dine at any of the
institute's four restaurants: the award-winning American Bounty, The
Escoffier, St. Andrew's Café, and The Caterina de Medici Dining Room.
Reservations are required, and jackets are de rigueur for men

Franklin Delano Roosevelt National Historic Site (Hyde Park, tel. 914/229–
9115 for tour information). The Roosevelt family estate, retreat of our 32nd
president, is in Hyde Park. Here visitors will find the setting of some of
Roosevelt's "fireside chats," as well as many of his personal effects,
including his wheelchair and books. The graves of the president and his wife,
Eleanor, are in the Rose Garden, next to the house. The FDR Library and
Museum are also on the grounds.

Hudson Valley Wineries. There are a number of notable wineries on both sides of the river. Most are open to the public—some by appointment—and some have regular tours. Among them are *Cascade Mountain Vineyards*, on Flinthill Road in Amenia (tel. 914/373–9021); *Millbrook Vineyards*, on Wayne and Shunpike roads in Millbrook (tel. 914/677–8383); *Brotherhood* (America's oldest winery), in Washingtonville (tel. 914/496–9101); and *Clinton Vineyards*, in Clinton Corners (tel. 914/266–5372).

Olana State Historic Site (Hudson, tel. 518/828–0135, reservations advised). The home of Hudson River School artist Frederick Edwin Church commands a stunning view of the river. The Persian-style mansion is surrounded by gardens and carriage trails. The house, designed by the artist and built between 1870 and 1891, is shown by guided tour only, May through October, but the grounds are open year-round for outdoor pursuits such as walking, running, and cross-country skiing. Olana is outside the city of Hudson, near the Rip Van Winkle Bridge.

The Shaker Museum (Chatham, tel. 518/794–9100). This off-the-beaten-track museum in the hamlet of Old Chatham houses the largest collection of Shaker artifacts in the United States. Over 40,000 items, from baskets to wagons, are on display in the eight buildings that make up the exhibition. A museum shop featuring reproductions of Shaker furniture and a small restaurant are on the grounds.

The United States Military Academy (tel. 914/938–2638 for tour information). Known simply as West Point, the academy has been the training ground for U.S. Army officers since 1802. The site is also the country's oldest military base in continuous operation. Athletic events (especially the yearly contest between the Army and Navy football teams) draw many visitors to the post. There's also an outstanding military museum.

Tourist Information

Hudson River Valley Association (42 Catherine St., Poughkeepsie 12601, tel. 800/232–4782).

Reservation Service

Bed and Breakfast USA, Ltd. (Box 606, Croton-on-Hudson 10520).

Anthony Dobbins Stagecoach Inn

Since 1740, only three families have owned the Anthony Dobbins Stagecoach Inn. The present proprietor, Margo Hickock, takes pleasure in imagining what the original inn—complete with common room and bundling boards—must have been like. In its present incarnation as a bed-and-breakfast, the inn is no doubt a great deal more comfortable than its 18th-century predecessor. It even has an elevator.

The house is charmingly furnished with English antiques, some of which are family heirlooms. "Nothing matches, but everything fits," says Margo, a former fashion model who once ran a spa for the Gabor sisters and now guides aspiring young models.

Even the furnishings are steeped in history. Margo's family is descended from both Wild Bill Hickok and William Penn, and the room named for Mr. Penn boasts a bed that belonged to the founder of the Crown Colony of Pennsylvania. The Hickok Room has twin canopy beds and an antique love seat, and, with the neighboring Green Room, which has a fireplace, can be made into a double suite. The Blue Room, with flowered wallpaper and Williamsburg-blue trim, features an antique brass bed, fireplace, sun deck, and private bath.

Among the many artful touches are all-cotton sheets; antique lace-trimmed, linen hand towels; and homegrown flowers placed in each room throughout spring and summer. A collection of Currier and Ives prints and paintings of horses adorns the inn's spacious entry hall, but for the real thing, visitors need only walk half a block to the race track. Goshen is known as the Cradle of the Trotters, and the harness track here is the nation's oldest. Tennis courts are also a short walk away, and hot-air-balloon rides can be arranged at a nearby airport.

Address: *268 Main St., Goshen, NY 10924, tel. 914/294-5526.*
Accommodations: *2 double rooms with baths, 1 double suite.*
Amenities: *Air-conditioning in 2 rooms, TV in common rooms, fruit and candy in each room.*
Rates: *$65–$130; Continental breakfast, afternoon tea. No credit cards.*
Restrictions: *Smoking in sun room only, no pets, 2-night minimum on weekends.*

The Inn at Shaker Mill

The Inn at Shaker Mill is an unusual establishment for two reasons: its Shaker decor and its gregarious host, Ingram Paperny.

As befits a converted 1823 Shaker mill, the rooms are simply furnished in a comfortable but utilitarian style. Pegboards hang from the plaster walls, and in the Shaker tradition the common room has a barrel roof—though it also boasts a glass wall that looks out on the mill's brook and waterfalls.

After 25 years in the business Mr. Paperny has been called the doyen of New England innkeepers. A stay at the inn is like spending time in the home of a fascinating new friend. As might be expected of a former consultant to the United Nations, Paperny is an internationalist, and he relishes playing host to an eclectic bunch of visitors. During summer he brings European hiking and cultural groups to the United States, acts as their tour leader and host, and encourages them to mix with the American guests at the inn. He is also a woodworker and is responsible for all the carpentry done in the building.

The inn is unique in another way: It charges per person, so singles who want to get away from the city can retreat to a place that doesn't put the emphasis on couples (which isn't to say that a room overlooking the waterfalls wouldn't serve as a romantic retreat for two). Also, several of the rooms are large enough to accommodate families: The stone-wall, wood-beam suites on the third floor can sleep six.

The inn's hospitality extends to meals as well. Breakfasts include juice, fresh fruit, cereals, yogurt, cheese, bagels, muffins, breads, and eggs. Dinners vary with the whim of the chef—one night it might be a West Indian spread, another night, Chinese—and include wine. On Saturday nights in summer there are outdoor barbecues.

Address: *Cherry La., off Rte. 22, Canaan, NY 12029, tel. 518/794–9345, fax 518/794–9344.*
Accommodations: *20 double rooms with baths.*
Amenities: *Restaurant, air-conditioning in some rooms; swimming pond, sauna.*
Rates: *$75–$300; full breakfast. MC, V.*
Restrictions: *No smoking in dining room.*

Le Chambord

Although it is housed in an 1863 Georgian mansion one minute from the Taconic Parkway, Le Chambord could easily be the focal point of an antebellum Southern plantation. In fact Scarlett O'Hara would feel right at home on its pillared veranda. The mansion's involvement with things Southern is more than skin-deep, however: The trap door under the inn's bar leads to a former stop on the Underground Railroad.

Miss O'Hara was not far from the mind of innkeeper Roy Benich when he named the latest additions to Le Chambord: Tara Hall, containing 16 rooms; and Butler Hall, which has corporate and banquet facilities. Both structures are in keeping with the genteel traditions of the opulent dining and banquet rooms and the nine handsome bedrooms in the main building.

Mr. Benich, a former art-and-antiques dealer, has designed Le Chambord for aesthetic appeal and treats it as his home. He chooses all the art and antiques for the inn, and his taste is impeccable. Not many dining rooms can boast a $20,000 antique Chinese breakfront, and not many bedrooms and sitting rooms have sofas and wing chairs covered in imported floral tapestries. For the cost of each of these chairs, "you can furnish two Holiday Inn rooms and have $200 left over," laughs Benich. No expense has been spared

in selecting furniture and accessories—or food and wine, for that matter.

Mr. Benich's focus on visual delights is shared by his Parisian chef; Henry Benveniste. The two have collaborated on an elegant menu that satisfies both the palate and the eye.

Despite such luxuries, the inn is quite affordable. True, the wine list offers a 1929 Château Lafite Rothschild for $1,500, but there are also good wines in the $15 range.

Address: *2075 Rte. 52, Hopewell Junction, NY 12533, tel. 914/221–1941.*
Accommodations: *25 double rooms with baths.*
Amenities: *Restaurant, air-conditioning, cable TV in rooms; facilities (including fax) for corporate meetings, health club.*
Rates: *$105; Continental breakfast. AE, DC, MC, V.*
Restrictions: *No pets, closed Christmas Day.*

Simmons Way Village Inn

Simmons Way Village Inn, set on a wide expanse of lawn in the middle of Millerton, was built by the village's first merchant in 1854 and was transformed into a handsome country inn in 1983.

Current owners Richard and Nancy Carter (he is a management consultant and educator, she is a bank vice president) bought Simmons Way in 1987 with the idea of running an inn that combined "European civility and American comfort" and served the best in international cuisine.

There are two common rooms on the first floor, one of which opens onto the inviting front porch, where guests may eat breakfast in the warmer months. The main dining room was added in 1986 but is hard to distinguish from the original structure.

The bedrooms (six on the second floor and three on the third) are furnished with English and European country antiques. Each has its own charm; but Room 5, with its rose-floral wallpaper, queen-size antique iron bed, embroidered bedspread, wicker love seat, and 6-foot French bathtub with hand-held shower is perhaps the most romantic. Room 2, the Bridal Suite, offers a private covered porch, marble fireplace, and queen-size crown-canopy bed; and Room 4 has peach walls, an English brass canopy bed, swag curtains, and a stripped-pine armoire.

If one can bear to leave these lovely rooms (where breakfast may be served, if desired) and venture beyond the inviting front porch, the surrounding area is well worth exploring. A swimming pond is 3 miles away, golf courses are close by, and the inn offers special weekday packages that include tickets to the nearby Lime Rock (auto) Race Track—where you might just catch a glimpse of Paul Newman, who frequently races there.

Address: *33 Main St., Millerton, NY 12546, tel. 518/789-6235.*
Accommodations: *9 double rooms with baths, 1 suite.*
Amenities: *Restaurant, air-conditioning, banquet facilities, cable TV and phone in common room, complimentary sherry.*
Rates: *$95–$150; full breakfast. AE, MC, V.*
Restrictions: *Smoking in designated areas only, no pets, 2-night minimum on weekends May 1–Nov. 1, 3-night minimum on holiday weekends.*

Troutbeck

This Tudor-style manor house set amid 425 gracious acres outside the hamlet of Amenia figured prominently in American literary and political history. It was once home to Myron B. Benton, whose circle of friends included Emerson, Thoreau, and John Burroughs. The estate served as a gathering place for the likes of Sinclair Lewis, Teddy Roosevelt, and Lewis Mumford in the early 20th century, and black leaders formed the NAACP under its roof.

Today Troutbeck also serves the movers and shakers—the elite of the corporate world—as a conference center during the week. On weekends, however, it is transformed into one of the area's most romantic country inns, the vision of genial innkeeper Jim Flaherty and his partner, Bob Skibsted.

Guests lack nothing here. The Troutbeck package includes three gourmet meals a day, an open bar, and access to all sorts of recreational activities, ranging from tennis, swimming (indoor and outdoor), fishing, and cross-country skiing to strolling through walled gardens and watching video movies or major sports events on satellite TV.

Most guest rooms are suitably romantic, although the rooms in the main house seem more so. For the premium prices charged by Troutbeck, guests might prefer a canopied, fireplaced, sun-porch

room in the manor house (with its leaded-glass windows, 12,000-book oak-panel library, and comfortable English country appointments) to the Americana offered in the neighboring Century Farmhouse rooms. Of course, guests in both buildings have access to all the inn's amenities.

If you can tear yourself away from the estate the surrounding area is prime antiquing territory, and guests can take elegant prepared picnics with them on excursions. The inn will also transport guests to concerts at Tanglewood, dance performances at Jacob's Pillow, and Shakespeare at The Mount.

Address: *Box 26, Leedsville Rd., Amenia, NY 12501, tel. 914/373-9681, fax 914/373-7080.*
Accommodations: *29 double rooms with baths, 5 doubles share 3 baths.*
Amenities: *Restaurant, air-conditioning, banquet facilities.*
Rates: *$375–$475; three meals, wines, and spirits. AE.*
Restrictions: *Pipes and cigars not permitted in dining rooms, no pets, closed weekdays for conferences.*

The Bird and Bottle Inn

The Bird and Bottle Inn in Garrison predates the Revolutionary War and was once a way station on the old Albany–New York post road. Today it is a homey but sophisticated country inn and restaurant with a well-deserved international reputation—and it's only an hour from Manhattan.

The inn's owner, Ira Boyar, has been in the hospitality industry for over 25 years, and he applies his expertise to all aspects of the inn, from marketing to menu choices.

All the elegantly Colonial rooms have fireplaces. The Emily Warren Room offers a queen-size canopy bed draped in rose-color fabric. The John Warren Room boasts the original wainscoting and fireplace, and the bathroom has a view of a stream.

The suite's queen-size canopy bed is draped with English-style chintz, and a braided rug dresses the wide-board pine floors. The cottage suite, 50 yards from the inn, appeals to couples seeking a secluded getaway.

Address: *Old Albany Post Rd. (Rte. 9), Garrison, NY 10524, tel. 914/424-3000, fax 914/424-3283.*
Accommodations: *2 double rooms with baths, 1 suite, 1 cottage.*
Amenities: *Restaurant, air-conditioning,*
Rates: *$195–$215; breakfast and dinner. AE, DC, MC, V.*
Restrictions: *No pets, 2-night minimum on weekends with Sat. reservation, closed first 2 weeks in Jan.*

The Crary House

Innkeeper/law student Juliette Crill is famous for her muffins. They are served as part of the Continental breakfast offered at the Crary House, a center-hall-Colonial bed-and-breakfast in Columbia County. Juliette and her partner, Joan Damiani, restored the house themselves, and welcomed their first guests one month after the closing. Its features include wide-board floors; three porches (complete with wicker chairs); and informal country, antique, and reproduction furniture. "It's a place you can bring the kids to and not have to worry," says Juliette.

The one disadvantage to the Crary House is its location, on a main thoroughfare. Weekend traffic along Route 23 makes this inn something less than a secluded retreat.

Address: *Rte. 23, Craryville, NY 12521, tel. 518/325-5888.*
Accommodations: *1 double room with bath, 2 doubles and 1 single share 1 bath, 1 suite.*
Amenities: *Mini-refrigerator in Peach Room.*
Rates: *$40–$70; Continental breakfast. MC, V.*
Restrictions: *Smoking in public rooms only, no pets, 2-night minimum on holiday weekends.*

Hudson House, A Country Inn

From the foot of Main Street in the charming 19th-century village of Cold Spring, this 1832 inn (the second oldest inn in continuous operation in the state) takes in spectacular views of the Hudson River, West Point, and Storm King Mountain. Visitors here should request a room facing the river.

The entire inn, from the wood-panel bar and sitting area downstairs to the 15 guest rooms, was renovated in 1981. Many rooms are furnished with old-fashion painted-iron beds (quite a few have twin beds), and all feature country decor and accessories. River-view rooms on the second floor open onto a wraparound porch. One of the two suites, with twin beds in one room and a double in the other, has just one bathroom and is best suited for a family.

Guests without cars will find the Hudson House an ideal spot for a weekend of antiquing and exploring on foot—the railroad station is just 500 feet from the inn's door.

Address: *2 Main St., Cold Spring, NY 10516, tel. 914/265-9355.*
Accommodations: *11 double rooms with baths, 2 suites.*
Amenities: *Restaurant, air-conditioning in some rooms.*
Rates: *$65–$175; Continental breakfast midweek, full on weekends. AE, MC, V.*
Restrictions: *No pets, 2-day minimum on weekends.*

The Martindale Bed and Breakfast Inn

The Martindale Bed and Breakfast Inn is located in rural Columbia County. The 137-year-old building is a Hudson Valley "bracket house," a hybrid of Southern, Victorian, and Federal architecture. It was in the same family for 134 years before it began its new life as a bed-and-breakfast. It is now supervised by innkeepers Terry and Soll Berl—a retired teacher and a physician, respectively.

The Berls opened up a warren of small, dark spaces and turned it into a comfortable, airy, and elegant B&B. The wide-board floors found throughout are originals, and the chestnut molding was fashioned from trees growing on the property when the house was built.

Guest rooms have antique-brass or four-poster oak beds and are graced with 19th-century prints and dried-flower wreaths. The antiques-furnished sitting room has a TV, VCR, and CD player, but guests often prefer to pass the time in Terry's homey kitchen.

Address: *Rte. 23, Craryville, NY 12521, tel. 518/851-5405.*
Accommodations: *3 double rooms with baths, 1 suite.*
Amenities: *TV/VCR in parlor, dinner available with 24-hour's notice.*
Rates: *$60–$95; full breakfast. No credit cards.*
Restrictions: *Smoking on veranda only, 2-day minimum on weekends June–Labor Day and Oct.*

Pig Hill Inn

There aren't any real pigs in residence, and the Federal-style building wasn't built on a hill named for swine, but owner Wendy O'Brien's affection for porkers is evident throughout Pig Hill Inn: There's a painted-piggy floor cloth in the entryway, and folk-art pig carvings are set amid antiques throughout the inn's three floors.

Each guest room is unique. Room 1 imparts a rustic feeling, with Indian rugs, antlers hung above the fireplace, and a settee made from birch logs. Room 6 contains a full four-poster bed and inviting burgundy wing chairs, and Room 7 has its own wood-burning stove and a stunning antique pine armoire.

The downstairs sitting room has rag rugs, comfortable chairs, and a collection of classic children's books, including *Charlotte's Web*, the main character of which is a pig named Wilbur. The fictional Wilbur had to settle for slops in the barn, but guests at Pig Hill are pampered with breakfast in bed of shirred eggs and freshly baked breads or maybe a spinach-filled souffle roll.

Address: *73 Main St., Cold Spring, NY 10516, tel. 914/265–9247.*
Accommodations: *4 double rooms with baths, 4 doubles share 2 baths.*
Amenities: *Air-conditioning, fireplaces in some rooms, dinner available.*
Rates: *$90–$140; full breakfast: AE, D, DC, MC, V.*
Restrictions: *No smoking, no pets.*

Plumbush Inn

Plumbush, once the estate of American-born marquise Agnes Rizzo dei Ritii, was transformed into an elegant Hudson Valley restaurant in 1976. Several years later, Swiss-born owners Giere Albin and Ans Bender, who grew up in the hotel-and-restaurant business, decided to convert the Victorian mansion's unused second floor to overnight accommodations.

The walls of the Marchesa Suite are covered with flowered paper; the room is furnished with a large iron-and-brass bed and Victorian settee and has a full bath. Two smaller rooms have similar Victorian appointments and private baths.

Breakfast includes homemade croissants, pastries, jams, juices, coffee, and tea and may be served in the guest rooms or on the small downstairs porch. "We're very flexible," says Ans.

Local attractions include lush golf courses, state parks for hiking and cycling, and the antiques shops in Cold Spring, five minutes away.

Address: *Rte. 9D, Cold Spring, NY 10516, tel. 914/265–3904.*
Accommodations: *2 double rooms with baths, 1 suite.*
Amenities: *Restaurant, air-conditioning, cable TV in sitting room.*
Rates: *$95–$125; Continental breakfast. AE, MC, V.*
Restrictions: *Smoking in restaurant area only, closed Mon. and Tues.*

The Swiss Hutte

At the foot of the Catamount Ski Area, in a picture-perfect setting, is the Swiss Hutte, a chalet that's more reminiscent of the Alps than of the Berkshires.

Gert and Cindy Alper are the energetic couple who have owned the inn since 1986. Swiss-born Gert, who started his training at 15, as a chef's apprentice, runs the kitchen, while Cindy oversees the dining room and lodgings.

There are two bedrooms in the inn itself, with 16 more in the nearby motel. Although the motel rooms are large, bright, and have private terraces, their ambience is typical of motels. The charm of the Swiss Hutte, however, has more to do with its setting, service, and food than with its bedrooms. Gert's Continental specialties are irresistible, and guests can always work off the calories on the inn's tennis courts or in its pool during summer. In winter a day on the slopes could easily justify a second helping of the inn's famous raspberry-cream pie.

Address: *Rte. 23, Hillsdale, NY 12529, tel. 518/325–3333.*
Accommodations: *15 double rooms with baths, 1 double suite.*
Amenities: *Restaurant, airconditioning, phones and TV in rooms.*
Rates: *$150–$160, MAP. MC, V.*
Restrictions: *2- or 3-night minimum on holiday weekends, depending on season, closed mid-Mar.– mid-Apr.*

The Village Victorian Inn

With a chandelier right out of *Gone with the Wind* in the spacious front entry hall, flowered wallpaper and an Oriental rug in the parlor, and fishnet-canopy beds heaped with heart-shape, lacy throw pillows, "romantic" seems to be the only word to describe Rhinebeck's circa 1860 Village Victorian Inn. The inn is on the National Register of Historic Places, and it reflects the dream of owners Judy and Richard Kohler to restore the house to its original elegance.

All the guest rooms are lovely. The Blue Room, with its king-size bed and working fireplace, is often chosen by honeymooners. The Green Room has an intricately carved queen-size, Victorian bed and a mirrored armoire. The focal point of the Red Room is an extraordinarily elaborate antique brass bed.

Guests who can be lured from the wicker chairs on the front porch enjoy local antiquing or watching vintage aircraft in action at the Old Rhinebeck Aerodrome, 4 miles away.

Address: *31 Center St., Rhinebeck, NY 12572, tel. 914/876–8345.*
Accommodations: *5 double rooms with baths.*
Amenities: *Air-conditioning.*
Rates: *$120–$170; full breakfast. AE, MC, V.*
Restrictions: *Smoking in parlor and on porch only, no pets, 2-night minimum on weekends, 3-night minimum on holiday weekends.*

Eastern Long Island

The eastern end of Long Island first attracted English colonists in the 1640s. They fled the harsh New England winters for the ocean-tempered island, and founded the towns of East Hampton and Southampton. The East Hampton area (called Maidstone by these settlers) was purchased from the Shinnecock tribe for 20 coats, 24 hatchets, 24 hoes, 24 looking glasses, and 100 tools the tribe would use for making wampum. The vacationtime invasion of the farming communities on the island's bucolic eastern end began in the late-19th century and mushroomed when the Long Island Railroad started service to the region from Manhattan's Pennsylvania Station.

Today the ocean is the area's big draw. Those not lucky enough to own beachfront property "south of the highway" (the Montauk Highway) have access to miles of white, sandy public beaches. Although the beaches are free, passes are required for parking. A number of bed-and-breakfasts and inns offer free passes to guests. One pleasant way to avoid parking charges is to bike to the beach.

In summer the South Fork, from Southampton to Montauk, is one big—and somewhat crowded—playground for the tan, chic, and well-heeled. Summer housing is expensive, though there are a few notable bargains. The main thoroughfare to the eastern end of the island is Route 27, a two-lane nightmare on summer weekends. For those who don't want to drive, there's the Hampton Jitney bus and limousine service from Manhattan (tel. 212/936-0440) and a local airport, as well as numerous marinas for docking the family yacht.

Summer in the area brings warm ocean breezes, boutiques, chic night spots, and roadside stands brimming with the bounty of Long Island's farms. It's a wonderful time here, but the beach is still there the rest of the year, and nothing is as crowded—something to consider when planning your trip. The ocean sometimes remains warm enough for swimming into October, and restaurant reservations are certainly easier to come by out of season.

Not all of Eastern Long Island is trendy and developed. The North Fork is an agricultural area, with some of the state's most productive farms. Thanks to conservationists more than 6,800 acres on the South Fork have been turned into nature preserves. Eastern Long Island's salt marshes, dunes, pine barrens, woodlands, and grasslands are home to many endangered species of flora and fauna, and preservationists are determined that at least part of the island will stay as it was in the 1600s, when the first big real-estate deal was completed.

Places to go, sights to see

Home Sweet Home (East Hampton, tel. 516/324–0713). The childhood home of poet John Howard Payne, who wrote the song "Home Sweet Home" in the early 1800s, is now a museum in a simple, 1660 rough-shingle house, which features a three-century collection of furnishings and a 19th-century windmill.

Long Island Wineries. The area claims a dozen wineries. Climate and the makeup of the soil here provide unique growing conditions, and the area is fast becoming a source of award-winning wines. The town of Cutchogue is home to five wineries, including *Bedell Cellars* (tel. 516/734–7537), *Bidwell Vineyards* (tel. 516/734–5200), *Hargrave Vineyard* (tel. 516/734–5158), *Peconic Bay Vineyards* (tel. 516/734–7361), and *Pugliese Vineyards* (tel. 516/734–5983). Peconic offers *Lenz Winery* (tel. 516/734–6010), *Pindar Vineyards* (tel. 516/734–6200), and *Soundview Vineyards, Inc.* (tel. 516/624–9463). Other North Fork vineyards include *Jamesport Vineyards* (Jamesport, tel. 516/722–5256), *Mattituck Hills Winery* (Mattituck, tel. 516/298–5964), and *Pallmer Winery* (Aquebogue, tel. 516/722–4080). The South Fork vineyards are *Bridgehampton Winery* (Bridgehampton, tel. 516/537–3155) and *Le Reve Winery* (Southampton, tel. 516/726–7555). Many vineyards offer tours and tastings.

Mashomack Preserve (Shelter Island, tel. 516/749–1001). The Nature Conservancy, a nonprofit organization that manages the world's largest privately held nature preserve, protects and maintains a 2,039-acre, pristine salt marsh on Shelter Island. The marsh is a habitat for a number of endangered species, including the osprey and the oystercatcher. Osprey nesting areas may be observed (and should be left undisturbed) all over the island. The preserve is open for hiking every day but Tuesday, and guided walks are offered.

Summer Festival, John Drew Theater of Guild Hall (East Hampton, tel. 516/324–4050). The festival features the best of Broadway; concerts; a film series; and lectures on the arts, the environment, and politics. Memberships, subscriptions, and single-event tickets are available.

Whale Watch Cruises (Montauk, tel. 516/728–4522). The Okeanos Ocean Research Foundation, a nonprofit marine-science organization, runs daily trips from May through September on its 90-foot cabin cruiser, *Finback II*, which is staffed by trained volunteers. Usually several whales are spotted on each voyage (about 20 miles out to sea from Montauk Point). Sighting a mother whale showing off her calf could be the high point of an Eastern Long Island vacation.

Tourist Information

East Hampton Chamber of Commerce (4 Main St., East Hampton 11937, tel. 516/324–0362, for information on Wainscott, East Hampton Village, Springs, Amagansett, and Montauk). **Sag Harbor Chamber of Commerce** (Box 116, Sag Harbor 11936, tel. 516/725–0011). **Shelter Island Chamber of Commerce** (Box 598, Shelter Island 11964, tel. 516/749–0399). **Southampton Chamber of Commerce** (76 Main St., Southampton 11968, tel. 516/283–0402). **Westhampton Chamber of Commerce** (Box 626, Westhampton Beach, 11978, tel. 516/288–3337).

The Huntting Inn

Huge elms and maples surround the Huntting Inn, a pre-Revolutionary landmark set on 2½ acres in the midst of East Hampton Village. The 18th-century house, originally a saltbox, was built by the Church of England for the Reverend Nathaniel Huntting. In 1751 Huntting's widow, probably short of cash, turned her home into a public house, and it's been an inn ever since. During the American Revolution it became the only neutral meeting ground in the area.

Innkeeper Linda Calder (who also manages Hedges' Inn, owned by the same corporation) has been here since 1980. Her degree from the Fashion Institute of Technology in New York City comes in handy in matters of inn decor. Her warmth, boundless energy, and good humor are evident as she tends to the needs of guests in the two inns.

The inn's dining room will look familiar to Manhattan's restaurant cognoscenti—it's run by the Palm Restaurant and has similar decor, including a pressed-tin ceiling, oak wainscoting, wide-board floors, bentwood chairs, a brass-rail bar, and drawings of celebrities lining the walls. As at the Palm, steaks and lobsters come in colossal proportions.

Guest rooms have cotton-chintz wall coverings (many designed by Laura Ashley). A number of antique beds are brass, iron, or a combination of both. One of the most charming rooms here is also the smallest, with a single brass-and-iron bed, a hand-crocheted bed cover, and lace curtains. The suite, done in a blue-and-white scheme, has wicker furnishings with flowered cushions, and balloon shades on the windows. It also offers a king-size bed and a queen-size pull-out couch to accommodate families.

Across the street you'll find public tennis courts, and several golf courses are located nearby. The inn provides guests with town stickers for parking in beach areas. The main village beach features a pavilion with lifeguards and refreshments. Other beaches in the area are more secluded but have few or no amenities. The inn lies within walking distance of all of East Hampton's shops, theaters, and museums.

Address: *94 Main St., East Hampton, NY 11937, tel. 516/324–0410, fax 516/324–8751.*
Accommodations: *17 double rooms with baths, 3 single rooms with baths, 1 suite.*
Amenities: *Restaurant, air-conditioning.*
Rates: *$95–$250; cold buffet breakfast. AE, MC, V.*
Restrictions: *No pets, 2-night minimum on weekends May–June and Sept.–Oct., 3-night minimum on weekends July–Aug., 5-night minimum July 4 and Labor Day weekends, closed Jan. 1–mid-Mar.*

Ram's Head Inn

Ospreys nest atop the telephone poles by this inn on Shelter Island. A yellow and white awning shelters the patio, and a beached rowboat sits in a children's play area on the wide front lawn. The voice of Billie Holiday is often heard in the dining room. The 1929 center hall Colonial-style building is all weathered shakes, white trim, and green shutters. Guests can walk to a gazebo by the tennis courts, and a grassy path leads down to 800 feet of beachfront on Coecles Harbor. Summer guests are cooled by bay breezes.

In the 1940s the nuclear physicists Enrico Fermi, J. Robert Oppenheimer, and Edward Teller attended a conference on the foundations of quantum mechanics here. The event is remembered with a framed document hanging in the entrance hall. Today guests will find the Ram's Head a serene setting for a meeting, an executive getaway, a family retreat, or a romantic weekend à deux.

Owners James and Linda Ecklund and innkeeper Brian Moorehead collaborate in running the place, and each fills in wherever necessary to make sure guests are taken care of. The Ecklunds bought the inn in a rather "decayed state," as they put it, and have spent the last 12 years restoring it.

The common rooms are often flooded with natural light. The lounge, decorated in a nautical theme, features ships' lanterns and a model sloop on the mantel. Green wicker couches have flowered cushions, and the library is the perfect spot for a rainy-day read. Here framed sheet music lines the walls, and a piano occupies an honored place. Every Sunday from 7 to 11 PM, a local jazz group livens the atmosphere. The dining-room menu stresses fresh seafood creatively prepared and presented. Specialties include shellfish bisque garnished with caviar and lobster, and braised red snapper accompanied by oyster mushrooms and artichokes.

Guest rooms are simple, bright, and airy. Those with a water view are often requested, but in summer the harbor can be glimpsed only through the leaves of majestic oak trees.

Address: *Ram Island Dr., Shelter Island Heights, NY 11965, tel. 516/749–0811.*
Accommodations: *5 double rooms with baths, 4 doubles share 2 baths, 4 suites.*
Amenities: *Restaurant, free use of boats and tennis court.*
Rates: *$76–$175; Continental buffet breakfast. AE, MC, V.*
Restrictions: *Smoking in lounge only, pets permitted with prior arrangement, 3-night minimum on holiday weekends, 2-night minimum other weekends, closed mid-Nov.–mid-Apr.*

The 1770 House

At various times in its history the 1770 House, actually a 1740 Colonial built for one of East Hampton's earliest families, has been a general store; a dining hall for students at the Clinton Academy next door; and, finally, an inn that had its heyday in the 1940s and '50s. When Sidney and Miriam Perle bought it, in 1977, it had been in a state of decline for several years. The Perles—he was in the retail business, and she ran a cooking school—were undaunted by the formidable restoration needed to return the building to its former glory.

Guest rooms have been furnished with fine antiques from various periods and origins. One room has a fireplace and an English-style, carved canopy bed. Another has an early American highboy. The inn's elegant library features English-pine paneling and a fireplace. The dining room has raspberry walls, and displays the owners' extensive collection of clocks and apothecary jars. "The kitchen," jokes Miriam, "is painted smoked-salmon."

The Perles' well-kept secret, named the nearby Philip Taylor House, is the family's private residence. Here, three opulent bedrooms are available to guests. Miriam's description of the house is forthright: "This is a drop-dead house." The core of the house was built in 1650; at the turn of this century its owners transformed it into a beige-stucco Elizabe-

than minipalace. Were she alive today, Marie Antoinette would most likely lose her head over the French antiques in the Boxwood Room—so named because it overlooks the English boxwood and Italianate columned garden. The Pear Tree Room, in the 1650 wing of the house, has massive ship's beams of English pine and a queen-size canopy bed. The Wisteria Room boasts an English-pine canopy bed and pine armoire. The house is filled with intricately crafted wood, architectural embellishments, and a museum-quality collection of antiques from seven historic periods.

Address: *143 Main St., East Hampton, NY 11937, tel. 516/324–1770.*
Accommodations: *10 double rooms with baths, 2 suites.*
Amenities: *Restaurant, air-conditioning.*
Rates: *1770 house, $95–$225; call ahead for Philip Taylor house rates; Continental breakfast. MC, V.*
Restrictions: *Smoking discouraged, no pipes or cigars, no pets, 4-night minimum on summer weekends, 2-night minimum other weekends.*

The Village Latch Inn

The theatrical air to the 5-acre compound that makes up the Village Latch Inn is no accident. Owner Marta White spent her life in the theater, and she revels in setting a stage. Her husband and fellow innkeeper, Martin, is a photographer who used to work in commercial films. The main house is "old Southampton, turn-of-the-century, Gatsby-style," says Marta. The circa 1900 building, once the annex to Southampton's most opulent hotel, may have been of Sanford White design. Near the main house are what Marta refers to as the "outbuildings," which were part of the old Merrill Lynch estate. These include the Terry Cottage, which features a comfortable living room with flowered wallpaper and Victorian dining room; the Potting Shed, where the first U.S. locomotive was built and which is now used for corporate meetings; six modern duplexes with private decks; and two other large houses connected by a Victorian greenhouse. One of these houses has a distinguished collection of Mexican folk art.

The living room in the main house could be the set of a movie—perhaps *Around the World in 80 Days with Auntie Mame.* Plush leopard-print cushions and gold- and silver-threaded pillows are tossed artfully on the couches. Balinese marionettes hang from the walls. It's all eccentric, eclectic, and artsy—and it all works.

No guest room resembles another, and Marta is always changing things. "If I'm not creating space, then it's boring," she comments. The rooms are decorated with a collection of antiques from different periods. Despite its lavishness, the inn is cozy—the sort of place where guests can help themselves to coffee or a cold drink any time of the day, even if the sign says KITCHEN CLOSED.

A number of the buildings can be rented to groups, and the facilities have been used for everything from fashion shoots to family reunions. The greenhouse is the perfect setting for an intimate wedding.

Address: *101 Hill St., Southampton, NY 11968, tel. 516/283–2160 or 800/54–LATCH.*
Accommodations: *27 double rooms with baths, 6 suites, 6 duplexes.*
Amenities: *Lunch catering on request, air-conditioning, cable TV and phones in rooms on request; swimming pool, tennis courts.*
Rates: *$85–$350; Continental breakfast. AE, DC, MC, V.*
Restrictions: *Pets only with prior arrangement, 3-night minimum July and Aug. weekends, 2-night minimum other weekends.*

Bassett House

A portrait of humorist Will Rogers, who believed that "friends are merely strangers who haven't met," occupies a prominent spot in Bassett House, an 1830 Colonial-style building on the outskirts of East Hampton. Rogers is innkeeper Michael Bassett's hero. Michael, a former photographer, has created a relaxed place. His taste in decorating runs to the eclectic. World War I Red Cross posters deck the halls, and in the living room an old cookstove stands next to a doctor's scale.

Guest rooms too contain furniture from a variety of periods. Room 5 has an oak spindle bed and a fireplace; the suite is furnished with a painted oak Victorian bed and matching dresser. Don't expect the decor to be exactly the same when you get there—rooms change according to Bassett's whim.

Address: *Box 1426, 128 Montauk Hwy., East Hampton, NY 11937, tel. 516/324-6127.*
Accommodations: *7 double rooms with baths, 1 double and 2 singles share 2 baths, 2 suites.*
Amenities: *Air-conditioning, cable TV in some rooms. Well-behaved pets allowed with prior arrangement.*
Rates: *$65–$150; full breakfast. MC, V.*
Restrictions: *2-night minimum on summer weekends, 4-night minimum holidays.*

Hedges' Inn

If you're up early enough, you might see pheasants searching out breakfast in the front yard of Hedges' Inn. The property sits across from a greensward and pond where cattle grazed in the mid-1600s, when the area was first settled. In winter, when skaters glide over the frozen pond, the vista is a Currier and Ives print brought to life.

The inn, now owned by the Palm Management Corporation, was built as a private residence, in 1774. A varied selection of flowers in brilliant hues lines the brick path to the columned front porch, where visitors can ease themselves into green-cushion wicker chairs and enjoy the passing scene. Guest rooms are attractively furnished with antiques, patchwork quilts, and frilly shams and throw pillows. You sit down to breakfast at English-pine tables adorned with baskets of blooms, in a small, sunny dining room. A buffet is set on a carved-pine hutch. Those who dine at the Inn's Palm Restaurant may sample the gargantuan lobsters and steaks.

Address: *74 James La., East Hampton, NY 11937, tel. 516/324-7100.*
Accommodations: *11 double rooms with baths.*
Amenities: *Restaurant, air-conditioning.*
Rates: *$85–$150; cold buffet breakfast. AE, MC, V.*
Restrictions: *No pets, 3-night minimum on July and Aug. weekends, 5-night minimum July 4 and Labor Day weekends, closed winter.*

The Hill Guest House

Built around 1890, the Hill Guest House is the Hamptons without frills. Located a mile from the village of Southampton and a two-minute drive from the beach, the house offers clean and pleasant accommodations at low rates. Owners Mauro and Ronnie Salerno have been here since 1964, when they came for a two-week vacation at the guest house and ended up buying it. Mauro was in the meat business ("Selling rooms is the same as selling sausages," he says with a laugh) and today spends his spare time playing golf, swimming, and serving as a hospital volunteer. Ronnie is a gourmet cook and "does *The New York Times* crossword puzzle in ink," boasts Mauro.

The rooms have twin beds (which can be pushed together); most beds are made of antique iron painted to match the decor. The front porch has painted wicker chairs, and on cool evenings the living-room fireplace is the cheery focal point of the inn.

Address: *535 Hill St., Southampton, NY 11968, tel. 516/283–9889 or 718/461–0014 (Nov.–Apr.).*
Accommodations: *1 double room with bath, 2 doubles share 1 bath; 3 doubles share 2 hall baths.*
Rates: *$55–$75; breakfast extra. No credit cards.*
Restrictions: *No pets, 2-night minimum on weekends June and Sept., 3-night minimum on July and Aug. weekends, closed Nov.–Apr.*

The Maidstone Arms

The original settlers of East Hampton called the village Maidstone, after their native village in England, so it's not surprising that the Maidstone Arms has the air of a British seaside resort. The Victorian inn, built in the 1830s, features porches with white-wicker furniture, green-and-white–stripe awnings, and an English perennial garden—the perfect spot for tea on a balmy afternoon. Since 1979 Donna Cullum has been the able innkeeper. Gary Reiswig, a city planner, and his wife, Rita, a psychotherapist, own the inn.

Rooms are decorated in Victorian style. Some walls are stenciled, and others have wallpaper with a flower motif. White dotted-swiss curtains and lots of wicker complete the furnishings. One suite has its own sun porch. One of the two cottages (which are rented by the week during the summer) has a queen-size sleigh bed and a fireplace.

Address: *207 Main St., East Hampton, NY 11937, tel. 516/324–5006.*
Accommodations: *12 double rooms with baths, 7 suites.*
Amenities: *Restaurant, air-conditioning, cable TV in rooms; limo service from jitney, train, and East Hampton airport.*
Rates: *$95–$230; Continental breakfast. AE, MC, V.*
Restrictions: *No pets, 3-night minimum on holiday weekends, 2-night minimum other weekends, closed mid-Jan.–Apr. 1.*

Mill House Inn

In the shadow of East Hampton's landmark windmill, across from the village green, is the appropriately named Mill House Inn. This 1790 saltbox reminiscent of New England architecture was converted to a Dutch Colonial in 1890. Innkeepers Barbara and Kevin Flynn left California—she was a software engineer, he was a manager of a steamship company—to buy a bed-and-breakfast "back East." Now they preside over this charming place, where clematis climbs the screened porch and geraniums sprout from the window boxes.

Barbara stenciled the walls and is also responsible for the guest-room curtains, some made of Laura Ashley fabrics. Rooms have Colonial-period antiques, including a queen-size canopy and a four-poster. Guests breakfast on walnut waffles or French toast with cream cheese and apricot preserves. To work off breakfast they borrow the inn's bikes and pedal to the beach.

Address: *33 N. Main St., East Hampton, NY 11937, tel. 516/324–9766.*
Accommodations: *6 double rooms, with baths, 2 doubles share bath.*
Amenities: *Beach passes.*
Rates: *$75–$145; full breakfast, afternoon beverages. AE, MC, V.*
Restrictions: *No smoking in bedrooms, no pets, 3-night minimum on weekends, 4-night minimum on holiday weekends June–Aug.*

The Old Post House Inn

The Old Post House is New York State's oldest privately owned and occupied English wood-frame house. Innkeepers Ed and Cecille Courville (he's a retired executive) share wonderful stories with their guests about the building's history (ask about the archaeological dig in the basement). The beams in the common room of the building date from the early 1700s, and a chimney brick found during the inn's restoration is thought to date from 1684.

Furnished with American antiques, the guest rooms are named for local historical figures. The charming Lizbeth White Room displays a Dresden Plate quilt (many of the inn's quilts are for sale). The Lion Gardiner Room has flowered wallpaper, a four-poster bed, and an afghan-covered blanket chest. Guests breakfast in the common room or take trays out to the porch. The nearby Methodist church sounds its carillon each day at noon—a perfect old-fashion accompaniment to this old-fashion village inn.

Address: *136 Main St., Southampton Village, NY 11968, tel. 516/283–1717.*
Accommodations: *7 double rooms with baths.*
Amenities: *Air-conditioning.*
Rates: *$80–$160; Continental breakfast. AE, MC, V.*
Restrictions: *No pets, 2-night minimum on weekends June–Sept., 3-night minimum on holiday weekends.*

Pennsylvania

The Inn at Phillips Mill

Pennsylvania

NEW YORK

0   20 miles
0   30 km

N

Sayre

New Milford   Starlight

Wysox   Lake Como

Dushore   Tunkhannock   81   Beach Lake

220   Scranton   Hawley

                                        Lake   Tafton
                                    Wallenpaupack
Wilkes-Barre   84   Promised Land
                                                    Pond   Milford
ort   S. Sterling
                                    La Anna   BUSHKILL AND
Bloomsburg   Blakeslee   Canadensis   DELAWARE WATER
                    Corners   Mt. Pocono   GAP NATIONAL
                            Pocono   REC. AREA
                    80   Manor   Analomink
Hazleton   Lake   Tannersville
                    Harmony   Stroudsburg
nbury   Jim Thorpe

        Tamaqua   Palmerton

        81   NEW JERSEY

                            Bethlehem
                Fogelsville   Upper
                                    Allentown   Black Eddy
                    Mertztown
                                            9   Erwinna
                78
Lebanon   422   New
Hershey   Reading   Hope
                Adamstown   Doylestown   Washington
        Lititz   Ephrata   Pottstown   Schwenksville   Crossing   Trenton
Mt. Joy   76   Morrisville
            Bird in Hand Churchtown   Valley   Narristown   Falsington
                Intercourse   Forge
Lancaster   Exton   30
        Strasburg   Glenloch
                        West Chester   Gradyville   Camden
            Kennett Square   Chadds Ford   Philadelphia
83   Avondale   Fairville
            1

The Poconos

Though the Poconos are best known as the Honeymoon Capital of the World, the land of the glitzy motel, with heart-shape beds, hot tubs, and bottomless champagne glasses, the "other" Poconos may be Pennsylvania's best-kept secret. The northeast corner of the state, bordering the Delaware River, encompasses 2,400 square miles of mountainous wilderness, with lakes, streams, waterfalls, woods, and enchanting country inns.

The region consists of four counties: Carbon, Monroe, Pike, and Wayne. The discovery of anthracite coal in Carbon County led to its development as a mining region, a railroad center, and a land of opportunity for European immigrants. The town of Mauch Chunk, founded in 1815 (now called Jim Thorpe, after the great Native American athlete), became home to a dozen coal and railroad millionaires. Monroe County, along the Delaware River, was first inhabited by the Delaware and Shawnee tribes, then settled by the Dutch in 1659, and by the English and Germans a century later. In the 1820s people began visiting the Poconos in summer for the crisp mountain air. Boardinghouses were built along the Delaware Water Gap, Monroe County developed a small resort industry, and by 1900 thousands were coming each summer from Philadelphia and New York City.

A back-roads drive through the woodlands and rolling hills will turn up dairy farms and quaint villages, country stores and lots of antiques and crafts shops. In winter there's downhill and cross-country skiing, ice skating, snowmobiling, and sledding. In summer there's theater, golf and tennis, boating, swimming, horseback riding, and hiking. And any time after a full day, you'll find a good night's sleep in a country inn.

Places to go, sights to see

Bushkill Falls (Bushkill, tel. 717/588–6682). The Niagara of Pennsylvania, on 300 acres, has trails leading to eight waterfalls. There's an exhibit of Pennsylvania wildlife, and there are picnic grounds, fishing, paddleboats, and a silversmith shop.

Grey Towers (Milford, tel. 717/296–6401). You can tour the house and gardens of the stone ancestral home of Gifford Pinchot, first chief of the U.S. Forest Service and twice governor of Pennsylvania.

Jim Thorpe (Rte. 209). This late-Victorian mountain-resort town, once called Mauch Chunk (from the Native American *Machktschunk*, Mountain of the Sleeping Bear), has first-rate antiques shops and galleries, the Asa Packer Museum, St. Mark's Church, Flagstaff Park, the Overlook, and a restored railroad station.

Lake Wallenpaupack (between Greentown and Hawley). Year-round activities along the 52-mile shoreline of the largest recreational lake in the state include water skiing, swimming, boating, fishing, snowmobiling, ice skating, cross-country skiing, and ice fishing. Hiking trails lead to scenic overlooks.

Pocono Indian Museum (Bushkill, tel. 717/588–9164). Exhibits of artifacts and crafts and a replica of a longhouse trace the history of the Delaware Indians.

Pocono Inn-to-Inn Bicycle Tours (Jim Thorpe, tel. 717/325–3655). Pocono Whitewater Adventures sponsors two- to five-day tours from inn to country inn.

Promised Land State Park (10 mi north of Canadensis, tel. 717/676–3428). This natural forest and recreational area of 11,010 acres, filled with deer, bear, and smaller game, has seasonal sports, picnic grounds, and 25 miles of marked hiking trails.

Quiet Valley Living Historical Farm (Stroudsburg, tel. 717/992–6161). Authentically costumed "family members" reenact farm life in a 1765 log house. Demonstrations include spinning, baking, gardening, and tending the animals.

Ski areas and resorts

You'll find beginner, intermediate, and expert trails in the region. All have ski schools, rentals, cross-country ski trails, ice skating, and night skiing. Many offer indoor swimming, tennis, racquetball, and entertainment. Inquire about midweek packages.

Alpine Mountain, Analomink, tel. in PA, 717/595–2150; outside PA, 800/233–8240. **Big Boulder,** Blakeslee, tel. 717/772–0101. **Blue Mountain Ski Area,**

Palmerton, tel. 215/826–7700. **Camelback,** Tannersville, tel. 717/629–1661. **Fernwood,** Bushkill, tel. 717/588–9500. **Jack Frost Mountain,** Blakeslee, tel. 717/443–8425. **Mount Airy Lodge,** Mt. Pocono, tel. in PA, 717/839–8811; outside PA, 800/441–4410. **Mount Tone,** Lake Como, tel. 717/798–2707. **Pocono Manor Inn and Gold Resort,** Pocono Manor, tel. in PA, 717/839–7111; outside PA, 800/233–8150. **Shawnee Mountain,** Shawnee-on-Delaware, tel. 717/421–7231. **Split Rock Resort,** Lake Harmony, tel. in PA, 717/722–9111; outside PA, 800/255–7625. **Tanglwood,** Tafton, tel. in PA, 717/226–9500; outside PA, 800/341–5700.

Tourist Information

Pocono Mountains Vacation Bureau, Inc. (Box CIB, Stroudsburg 18360, tel. 717/424–6050 or 717/421–5791, 24-hour ski hotline, 717/421–5565).

The French Manor

The 43-acre setting is aristocratic and the views exquisite. Rolling hills and mountain ranges reveal themselves periodically as you drive up the winding, wooded road toward the crest of Huckleberry Mountain to the fieldstone manor house with a slate roof, copper-mullioned windows, and arched oak door.

It was built between 1932 and 1937 as a summer residence for mining tycoon and art collector Albert Hirschorn, who modeled it after his château in southern France. After changing hands several times, the house became an inn in 1985 and in 1989 was bought by Walter and Lois Nebel, whose background was in data processing.

The 27-foot-high Great Room, with a vaulted cherry-wood ceiling and a mammoth plastered-stone fireplace at each end, makes a spectacular restaurant. French doors with leaded glass open onto a slate terrace that has a sweeping view of the countryside. The guest rooms, named after European cities, have cypress-panel walls and ceilings and are decorated in a mix of contemporary style and French antique reproductions. "Venice" has an ornate headboard on its king-size bed. Baths have old-fashion tile with pedestal sinks. The carriage-house suite, recently renovated, is furnished like the manor house but has smaller rooms. Though it is secluded, its feeling of newness makes it not nearly as nice as the larger house.

Dinner on weekends, an eight-course gourmet feast, might include marinated mussels or a pastry puff filled with seafood Newburg. There's always a salad and a palate-clearing sorbet. Then you might try fresh salmon with hollandaise sauce, lamb chops with herbs and butter, or a light veal Marsala. After a selection of imported cheeses, a dessert tray of home-baked cakes arrives.

With grandiose views as a backdrop, you can take peaceful walks or go cross-country skiing. Golf, horseback riding, and other recreations are nearby. The medieval atmosphere of the house—and the thoughtful service of the Nebels and their staff—create the timeless feeling that you have really gotten away from it all.

Address: *Box 39, Huckleberry Rd., South Sterling, PA 18460, tel. 717/676-3244.*
Accommodations: *4 double rooms with baths, 2 doubles share 1 bath, 1 suite.*
Amenities: *Restaurant open daily for lunch and dinner, air-conditioning in bedrooms, TV in lounge; croquet.*
Rates: *$110–$325; Continental breakfast, dinner. AE, MC, V.*
Restrictions: *Smoking in public areas only, no pets, BYOB, closed last 2 weeks of Mar.*

The Inn at Meadowbrook

Guests who arrive at The Inn at Meadowbrook after dark are often relieved to find they aren't lost. On the long and winding 4½ wooded miles from Tannersville you may begin to think you've missed it, but suddenly, around a corner, there it is, blanketed by soft light and trees and chirping night sounds: a white clapboard manor house with green trim. And just across the road is a white mill house that's part of the inn. If you're going to get pleasantly lost anywhere in the Poconos, this is the place to do it.

For many years the 1867 house and its 43 acres were a horse farm, and in 1985 Kathy and Bob Overman bought the estate and turned it into a bed-and-breakfast. Kathy, an artist who loves to garden, has given each of the guest rooms a distinctive decor. On weekdays Bob commutes to his aluminum business in Wilkes-Barre, and on weekends he's the inn's gourmet chef.

The light-flooded parlor is decorated in soft browns and greens, with chintz fabrics. You can curl up with a book on the leather sofa or in wing chairs that face the fireplace, or you can simply gaze out the windows at the pond, gazebo, and mill house. The spacious hunter-green dining room, added in the '20s, is a setting out of *The Great Gatsby*, with 15-foot ceilings, arched columns, and tall Palladian windows on three sides framing the gardens, the rushing brook with footbridge, and a pond. French doors open onto the terrace for dining in warm months.

The guest rooms are furnished with English and American antiques and country pieces. There are patchwork quilts, lots of books, wicker chairs, and convenient reading lamps. Room 9, a favorite of guests, has rich burgundy paisley draperies, hunter-green walls, an antique brass bed, and a view of the stables.

On the inn's own grounds you can swim, fish, play tennis, ice-skate, and take leisurely walks with a picnic lunch. The nearby Meadowbrook Equestrian Center boards about 30 horses in its stables, and Bob and Kathy can arrange horseback riding and carriage and sleigh rides. The area also has its share of antiques shops and flea markets.

Address: *RD 7, Box 7651, Cherry Lane Rd., Stroudsburg, PA 18301, 717/629–0296.*
Accommodations: *10 double rooms with baths, 6 doubles share 2 baths.*
Amenities: *Restaurant, TV and VCR in recreation room; swimming pool, 2 tennis courts, shuffleboard.*
Rates: *$50–$85; full breakfast. AE, MC, V.*
Restrictions: *Smoking in common rooms only, no pets, 2-day minimum on weekends.*

The Inn at Starlight Lake

The hamlet of Starlight, nestled in the foothills of the Moosic range, was once a railroad stop, and in 1909 this Adirondack-style lodge was built on the lake nearby to serve passengers. Today the sprawling white-and-green clapboard inn looks much as it did around the turn of the century, and it's just as peaceful. Jack and Judy McMahon have been innkeepers here since 1974. Before that they lived in New York City and worked in the theater, where they met while performing.

The rambling parlor, with its wood-burning stove, stone fireplace, and baby-grand piano, sets the homey, lodgelike mood. There's a comfortable mixture of antiques, Mission oak furniture, and well-lived-in pieces, with numerous Tiffany-style lamps for reading. In winter you might expect Bing Crosby to step out and warble "White Christmas."

Guest rooms on the second and third floors are simple and unpretentious, with framed prints on floral-papered walls, crocheted doilies, and lots of magazines. You'll find iron beds and marble-top dressers, but mostly a hodge-podge of old and not-so-old furniture. A row of recently renovated cottages is furnished with wicker and antique reproductions. The suite has a king-size bed and a whirlpool bath for two; above it is another charming room with an iron bed and a fieldstone fireplace.

Cordon Bleu chef Michael O'Neill presides in the dining room. He offers such choices as duck with two sauces; pheasant stuffed with pheasant mousse; and a seafood sausage made of scallops, shrimp, and fillet of sole. Everything served is made on the premises, including breads, pastas, ice cream, and pastries.

No motors are allowed on the 45-acre lake, so it's quiet and crystal clean for swimming and fishing. On occasional murder-mystery weekends, whodunits are performed by the Starlight Players. In winter there's ice skating, and the McMahons' son, a certified ski instructor, can take you down the property's slopes or show you the best trails for cross-country skiing. On crisp autumn mornings you are likely to see deer or flocks of wild turkeys through the early mist.

Address: *Starlight, PA 18461, tel. 717/798-2519.*
Accommodations: *20 double rooms with baths, 2 doubles share bath, 1 suite.*
Amenities: *Restaurant, TV and VCR in sun-room, baby-sitting arranged; tennis court, canoes, bicycles.*
Rates: *$115–180; full breakfast, dinner. MC, V.*
Restrictions: *No smoking in dining room, no pets, 2-day minimum in season, 3-day minimum on holidays, closed first 2 weeks in Apr.*

The Beach Lake Hotel

In 1986 Roy and Erika Miller, lovers of antiques, restoration, and cooking, left their careers in health administration to become keepers of this Victorian country inn. The mustard-colored, clapboard two-story building in the sleepy village of Beach Lake began as a hotel and tavern around 1859. The antiques-filled lobby, with wainscoted walls and ceilings, was once a general store. The inn is furnished throughout with Victorian oak and walnut, and everything is for sale. The parlor has a 15-foot ceiling, a velvet sofa, and a grandfather clock. In the formal dining room lace tablecloths and crystal-globe lamps on each table enhance the dinners prepared by Erika Thursday through Monday. The guest rooms, each unique, have carved headboards, lace-canopy beds, rocking chairs, armoires, and imported lace curtains. There are pedestal sinks in the bathrooms. Though the lake is only a short walk away, and ski areas are nearby, you might want to spend your time on the upstairs porch just rocking or reading.

Address: *Box 144, Main and Church Sts., Beach Lake, PA 18405, tel. 717/729–8239.*
Accommodations: *6 double rooms with baths.*
Amenities: *Restaurant, air-conditioning in bedrooms, pub with TV.*
Rates: *$85; full breakfast. MC, V.*
Restrictions: *Smoking in public areas only, no pets, 2-day minimum on holiday weekends.*

Cliff Park Inn

This historic country inn, built as a homestead in 1820, has been in innkeeper Harry W. Buchanan's family for four generations. The three-story white-clapboard Colonial building with green trim is a mile west of Milford, and its 560 acres overlook one of the country's first golf courses. In the main parlor you'll find a wealth of Victorian family heirlooms, Buchanan ancestral portraits, and a stone fireplace. Guest rooms are decorated with family antiques and reproductions; some have porches that overlook the golf course. Three nearby cottages, ideal for families or groups, have exposed beams, large fieldstone fireplaces, and eclectic furnishings. The chef is a member of the renowned *Chaîne des Rôtisseurs*, a society of chefs. The inn's maple-shaded veranda is a favorite gathering place. There you can watch the golfers and the deer that come at dusk.

Address: *RD 2, Box 8562, Cliff Park Rd., Milford, PA 18337, tel. 717/296–6491 or 800/225–6535, fax 717/296–3982.*
Accommodations: *19 double rooms with baths.*
Amenities: *Restaurant, air-conditioning in bedrooms, phones in bedrooms, conference facilities, TV and VCR in meeting rooms; golf course, pro shop, stable for boarding horses.*
Rates: *$100–$125; full breakfast, dinner. AE, D, DC, MC, V.*
Restrictions: *No pets.*

Harry Packer Mansion

In 1874 Asa Packer, founder of the Lehigh Valley Railroad, built this Victorian mansion as a wedding present for his son. The imposing building of brick, stone, and New England sandstone, trimmed with cast iron, overlooks the Victorian village of Jim Thorpe. Inside, the library, formal parlors, and dining room are paneled in solid mahogany, and the parquet floors are inlaid with five different woods. Tiffany windows, bronze chandeliers, and intricately carved mantels add to the Gothic-novel grandeur. The guest rooms have high-back Victorian beds and tall bay windows with lace curtains. Robert and Pat Handwerk moved here from Philadelphia, where he was an urban planner and she was a marketing executive. They restored the mansion and carriage-house to its former glory and have been innkeepers since 1984. Jim Thorpe is chock-full of interesting shops, and there's skiing 10 minutes away. On weekends guests match wits to solve a murder mystery.

Address: *Packer Hill, Jim Thorpe, PA 18229, tel. 717/325–8566.*
Accommodations: *5 double rooms and 2 loftrooms with baths, 5 doubles share 2 baths, 1 suite.*
Amenities: *TV in common area, local tours arranged.*
Rates: *$75–$110; full breakfast. MC, V.*
Restrictions: *Smoking in sitting room only, no pets, 2-day minimum on holidays.*

The Overlook Inn

Just outside Canadensis is a yellow three-story inn with a porch around it so high that when you're on it you feel as though you're up in the pines. Arthur and Debbie Bolger and David and Valerie Escalet, innkeepers who grew up in the business, have furnished the guest rooms in this 1870 Victorian farmhouse in a mix of early American reproductions and Victorian antiques. The rooms downstairs, though dark, are cozy. On cool evenings, a fire crackles in the stone fireplace in the living room, and from the window seat in the library you might see deer grazing on the lawn. Nothing's fussy here, yet meals in the dining room do attract a well-dressed following. Chef Pierre is famous for his creations— particularly his popovers in the morning. The Bolgers or the Escalets will gladly point you to the trails for cross-country skiing on the inn's 15 wooded acres or help you plan a drive down scenic back roads.

Address: *Dutch Hill Rd., Canadensis, PA 18325–9755, tel. 717/595–7519 or 800/441–0177, fax 717/588–7519.*
Accommodations: *18 double rooms with baths, 2 suites.*
Amenities: *Restaurant, air conditioners available, telephones in rooms, TV in library; swimming pool, conference facilities.*
Rates: *$65–$100; breakfast, high tea, dinner. AE, MC, V.*
Restrictions: *No pets, 2-day minimum on weekends.*

Pine Knob Inn

This board-and-batten 1847 inn, painted bishop's gray, is on 10 wooded acres. Scott Frankel, discouraged with the impersonality of large hotels he had worked in, became innkeeper here with his wife, Annie, in 1988. The place is rambling, but inside it feels cozy and old-fashioned, with homey Victorian antiques and reproductions. There's a fieldstone fireplace in the parlor, and the dining room is a warm, Mildred Pierce kind of place—You wonder if apple pies are baking nearby. On shelves and sideboards are the 107 cookie jars that Annie has collected. Guest rooms have carved headboards, brass beds, and Annie's homemade quilts. The Pineapple Room has a step-down bathroom with a claw-footed tub. Three adjacent cottages are furnished similarly, and the barn has been converted into an art gallery and workshop. From the pool it's only a few steps down to the rapids in Brodshead Creek. You're likely to find artists here at their easels, capturing blazing colors in autumn or the buds in spring.

Address: *Rte. 447, Canadensis, PA 18325, tel. 717/595-2532.*
Accommodations: *18 double rooms with baths, 5 doubles share 2 baths.*
Amenities: *Restaurant open daily except Mon. for breakfast and dinner, TV in parlor; swimming pool, tennis court, ski instruction, conference facilities.*
Rates: *$144 MAP; MC, V.*
Restrictions: *No pets, 2-day minimum on holiday weekends.*

The Settler's Inn

This rambling Tudor-style grand hotel built in 1927 has been restored as a country inn. It's on a well-traveled bend of Route 6, five minutes from Lake Wallenpaupack, but once you enter the high-ceilinged living room, with its chestnut beams and massive stone fireplace, you will forget about the location. Antique marble-top tables, Victorian chairs and sofas evoke the atmosphere of an English country hotel. The rooms, furnished with "early attic" antiques, also have handmade quilts and early American memorabilia. The popular dining room is the domain of Grant Genzlinger, who's not only chef/innkeeper but also a student of ancient Chinese languages. He and his wife, Jeanne, have been innkeeping for 20 years, and 10 of them have been spent here. The location is ideal for getting to winter or summer sports, and the town has enough antiques shops to keep you browsing for days.

Address: *4 Main Ave., Hawley, PA 18428, tel. 717/226-2993.*
Accommodations: *15 double rooms with baths, 3 double suites.*
Amenities: *Restaurant, air-conditioning, TV in sitting room, 2 meeting rooms, 1 large banquet room.*
Rates: *$65-$80; full breakfast. AE, MC, V.*
Restrictions: *Ask about pets.*

New Hope/Bucks County

*Since the 1930s, when Bucks County was discovered by
Broadway's smart set, the area has been a popular retreat
from the hectic urban pace. The rolling hills, stone barns,
and quaint covered bridges that once attracted George S.
Kaufman, Dorothy Parker, and Oscar Hammerstein can
still be found here in abundance. But easy access from
Philadelphia (one hour) and New York (two hours) has
brought crowds and traffic jams on summer weekends.*

*Despite its rapid growth, much of Bucks County's 625
square miles remain bucolic. The sleepy, sylvan beauty of
the 18th- and 19th-century villages and the lush banks of
the Delaware River make it an enchanting place to explore.
You'll see many of Pennsylvania's famous "bank barns"
(built against a bank or hill, so wagons could roll right
into the loft). Stray off the beaten path and you will
discover ageless scenic roads that centuries ago were the
forest trails of the Leni-Lenape Indians. George
Washington's Continental Army later used these roads to
reach the Delaware River, which they crossed on an icy
Christmas Eve, in 1776.*

*New Hope, settled in the early 1700s, is the heart of Bucks
County. This idyllic village on the Delaware River is
a tapestry of stone houses, narrow streets and alleys,
hidden courtyards, and charming restaurants. Doylestown,
the county seat, an important coach stop in the 18th
century, is today a showcase of American architecture and
fine museums of Americana.*

*Bucks County is the place to relax, with a ride on
a mule-drawn barge along the Delaware canal or on
a horse-drawn carriage along a country lane. You can visit
art galleries and crafts emporiums, wineries, flea markets,
farm markets, and historic sights. In fall you can attend
auctions, take in the foliage, and browse through one of the*

largest concentrations of antiques shops in the country. In summer there's canoeing, tubing, hiking, horseback riding, and an old and famous summer-stock theater. In any season, after a day of exploring, the country inns and bed-and-breakfasts are one of Bucks County's greatest pleasures.

Places to go, sights to see

Bucks County Carriages (tel. 215/862–5883) offers 30-minute tours of New Hope in horse-drawn carriages, daily in summer and weekends only in spring and fall.

Bucks County Playhouse (New Hope, tel. 215/862–2041), housed in a mid-18th-century mill, presents Broadway drama and musical hits. The season runs from May through Christmas.

Bucks County Vineyards and Winery (3 mi south of New Hope, tel. 800/362–0309; in PA, 800/523–2510) is open for tours and wine tastings.

Fonthill (Doylestown, tel. 215/348–9461) was designed and constructed by Henry Chapman Mercer, a leader in the arts and crafts movement, a noted antiquarian and archaeologist, and a pioneer ceramicist. Built with all the grandeur of a medieval castle, the house contains collections of decorative tiles, prints, prehistoric pottery, and memorabilia.

Ghost Tours of New Hope (tel. 215/357–4558) consist of one-hour walks by lantern lights to explore the haunted spots of the area.

Historic Fallsington (Fallsington, tel. 215/295–6567) is the 300-year-old village where William Penn attended Quaker meetings. The restored buildings span three centuries.

Mercer Museum (Doylestown, tel. 215/345–0210) contains a collection of early Americana, tools, and implements of trades and crafts before mass production. There are antique vehicles, a log house, and a 14,000-volume library.

Moravian Pottery and Tile Works (Doylestown, tel. 215/348–6722) is now restored as a living-history museum; here you can watch tiles being made.

New Hope Mule Barge Co. (tel. 215/862–2842) offers one-hour excursions on the Delaware Canal, through the countryside, and past 18th-century cottages and artists' workshops.

Parry Mansion (New Hope, tel. 215/862–5652), a restored stone house built in 1784 by Benjamin Parry, a prosperous merchant and mill owner, is furnished in period antiques that date from the late-18th to the early 20th century.

Pearl S. Buck House (Hilltown, tel. 215/249–0100 or 215/242–6779), the home of the Pulitzer- and Nobel Prize-winning author has its original furnishings, including many Chinese artifacts.

Peddler's Village (Lahaska, tel. 215/794–7055) is a re-created 18th-century village of 62 old-fashion country shops and "early American" restaurants.

Pennsbury Manor (Morrisville, tel. 215/946–0400) is William Penn's reconstructed 17th-century country estate. The estate's 43 acres contain the manor house (with period furnishings), outbuildings, livestock, and gardens.

Quarry Valley Farm (Lahaska, tel. 215/794–5882) is a working farm with many animals to pet.

Rice's Sale and Country Market (Solebury, tel. 215/297–5993) offers bargains in clothing, antiques, linens, shoes, and plants Tuesday from dawn to 1 PM.

Washington Crossing Historic Park (tel. 215/493–4076) has the old McConkey's Ferry Inn, replicas of Durham boats (the type George Washington used), a restored gristmill, a wildflower preserve with displays, lectures, and trails.

Tourist Information

Bucks County Tourist Commission (152 Swamp Rd., Doylestown 18901, tel. 215/345–4552). **New Hope Borough Information Center** (Box 141, 1 W. Mechanic St., New Hope 18938, tel. 215/862–5880).

Barley Sheaf Farm

Turn off well-traveled Route 202 10 minutes from New Hope, and you will see sheep grazing in the pastures on either side of a sycamore-flanked lane. At the end is Barley Sheaf Farm, the 1740 mansard-roof, fieldstone house that in the '30s was the hideaway of playwright George S. Kaufman. Today this charming 30-acre farm, though just around the bend from the bustling antiques shops of Peddler's Village, manages to retain the quiet gentility that prevailed when Lillian Hellman, Alexander Woollcott, and Moss Hart visited here.

The swimming pool, a duck pond, and the bank barn add texture and a relaxed appeal to the house and grounds, which have been designated a National Historic Site. Until 1979 this was the home of innkeepers Don and Ann Mills, who then decided to open their farm to travelers. Barley Sheaf Farm was Bucks County's first B&B, and with good reason it has become one of the most noted.

The house and adjacent cottage are furnished in a mixture of English and American antiques, with rich Oriental rugs scattered over the wide-plank floors. Guests gather in the common room, by the fire, for chess, checkers, and conversation.

The bedrooms on the second and third floors have elegant views. The rooms are decorated with floral prints and brass-and-iron beds. Personal touches complement the antique furnishings: doll collections, family photographs, and paintings by Ann. Don was president of a fragrance company before retiring to Barley Sheaf, and perfume bottles decorate the antique bureaus.

The cottage is cozy, and in winter months there's always a crackling fire. The three bedrooms here are decorated with American folk art, both antique and reproduction. Each room has sloping eaves, hooked rugs, and antique pine furniture. Though the rooms are small, the cottage is perfect for families.

You should expect to hear noises in this rural setting—the noises of a working farm—sheep, chickens, and the occasional tractor. But that means you can count on the abundant breakfasts (which include eggs, bread, jams, and honey) to be farm fresh.

Address: *Box 10, Rte. 202, Holicong, PA 18928, tel. 215/794–5104.*
Accommodations: *7 double rooms with baths, 2 suites.*
Amenities: *Air-conditioning in bedrooms, TV in study; swimming pool, badminton, croquet, meeting room and kitchen in barn.*
Rates: *$90–$175; full breakfast. V.*
Restrictions: *No pets, 2-day minimum on weekends, 3-day minimum on holidays, closed mid-Dec.–early Jan.*

Evermay-on-the-Delaware

Thirteen miles north of New Hope is Evermay-on-the-Delaware, a romantic country hotel with a carriage house and cottage set on 25 parklike acres between the river and the canal. Here Victorian elegance is still very much in fashion.

The mansion, which is on the National Register of Historic Places, was built in 1720, and had a third floor added in 1870. From 1871 through the early 1930s, it was a popular country hotel. It was abandoned for many years and then bought by veteran innkeepers Fred Cresson and Ron Strouse. After meticulous restoration, they reopened it in March 1982. You will find Fred and Ron to be unobtrusive, genteel hosts; their style is in keeping with the hotel's tradition of understated elegance.

In the stately wainscoted double parlor you can meet for afternoon tea or for an aperitif in the evening. The fireplace is inset with Mercer tiles, and there are crystal chandeliers, tapestry rugs, a Victorian grandfather clock, and brocade camelback settees. Breakfast is served in a conservatory off the back parlor. The bedrooms, carefully decorated with Victorian antiques and named after Bucks County notables, have wide-plank squeaky floors; some retain their original fireplaces. Carved walnut beds, massive headboards, marble-top dressers, Victorian wallpaper, and fresh fruit and flowers

are everywhere. Ask for one of the six bedrooms in the main house that face the river. The carriage house may be preferable for groups traveling together. It has a two-bedroom suite with sitting room and bath on the second floor and two double rooms on the ground floor.

A weekend stay at the Evermay is incomplete without the seven-course prix fixe dinner, which is mandatory one night. Ron, a gourmet chef who trained with James Beard, serves unforgettable French and northern Italian dishes.

The Evermay is ideally located for enjoying the countryside in any season. If you venture out into the meadows or into the old barn you will run across sheep and peacocks. Fred and Ron keep a canoe across the road for paddling on the Delaware, and in warm weather there's croquet on the lawn.

Address: *River Rd., Erwinna, PA 18920, tel. 215/294–9100, fax 215/294–8249.*
Accommodations: *14 double rooms with baths, 1 suite.*
Amenities: *Restaurant, air-conditioning and phones in bedrooms; hookups for modem.*
Rates: *$70–$175; full breakfast, afternoon tea. MC, V.*
Restrictions: *No pets, 2-day minimum with Sat. reservation, 3-day minimum on holidays, closed Christmas Eve.*

The Inn at Fordhook Farm

The Inn at Fordhook Farm, set on 62 acres a mile and a half from the center of Doylestown, is the Burpee family estate. There's a bank barn and a carriage house, surrounded by the fields and meadows where W. Atlee Burpee first tested seeds for his company before the turn of the century. The oldest part of the fieldstone-and-plaster house with a mansard roof dates from 1740. Through the years, additions were carefully made to blend architecturally with the original structure.

Burpee's grandchildren, Blanche Burpee Dohan and her brother Jonathan Burpee, grew up here. Thinking that a bed-and-breakfast would be a good way to preserve the family home, they opened it to guests in 1985. When Burpee family members gather here on holidays, guests are encouraged to join in the festivities.

The house, furnished throughout with a mixture of English and American antiques, is a living legacy of photographs, china, furniture, grandfather clocks, and other Americana. In the dining room, the mantel is inlaid with Mercer tiles, and the long mahogany table is set with heirloom china each morning for breakfast. French doors open to a large terrace shaded by 200-year-old linden trees, with a view of the broad, sweeping lawn. In the bedrooms, you will find floral prints, quilts, 19th-century four-poster beds, window seats, family photographs and portraits, fresh flowers, and panoramic views.

The carriage house is a spacious two-bedroom suite not quite as carefully decorated as the main house, but ideal for a family or for two couples. The chestnut-paneled Great Room there, once a study, has a vaulted ceiling and Palladian windows, and children's books, photographs, and other Burpee memorabilia everywhere. Seeds are still tested on 2 acres beside the carriage house, and in spring and summer you will view bursts of color in the gardens outside your window.

The style at Fordhook Farm is a quiet, casual elegance. When Blanche and Jonathan are away, it is in the capable hands of Elizabeth Romanella, who worked for the Philadelphia Museum of Art for 12 years. She will suggest walks for you if you're not spending the evening by the fireplace with the family albums.

Address: *105 New Britain Rd., Doylestown, PA 18901, tel. 215/345–1766.*
Accommodations: *3 double rooms with baths, 4 doubles share 2 baths.*
Amenities: *Air-conditioning in bedrooms, conference room.*
Rates: *$90–$165; full breakfast. AE, MC, V.*
Restrictions: *No smoking, no pets, 2-day minimum on weekends, 3-day minimum on holidays.*

Inn at Phillips Mill

Perched at a bend in the road, in a tiny hamlet on the Delaware Canal near New Hope, is a 1750 stone inn that looks like an illustration from Grimm's Fairy Tales. There may be no country inn with a setting more romantic than the Inn at Phillips Mill. Built as a barn and a gristmill, it once stood next to the village piggery—a copper pig with a wreath around its neck now welcomes you from just above the deep-blue door.

Around the turn of the century, landscape painter William Lathrop bought the gristmill and started Bucks County's first artists' colony. In the early 1970s, the building and its walled garden caught the imagination of Brooks and Joyce Kaufman. Thinking it had the look of a European village, they bought it; Brooks, an architect, started the renovation, and Joyce began doing the interior. They opened in 1977.

The guest rooms are small, but they will enchant you. Some are tucked imaginatively into nooks and under eaves, and each is whimsically furnished. There are brass and iron and late 19th-century four-poster beds, an eclectic mix of antiques, wicker, quilts, dried bouquets, hand-painted trays, embroidered cloths on night tables, Provençal fabrics, floral wallpapers, and oil paintings. The cottage, also decorated in a mix of French country and American antiques, has a bedroom, a bath, and a living room with a stone fireplace. If you wish, breakfast will be delivered to your bedroom door in a big basket. When you lift the blue-and-white checkered cloth, you will find a pot of coffee or tea, flaky croissants, and coffee cake with cherry jam.

Phillips Mill is famous for its restaurant, and rightly so. The candlelit tables in the three dining rooms are intimately nestled into nooks and crannies, under low, rough-beamed ceilings. The menu is French and may feature tournedos of beef served with an artichoke bottom, a salmon napoleon in watercress sauce, and pork chops stuffed with fresh prunes. Two pastry chefs on the premises prepare blond chocolate mousse with a chocolate sauce, lemon meringue ice cream pie and other, more exotic desserts.

The winding backroads are perfect for hiking, bicycling, or driving to see the fall foliage.

Address: *N. River Rd., New Hope, PA 18938, tel. 215/862–2984.*
Accommodations: *6 double rooms with baths, 1 suite.*
Amenities: *Restaurant, air-conditioning in bedrooms; swimming pool.*
Rates: *$68–$78; Continental breakfast extra. No credit cards.*
Restrictions: *No pets, BYOB, 3-night minimum on holiday weekends, closed early Jan.–early Feb.*

The Wedgwood Inn

Y ou can't miss the Wedgwood Inn. This hip-gabled 1870 Victorian clapboard house on a tree-lined street is only two blocks from the center of New Hope, and it's painted bright Wedgwood blue. It has a large veranda loaded with pots of flowers and hanging ferns, a porte-cochère, and garden walks that wind around to a gazebo. A recent addition next door, called Umplebe House after the town miller, an early owner, was built of plaster and stone about 1830 in the Classic Revival tradition. It has walls that are 26 inches thick, brick walkways through flowering gardens, and a carriage house in back.

The innkeeping business seemed a logical profession for owners Nadine Silnutzer and Carl Glassman. They like collecting china and gardening, and they delight in finding American and English antiques at auctions and flea markets. So they opened their bed-and-breakfast in 1982 as a way to work together while pursuing their interests, and they enjoy innkeeping so much that they even run seminars and apprenticeship programs for prospective innkeepers.

Wedgwood pottery, paintings, handmade quilts, and fresh flowers are everywhere in the sunny interior. The parlors in both houses have coal-fed fireplaces and plush Victorian sofas and chairs. The windows are covered with lace swag curtains. Per-

sian rugs lie on hardwood floors. Both houses have quirky odd-size bedrooms with bay windows and Victorian antiques, brass beds, and four-posters (one is a marvelous queen-size 1850 mahogany sleigh bed). Bedrooms are cooled by old-fashioned ceiling fans in addition to air-conditioning. The circa-1890 carriage house has a small sitting room and a glass-enclosed porch, a kitchenette, and a four-poster in the loft that overlooks a small deck. It's a private retreat that's ideal for reading a novel, or maybe writing one.

Days begin casually with a "Continental plus" breakfast, served in the sun porch, the gazebo, or if you prefer, in bed. If you ask, Carl and Dinie will get you theater tickets, make dinner reservations, arrange picnics, dinner in the gazebo, or a moonlight carriage ride.

Address: *111 W. Bridge St., New Hope, PA 18998, tel. 215/862–2570.*
Accommodations: *10 double rooms with baths, 2 doubles share a bath, 2 suites.*
Amenities: *Air-conditioning in bedrooms, TV in parlors, concierge services; free swimming and tennis privileges at nearby club, complimentary carriage rides.*
Rates: *$75–$140; Continental breakfast, afternoon tea. No credit cards.*
Restrictions: *No smoking indoors. 2-day minimum on weekends, 3-day minimum on holiday weekends.*

The Whitehall Inn

Ten minutes southwest of New Hope and five minutes from Peddler's Village is the Whitehall Inn, a white plaster-over-stone manor house, circa 1794, set on 12 rolling acres, with a huge white barn and stables at the side. It is one of the most peaceful and secluded inns you will find in Bucks County.

Two transplanted Oklahomans, Mike and Suella Wass, are responsible for transforming the house into an elegant bed-and-breakfast. In 1985, after long and careful planning, Mike left his corporate career in human resources and Suella hers as a speech pathologist to take up innkeeping. Suella comes from a long line of good Southern cooks, and her elaborate candlelight breakfast is a meal you are bound to remember.

Inside the house, past the sun-room, are high ceilings, Oriental rugs on wide-plank floors, and windows with deep sills. The parlor has a fireplace, a late-19th-century pedal organ, comfortable contemporary sofas with lots of Victorian lamps, and the soothing sounds of antique clocks ticking everywhere. The bedrooms (four with fireplaces) are furnished in a mixture of late Victorian and American country antiques. You will find a basket of apples, a bottle of Bucks County wine, and Crabtree and Evelyn soaps, colognes, and shampoos. The linens are imported, and in winter, you will sleep between flannel sheets.

Heirloom china and ornate Victorian sterling flatware are used for breakfast, a beautifully orchestrated four-course feast, with lighted tapers on the table and sideboards. The Wasses keep your menu on file, so you'll never get a repeat unless you make a special request.

High tea is served at 4 each afternoon with crystal, china, and silver. In summer you can relax by the pool, play tennis, or go horseback riding. In October, you can walk in the gardens or fields, enjoy the foliage, then spend evenings by the fire in the candlelit parlor.

The Whitehall Inn may appeal most to well-seasoned travelers with epicurean tastes. Special events are traditional: gourmet picnics, Baroque concerts at tea, and a New Year's Eve candlelight concert with champagne. Chocolate Lovers' Weekend is one of the most popular; everything on the menu is made with chocolate.

Address: *RD 2, Box 250, Pineville Rd., New Hope, PA 18938, tel. 215/598–7945.*
Accommodations: *4 double rooms with baths, 2 doubles share bath.*
Amenities: *Air-conditioning in bedrooms; swimming pool, tennis.*
Rates: *$120–$160; full breakfast, high tea. AE, DC, MC, V.*
Restrictions: *No smoking, no pets.*

Ash Mill Farm

Ash Mill Farm, on 11 pastoral acres, is 10 minutes by car from both New Hope and Doylestown. As you turn up the long drive off Route 202, you will pass sheep grazing in the meadows and then come to the charming buff plaster-over-stone 1790 Federal manor house with the large veranda. When Jim and Patricia Auslander moved from New York City and became innkeepers in 1989, Jim traded in legal briefs for cookbooks and Patricia called upon her corporate managerial skills. They refurbished Ash Mill with eclectic treasures collected from Ireland and England, American antiques, and Shaker reproductions. The downstairs rooms have high ceilings, random-width floors, and deep-set windows; the bedrooms have tranquil views, rag rugs, canopy beds, and antique Irish armoires. You will find down comforters in winter and terry robes for after your bath. And if you've had enough tranquillity, antiques shops and Peddler's Village are only minutes away.

Address: *Box 202, Rte. 202, Holicong, PA 18928, tel. 215/794-5373.*
Accommodations: *3 double rooms with baths, 2 doubles share 1 bath, 1 suite.*
Amenities: *Air-conditioning in bedrooms, breakfast in bed on request.*
Rates: *$75–$125; full breakfast, afternoon tea, complimentary brandy. D, MC, V.*
Restrictions: *Smoking on veranda only, no pets, 2-day minimum with Sat. reservation, 3-day minimum on holiday weekends.*

Bridgeton House

At the foot of the bridge to Milford, New Jersey, is a three-story 1836 Federal brick building that has been a residence and a general store. In 1982, with a dozen years of inn experience behind them, Beatrice and Charles Briggs completely transformed it into a terra-cotta-colored bed-and-breakfast. You will find American country antiques, reproductions, and contemporary furnishings. Five rooms on the riverside have four-posters, country quilts, and screened-in private porches with breathtaking views of the morning mist. A spiral staircase leads to a huge third-floor penthouse suite so ultra-high-tech you might think you were in Manhattan. But the view—as though you're suspended over the Delaware—tells you otherwise. In winter, the cozy sitting room is a perfect place to gaze out at the snow falling on the river. In summer, you can watch people paddle canoes and float lazily along in inner tubes, or you might even indulge, yourself.

Address: *River Rd., Upper Black Eddy, PA 18972, tel. 215/982-5856.*
Accommodations: *5 double rooms with baths, 3 suites.*
Amenities: *Air-conditioning in bedrooms, fireplaces in dining room and in suites.*
Rates: *$65–$175; full breakfast. No credit cards.*
Restrictions: *No smoking indoors, no pets, 2-day minimum on weekends, 3-day minimum on holiday weekends, closed Dec. 24–25.*

Bucksville House

This gem of a bed-and-breakfast on 5½ acres in northern Bucks County was once a stagecoach stop. Innkeepers Barbara and Joe Szallosi restored the 1795 Colonial fieldstone-and-stucco house while she wasn't teaching and he wasn't doing carpentry. The living room is decorated in English and American antiques, and in the den (once the tavern), you will find a coal stove to curl up in front of. The dining room, once the old wheelwright shop, has a walk-in fireplace, a Mercer tile floor, and a long country table. Dried herbs and antique baskets hang from the beams of the low ceiling. In the bedrooms, antiques blend nicely with reproductions handcrafted by Joe—cupboards and pencil-post beds. Grapes grow on an arbor near the gazebo, and Joe makes his own wine. Chances are, he will bring a bottle up from the cellar for you to sample. At Lake Nockamixon, a mile away, there's swimming, sailing, horseback riding, and cross-country skiing.

Address: *Rte. 412 and Buck Dr., Kintnersville, PA 18930, tel. 215/847-8948.*
Accommodations: *3 double rooms with baths, 1 suite.*
Amenities: *Air-conditioning in bedrooms, cable TV in den, fireplaces in 2 bedrooms.*
Rates: *$85–$120; full breakfast. AE, MC, V.*
Restrictions: *No smoking, no pets.*

Highland Farms

Bordering the Doylestown Country Club golf course is the 1740 fieldstone country manor that was once home to lyricist Oscar Hammerstein. Innkeepers John and Mary Schnitzer bought the estate and opened it as a bed-and-breakfast on Valentine's Day, 1988. The elegant, high-ceilinged rooms are furnished in American and English antiques. Flanking a foyer with a grandfather clock and a Victorian pierglass are a spacious parlor and a formal dining room. Wicker and ferns fill a sun-room that overlooks a white carriage house, bank barn, and a 60-foot pool. The library is richly decorated with green velvet sofas and chairs and a collection of Hammerstein memorabilia. You can spend cozy evenings by the fire here enjoying a game of chess or watching a musical film from the video collection. The bedrooms have flowered curtains and canopy beds, and each has a magnificent view. You will wake to the aroma of fresh hazelnut coffee and, in late summer, the sight of corn growing "as high as an elephant's eye."

Address: *70 East Rd., Doylestown, PA 18901, tel. 215/340-1354.*
Accommodations: *2 double rooms with baths, 2 doubles share bath.*
Amenities: *Air-conditioning in bedrooms, cable TV, VCR, and phone in library; swimming pool, tennis court.*
Rates: *$98–$114; full breakfast. MC, V.*
Restrictions: *Smoking in library only, 2-day minimum on weekends, 3-day minimum on holidays.*

Isaac Stover House

Thirteen miles north of New Hope, the Isaac Stover House, on 13 tranquil acres, overlooks the Delaware River. The stately exterior of this Victorian Federal mansion hardly prepares you for the highly theatrical decor inside. When radio and TV personality Sally Jessy Raphael opened her bed-and-breakfast in 1988, she decorated it with a mishmash of antiques, treasures from her travels, and a rich, ever-expanding clutter of Victoriana. It works. Jokingly, Sally calls it "Nouveau Bordello." Faux marble arches in the foyer, real black marble fireplaces, red velvet settees, and lush moiré draperies in the parlor transform the house into a whimsical stage setting. Bedrooms have their own fanciful themes, such as Emerald City and Loyalty Royalty. Each bed has a thick down comforter and mountains of pillows (where chocolate truffles await you). After your sumptuous three-course breakfast, innkeeper Susan Tettemer, a veteran of other Bucks County inns, will gladly help plan your daily outings.

Address: *Box 68, River Rd., Erwinna, PA 18920, tel. 215/294-8044.*
Accommodations: *4 double rooms with baths, 2 suites.*
Amenities: *Air-conditioning in bedrooms, cable TV and phone in 2nd-floor alcove, picnics provided.*
Rates: *$100–$250; full breakfast and afternoon tea. AE, MC, V.*
Restrictions: *No smoking in bedrooms, no pets, 2-day minimum on weekends.*

The Logan Inn

This Colonial tavern and inn in the heart of New Hope was established in 1727. Legend has it that George Washington stayed here five times. Restaurateur Steve Katz recently bought the shuttered fieldstone inn, and with innkeeper Gwen Davis, embarked on a major renovation. Wide hallways lead into spacious bedrooms with four-posters, and Victorian and Colonial reproductions. Lace curtains and baskets of flowers fill the deep-set window embrasures that overlook the river and the village's main thoroughfare. The tavern has a Colonial fireplace, a dartboard, and restored 18th-century murals of hunting scenes. A wall of stained glass gives a Victorian elegance to the Garden Dining Room. The Logan is within easy walking distance of all area sights. Gwen, a longtime resident who has worked with the historical preservation society, will fill you in on local lore, arrange tours, and get tickets to nearby attractions.

Address: *10 W. Ferry St., New Hope, PA 18938, tel. 215/862-2300.*
Accommodations: *15 double rooms with baths, 1 suite.*
Amenities: *Restaurant, tavern, air-conditioning in bedrooms, cable TV and phones in bedrooms, 1 meeting room with kitchen in annex.*
Rates: *$95–$125; full breakfast. AE, MC, V.*
Restrictions: *No pets, 2-day minimum on weekends Memorial Day–Labor Day, 3-day minimum on holiday weekends.*

Pineapple Hill

This cream-colored clapboard and stucco bed-and-breakfast on 5 acres is tucked between two sections of Washington's Crossing State Park. Linda and Hal Chaize, originally from New York, stayed in the 1790 Colonial house on the canal, with its deep-set windows and thick walls and fell in love with its charm. In early 1989, when they were told the inn was for sale, they decided immediately to buy it. The common room has random-width pine floors adorned with Oriental rugs, a collection of pewterware, and teal-blue wing chairs flanking the fireplace. Breakfast is served here at a long Colonial table to the sounds of classical music. The bedrooms, with old wainscoting doors and Colonial wrought-iron hardware, are furnished with American country antiques and reproductions. (Mind the low ceilings!) Out back is the jewel of Pineapple Hill: a swimming pool idyllically set in the preserved ruins of a stone barn. Linda is helpful in suggesting the best routes for hiking, cross-country skiing, and for seeing the fall foliage.

Address: *1324 River Rd., New Hope, PA 18938, tel. 215/862-9608.*
Accommodations: *2 double rooms with baths, 2 doubles share a bath.*
Amenities: *Air-conditioning in bedrooms; swimming pool.*
Rates: *$80–$100; Continental breakfast weekdays, full breakfast weekends. AE, MC, V.*
Restrictions: *No smoking, no pets, 2-day minimum on weekends, 3-day minimum on holidays, closed Christmas.*

Pinetree Farm

Two miles outside Doylestown is a white stucco-and-fieldstone 1730 Quaker farmhouse that has been carefully restored by innkeepers Joy and Ron Feigles. Joy jokes that she majored in hotel management "and then 29 years later we bought an inn." The interior is white, light, and airy, and it's decorated with American Colonial antiques and reproductions and lots of wicker. A solarium overlooks the swimming pool and 16 acres of pine trees. The bedrooms have stenciling, Oriental rugs, marble fireplaces, writing desks, four-poster beds, iron beds, and, in the Pink Room, a canopied white twig bed that's a masterpiece. Stuffed toy lambs are perched on each bed; the deep window seats have mounds of pillows to curl up into, and the view makes you want to reread Jane Austen. The Feigles, lifelong residents of Doylestown, have plenty of suggestions if you should want to explore nearby villages or shop for antiques.

Address: *2155 Lower State Rd., Doylestown, PA 18901, tel. 215/348-0632.*
Accommodations: *2 double rooms with baths, 2 doubles share 1 bath.*
Amenities: *Air-conditioning in bedrooms, cable TV in study; swimming pool, tennis court.*
Rates: *$115–$130; full breakfast. No credit cards.*
Restrictions: *No smoking, no pets, 2-day minimum on weekends, 3-day minimum on holiday weekends.*

The Brandywine River Valley

About an hour from Philadelphia, where southeastern Pennsylvania meets northern Delaware, the Brandywine River flows lazily from West Chester to Wilmington, through rolling hills where streams wind through dense woodlands. The pastoral valley has sheltered artists and millionaires, Revolutionary War soldiers and slaves on the Underground Railroad. Today it looks much as it did 250 years ago.

Beginning in 1623 the Dutch, the Swedes, and the English moved in successively, coexisting with the Leni-Lenape Indians, the region's earliest residents. But it was not until 1682 that William Penn and the English finally stabilized the region. Quaker millers and farmers began to settle here in the early 1700s. Powder mills supplied munitions for George Washington's army, and in the fall of 1777 more than 30,000 soldiers fought the Battle of Brandywine. After a resounding defeat Washington's army camped over the winter at nearby Valley Forge until that famous Christmas crossing over the Delaware River.

Early in this century the illustrator Howard Pyle and other artists began building the reputation of the Brandywine School, dominated today by three generations of Wyeths—N. C., Andrew, and James. A century before the Wyeths began capturing the local landscape on canvas, the du Pont family was ornamenting it with grand mansions and gardens. Pierre-Samuel du Pont, the patriarch, escaped with his family from post-Revolutionary France and settled in northern Delaware. His son Eleuthère Irénée (E. I.) founded the Du Pont Company in 1802 and made the family fortune, first in gunpowder and iron, later in chemicals and textiles (see Delaware, The Wilmington area).

Log cabins, 18th-century stone farmhouses, and the ornate estates of the du Ponts are all reminders of the past. Today you can visit world-famous formal gardens and museums of the decorative arts. You can explore backcountry roads and antiques shops (without the crowds that you find in Bucks County), then check into a restful country inn.

Places to go, sights to see

Brandywine Battlefield State Park (Chadds Ford, tel. 215/459–3342) is where British troops defeated the Continental Army in the fall of 1777. On the site are two restored farmhouses that once sheltered Washington and Lafayette.

Brandywine River Museum (Chadds Ford, tel. 215/388–7601). This restored Civil War–era gristmill, on the banks of the Brandywine River, now houses a collection of landscape paintings, American illustrations, and works by three generations of Wyeths. Outside are gardens and nature trails.

Frankin Mint Museum (Franklin Center, tel. 215/459–6168). The world's largest private mint creates collectibles—books, records, jewelry, furniture, porcelain, bronzes, and crystal.

Longwood Gardens (Kennett Square, tel. 215/388–6741) boast some 350 acres of magnolias and azaleas in spring; roses and water lilies in summer; fall foliage; and winter camellias, orchids, and palms in a 19th-century arboretum.

Valley Forge National Historical Park (Valley Forge, tel. 215/783–7700) consists of the 3,500 serene acres where George Washington's army endured the winter of 1777–1778; it has picnic areas and 6 miles of paved trails.

Tourist Information

Tourist Information Center for the Brandywine Valley (Rte. 1, Kennett Square 19348, tel. 215/388–2900 or 800/228–9933). **Valley Forge Convention & Visitors Bureau** (Box 311, Norristown 19404, tel. 215/278–3558).

Reservation Services

B&B of Chester County (Box 825, Kennett Square 19348, tel. 215/444–1367). **B&B Connections** (Box 21, Devon 19333, tel. 215/687–3565 or 800/448–3619). **B&B of Philadelphia** (Box 252, Gradyville 19039, tel. 215/358–4747 or 800/733–4747). **B&B of Valley Forge/Philadelphia** (Box 562, Valley Forge 19481-0562, tel. 215/783–7838).

Duling-Kurtz House and Country Inn

On a country road midway between Valley Forge and the Brandywine Battlefields is the Duling-Kurtz House & Country Inn. Down a driveway lined with converted gas street lamps are formal gardens, a Victorian-style gazebo, and a footbridge that crosses a stone-lined brook. The 1830s farmhouse and the adjacent barn, both white plaster over fieldstone, were elegantly restored and opened in 1983. Raymond Carr and David Knauer, who did the restoration, named the property after their mothers. Today Carr, the sole owner, runs a real-estate corporation; though he probably won't be around when you step into the parlor, his staff will be on hand to greet you.

The guest rooms (in the barn) have been restored and furnished in Williamsburg period reproductions. You will find marble-top sinks; Oriental rugs; writing desks; and canopied, brass, and four-poster beds. One suite has its own courtyard; two have working fireplaces. Rooms are named for historic figures: Honeymooners often request the George Washington Room, with its king-size, cherry-wood canopy bed and a step-down bathroom with a claw-foot tub. A Continental breakfast served on china is brought to your room, along with fresh flowers and the morning paper.

A sheltered brick walkway connects the barn and the farmhouse restaurant, which is also furnished with Colonial antique reproductions. Near the entrance you'll discover an unusual 18th-century beehive bread oven. Four of the dining rooms have stone fireplaces, which are used on chilly nights, and richly mullioned windows detail the bar and porch dining areas. The menu features regional fare.

You can stroll through peaceful wooded areas adjoining the inn, and when it's warm you can enjoy tea in the gazebo. Museums and battlefields are not far away, and Ray and his staff will point you to the best antiquing and skiing. Duling-Kurtz is probably best suited for mature travelers who want the intimacy of an inn as well as the anonymity and more formal luxuries usually found only in larger establishments.

Address: *146 S. Whitford Rd., Exton, PA 19341, tel. 215/524–1830, fax 215/524–1358.*
Accommodations: *15 double rooms with baths, 3 suites.*
Amenities: *Restaurant open Mon.– Sat., air-conditioning in bedrooms, cable TV and phones in bedrooms, room service; 3 conference rooms with catering.*
Rates: *$80–$130; Continental breakfast. AE, MC, V.*
Restrictions: *No pets, closed Christmas and New Year's Day.*

Fairville Inn

In the heart of Andrew Wyeth country, on the road between Winterthur Museum and Longwood Gardens, this country-house inn set on 5½ acres behind a split-rail fence is surrounded by estates, beautiful gardens, and miles of country back roads. The hub of the inn is a cream-colored 1826 Federal plaster-over-double-brick house with black shutters. A Victorian-style veranda across the front makes an open porch on the second floor. In back are the barn and carriage house, smaller clapboard and fieldstone buildings that were recently constructed by an Amish family who live nearby.

Swedish-born Ole Retlev and his wife, Patricia, both former ski instructors, owned two different inns in Mt. Snow, Vermont. But, as Ole explains, "There's more to draw travelers here on a year-round basis." So, in 1986, they moved to the Brandywine River Valley and opened the Fairville Inn.

The rooms are bright and airy, appealingly furnished with Queen Anne and Hepplewhite reproductions. Before the fireplace in the living room are two blue velvet settees, with a large copper-top coffee table between them. An antique Swedish linen cupboard, flowered draperies, and potted plants give the room an understated "relaxed formal feel," as Ole calls it. The bedrooms in the main house, all of quirky size and

shape, are done in light, elegant country colors. They are carpeted, and each has a working fireplace. You will also find four-poster beds, canopy beds, settees, writing desks, floral wallpapers—and fresh roses. The four rooms in the barn are somewhat smaller. Siding from the old barn has been used for mantels and paneling, and some of the sinks have copper drainboards.

Some of the four rooms and two suites in the carriage house have private terraces and balconies that overlook a pond and rolling farmland. They are at the back of the property and away from traffic noise. With cathedral ceilings and old barn timbers for beams and mantels, they are also the most architecturally interesting.

You can spend winter afternoons taking in the museums, browsing through antiques shops, or sitting before the fire with tea and home-made cookies. In warmer months, you can enjoy canoeing or tubing down the Brandywine River, hiking, or attending the polo matches.

Address: *Box 219, Rte. 52, Fairville, PA 19357, tel. 215/388–5900.*
Accommodations: *13 double rooms with baths, 2 suites.*
Amenities: *Air-conditioning, cable TV, and phones in bedrooms.*
Rates: *$95–$150; Continental breakfast, afternoon tea. AE, D, MC, V.*
Restrictions: *No pets.*

Sweetwater Farm

Fifteen minutes east of Chadds Ford at the end of a circular driveway is a stately 1758 Georgian fieldstone manor house with shutters the color of lemon custard. Sweetwater Farm once sheltered weary Revolutionary War soldiers and the Marquis de Lafayette, and was a refuge for slaves on the Underground Railroad. It is probably the finest country inn in the Brandywine Valley.

In the fields around the 16-room house thoroughbreds and sheep graze amid wildflowers. From each window there are views of majestic maples on the 15 lush acres, and of the 50 undeveloped acres beyond. Though Jonathan Propper and Mike Gretz are both from the area and accustomed to its charm, they couldn't help but be drawn to this gentleman's farm; they bought Sweetwater in October 1989 and have been its innkeepers since.

Inside you will find tall, deep-set windows and a sweeping center-hall staircase. Almost every room has a wood-burning fireplace, random-width floors of oak and pine, and original paintings. Rustic Pennsylvania primitive pieces are mixed with authentic 18th- and 19th-century antique furnishings. The nine guest rooms have handmade quilts and fine linens on canopy beds and four-posters, embroidered spreads, dried-flower wreaths, and hidden nooks containing odd collectibles.

There's a library, with a fireplace and wall of books, a formal parlor, a sun-room with TV, and a "boardroom" for small business meetings and luncheons. In warm weather, the broad back veranda overlooking the fields and the swimming pool is a favorite spot.

Breakfast, served before the kitchen fireplace, features homemade muffins, sausage, and fresh eggs. On Saturday, chef Guillermo Pernot, who cooked at New York's Four Seasons, prepares an elegant prix-fixe dinner. Five cottages, also furnished in American antiques, are the ultimate romantic hideaways, with fireplaces, kitchens, and four-poster canopied beds. Museums, historic houses, and antiques shops are all nearby.

Address: *50 Sweetwater Rd., Glen Mills, PA 19342, tel. 215/459–4711, fax 215/358–4945.*
Accommodations: *3 double rooms with baths, 3 doubles share 1 bath. 3 suites, 5 cottages.*
Amenities: *Air-conditioning and phones in bedrooms; swimming pool, 9 boarding stalls, exercise ring, 2 conference rooms.*
Rates: *$125–$155; full breakfast. AE, MC, V.*
Restrictions: *No smoking in bedrooms, BYOB, 2-night minimum with Sat. reservation, 3-day minimum on holiday weekends.*

The Whitethorne

Up a long country lane that's edged by meadows and a post-and-rail fence is a 1732 Colonial fieldstone manor house that was once a stop on the Underground Railroad. This whitewashed three-story house is set on 20 acres of farm and woodlands, north of Kennett Square, and it's wedged against a nature preserve of more than 400 acres. Though the setting is stately and elegant, you will find nothing fancy here. Just peace and quiet. Jim and Marianne Hoy, the enthusiastic hosts, say that's what appeals most to urbanites.

The Hoys, who are only the seventh family to own the house, have lived here for 10 years. Five years ago when they opened the inn, neither had stayed in a bed-and-breakfast, but they saw it as a great way to share their house. These days, Jim, a retired labor negotiator for Bell Atlantic, divides the chores of running the Whitethorne with Marianne.

After you cross the brick terrace, surrounded by boxwood and a wrought-iron railing, you enter a living room painted Wedgwood blue that's filled with family photographs and mementos and decorated with English antiques and contemporary furnishings. The bedrooms have comfortable chairs for reading, crocheted spreads on four-poster beds, and elegant flowered 18th-century-reproduction wallpaper. Original locks, hardware, and woodwork are to be found throughout, and a basket of soaps and folded towels is on each bed.

Guests often begin the day by gathering around the fireplace in the kitchen while Marianne prepares breakfast. It's an elegant feast, complete with crystal, that might include broiled catfish, Dijon chicken, or eggnog-batter French toast with sautéed mushrooms.

In winter, there's cross-country skiing, and in warmer months, you can walk in the woods, bird-watch, or picnic. Jim and Marianne have canoes and bicycles on hand for you to use. He will show you the best place to launch your inner tube, then be downriver a few hours later to pick you up. They can arrange horseback riding, hot-air-balloon rides, carriage rides, and your reservations for dinner. In summer, they host barn dances in a nearby 1806 stone barn, and often, on clear nights, they bring the radio out on the terrace for dancing under the stars.

Address: *Box 92 (Rte. 842), Unionville, PA 19375, tel. 215/793–1748.*
Accommodations: *1 double room with bath, 2 doubles share a bath.*
Amenities: *Air-conditioning in bedrooms, TV and VCR in sitting room; stalls for boarding horses.*
Rates: *$75; full breakfast. No credit cards.*
Restrictions: *No smoking indoors, no pets.*

The Bankhouse Bed and Breakfast

Just outside West Chester is an 18th-century stucco-over-stone house built into the bank of a hill. It once housed the servants of a large estate. Innkeepers Diana and Michael Bové, who both worked in media services at a nearby university, opened their home to travelers in 1988, and Diana now manages the bed-and-breakfast full-time. You enter the second-floor guest rooms by an outside staircase. The homey upstairs sitting room has an extensive collection of books, games, and brochures; and bedrooms are decorated with 19th-century oak antiques, stenciling, and fresh roses from Diana's English gardens. Guests often linger in the narrow dining room over a hearty country breakfast; through one deeply recessed window, you look down over the pond to the split-rail fence that borders a meadow across the road. You can spend your time gazing at the scenery; or you can explore the quaint shops in West Chester, canoe the Brandywine, or bike down country lanes.

Address: *875 Hillsdale Rd., West Chester, PA 19382, tel. 215/344–7388.*
Accommodations: *2 double rooms share a bath.*
Rates: *$60; full breakfast. No credit cards.*
Restrictions: *No smoking, no pets.*

Bed and Breakfast at Walnut Hill

This white clapboard-and-fieldstone Pennsylvania mill house just outside Kennett Square was built in 1844. Proprietors Tom and Sandy Mills, who have lived here for 28 years, opened it as a bed-and-breakfast in 1987. Across the crooked little road, beyond horses grazing in the meadow, is a creek, where it's so quiet you can hear every trickle as you watch for Canada geese, deer, or the occasional red fox to meander across the meadow. The house is warmly decorated with early 19th-century country antiques and reproductions; you'll find bunches of dried herbs and flowers hanging, pie safes, and a New England whaler's lamp over the table. The bedrooms are furnished with writing desks, Victorian wicker, and pencil-post beds. The paneling throughout is made from old barn siding. Sandy and Tom are glad to offer tips on the best routes for biking, or hiking, or touring.

Address: *214 Chandlers Mill Rd., Avondale, PA 19311, tel. 215/444–3703.*
Accommodations: *2 double rooms and 1 single share 1 bath.*
Amenities: *Air-conditioning in 1 bedroom, TV in family room, indoor hot tub.*
Rates: *$50–$65; full breakfast. No credit cards.*
Restrictions: *Smoking in common room only, no pets.*

Highpoint Victoriana

About 5 winding miles outside Skippack is Highpoint Victoriana, a hip-roofed, red-brick three-story house that has been restored to its 1901 elegance by innkeepers Debbi and Albert Slotter. The sitting room has a wood stove, marble-top tables, and plush 1860 rococo chairs and settees; sliding doors open to a formal dining room, and there's a pump organ in the alcove that you are welcome to play. But one nonpaying guest, a bodiless friendly spirit, has a fondness for Big Band music, and you may be greeted with faint strains of it at breakfast. All the rooms have rich reproduction Victorian wallpapers with natural wood trim. In the bedrooms, you will find oak headboards, washstands, and writing desks. From the swing on the wraparound porch there is a magnificent view of farmland. You can hike, browse through the many antiques shops in Skippack, visit nearby Valley Forge, or ski at Spring Mountain.

Address: *723 Haldeman Rd., Schwenksville, PA 19473, tel. 215/287-6619.*
Accommodations: *3 double rooms and 1 single share 2 baths.*
Amenities: *Air-conditioning in bedrooms.*
Rates: *$60–$70; full breakfast. MC, V.*
Restrictions: *Smoking in public areas only, no pets.*

Meadow Spring Farm

Just minutes north of Kennett Square and Longwood Gardens, up a country lane past grazing cows, is the brick Colonial 1836 house of this 200-acre working farm. Anne Hicks arrived here as a bride 43 years ago, raised five children, and in 1984 opened it as a bed-and-breakfast. She's an accomplished cook, craftswoman, and collector of dolls and family antiques. You'll find big, sunny farmhouse bedrooms, with fireplaces, Amish quilts, family photographs, a Chippendale bed with a crocheted canopy, and a carved sleigh bed with a headboard 7 feet tall. The two rooms over the garage, recent additions, lack the warmth of those in the farmhouse. Anne serves breakfast on the long mahogany table in the dining room, or in the solarium, a glassed-in porch overlooking the flower gardens. You may want to take a hayride or, in winter, enjoy the solarium's hot tub. With Sparky, the farm dog, you can stroll through the meadows or visit the pigs, lambs, and horses in the barns.

Address: *201 E. Street Rd. (Rte. 926), Kennett Square, PA 19348, tel. 215/444-3903.*
Accommodations: *3 double rooms with baths, 2 doubles share bath, 1 single shares bath.*
Amenities: *Air-conditioning in bedrooms, TV in bedrooms, game room with pool table and table tennis, hot tub, kitchen and laundry privileges; swimming pool.*
Rates: *$35–$65; full breakfast. No credit cards.*
Restrictions: *No pets.*

Pace One

Set in a secluded hamlet, Pace One makes a charming base from which to explore the nearby museums and countryside. Innkeeper Ted Pace, who comes from a family of restaurateurs, bought the four-story 1740 fieldstone barn 13 years ago and transformed it into a country inn. You'll find the original hand-hewn poplar beams and walls that are 2-feet thick, hung with the work of local artists. Dormer windows make the six guest rooms cozy; they're furnished with Shaker-style oak beds, dressers, and small writing tables, handmade by a local craftsman. Downstairs, the heart of Pace One, is an excellent restaurant and a taproom that has the feel of an authentic Colonial tavern. In a labyrinth of intimate dining areas Ted serves what he calls "country imaginative" cooking. Pace One maintains the highest standards of service and cuisine, yet Ted and his staff are not stuffy—the atmosphere is warm and casual.

Address: *Box 108, Thornton and Glen Mills Rds., Thornton, PA 19373, tel. 215/459-3702, fax 215/558-0825.*
Accommodations: *7 double rooms with baths.*
Amenities: *Restaurant, air-conditioning and phones in bedrooms, free use of nearby tennis and racquetball courts, 3 conference rooms with catering.*
Rates: *$65–$85; Continental breakfast. AE, DC, MC, V.*
Restrictions: *No pets, closed Christmas and New Year's Day.*

Stottsville Inn

A half hour north of Longwood Gardens, along a lovely winding drive through pastureland and wooded hunt country, is the elegant 1858 Stottsville Inn. This three-story fieldstone Victorian building with a porch across the front has been the site of many a marriage proposal. It has wide hallways, ceiling fans, old photographs and ledgers, velvet settees, and a Victorian pump organ. The rooms are romantically furnished with Victorian antiques and reproductions: high, carved headboards, marble-top dressers, and Amish quilts. The formal gardens and the flower-filled kissing arbor are maintained by a pro from Longwood Gardens. Diana and Geno Principe bought Stottsville and became innkeepers here in 1990 after managing larger hotels and restaurants in New Hampshire. Diana will be glad to fill you in on the romantic history of the inn, and she can guide you to nearby golf courses, hiking trails, and the best antiques shops.

Address: *Box 67, Rte. 372 and Strasburg Rd., Pomeroy, PA 19367, tel. 215/857-1133, fax 215/857-9316.*
Accommodations: *11 double rooms with baths.*
Amenities: *Restaurant, air-conditioning in bedrooms, TV and phones in bedrooms; conference facilities.*
Rates: *$50–$70; Continental breakfast. AE, DC, MC, V.*
Restrictions: *No pets, closed Christmas.*

Lancaster County/Amish Country

*Lancaster County, the Pennsylvania Dutch country, is 65
miles west of Philadelphia. In the wilderness of the early
18th century, this vast, rolling farmland became home to
the so-called plain people—the Amish, Mennonites,
Dunkards, and Brethren—German and Swiss immigrants
escaping religious persecution. The Pennsylvania Dutch
population consists of about 20 sects, and they aren't
Dutch at all; the name comes from "Deutsch," or German.
They came to Pennsylvania to live, work, and worship in
harmony. Today, in clinging to a centuries-old way of life,
their descendants in their traditional dress have turned
their backs on the modern world—and have attracted the
world's attention. In this patchwork quilt of cultures many
small farms are still worked with horses and mules, and
buggies are a frequently seen mode of transportation. Few
power lines disturb the tranquil countryside.*

*The Amish are a prime attraction of, though not the only
lure to, the area. Lancaster (which the English named after
the city in Lancashire) is an intriguing town of restored
Colonial homes, taverns, shops, and centuries-old churches.
It is the nation's oldest inland city, dating from 1710, and
it was the nation's capital for one day during the
Revolution, when Congress fled Philadelphia after the
Battle of Brandywine.*

*The region can be hectic, especially on summer weekends.
Busloads of tourists on their way to souvenir and crafts
shops and outlet stores often jam Routes 30 and 340, the
main thoroughfares. But there is still charm here if you
take the back roads, getting off the well-trodden path. Here
on country lanes you will find the general stores, one-room
schoolhouses, and hand-painted signs advertising quilts or
produce and eggs outside Amish farms.*

What attracts travelers to this simpler, more peaceful world is the opportunity to sample an authentic early American way of life. The plain people are unique folk who seek to be at peace with themselves, their neighbors, their surroundings, and their God. Observing this extraordinary lifestyle can be a fascinating and provocative experience.

Places to go, sights to see

Abe's Buggy Rides (Bird-in-Hand, no tel.). Abe will give you background information on the Amish during a 2-mile spin down country roads in an Amish family carriage.

Amish Country Tours (between Bird-in-Hand and Intercourse, tel. 717/392–8622) offers a variety of tours conducted in large buses or minivans. Most popular are the two- and four-hour Amish farmland trips.

The Amish Homestead (Lancaster, tel. 717/392–0832) is a house-and-farm tour that provides an introduction to Amish life. (It is a simulated enterprise and is not Amish-run.) You'll learn about Amish origins, worship, courtship, marriage, and honeymoon rituals.

Central Market (Lancaster, tel. 717/291–4739). One of the oldest covered markets in the country is located in Lancaster. This is where the locals shop for fresh produce, meats, and baked goods.

Ephrata Cloister (Ephrata, tel. 717/733–6600) presents a look at a religious communal society of the 1700s best known for its publishing center, a cappella singing, Fraktur (ornate decorative calligraphy), and Medieval-style German architecture.

Green Dragon Farmers Market and Auction (Ephrata, tel. 717/738–1117) is a traditional agricultural market, where Amish and Mennonite farmers sell meats, fruits, vegetables, fresh-baked pies, and dry goods at 450 indoor and outdoor stalls.

Lititz. This town was founded by Moravians who settled in Pennsylvania to do missionary work. Along a tree-shaded main street are 18th-century cottages and shops selling antiques, crafts, and clothing. Nearby are the *Julius Sturgis Pretzel House* (tel. 717/626–4354), the nation's oldest pretzel bakery, and the Wilbur Chocolate Company's *Candy Americana Museum outlet* (tel. 717/626–1131 or 626–0967).

Pennsylvania Farm Museum of Landis Valley (Lancaster, tel. 717/569–0401) offers displays on Pennsylvania rural life and folk culture before 1900.

People's Place (Intercourse, tel. 717/768–7171) is an excellent introduction to the Amish, Mennonites, and Hutterites, which includes a hands-on exhibit on transportation, dress, and schools and on the effects of growing old and mutual aid in these communities.

Strasburg Rail Road (Strasburg, tel. 717/687–7522). Wooden coaches are pulled by a steam locomotive on this scenic 9-mile excursion.

Wheatland (1½ mi east of Lancaster, tel. 717/392–8721) is the restored 1828 Federal mansion of James Buchanan, the only U.S. president from Pennsylvania.

Wilbur Chocolate Museum and Outlet (Lititz, tel. 717/626–0967), one of the suppliers for Godiva chocolates, offers a candy-making demonstration (with free samples) and a small museum of candy-related memorabilia.

Tourist Information

Mennonite Information Center (2209 Millstream Rd., Lancaster 17602, tel. 717/299–0954). **Pennsylvania Dutch Visitors Bureau** (Dept. 2064, 501 Greenfield Rd., exit off Rte. 30, Lancaster 17601, tel. 717/299–8901).

Reservation Services

Bed & Breakfast of Lancaster County (Box 19, Mountville 17554, tel. 717/285–7200). **Hershey Bed & Breakfast Reservation Service** (Box 208, Hershey 17033, tel. 717/533–2928).

Churchtown Inn

Across from the historic church in this tiny Pennsylvania Dutch village is the Churchtown Inn, a circa-1735 Georgian fieldstone inn and carriage house. From 1804 to 1853 the inn was the home of Edward Davies, a member of the 25th Congress and a state legislator. Once you enter the restored mansion you will know it was built for the gentry.

To the right of the entryway are two parlors with Victorian antiques and original ornate mantels. Here each evening, innkeepers Jim Kent and Stuart and Hermine Smith entertain guests with music and conversation. Before opening their bed-and-breakfast, in April 1987, the three stayed at 150 B&Bs in six states to pick up ideas. Back in New Jersey Hermine was a health-food retailer, Stuart was a choral director whose choirs appeared at Lincoln Center and Carnegie Hall, and Jim was an accountant and ballroom-dancing teacher. (He'll gladly give you a quick lesson.) Stuart is known to delight guests with a concert on the grand piano, or he might wind up an antique music box from the inn's fine collection.

The 15-room center-hall mansion is decorated throughout with European and American antiques. The glassed-in garden room, where breakfast is served, overlooks farmland and a distant mountain range. A onetime summer kitchen with a walk-in fireplace has been converted into a den with a TV and VCR. Guest rooms have antique marble sinks; and brass or iron, sleigh or carved, or four-poster canopy beds. You'll find wardrobes, washstands, and TV cabinets handmade by an Amish craftsman. Each room has a sitting area. The dormer rooms on the third floor are cozy but have low ceilings.

On many weekends special packages are offered that include scheduled events. These vary from Victorian balls, carriage rides, and murder mysteries to authentic Amish wedding feasts, barbecues with music, cabaret, classical string quartets, and festive holiday dinners.

The inn is close to antiques and crafts markets, the Reading outlets, and Amish farms. There are also biking, hiking, fishing, and cross-country skiing in nearby French Creek state park.

Address: *Rte. 23, Churchtown (2100 Main St., Narvon, PA 17555), tel. 215/445-7794.*
Accommodations: *6 double rooms with baths, 2 doubles share a bath, 1 suite in carriage house.*
Amenities: *Air-conditioning and TV in 6 rooms; TV in den.*
Rates: *$49–$125; full, 5-course breakfast. MC, V.*
Restrictions: *Smoking in reception room only, no pets, 2-night minimum on weekends, ?-night minimum on holiday weekends.*

Clearview Farm Bed and Breakfast

Up a winding road along the base of a mountain ridge in northern Lancaster County is a beautifully restored three-story limestone farmhouse built in 1814. It sits on 200 acres of peaceful Pennsylvania farmland, and there's a huge bank barn nearby. There's also a pond out front that's the domain of two swans. The setting of Clearview Farm is elegantly pastoral; it's the kind of place you want to keep secret.

Mildred and Glenn Wissler bought the house when they married 31 years ago. Glenn is a farmer who also has a good eye for color, and Mildred is a talented decorator who grew up learning about her father's antiques business. After working together to choose the right furnishings and decorations, they opened the bed-and-breakfast in 1989.

Country antiques and collectibles are mixed with exquisite Victorian furnishings throughout. You'll find a fireplace in the den, and there are hooked rugs on the original random-width floors. Exposed beams and limestone walls give the kitchen a homey feel. Guest rooms are lushly textured with lots of colors and patterns. The Royal Room has an ornately carved walnut Victorian bed, a Victorian étagère displaying turn-of-the-century knick-knacks, Victorian chairs, and marble-top tables. The Princess Room is lavished with lace, a canopy bed, a Victorian marble-top dresser and a washstand. The Garden Room has an antique iron and brass bed in an alcove of flowered draperies, a French marble-top dresser, and a wicker chaise and chair. In the rooms on the third floor, hand-pegged rafters and limestone walls are exposed. Here you'll find homemade quilts, country antiques, and a doll collection.

Breakfast is served by candlelight in the formal dining room or in the screened porch that overlooks the fields. The dining room has elegant draperies and Victorian-print wallpaper. Six days a week, Mildred prepares a full country breakfast, and on Sunday, Continental breakfast.

The mountain ridge behind the house is great for hiking or quiet walks. In autumn, you can enjoy the fall foliage by car or by bike—just follow Clearview Road; it's truly one of those scenic back roads you always hear about. Nearby are Wahtney's Inn (an excellent restaurant), farmers' markets, and five antiques malls.

Address: *355 Clearview Rd., Ephrata, PA 17522, tel. 717/733–6333.*
Accommodations: *3 double rooms with baths, 2 doubles share bath.*
Amenities: *Air-conditioning in rooms, TV in family room.*
Rates: *$55–$69; full breakfast. MC, V.*
Restrictions: *No smoking indoors, no pets.*

Limestone Inn

I n the very heart of the Amish country, in Strasburg's historic district, is the Limestone Inn. This elegant bed-and-breakfast, listed on the National Register of Historic Places, was built about 1786 as a merchant's residence. From 1839 to 1860 the principal of the noted Strasburg Academy boarded about 50 boys here. After the Civil War, the house served as an orphanage.

The 14-room house, based on a symmetrical five-bay Georgian plan, has a central hallway. The building also has some Germanic overtones, and details like the pent roof and the decorative stonework called "tumbling" between the second-floor windows give the inn a distinctive architectural sense.

Innkeepers Jan and Dick Kennell are both natives of New Hampshire. Friends who ran a B&B gave them the idea of establishing their own, and they opened the Limestone in May 1985. Dick was with the Department of Agriculture and Forestry in Washington, DC, for 30 years; and Jan, who is versed in Colonial history, was a tour guide in Annapolis.

Though antique clocks in the elegant rooms tick away, time stands still. The inn is furnished with Colonial and primitive family antiques and reproductions, and you'll find whitewashed walls, wide-planked wavy floors, and Williamsburg colors in every room. In the keeping room there are woven woolen rugs, lots of books and folk art, and settees in front of the fireplace. A spinning wheel stands in the corner. There are old family photographs and a player piano in the living room. Up the steep, narrow stairs you'll find the guest rooms, with old pegged doors, quilts, trunks, and Wilbur chocolates under your pillow. On the third floor, the original numbers on the doors show where boys from the academy once slept.

For the multicourse breakfast, served in the dining room at a long table set with a lace cloth, Dick, an excellent chef, may whip up his French toast and sourdough pancakes. He and Jan often serve their guests in period costumes.

The Limestone Inn is quiet and homey—not the kind of self-consciously decorated place where you feel ill at ease about exploring. It's close to horseback-riding and antiquing facilities. And the Kennells have Amish friends nearby who have quilts for sale for less than you'd pay for them in commercial centers.

Address: *33 E. Main St., Strasburg, PA 17579, tel. 717/687–8392.*
Accommodations: *6 double rooms share 3 baths.*
Amenities: *Air-conditioning.*
Rates: *$65–$80; full breakfast. AE.*
Restrictions: *No smoking in bedrooms, no pets, 2-night minimum on holiday weekends.*

Smithton Country Inn

Twelve miles north of Lancaster is the best inn in all of Pennsylvania Dutch country: the historic Smithton Country Inn, which began taking in lodgers in 1763. It was built by Henry and Susana Miller, who were householders, or "outdoor members," of the Ephrata Community, an 18th-century Protestant monastic sect. Stone walls and flower gardens surround the fieldstone building that is on a hill overlooking the Ephrata Cloister.

Innkeeper Dorothy Graybill is Pennsylvania Dutch. A native of Ephrata, she's director of a local art center, a gardener, and a craftsperson. In 1983, she bought Smithton, attentively restored it down to the most minute detail, and reopened it.

At dusk, lamps are lit in each window. The first floor has a Great Room and library to the right, and the Tavern Room, where breakfast is served, to the left. Upstairs, guest rooms are individually decorated, but in each you'll find a working fireplace, antique or handmade reproduction furniture, handmade quilts, reading lamps, stenciling, minirefrigerators, and chamber music. Feather beds are kept in trunks for guests who request them. Flannel nightshirts, coordinated to the color scheme of the room, hang on wooden pegs behind the doors. Many rooms have canopy beds, some have whirlpool baths.

The attached duplex suite has its own entrance. Inside there's a living room, a kitchenette, a queen-size bed, a twin cupboard bed, and a whirlpool bath.

Numerous decorative influences come from the nearby Ephrata Cloister. The hand-hewn doors are pegged and have wooden hardware. Dorothy's partner, Allan Smith, handplaned the old floorboards and made the clay tiles for the bathrooms and a Cloister-inspired buffet for the Tavern Room.

Guest's enjoy Smithton's breakfast, served by candlelight—usually a plate of fresh fruit, juice, Pennsylvania Dutch waffles, and pastry. Afterward, Dorothy gives tips on the proper etiquette when meeting the plain people of Lancaster County.

Address: *900 W. Main St., Ephrata, PA 17522, tel. 717/733-6094.*
Accommodations: *7 double rooms with baths, 1 suite.*
Amenities: *Air-conditioning in bedrooms.*
Rates: *$65–$170; AE, MC, V.*
Restrictions: *No smoking, inquire about pets, 2-night minimum with Sat. reservation and on holidays.*

Adamstown Inn

Adamstown, the antiques capital of Pennsylvania, is 20 minutes northeast of Lancaster. This three-story yellow-brick Victorian house is on a residential street in the heart of the antiques district. It was built in 1838 and rebuilt in 1925. Tom and Wanda Berman, both avid antiques collectors, left Baltimore and their banking careers to open a bed-and-breakfast in April 1989. You'll find leaded-glass windows and doors, magnificently refinished chestnut woodwork, and wallpaper in Victorian motifs. Each guest room is decorated with family heirlooms, handmade quilts, lace curtains, Oriental rugs, and fresh flowers. Baskets of towels and soaps sit on Victorian beds. One room has a two-person whirlpool bath. On summer weekends more than 2,000 antiques dealers exhibit their wares in Adamstown. You can browse through stalls, or, if you're looking for something specific, the Bermans can direct you. They'll also point you to nature trails and biking paths.

Address: *62 W. Main St., Adamstown, PA 19501, tel. 215/484–0800 or 800/594–4808.*
Accommodations: *4 double rooms with baths.*
Amenities: *Air-conditioning in rooms, cable TV in 3 bedrooms, morning coffee, tea, or hot chocolate, off-street parking.*
Rates: *$60–$95; Continental breakfast. MC, V.*
Restrictions: *Smoking in mud room only, no pets, 2-night minimum on holiday weekends.*

The Cameron Estate Inn

On 15 wooded acres 15 miles west of Lancaster is a red-brick Federal mansion built in 1805, listed on the National Register of Historic Places. A trout-stocked stream flows beneath an arched stone bridge nearby, and the veranda overlooks a sweeping lawn. Between towering oaks you can see an 18th-century church and Amish farms. Abe and Betty Groff, longtime area residents, opened their country inn in 1981 after Betty had started a restaurant in her home 5 miles away. Wide hallways and a central staircase lead to guest rooms furnished with Williamsburg reproductions. Seven of the bedrooms have working fireplaces; in all of them you'll find quilts, four-posters, sitting areas, and writing desks. The restaurant here serves exquisite French-American fare, and Groff's Farm Restaurant is famous for its Pennsylvania Dutch cuisine.

Address: *Donegal Springs Rd., RD 1, Box 305, Mount Joy, PA 17552, tel. 717/653–1773.*
Accommodations: *16 double rooms with baths, 2 doubles share bath.*
Amenities: *Restaurant, air-conditioning in rooms, TV and VCR in sitting area, conference facilities in restaurant; bicycles, access to swimming pool and tennis courts.*
Rates: *$55–$105; Continental breakfast. AE, DC, MC, V.*
Restrictions: *No pets.*

Doneckers

The Guest House at Doneckers is a trio of joined turn-of-the-century brick Victorian houses across from the Restaurant at Doneckers. It's part of the "town within a town" developed by Bill Donecker that has a department store, a noted French restaurant, two bed-and-breakfasts (the recently opened 1777 House is a few blocks away), and a warehouse mall of artists, craftspeople, antiques, and art galleries called Artworks. The inn is furnished with French and American antiques, and antique hooked rugs hang on the stenciled walls. In the bedrooms you will find sinks in reproduction Victorian vanities, upholstered headboards, and fresh fruit. Some suites have fireplaces and/or whirlpool baths. Doneckers is neatly packaged; you never have to get in your car. But if you should venture forth, the authentic Amish countryside is only minutes away.

Address: *318 N. State St., Ephrata, PA 17522, tel. 717/733-8696, fax 717/733-4248.*
Accommodations: *13 double rooms with baths, 2 doubles share bath, 4 suites.*
Amenities: *Restaurant open Thurs.–Tues., air-conditioning in rooms, cable TV in common room.*
Rates: *$59–$130; Continental breakfast. AE, MC, V.*
Restrictions: *No pets, 2-night minimum on holiday weekends, closed Christmas.*

General Sutter Inn

This three-story, red-brick inn, built in 1764 in Georgian style, overlooks the village square. It's said to be the oldest Pennsylvania inn in continuous operation. Originally known as Zum Anker, the name was changed in 1930 to honor John Augustus Sutter, the Gold Rush pioneer who retired to Lititz. Richard Vetter was an Episcopal priest and then a headmaster before becoming innkeeper here with his wife, Joan, in 1980. Inside, the decor is decidedly Victorian. In the parlor, there are medallion-backed sofas before the fireplace, marble-top tables, a pump organ, and crystal parlor lamps. Lovebirds and finches twitter in Victorian wire cages. Guest rooms are decorated with antique country and Victorian furnishings. The General Sutter is frayed around the edges just enough to add to its authenticity. There's a spacious tree-shaded terrace out front, where you can relax and watch the passing parade of villagers, and it's only a short walk to the Wilbur Chocolate Factory (the maker of Godiva chocolates) and the town's lovely Moravian Square.

Address: *14 Main St., Lititz, PA 17543, tel. 717/626-2115.*
Accommodations: *8 double rooms with baths, 2 suites.*
Amenities: *Restaurant, coffee shop, air-conditioning in rooms, TV and phones in rooms, library, 2 conference rooms can be combined.*
Rates: *$70–$90. AE, MC, V.*
Restrictions: *No pets.*

The King's Cottage

ucked away in a quiet residential corner of Lancaster is a Spanish Mission Revival house, built in 1913, that's listed on the National Register of Historic Places. Hosts Jim and Karen Owens opened their bed-and-breakfast in 1987. He's an engineering consultant and she's a former educator. The interior is a successful blend of many different architectural styles: The living room has an Art Deco fireplace, the elegant library is Georgian-influenced, the bright and cheerful Florida Room has rattan furniture and ceiling fans, and the dining room has a crystal chandelier and fine Chippendale reproductions. The guest rooms are furnished in 18th-century reproductions with some antiques. Inside antique wardrobes, you'll find fluffy terry-cloth robes. The Princess Room has three walls of windows and a private balcony that overlooks the water garden. Karen and Jim will be glad to give you directions for sightseeing and make arrangements for you to have dinner with an Amish family.

Address: *1049 E. King St., Lancaster, PA 17602, tel. 717/397–1017.*
Accommodations: *7 double rooms with baths.*
Amenities: *Air-conditioning in rooms, cable TV in library; off-street parking.*
Rates: *$75–$105; full breakfast, afternoon tea. MC, V.*
Restrictions: *No smoking, no pets, 2-night minimum on weekends.*

Patchwork Inn

hree miles east of Lancaster is Patchwork Inn, a pre–Civil War Victorian clapboard farmhouse with deep blue shutters. When Lee Martin retired from the Marine Corps, he and his wife, Joanne, wanted to turn their love for country antiques and quilt collecting into practical use. They opened their bed-and-breakfast in 1987, and Lee, now a widower, enjoys giving guests tips about bidding at auctions and showing them how to tell the quality of a good quilt. In the living room, you'll find contemporary sofas and rocking chairs before the stone fireplace. There are extensive collections—including one of old phones—and quilts everywhere. Lee has more than 60 he displays and puts on beds. Guest rooms have ceiling fans and are furnished with antique oak. The suite, with a small kitchenette, has its own private entrance. You can visit farmers' markets, crafts shops, and Amish farms nearby.

Address: *2319 Old Philadelphia Pike, Lancaster, PA 17602, tel. 717/293–9078.*
Accommodations: *1 double room with bath, 2 doubles share bath, 1 suite.*
Amenities: *Air-conditioning in bedrooms, TV in suite; off-street parking.*
Rates: *$55–$75; Continental breakfast, afternoon tea. MC, V.*
Restrictions: *No smoking, no pets, 2-night minimum on holiday weekends.*

Swiss Woods

In northern Lancaster County, nestled in rolling, wooded hills that overlook a lake, is Swiss Woods. When you enter the white brick modified Swiss chalet, Debrah Mosimann will greet you with a glass of chilled Swiss-made sparkling cider. She's a Lancaster County native who met her husband, Werner, in Austria while working with an interdenominational mission. They built their bed-and-breakfast on 30 acres of family-owned land and opened it in 1986. Swiss Woods is bright and airy, with natural woodwork, and it's decorated in country contemporary style. In the common room, there's a large sandstone fireplace to curl up in front of; in the bedrooms, you'll find handmade Swiss rugs, goose-down covers, and Swiss chocolates. Two rooms have whirlpool baths, and every room has either a balcony or a patio from which you can enjoy a spectacular view. The Mosimanns keep a canoe for guests at the lake, and they will direct you to the best trails for hiking or biking.

Address: *500 Blantz Rd., Lititz, PA 17543, tel. 717/627–3358 or 800/594–8018.*
Accommodations: *6 double rooms with baths, 1 suite.*
Amenities: *Air-conditioning in bedrooms, TV in suite and in common room, kitchenette for guest use, dinner prepared on request.*
Rates: *$65–$100; full breakfast. MC, V.*
Restrictions: *No smoking, no pets, 2-night minimum on weekends, 3-night minimum on holidays.*

White Rock Farm Guest House

Eighteen miles southeast of Lancaster, deep in the Amish country, is White Rock Farm, a 150-acre working farm and the home of a young Mennonite family. Overlooking a scenic stream and a historic covered bridge, the white-stucco farmhouse, built in the 1860s, has been in Les Hershey's family for four generations. In 1987 Les and his wife, Lois, opened their home to travelers. Tending the crops and the 150 head of cattle keeps Les and Lois on the farm; Les is also a carpenter. Their bed-and-breakfast, they say, "is our way of traveling and meeting new people." Guest rooms are furnished with a mix of family antiques and contemporary pieces; one room has a bed made by a local Amish craftsman. You'll find homemade quilts, hooked rugs, and old trunks. You can relax on the porch that overlooks the manicured farmland or take walks along wooded trails. Lois can arrange for babysitting and direct you to Amish farms where crafts and quilts are sold. Among the pleasures at White Rock are falling asleep with the smell of newly cut hay drifting in the window and waking to the clip-clop of a passing horse and buggy.

Address: *154 White Rock Rd., Kirkwood, PA 17536, tel. 717/529–6744.*
Accommodations: *3 double rooms share bath.*
Amenities: *Air-conditioning in bedrooms; croquet.*
Rates: *$55; full breakfast. No credit cards.*
Restrictions: *No smoking, no pets, 2-night minimum on weekends.*

Gettysburg/York

Gettysburg and York are in the middle of Pennsylvania's east-west axis, near the Maryland state line. The Susquehanna River is the region's eastern border, and to the west is the Allegheny National Forest. Thousands of visitors are drawn each year to these two relatively small places that have been the sites of significant events in U.S. history.

Gettysburg dates from the early 1700s, when Samuel Gettys acquired 381 acres from the descendants of William Penn. Gettys' son James eventually had town lots drawn up and gave the area his family name. Every schoolchild knows that Gettysburg was the site of the bloodiest Civil War battle. The three-day encounter, in July 1863, claimed 51,000 lives and was a turning point in the war. Five months later President Abraham Lincoln dedicated the cemetery at Gettysburg and gave his famous address.

Thirty miles from Gettysburg is York, first settled in 1736 and named after the city of York, England. In Colonial days, its fields were so fertile that it was known as the Breadbasket of America. Between September 30, 1777, and June 28, 1778, York was the site of the nation's capital. During that period the Continental Congress met at the York Courthouse and adopted the Articles of Confederation, the first document to describe the Colonies as the United States of America.

A visit to Gettysburg and York today gives a unique insight into 18th- and 19th-century life. Gettysburg remains a small town of about 7,000 people, in the midst of apple orchards and rolling hills. Visitors can tour the historic battlefield and see the battle reenacted through various media. York, with a population of about 50,000, has preserved and restored much of its Federal and Victorian architecture. In both towns you will discover brick walkways, carved doors, stained-glass windows, and houses with cast-iron trim. You will find relatively unspoiled the surrounding gently sloping farmlands, where cannon once roared, rifles cracked, and drums rolled. Passing through villages you will see taverns, quaint shops, and inns with candle-lit windows, one of which may be your lodging for the night.

Places to go, sights to see

Battlefield Bus Tours (Gettysburg, tel. 717/334–6296). This 2-hour, 23-mile tour with taped commentary narrated by Hollywood personalities creates a "you are there" experience.

Eisenhower National Historic Site (tel. 717/334–1124). At the Gettysburg Visitor Center you can purchase tickets and board shuttle buses to visit the farm home of President and Mrs. Dwight D. Eisenhower. The 495-acre estate includes a 15-room Georgian-style home, an 1887 bank barn, and lots of memorabilia.

General Lee's Headquarters (Gettysburg, tel. 717/334–3141). Lee and his staff made their battle plans in this fieldstone house in Gettysburg, which now contains a fine collection of Civil War uniforms and relics.

Gettysburg National Military Park (tel. 717/334–1124) consists of the historic 3,500 acres where the Battle of Gettysburg was fought. The best way to see it is from your car, following a step-by-step narrated tour. Licensed battlefield guides can be engaged at the visitor center, which is a good place to begin your tour.

Golden Plough Tavern (York, tel. 717/845–2951). This Germanic half-timber building dating from 1741 contains a fine collection of furnishings from the early 18th century.

Jennie Wade House & Olde Town (Gettysburg tel. 717/334–4100; outside PA, 800/447–8788). The home of Gettysburg's heroine, the battle's only civilian casualty, has been carefully restored. Behind the house is a re-created village courtyard with shops of the era.

Lincoln Room Museum (Gettysburg, tel. 717/334–8188). The house and bedroom where Lincoln finished the final draft of his Gettysburg Address have been preserved, with many original furnishings.

York County Colonial Courthouse (York, tel. 717/846–1977). Artifacts and memorabilia are displayed in this reconstruction of the building where the Continental Congress adopted the Articles of Confederation, in 1777.

Tourist Information

Downtown Information Center (Colonial Courthouse, 205 W. Market St., York 17405, tel. 717/846–1977). **Gettysburg Travel Council** (35 Carlisle St., Gettysburg 17325, tel. 717/334–6274). **York County Convention and Visitors Bureau** (1 Market Way E., Box 1229, York 17405, tel. 717/848–4000).

The Bechtel Mansion Inn

In 1897 East Berlin's leading businessman built this 28-room Queen Anne mansion in the center of town as a residence for his family. It's such a fanciful, through-the-looking-glass place that you'll know it at once. The yellow-brick-and-white-trim building has a high pointed turret, a long curved porch, and lush Victorian gardens.

Owners Charles and Mariam Bechtel live in Fairfax, Virginia, where he is a manager for Bell Atlantic; but every weekend they are resident hosts. Charles grew up on a farm near East Berlin and will give you inside tips on touring the countryside. Innkeeper Ruth Spangler, who is always on hand, is knowledgeable about local history and customs.

The Bechtel, which became an inn in 1983, has been carefully furnished with American and European 19th-century antiques. It's on the National Register of Historic Places. Guests with a love of art and architecture will appreciate the intricate craftsmanship that went into the building and restoration of the house. Many rooms have original brass chandeliers. The Victorian parlor has vertical shutters, sliding pocket doors, and a handsome mantel—all in elegant cherry wood. The dining room has etched-glass windows and a large window seat. The breakfast room was the original kitchen, and you'll find French windows in the chimney corner, and

handmade furniture, pottery, and paintings by local artists throughout the house.

Each bedroom is furnished in antiques, has handmade Pennsylvania quilts, lace curtains, and a brass chandelier. In many you will find built-in wardrobes with full-length mirrors, and two have private balconies. Bathrooms retain their original ornate Victorian decor (though the plumbing is new). One of the most popular is the Sara Leas Room, with its turret-shape bay window and view of East Berlin's National Historic District.

You can easily spend a weekend exploring the Bechtel's nooks and crannies. Its location—almost equidistant from York, Gettysburg, and Hershey—makes it an ideal base for touring the area.

Address: *400 W. King St., East Berlin, PA 17316, tel. 717/259-7760.*
Accommodations: *4 double rooms with baths, 2 doubles share a bath, 2 suites.*
Amenities: *Air-conditioning in bedrooms, TV and VCR in common areas, gift shop in carriage house.*
Rates: *$77.50–$125; Continental breakfast, afternoon tea. AE, D, MC, V.*
Restrictions: *No smoking indoors, no pets, 2-night minimum on holiday weekends.*

The Brafferton Inn

A stay at the Brafferton Inn may be the pleasantest way to get a full sense of Gettysburg's historical richness. The 14-room stone house built in 1786, the first residence in town, faces a mid-19th-century street and has a seven-room pre–Civil War clapboard addition in back. On the first day of the battle, a bullet shattered an upstairs window. It lodged in the mantel and is still there today. During the war, services were held here while the church was being used as a hospital. And just down the street is the house where Lincoln completed his Gettysburg Address.

Mimi and Jim Agard purchased the property in the early 1980s, completely restored it, and in April 1985, opened the historic bed-and-breakfast inn. It is now listed on the National Register of Historic Places. Jim, who is chairman of the art department at Gettysburg College, had previously restored five houses in Vermont. And prior to becoming an innkeeper, Mimi was in public relations in New York City.

The inn has high ceilings, oversize doors, and odd nooks, turns, steps up and steps down that will constantly surprise you. It glows with Colonial colors. Above the original fireplace in the living room is an 1860 portrait of Robert E. Curtis, Jim's forefather. Here you'll also find wing chairs, a chimney cupboard, a player piano, and a primitive mural on four walls that depicts the area's historic buildings.

An atrium connects the stone house to the addition. This area, with brick floors and walls, is decorated with primitive pieces, pottery, and Oriental and hooked rugs. Farm implements are displayed on the walls, and opened antique cupboards are filled with old books. Down a wooden walkway is a deck where dahlias, zinnias, petunias, and marigolds are grown.

The guest rooms, with 18th-century stenciling on whitewashed walls, are furnished with country antiques and family pieces. You'll also find oil paintings, prints, and drawings— many by Jim's father, an artist. A local potter made the basins for washstands and dressers that have been transformed into sinks.

After a candlelight breakfast set to classical music, you can relax in the atrium while you plan the day. The inn is an easy walk from the battlefield, shops, and restaurants.

Address: *44 York St., Gettysburg, PA 17325, tel. 717/337–3423.*
Accommodations: *6 double rooms with baths, 5 doubles share 2 baths.*
Amenities: *Air-conditioning in bedrooms; off-street parking.*
Rates: *$70–$95; full breakfast. MC, V.*
Restrictions: *Smoking in atrium only, no pets.*

The Doubleday Inn

The Doubleday Inn is set amid the breastworks of the Gettysburg Battlefield and offers Civil War enthusiasts a bird's-eye view of where it all began. The white-clapboard Colonial-style house, built in 1929, sits on the Oak Ridge section of the Gettysburg Battlefield.

Sal Chandon, a recording engineer, and his wife, Joan, who worked for Jim Henson of Muppets fame, had been looking for a business to work in together. Sal's passion for the Civil War brought them to Gettysburg, where Joan's brother is a licensed battlefield guide. In spring 1987, they bought the property, which is within the national park, renovated the house completely, and became innkeepers. They named the inn after Abner Doubleday, who fought that first day of the battle.

The main parlor, whose windows overlook the sloping battlefield, has authentic period furnishings—an 1880s Victorian couch, a turn-of-the century pump organ, and a claw-foot coffee table. Civil War–related memorabilia can be found throughout the house, along with amusing period treasures, such as a stereoscope and a magic lantern that Joan and Sal like to demonstrate for their guests. The bedrooms are decorated in a mix of antique Victorian and country French, and you will find four-posters, brass beds, iron beds, and an oak pineapple bed.

You can browse through the 600-book library devoted to the battle and on Wednesday and Saturday evenings join in a discussion led by a Civil War historian. Often, Joan's brother drops by to meet guests and answer questions.

An elaborate home-cooked breakfast is served by waitresses in period dress in the formal dining room, complete with candlelight, crystal, and odd pieces of turn-of-the-century china. From 4 to 6 each afternoon, tea, drinks, and hors d'oeuvres are served in the main parlor. There are three outdoor patios and a screened-in porch where the Chandons entertain guests with barbecues on special occasions.

Sal and Joan are the kind of enthusiastic hosts who will make dinner reservations, arrange tours, and share tips on local antiquing.

Address: *104 Doubleday Ave., Gettysburg, PA 17325, tel. 717/334–9119.*
Accommodations: *5 double rooms with baths, 4 doubles share 2 baths.*
Amenities: *Air-conditioning, turndown service; picnics available.*
Rates: *$69–$94; full breakfast, afternoon tea. MC, V.*
Restrictions: *No smoking, no pets, 2-night minimum on holiday weekends.*

The Mercersburg Inn

Mercersburg, at the foot of the Blue Ridge Mountains, is a historic village off I-81, an hour and a half from Washington, DC. This country inn, on the outskirts of town, is an impressive Classic Revival red-brick structure with white trim, adorned with numerous porticoes, porches, and terraces.

Owner Fran Wolfe grew up in Delaware, where her mother operated a guest house. Fran later completed a series of restoration projects, including a 150-year-old log cabin in North Carolina; then, in 1986, she tackled this estate, transforming it into an elegant inn.

It's the kind of place where you expect something romantic has either already happened or will. In the entrance hall, twin staircases wind dramatically to the second floor, and rose and green Scaglioli columns accent the chestnut wainscoting. The Classic Arts and Crafts sun-room has a tiled floor and fireplace, high beamed ceilings, and a wall of broad windows. It's done in peach and blue, with white wicker furniture and flowered upholstery and curtains. You can sit back on the deep window-seat cushions and admire the stately grounds.

Restored antiques and locally handmade pieces fill the spacious guest rooms. You will find four-poster, canopy, brass, and king-size beds. Some rooms have fireplaces, others have private balconies with views of the mountains. In the tiled, high-ceilinged bathrooms there are antique needle showers, pedestal sinks, and free-standing tubs. Each bathroom has been meticulously restored to its turn-of-the-century grandeur.

In the formal mahogany-paneled dining room, there's a deep green marble fireplace, leaded-glass built-in cabinets, Tiffany stained-glass light fixtures, and parquet floors. Here, the award-winning restaurant known as The Morel serves six-course dinners and an à la carte menu of regional New American cuisine.

A bit farther north is a pocket of Amish country that most tourists never hear about. Fran can tell you how to get to the Gettysburg Battlefield and to the Amish market that's held each Wednesday.

Address: *405 S. Main St., Mercersburg, PA 17236, tel. 717/328–5231.*
Accommodations: *15 double rooms with baths.*
Amenities: *Restaurant open Wed.–Sun., air-conditioning and phones in bedrooms, TV and VCR in game room, conference room.*
Rates: *$105–$175; Continental breakfast. AE, MC, V.*
Restrictions: *No smoking indoors, no pets, 2-night minimum on fall-foliage weekends and holidays.*

Beechmont Inn

This 1834 Federal red-brick town house, with black shutters and window boxes overflowing with flowers, is on a tree-lined street in Hanover, about 13 miles south of Gettysburg and York. In 1986 Monna Hormel, a veteran bed-and-breakfast guest, left a career in retailing to open this inn. She has furnished it with elegant Federal-period antiques and replicas. In the library are 18th-century books and a collection of Civil War memorabilia. One suite has a marble fireplace, and the others have small kitchenettes. Up the winding staircase, guest rooms have four-poster beds, writing desks, and lace curtains. During warmer months you can relax in the old-fashion glider in the landscaped courtyard; and some morning, should you decide not to join the other guests in the dining room, you can enjoy breakfast in bed. This area is a gold mine of antiques shops, and hiking and swimming are nearby.

Address: *315 Broadway, Hanover, PA 17331, tel. 717/632–3013.*
Accommodations: *4 double rooms with baths, 3 suites.*
Amenities: *Air-conditioning in bedrooms, phone in bedrooms, accessible to handicapped; off-street parking, bicycles.*
Rates: *$70–$95; full breakfast, afternoon tea. AE, MC, V.*
Restrictions: *Smoking in guest rooms only, no pets, 2-night minimum on weekends.*

Emig Mansion

This elegant Victorian Greek Revival mansion, 10 minutes north of York, is a treat to the senses. It has gorgeous leaded and stained-glass windows, intricate inlaid flooring, ornate molding, and Victorian antiques throughout. Breakfast is served in an oval bay with curved-glass windows at one end of the formal dining room or at the walnut dining table that's long enough to seat 30. In guest rooms you will find brass, iron, and massively carved beds. Two rooms have fireplaces. This house was built in 1850 by John Emig, Jr., who made his fortune producing the commercial wagons that hauled goods along 19th-century roads. Innkeeper Jane Llewellyn, who also sells real estate, bought and extensively restored the mansion several years ago. She opened it as a bed-and-breakfast in June 1984. There are antiques shops and factory outlets nearby. Or you can just relax on the expansive porch and gaze across the road at the old wagonworks, just as the Emig family did 100 years ago.

Address: *Box 486, 3342 N. George St., Emigsville, PA 17318, tel. 717/764–2226.*
Accommodations: *3 double rooms with baths, 4 doubles share 2 baths.*
Amenities: *Air-conditioning in rooms; off-street parking, conference room.*
Rates: *$85–$110; full breakfast, afternoon tea. MC, V.*
Restrictions: *Smoking on balconies only, no pets.*

Fairfield Inn

This fieldstone structure with its two-story open gallery is in a sleepy little village 8 miles west of Gettysburg. Built as a plantation home in 1757, it became a hotel and stagecoach stop in 1823. David Thomas managed a hotel in Washington, DC, before he bought the inn in 1976. Throughout you will find random-width floors, low ceilings, original brass hardware, crystal chandeliers, lace curtains, and a Williamsburg-influenced mix of antiques and reproductions. In the early-19th-century clapboard guest house across the street, your room may have a carved oak headboard, a spool-and-rope bed, or be totally Victorian. Grandfather clocks are everywhere. The house was used as a hospital for wounded Confederate soldiers, and the ghost of Major Samuel Starr is said to be still in residence. The inn is well known for its classic country fare. (In fact, Mrs. Dwight Eisenhower frequently chose to entertain here.) The Gettysburg battle sites are nearby, but you may be content just to relax in this carefully restored inn that is steeped in so much history.

Address: *Main St., Fairfield, PA 17320, tel. 717/642-5410.*
Accommodations: *6 double rooms share 3 baths.*
Amenities: *Restaurant, air-conditioning in common areas and 2 bedrooms; 1 meeting room.*
Rates: *$50-$65; Continental breakfast. AE, MC, V.*
Restrictions: *No smoking in dining room, no pets, closed Sun., Mon., 1st week Feb., and 1st week Sept.*

The Historic Farnsworth House Inn

Confederate sharpshooters once occupied this 1810 red-brick Federal house near the National Cemetery, and you can still see lots of bullet holes. Loring H. Shultz has owned the inn/restaurant since 1972. He sells Civil War prints and books in a shop next door, and he and his family opened the bed-and-breakfast in 1989. The lushly Victorian guest rooms have antique marble-top dressers, beds with fishnet canopies, ornate chandeliers, globe lamps, and Oriental rugs scattered before the fireplaces. A wicker-filled sun-room is the perfect place to relax; it looks out on gardens where, in summer, you can dine in the open air, alongside a stone-lined stream that provided water for both armies. The restaurant specializes in mid-19th-century food, and an excellent house specialty is a game pie of pheasant, duck, and turkey. In the attic and basement, the Shultzes display their collection of artifacts from daily life in the Civil War period. It is one of those quirky yet worthwhile attractions off the beaten path that most visitors to Gettysburg never have a chance to see.

Address: *401 Baltimore St., Gettysburg, PA 17325, tel. 717/334-8838.*
Accommodations: *5 double rooms with baths.*
Amenities: *Restaurant, air-conditioning in bedrooms, TV in sun-room.*
Rates: *$65-$80; full breakfast, afternoon tea. AE, D, MC, V.*
Restrictions: *Smoking in sun-room only, no pets.*

The Old Appleford Inn

This bed-and-breakfast, a few blocks from Lincoln Square, is a gray brick Italianate Victorian house built in 1867, with a carriage house in back. The house has a gabled roof and arched windows framed by black shutters. Frank and Maribeth Skradski, hosts since 1987, stayed here first as guests and fell in love with the place. Before starting a life of innkeeping, he was a research engineer in Illinois and she owned an antique clothing shop. There's a gracious Victorian parlor with a baby grand piano, a library with lots of books, Civil War memorabilia, and a wonderful collection of old Kodak cameras, and a plant-filled sun-room with a well-stocked fridge. Two of the guest rooms have working fireplaces, and all are decorated with Victorian antiques and brass beds, sleigh beds, iron beds, and beds so high you have to climb up into them. Throughout, Maribeth has found ingenious ways to display antique clothing. The Skradskis know how to respect your privacy, but will pull up a chair and enthusiastically ask about your explorations that day.

Address: *218 Carlisle St., Gettysburg, PA 17325, tel. 717/337–1711.*
Accommodations: *11 double rooms with baths, 1 suite.*
Amenities: *Air-conditioning in bedrooms; off-street parking.*
Rates: *$78–$98; full breakfast. AE, MC, V.*
Restrictions: *No smoking, no pets, 2-night minimum on weekends May–Nov.*

The Tannery Bed and Breakfast

Two blocks from the National Cemetery and the Visitor Center is a tan, Gothic-structured house with chocolate-brown trim and a gabled roof. In 1868, when a Mr. Rupp built the clapboard house, his tannery business was right next door. Charlotte Swope's grandfather bought the house in 1920, and she was born and raised here. After retiring from running a tire dealership, Charlotte and her husband, Jule, opened their bed-and-breakfast in May 1989 and named it after the tannery, which is no longer standing. In the early '20s, the interior of the house was completely renovated. The result was an interesting blend of periods: light, clean-lined modernism met lofty Victoriana, and the charm still manages to shine through. Guest rooms are decorated with soothing Williamsburg colors and new carpeting. You will find traditional reproductions and a handful of family antiques. There's a wide, airy porch where you can sit and rock and watch a world of Civil War buffs go by. The Tannery is a low-key kind of place that will appeal to mature travelers.

Address: *449 Baltimore St., Gettysburg, PA 17325, tel. 717/334–2454.*
Accommodations: *5 double rooms with baths.*
Amenities: *Air-conditioning in bedrooms, TV in sitting room; off-street parking.*
Rates: *$65–$85; Continental breakfast, afternoon tea. MC, V.*
Restrictions: *No smoking, no pets, closed Dec.–Mar.*

Off the Beaten Track

Century Inn

This hand-hewn stone building with a long porch and two large stone chimneys on either end is listed on the National Register of Historic Places. Since 1794, Century Inn has offered hospitality to travelers passing through this village 35 miles south of Pittsburgh. In 1945, Dr. and Mrs. Gordon Harrington restored the inn and furnished it with heirlooms and rare American antiques. Today, their daughter-in-law, Megin Harrington, continues the tradition. In the parlors are two identical fireplaces, a display of antique paperweights and glassware, and an original flag from the Whisky Rebellion that hangs above one mantel. The guest rooms are as carefully furnished with antiques as the public areas. Superb meals are served in the five dining rooms. In the Keeping Room (the original kitchen), the massive fireplace has a hand-forged crane and curious cooking utensils. Megin will gladly direct you to the best places for antiquing, boating, and skiing—which are all within a short distance.

Address: *Main St., Scenery Hill, PA 15360, tel. 412/945-6600 or 412/945-5180.*
Accommodations: *9 double rooms with baths, 3 suites.*
Amenities: *Restaurant with conference facilities, air-conditioning in bedrooms; tennis court, croquet.*
Rates: *$73–$118; full breakfast. No credit cards.*
Restrictions: *No pets, closed mid-Dec.–Feb. 14.*

Glasbern

You will understand why Al and Beth Granger chose this name (which means "glass barn" in Old English) when you see their country inn. Glasbern is a 19th-century German bank barn, tucked into a quiet valley 10 miles west of Allentown, and the Grangers have reconstructed it of stone, wood—and lots of glass. The Great Room resembles a lofty stone sanctuary, with a fireplace and hand-hewn beams that crisscross through the high, open spaces. Guest rooms are decorated traditionally, with standard antique reproductions, and in contemporary style with glass tables and wicker. Brick walkways lead to a farmhouse and a carriage house—both renovated and similarly decorated—there's a certain sameness about the decor. Some suites have whirlpool baths, kitchenettes, and private entrances. You can take carriage and sleigh rides; skiing, hiking, and antiquing are close by, but you may find you're content with just being on these 113 peaceful acres in the middle of nowhere.

Address: *RD 1, Box 250, Fogelsville, PA 18051-9743, tel. 215/285-4723 or 800/654-9296, fax 215/285-2862.*
Accommodations: *14 double rooms with baths, 7 suites.*
Amenities: *Restaurant with conference facilities open Tues.–Sat., air-conditioning in bedrooms, TV and phones in bedrooms; swimming pool, bicycles.*
Rates: *$95–$150; full breakfast. AE, MC, V.*
Restrictions: *No pets, 2-night minimum on fall weekends in suites.*

Longswamp Bed and Breakfast

This white clapboard Federal manor house is in a rural village about 15 minutes southwest of Allentown. Elsa and Dean Dimick restored the house, which was built in 1789, and opened it as a bed-and-breakfast in 1983. When they're not innkeeping, he's chief of medicine at the Lehigh Valley Hospital, and she's a professional chef. In the parlor, with its wood-pegged floors, deeply set windows, and settees before the fireplace, you can sit and enjoy the Dimicks' vast collection of books and music. The large, sunny guest rooms are decorated in a mix of Pennsylvania and Victorian antiques, with Amish quilts and one-of-a-kind antique iron beds. The cottage at the side, used in the Underground Railroad, is much more haphazardly decorated, with antiques and family hand-me-downs. Golf, tennis, and horseback riding are nearby, and the Dimicks can help you map out drives down scenic back roads through farmland or to antiques shops for browsing.

Address: *RD 2, Box 26, Main St., Mertztown, PA 19539, tel. 215/682–6197.*
Accommodations: *7 double rooms with baths, 4 doubles share 2 baths, 2 suites.*
Amenities: *Air-conditioning in bedrooms, TV in summer kitchen; hiking trails on 40 adjoining acres.*
Rates: *$60–$65; full breakfast, afternoon tea. MC, V.*
Restrictions: *No smoking in guest rooms, no pets.*

New Jersey

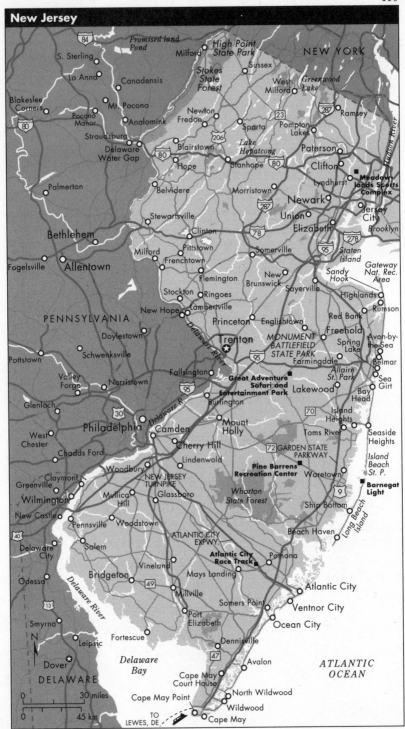

New Jersey

The Jersey Shore

Nowadays the 127-mile stretch of sandy beaches, bays, marshes, and inlets along the Jersey shore is one of the busiest vacation destinations in the country. It has been discovered, colonized, divided, subdivided, developed, renovated, and restored so many times that the few natural get-away-from-it-all places remaining are exceptions rather than the rule.

Swimming and water sports predominate in this area. Fishing, on the ocean or in the back bays, is convenient by party or charter boat. Murky visibility limits, but does not preclude, the joys of scuba. You're at most a short car trip away from golf, horseback riding, and tennis; and bicycling on most boardwalks is permitted during early morning hours.

Proximity to the beaches or bays (for boaters) is desirable, although beach areas tend to be noisy and busy at the height of the season. Admission to all New Jersey beaches, with the exception of those in Atlantic City, Wildwood, and Cape May Point, requires the purchase of a beach tag, which most bed-and-breakfasts provide free or for a small fee. Island Beach State Park in Ocean County, a 12-mile stretch of virtually pristine beaches and overgrown dunes, charges $2 to $5 per carload, with free admission on Tuesday.

If you'd like to side-step the crowds, visit during the off-season: September is the best month. The days then are shorter, the breezes cooler, the ocean warm and tranquil, and most restaurants and attractions are still open. May is also pleasant. The cold, quiet months of November and December are becoming popular for business retreats.

One component of a Jersey shore vacation is an evening in Atlantic City, where casino gambling has created a new

*style of adult-oriented entertainment and extravagance.
Unfortunately, the benefits from this "new" industry (back-
room gambling has existed in Atlantic City for more than
150 years) have yet to change the city's overall run-down
condition.*

Places to go, sights to see

Albert Hall (Waretown, tel. 609/971–1593). Locals gather here every
Saturday night at 8 in summer for concerts of folk music and old-time
Pinelands ballads and songs.

Allaire Village State Park (between Farmingdale and Lakewood, tel.
908/938–2371) is a 17th-century ironworks village surrounded by 3,000 acres.

Amusement parks. Boardwalk amusement rides are best in *Wildwood* and
Seaside Heights. The *Great Adventure* (tel. 908/928–1821) theme park,
southwest of Freehold, has the best roller coasters and an enclosed safari
park.

Cape May County Historical Museum (Cape May Court House, tel. 609/465–
3535). Period Victorian clothing and furniture, early whaling instruments,
and the lens from the Cape May lighthouse are among the variety of items in
this 1755 house.

Cape May County Park (Cape May Court House, tel. 609/465–5271),
a pleasantly landscaped park area, contains a picnic ground, playground, bike
trail, gazebo, tennis courts, and a petting zoo for kids. Free concerts are held
here in summer. It has facilities for the disabled.

Flea markets. Monmouth County flea markets and auctions include
Collingwood Auction & Flea Market (tel. 908/938–7941), in Howell; *The
Englishtown Auction* (tel. 908/446–9644), in Englishtown; and *Howell
Antique Village and Flea Market* (tel. 908/308–1105), on Rte 9, just north of
Rte. 195.

Garden State Arts Center (Holmdel, tel. 908/442–9200). Many of the
entertainers who perform in Atlantic City's casinos also appear here.

Leamings Run Botanical Gardens (Swainton, tel. 609/465–5871) consist of
27 spectacular theme gardens in Cape May County.

Lenox China factory (tel. 609/641–3700). China and giftware may be
purchased at retail prices at the site on Tilton Road in Galloway Township.
Bargain hunters should consider calling in October, when the store has an
annual week-long sale.

Lighthouses. At the northern end of the shore is the *Sandy Hook Light* (tel. 908/872–0092), the oldest continuously operating lighthouse in the country. *Navesink Twin Lights* (tel. 908/872–1814) is about 8 miles south, in Highlands. *Barnegat Light* (tel. 609/494–2016), the famous red-and-white tower built in 1858 and known as Old Barney, is at the northernmost end of Long Beach Island, in Barnegat Light State Park, which is expected to reopen in mid-1991 after repairs. The *Hereford Inlet Light* in North Wildwood (1st and Central Aves., tel. 609/729–1714) is the top floor of a small Victorian frame building.

Monmouth Battlefield State Park (Freehold, tel. 908/462–9616). Here Molly Pitcher earned her place in American history books.

Monmouth County Parks concert series (tel. 908/842–4000). Free and low-price evening concerts in various parks within the County Park system are presented June through August.

Noyes Museum (Oceanville, tel. 609/652–8848) has displays on New Jersey folklore and fine art.

Racetracks. Horse-racing fans can visit *Monmouth Park* (Oceanport, tel. 908/222–5100) and *Atlantic City Race Course* (McKee City, tel. 609/641–2190).

Sandy Hook (tel. 908/872–0092). Part of the Gateway National Recreation Area, Sandy Hook includes America's oldest operating lighthouse (built in 1764), public beaches, gun emplacements, an old Army weapon range and military encampment, a nature center, changing rooms and showers, and a fabulous view of New York Harbor.

South Jersey Regional Theater (Somers Point, tel. 609/653–0553) presents revivals, repertory, and original drama in Atlantic County.

Surflight Theater (Beach Haven, tel. 609/492–9477) offers summer-stock plays and Broadway revivals on Long Beach Island.

War games. The *Pine Barrens Recreation Center* (near Chatsworth, tel. 609/698–3333) offers weekly war games involving safe, nonprojectile-firing weapons.

Wineries. Worth visiting are *Renault Vineyard* (Egg Harbor City, tel. 609/965–2111) and *Balic Winery* (Mays Landing, tel. 609/625–2166.

Restaurants

In Monmouth County consider *Doris and Ed's* (Highlands, tel. 908/872–1565) for seafood, *Farmingdale House* (Farmingdale, tel. 908/938–7951) for genuine Northern Italian cuisine, and the *Fromagerie* (Rumson, tel. 908/842–8008) for French cuisine. *Harry's Lobster House* (Sea Bright, tel. 908/842–0205) serves excellent, sophisticated Continental fare, and *Harrigan's Pub*

(Sea Girt, tel. 908/449–8228) is an unpretentious tavern with inexpensive grilled seafood, chops, and chicken.

On Long Beach Island *Harvey Cedars Shellfish Company* (tel. 609/494–7112) serves steamed shrimp, clams, and simple flatfish in a casual atmosphere. *Romeo's* (tel. 609/492–0025) is a good Italian seafood restaurant, and *Terrace Tavern* (tel. 609/494–7051) serves inexpensive, generally well-prepared grilled seafood and tavern fare.

In Atlantic County, beyond Atlantic City, *Marriott's Seaview Resort* (tel. 609/652–1800), in Galloway Township, has a delicious seafood buffet and Sunday brunch. *Tre Figlia* (tel. 609/965–3303), in Pomona, is one of the region's best Northern Italian restaurants. *Little Rock Cafe* (tel. 609/823–4411) is a charming bistro in Ventnor. *The Clam Bar* (tel. 609/927–8783) in Somers Point (a short drive from Longport and Ocean City) has inexpensive steamed and fried seafood.

In Cape May County, north of Cape May City, the *Deauville Inn* (Strathmere, tel. 609/263–2080), a former speakeasy, does dockside surf-and-turf well. An inexpensive choice in Wildwood is the *Ravioli House* (tel. 609/522–7894). For dress-up hotel-style dining, Ocean City's *Flanders Hotel* (tel. 609/399–1000) serves American cuisine in dignified turn-of-the-century dining rooms. The *Whitebrier Inn* (Avalon, tel. 609/967–5225) offers surf-and-turf in a formal atmosphere, with some Continental and nouvelle items, and a good Sunday brunch.

Tourist Information

Atlantic City Visitors Bureau (Dept. of Public Relations, 2311 Pacific Ave., Atlantic City 08401, tel. 609/348–7044). **Cape May County Chamber of Commerce** (Box 74, Cape May Court House 08210, tel. 609/465–7181). **Long Beach Island–Southern Ocean County Chamber of Commerce** (265 W. 9th St., Ship Bottom 08753, tel. 609/494–7211). **Monmouth County Dept. of Public Information/Tourism** (27 E. Main St., Freehold 07728, tel. 908/431–7476). **New Jersey Division of Travel and Tourism** (CN 826, Trenton 08625, tel. 609/292–2470). **Ocean County Tourism Advisory Council** (CN 2191, Administration Bldg., Toms River 08753, tel. 908/929–2163).

Reservation Services

Bed & Breakfast Adventures (103 Godwin Ave., Suite 132, Midland Park, 07432, tel. 201/444–7409). **Northern New Jersey Bed & Breakfast/Temporary Lodgings** (11 Sunset Trail, Denville, NJ 07834, tel. 201/625–5129).

Normandy Inn

This huge Italianate villa with Queen Anne touches was built for Auden Ried, one of Spring Lake's mayors, around 1889 and became a guest house in 1909. In 1982 the inn was bought by Michael and Susan Inginio, who have slowly transformed it into a textbook of high-Victorian furnishings.

With the exception of a discordant pair of director's chairs in one guest room—which Michael admits "are not long for this world"—there are no reproductions or modern pieces of furniture in the Normandy. Everything is genuine American Victorian, from the formerly gaslit chandeliers, the magnificent dark rococo and French Revival bedroom sets to the Renaissance Revival parlor set carved with women's faces.

"We didn't think we'd get into anything like this, and we certainly didn't think we'd get so involved in period furnishings," Mike says. "Before we bought the inn, we had an ice-cream business in Toms River. We sold that, took a year off, thought about what we wanted, found this place, and, you know what they say, if you're going to do anything, you'd better do it right the first time." The Inginios also host B&B seminars and innkeeper workshops.

The Normandy, a two-minute walk from the beach, has become the standard against which the other bed-and-breakfasts in Spring Lake are measured. The inn's museum-quality furnishings create a formal atmosphere that the Inginios deliberately undercut, urging guests to relax. "To see a guest curl up on a sofa with a book is just what I want," he explains.

The five- to six-course hot breakfasts make it easy to skip lunch. All rooms have private baths; the tower room is built into the cupola, so its bathroom is down a flight of stairs. Guests staying in the tower room are provided with bathrobes. In the 1930s a garage was added, above which is a 2-bedroom apartment, in contemporary style, that's perfect for a family.

Address: *21 Tuttle Ave., Spring Lake, NJ 07762, tel. 908/449-7172.*
Accommodations: *15 double rooms and 2 singles with baths, 1 suite.*
Amenities: *Air-conditioning in bedrooms, cable TV in parlor and suite; bicycles, beach towels, on-site parking for 9 rooms, transportation to and from train and bus.*
Rates: *$92–$132; full breakfast. AE, MC, V.*
Restrictions: *No smoking in dining room; no pets, 2-night minimum July–Aug. and on weekends Mar.–Nov.; 3-night minimum on holiday weekends, 4-night minimum on weekends July–Aug.*

Pierrot by the Sea

This 1876 inn is a showplace of the skills of its owners, Richard and Catherine Burdo. Richard does professional Victorian restoration of buildings, furniture, and lighting, and Catherine is a fashion coordinator.

The restoration of Pierrot by the Sea is accurate to the high-Victorian era (1876–1890), including its color scheme, furnishings, chandeliers, woodwork, and stained glass. The one exception is a single 12-foot-tall mahogany reproduction of a bedroom set that Richard made to see how closely he could match the style. (He matched it perfectly.) "An architect who stayed with us begged us to sell it to him," Catherine says. "We told him it wasn't for sale."

The light wicker in the inn's first-floor parlor contrasts with the heavy woods and somber bedroom sets in the floors above. The bedrooms are light and airy, despite being furnished with Oriental rugs, flowered chintz draperies, and that highly carved walnut Victorian furniture. You can see the ocean from the majority of the rooms, and the inn is within walking distance of restaurants, the movies, outdoor amusements, and theater.

Before opening the Pierrot in 1984, the Burdos owned the Pierrot restaurant in Philadelphia. In the formal dining room of Pierrot by the Sea they serve multi-course Northern Italian dinners on weekends ($30 per person, bring your own Chianti), and their five-course hot breakfasts are the most elaborate served at any inn on Long Beach Island. Quiches and eggs Benedict compete with unusual cheese, herb, and sausage breads.

The modern beach block motels across the street clash jarringly with the Pierrot, and their proximity generates a degree of street noise on Saturday nights in summer, but the air conditioners, when turned on, mask the sound. By the end of 1991 the Burdos expect to add central air-conditioning and to complete three more private baths.

Address: *101 Centre St., Beach Haven, NJ 08008, tel. 609/492-4424.*
Accommodations: *4 double rooms with baths, 5 doubles share 2 baths, 1 suite.*
Amenities: *Air-conditioning in 3 bedrooms, cable TV in common room, fireplace in parlor; beach towels, beach tags, chairs.*
Rates: *$85–$125; full breakfast, afternoon tea. No credit cards.*
Restrictions: *No smoking indoors, no pets, 2-night minimum on weekends, 3-night minimum on holiday weekends, closed Nov.–Mar.*

Ashling Cottage

Goodi Stewart calls the style of her 1880 cottage Carpenter Gothic "because, as far as we can tell, the carpenter made it up as he went along." The intimate, unpretentious little house, which sits in the shadow of the old Colonial Hotel, is a block from the Spring Lake beach. There are no ocean views, and furnishings are mixed antiques and reproductions. Ocean breezes make air-conditioning unnecessary.

The atmosphere is easygoing, and innkeepers Goodi and Jack Stewart are experts at down-to-earth informality. "Jack's day gig is on the golf course," Goodi remarks. "Since he retired, he's become an expert at relaxation. We bought this place because I got jealous watching him on the couch reading the paper."

On warm days Goodi reads the paper in the solarium or chats with guests during their impromptu afternoon get-togethers. The inn has an extensive collection of games and books for whiling away quiet hours.

Address: *106 Sussex Ave., Spring Lake, NJ 07762, tel. 908/449–3553.*
Accommodations: *8 double rooms with baths, 2 doubles share a bath.*
Amenities: *Cable TV/VCR in parlor; bicycles, beach tags, on-site parking, transportation from train.*
Rates: *$73–$115; Continental buffet breakfast. No credit cards.*
Restrictions: *No smoking in bedrooms; 3-night minimum on weekends July–Aug. 2-night minimum other weekends, closed Jan.–Mar.*

BarnaGate Bed and Breakfast

If you can name the architectural style of this trim, pleasant 1896 Ocean City guest house, owners Frank and Lois Barna will be overjoyed. "We've had architects look it over and they can't figure it out," Lois says. "We call it seashore style." The exterior is vaguely Queen Anne, with a broad porch and bright burgundy awnings. Inside, a Second Empire oak dining room is the perfect setting to show off Lois's collections of spoons and bells. Frank collects John Wayne memorabilia, which he will show to interested guests.

Four blocks from the beach and convenient to Ocean City's busy downtown shopping area, the inn is reasonably priced by shore standards. Rooms have floral themes and

are dressed with country Victorian antiques and handmade quilts in pastel peach, rose, and mauve.

Leave the car at home: Frank will pick you up at the local bus terminal or the Atlantic City train station.

Address: *637 Wesley Ave., Ocean City, NJ 08226, tel. 609/391–9366.*
Accommodations: *1 double room with bath, 1 double with ½ bath, 3 double rooms share 2 baths.*
Amenities: *Cable TV in parlor; beach tags.*
Rates: *$60–$70; Continental breakfast. MC, V.*
Restrictions: *No smoking indoors, no pets, 2-night minimum on holiday weekends.*

Bayberry Barque

This 19th-century house was built in 1888 for a member of the Philadelphia Orchestra. Now it's an easygoing inn where Pat and Glenn Miller (he works for the state and doesn't play an instrument) live year-round with their three children.

The rooms are decorated in deep colors authentic to the period of the house and are filled with a blend of antiques, reproductions, bric-a-brac, wicker, and country Victorian furnishings that makes visitors feel at home. The striking 4-foot-by-8-foot stained-glass window on the landing of the open staircase is part of the original structure.

The inn is within walking distance of restaurants, boardwalk amusements, movies, a theater, nightclubs, and outdoor concerts, and it's just one block from the beach.

Address: *117 Centre St., Beach Haven, NJ 08008, tel. 609/492–5216.*
Accommodations: *2 double rooms with baths, 7 doubles share 2 baths.*
Amenities: *Ceiling fans in bedrooms, cable TV in living room; beach tags, Saturday-night wine-and-cheese parties in summer.*
Rates: *$80–$100; Continental breakfast. AE, MC, V accepted mid-June–mid-Sept.*
Restrictions: *No smoking indoors, no pets, 2-night minimum on weekends mid-June–mid-Sept., 3-night minimum on holiday weekends.*

Candlelight Inn

Paul DiFilippo and Diane Buscham, inspired by blissful stays in bed-and-breakfasts, sold their motel in order to transform this 1905 Queen Anne Victorian house into North Wildwood's first B&B, three blocks from the beach and boardwalk. "This is what we were meant to do," Diane says. "We enjoy everything about it. The people, the warmth—all of it."

Original stained-glass windows and converted brass gaslight fixtures adorn the house, which is furnished with period antiques. There's an 1855 Empire sofa and an Eastlake piano in the parlor, and on the veranda, a swing and hammock. The sun deck boasts a hot tub, for outdoor fun, and indoors guests enjoy murder-mystery weekends.

The bedrooms have lace curtains and Oriental carpets; all are wallpapered. The Oak, Pine, and Walnut rooms are furnished appropriately, as are Satin and Lace, Bay Window, and The Bride.

Address: *2310 Central Ave., North Wildwood, NJ 08260, tel. 609/522–6200.*
Accommodations: *7 double rooms with baths, 2 doubles share 1 bath with whirlpool tub.*
Amenities: *Air-conditioning in 3 bedrooms, cable TV in parlor, fireplaces in parlor and 2nd-floor foyer; off-street parking.*
Rates: *$85–$105; full breakfast. AE, D, MC, V.*
Restrictions: *No smoking indoors, no pets, 3-night minimum on weekends July–Aug.*

The Carriage House

The Carriage House, which was the pleasant home of Tom and Marie Bradley for more than 10 years, sits on a peaceful residential street in Spring Lake. By mixing antiques, reproductions, and modern furniture in pastel colors, the Bradleys have created a relaxed, country atmosphere.

The Bradleys like people and are experienced enough to know what people like. They encourage family visitors by keeping the room rates reasonable and accommodate visitors in every way they can. If eating in the dining room doesn't suit you, you can have your breakfast on the inn's large, open front porch, at a table on the front lawn, or in the cozy privacy of your own room. The large bedrooms in the front of the house have five windows each.

Address: *208 Jersey Ave., Spring Lake, NJ 07762, tel. 908/449-1332.*
Accommodations: *7 double rooms with baths, 2 doubles and 1 single share 1 bath, 1 suite.*
Amenities: *Air-conditioning in bedrooms, cable TV in living room; tennis passes, beach tags, beach towels, off-street parking, transportation from train.*
Rates: *$70–$90; Continental breakfast. No credit cards.*
Restrictions: *No smoking in public rooms, no pets, 2-night minimum on weekends May–Sept., 3-night minimum on holiday weekends.*

Cashelmara Inn

Built in 1901 for the U.S. Postmaster General, this deceptively small-looking gabled house boasts a proud Greek Revival porch that faces Sylvan Lake. Cashelmara is on the block between Ocean Avenue and the beach, overlooking Sylvan Lake. Marty Mulligan, a professional Irishman and technical representative for Eastman Kodak, was smitten by the near-perfect location, so he bought the house in 1986 and named it the Gaelic word for "house by the sea."

Overflowing with antiques, Oriental rugs, and period furnishings not so old that you can't relax in them, all the rooms have lake or ocean views. Cashelmara hosts mystery weekends and clambakes, as well as occasional afternoon wine-and-cheese parties.

Address: *22 Lakeside Ave., Avon-By-the-Sea, NJ 07717, tel. 908/776-8727.*
Accommodations: *13 double rooms with baths, 1 suite.*
Amenities: *Air-conditioning in 10 bedrooms, ceiling fans in all, fireplaces in parlor and suite, minirefrigerator in suite, cable TV in parlor; beach towels, reduced-rate beach tags, off-street parking, transportation to and from bus and train station.*
Rates: *$90–$100; full breakfast. AE, MC, V.*
Restrictions: *Smoking on porch only, no pets, 3-night minimum on weekends (4-night minimum on holiday weekends) Memorial Day–Labor Day, 2-night minimum on other weekends.*

The Chateau

The Chateau is four blocks from the beach, convenient to the Spring Lake railroad station, and across from the municipal park and lake, where there are tennis courts and a children's playground. Owner Scott Smith says he considers the Chateau, with its rambling complex of rooms, to be in a niche between a bed-and-breakfast and a hotel.

The Victorian-cottage exterior contrasts drastically with the interior, which has plush wall-to-wall carpeting and contemporary and wicker furnishings. Rooms are named after some of the hotel's more famous guests, such as Buster Keaton, Basil Rathbone, and Arthur Treacher. Twenty-two rooms and all the suites have wet bars, and many of the baths are marble.

Address: *5th and Warren Aves., Spring Lake, NJ 07762, tel. 908/974–2000, fax 908/974–2000, ext. 137.*
Accommodations: *40 double rooms with baths, 6 suites.*
Amenities: *Air-conditioning, cable TV, radios, telephones, and refrigerators in bedrooms; VCRs, wet bars, and oversize tubs in some rooms; fireplace in most suites; beach tags, on- and off-site parking; bicycle rental.*
Rates: *$79–$150; no breakfast served. AE, MC, V.*
Restrictions: *No pets, 3-night minimum on weekends June 21–Sept. 10.*

Conover's Bay Head Inn

Three porches adorn Ocean County's best known bed-and-breakfast, a shingle-style cottage built in 1905 that had become a hotel. Beverly and Carl Conover bought it about 22 years ago and began their bed-and-breakfast, inadvertently becoming leaders in the movement. Beverly hosts B&B seminars and teaches at a local college. Carl spent four years restoring a 1936 Elco cruiser.

You can see the water from many of the inn's windows; six guest rooms have ocean views, and two have views of the bay. Interiors are furnished in a mix of antiques and reproductions in English country style, with lots of chintz, spriggy wallpapers, and ruffled linens. An enclosed English garden was added to the grounds in May 1990. Special headboards were made for some of the beds, and one room, with oak furniture, has an ocean-view porch.

Address: *646 Main Ave., Bay Head, NJ 08742, tel. 908/892–4664.*
Accommodations: *12 double rooms with baths.*
Amenities: *Air-conditioning in bedrooms, turn-down service, fireplace in parlor; beach tags, beach towels, on-site parking, transportation to and from train station.*
Rates: *$110–$175; full breakfast, afternoon tea in cooler months. AE, MC, V.*
Restrictions: *No smoking indoors, no pets, 2-night minimum on weekends June–Sept., 3- and 4-night minimum on holiday weekends.*

Henry Ludlam Inn

Henry Ludlam has a small place in New Jersey's history books as the man who started the state's first public school. His 1804 house in the simple Federal style is now a bed-and-breakfast owned by Marty and Ann Thurlow. The house is decorated with country antiques and a variety of 18th- and 19th-century pieces in different woods. It sits on 55-acre Ludlam's Pond, which guests are encouraged to explore in the inn's canoe, catamaran, and inner tubes. Rods and reels are also available for amateur anglers, and less active guests can admire the lake from the gazebo.

The ambience at the inn is reminiscent of the Chesapeake Bay area: Were it not for the traffic along Route 47, you'd think you were in a Maryland backwater. Stone Harbor is 20 minutes away, and antiques shops are nearby.

Address: *Rte. 47, Dennisville (RD 3, Box 298, Woodbine, NJ 08270), tel. 609/861-5847.*
Accommodations: *4 double rooms with baths, 2 doubles share 1 bath.*
Amenities: *Air-conditioning in bedrooms, feather mattresses, fireplaces in 3 bedrooms, cable TV in parlor, fireside picnic baskets, dinner served Sat. Oct.–May; beach tags, beach towels, catamaran, inner tubes, canoe, fishing rods, off-street parking.*
Rates: *$75–$95; full breakfast, afternoon refreshments. AE, MC, V.*
Restrictions: *Smoking in common room only, no pets, BYOB, 2-night minimum on weekends July–Aug.*

Hollycroft

On a bluff hidden by trees above South Belmar's Lake Como, Hollycroft was built around 1900. Its log beams and brooding fieldstone fireplace suggest a Vermont log cabin or an Adirondack ski chalet. The lake can be seen from all but one of the guest rooms; one has a glassed-in porch.

Linda and Mark Fessler bought Hollycroft in 1985 and maintained its North Country mood throughout. The dining area has a minifridge that resembles an antique icebox, and the guest rooms are decorated with floral wallpaper, light woods, and brass and iron beds.

The inn is four blocks from the beach, and its proximity to Lake Como attracts anglers and bird-watchers. In the cooler months the Fesslers host mystery weekends, and it is a most atmospheric place for a family Christmas (BYOS—bring your own stocking).

Address: *506 North Blvd., South Belmar, NJ 07719, tel. 908/681-2254.*
Accommodations: *6 double rooms with baths.*
Amenities: *Air-conditioning in 4 bedrooms, 2 fireplaces in public areas; beach towels, off-street parking.*
Rates: *$85–$95; Continental breakfast. AE.*
Restrictions: *No smoking in bedrooms, no pets, 2-night minimum on weekends Memorial Day–Sept., 3-night minimum on holiday weekends.*

Inn at the Ocean

Betty Culbert, a former casino pit boss, bought this 1909 vacation home, tore out just about everything but the fireplace, and restored it with modern interiors in pastel shades. In 1989 she opened Atlantic City's first casino-era bed-and-breakfast inn, on the beachfront in the Chelsea section, about a mile south of the boardwalk casinos.

Her goal, she says, was to beat the casinos at a different game: "There's nothing in Atlantic City for the person who wants first-class rooms at an easygoing, more intimate pace, a place where you don't have to be a gambler to be treated right."

Even the smallest rooms have all the accessories of a casino hotel suite— hair dryer, cable TV, VCR, and whirl- pool bath. Breakfast is the five- course gourmet variety, with juices, fresh-baked breads, quiches, crepes, omelets, and fresh fruit.

Address: *109 S. Dover Ave., Atlantic City, NJ 08401, tel. 609/345–1717, fax 609/484–9223.*
Accommodations: *8 double rooms with baths, 2 suites.*
Amenities: *Air-conditioning, phones, washer, dryer, and refrigerator for guest use; massage; meeting areas; beach towels; beach chairs; bicycles; limo service; off-street parking.*
Rates: *$120–$250; full breakfast. AE, MC, V.*
Restrictions: *No pets.*

Sea Crest by the Sea

This whimsical Queen Anne–style bed-and-breakfast seeks to be just a little bit different from the pack. John and Carol Kirby opened Sea Crest in 1990. Its colorful rooms are inspired by characters and themes from fairy tales, history, literature, and such exotic realms as Casablanca and New Orleans.

The three-story house is furnished with French and English Victorian antiques in beautiful condition. Favorite guest rooms are the Victorian Rose, which boasts a carved Victorian American-walnut bed, and the Sleigh Ride Room, where there's a brass sleigh on the mantel. Located next door to the Normandy Inn, Sea Crest is close enough to the beach for guests to hear the surf from its wraparound porch.

Address: *19 Tuttle Ave., Spring Lake, NJ 07762, tel. 908/449–9031.*
Accommodations: *12 double rooms with baths.*
Amenities: *Air-conditioning and cable TV in bedrooms, fireplaces in 2 bedrooms and 2 in parlor, turn-down service, toiletries, player-piano recitals; croquet lawn, bicycles, beach towels, off-street parking, transportation to and from railroad station.*
Rates: *$100–$130; Continental breakfast, afternoon tea. MC, V.*
Restrictions: *Smoking on porch only, 2-night minimum mid-May–Sept., 3-night minimum on holiday weekends.*

The Seaflower

T his Dutch Colonial house has a breezy mix of antiques and seashore bric-a-brac. It's about half a block from the beach and boardwalk, in a sleepy residential area, away from the commercial district. Innkeeper Pat O'Keefe is a microbiologist, and her partner Knute Iwaszko is a chemist. One bedroom has a painted and stenciled floor; the others are refinished pine. "I'm wild about wallpaper and flowers," says Pat, and the rooms reflect that love.

Although scientific types do visit, "Most people are less interested in work," Pat says, "and more interested in running." Knute is a serious runner who can plan courses of any length (the shortest is about 20 feet—just far enough to collapse on the porch). He participates in many local races.

Address: *110 9th Ave., Belmar, NJ 07719, tel. 908/681–6006.*
Accommodations: *5 double rooms with baths, 2 doubles share 1 bath.*
Amenities: *sinks in bedrooms, TV, VCR, and games in parlor; beach tags, bicycles, off-street parking, transportation to and from railroad station.*
Rates: *$55–$95; full breakfast. No credit cards.*
Restrictions: *No smoking indoors, no pets, 2-night minimum on weekends Memorial Day–Labor Day, 3-night minimum on holiday weekends.*

The Studio

T he 1889 home of artist John F. Peto, the Studio is on the National Register of Historic Places and was restored with Victorian touches and many of Peto's paintings. It's in peaceful, historic Island Heights, on the Barnegat Bay, near Barnegat Peninsula beach resorts and Island Beach State Park. Visitors can walk to Bayshore beaches or sit in rocking chairs on the wraparound porch, looking out on Toms River.

Owner Joy Smiley, Peto's granddaughter, says guests just live in her enormous country kitchen, where breakfast is served. The bedrooms are carpeted with different colors— one with a river view has a beamed ceiling and a big double bed; another, with white-flowered spread and curtains, is big enough for three antique dressers and a desk. Joy says the quiet pace of the area makes it ideal for winter joggers, who can toast their toes on the specially designed "foot warmer" fireplace in the library. Artists and art historians are frequent guests.

Address: *102 Cedar Ave., Island Heights, NJ 08732, tel. 908/270–6058.*
Accommodations: *3 double rooms share 2 baths.*
Amenities: *Air-conditioning in 2 bedrooms, turn-down service, cable TV in parlor, fireplaces in studio and in library, baby-grand piano, small kitchen.*
Rates: *$50–$85; full breakfast. AE.*
Restrictions: *No pets.*

Victoria Guest House

Salvador Dalí was once a guest at this inn, which has grown to include a second 19th-century cedar-shake cottage in Beach Haven's historic district. Rooms here are informal, furnished with wicker, rag rugs, and a mix of antiques. A small heated outdoor pool was added for guests who don't want to walk one block to the beach.

Innkeepers Marilyn Miller, a former schoolteacher, and her husband, Leonard, a retired executive from United Technologies, are very sociable: They give bridge parties on Wednesday night and Saturday-evening wine-and-cheese gatherings, after which guests move to the porch to hear the outdoor concerts performed in the park across the street. Active in historic preserva-tion, the Millers give guests free tickets to the Long Beach Island Historical Society Museum, which is across the park. The inn is close to the well-known Summer Stock theater, restaurants, cinema, and outdoor amusements.

Address: *126 Amber St., Beach Haven, NJ 08008, tel. 609/492-4154.*
Accommodations: *12 double rooms with baths, 2 doubles share 1 bath.*
Amenities: *Air-conditioning in 2 bedrooms, complimentary Sun. New York Times; beach tags, beach chairs, bicycles, swimming pool.*
Rates: *$80-$110; Continental breakfast, afternoon tea. No credit cards.*
Restrictions: *No smoking indoors, no pets, 2-night minimum on weekends, closed Nov.-Apr.*

Along the Delaware

The Delaware River begins as a trickling brook in upstate New York and gathers momentum as it moves south, drawing the border between Pennsylvania and New Jersey. At the northwest corner of New Jersey it widens and forms the Delaware Water Gap, well known to canoeists, kayakers, and white-water enthusiasts. Just north of Trenton a historic park marks the spot where Washington crossed the river, which continues south through Philadelphia and empties into the broad basin of Delaware Bay.

The sites most interesting to tourists are concentrated along the 80 miles of river between the New York border and Washington's Crossing. Also of interest are Princeton, with its world-renowned university, and Lambertville, a small industrial village that is home to many of the artists, craftspeople, and restaurateurs of its neighbor across the river—New Hope, Pennsylvania. Lambertville is also where the Original Trenton Cracker Company turns out its famous walnut-size oyster crackers, found in seafood restaurants all along the East Coast. Lambertville, Stockton, and Frenchtown are good bases for antiquing and sightseeing in New Jersey and Pennsylvania. Flemington, about 10 miles east of Frenchtown, has a cluster of outlets, auctions, and antiques shops. Clinton, about 10 miles farther north, has a small historic area and is the site of a children's art festival. Still farther north are Hope and Fredon, nestled in a mountainous region that seems more a part of the Adirondacks than of New Jersey. Hot-air ballooning, water sports on the Delaware, spring and summer foliage-viewing, and skiing are highly recommended.

Places to go, sights to see

Ballooning. The still, windless mornings and tranquil twilight hours make this area perfect for hot-air ballooning, which costs from $135 to $150 per person for a 40- to 90-minute trip, transportation usually included. It's traditional to open a bottle of champagne at the finish, ask if your carrier supplies one. *Sky Promotions* (Pittstown, tel. 908/996–2195), near Clinton, operates year-round.

Gliders. For those who would rather not travel by balloon, *Eagle Ridge Soaring* (Blairstown, tel. 201/362–8311) offers trips in gliders.

Hiking and Biking. Though bicycles can be rented in the area, the steepness of the hills along the Delaware can be formidable. The Princeton area isn't quite so hilly, and the *Princeton University Cycle Club* (tel. 609/394–2221) meets every Sunday at 8 AM, weather permitting, at Forrestal Village, on Route 1. Hiking in state parks requires good boots, rugged clothing, sun protection for your head, and, from July through September, plenty of insect repellent.

McCarter Center of the Performing Arts (Princeton, tel. 609/683–8000). Notorious as one of the ugliest buildings on the Princeton campus, this theater presents memorable avant-garde and revival shows, as well as concerts and public lectures.

New Jersey State Museum (Trenton, tel. 609/292–6308). The dinosaur exhibit, the geology displays, the Native American artifacts, and the changing fine-arts exhibit at this museum make the drive into Trenton worthwhile.

Princeton University. *Orange Key Tours* (tel. 609/258–3603) employs undergraduates to show visitors around campus. Free tours leave daily from the Aclean House, next to Nassau Hall. *The Princeton Historical Society* (tel. 609/921–1854) gives tours of the university and its vicinity every Sunday at 2, starting from Bainbridge House (158 Nassau Street).

USGA Golf House Museum (Far Hills, tel. 908/234–2300). Housed in a Georgian Colonial–style mansion built in 1919, this museum and library is visited by golfers from all over the world. Two floors of exhibits lead you through the history of golf. There are special exhibits throughout the year.

Waterloo Village (Stanhope, tel. 908/347–0900). In this beautifully restored canal town in Stanhope shoppers will find a variety of craft items made by resident blacksmiths, potters, weavers, and candlemakers. The village's Indian museum displays and sells Native American crafts. The summer concert series, featuring a mix of jazz, classical, rock, and country-western music, is a big draw.

Wineries. New Jersey's wineries offer daily tours that end with tastings for those 21 and older. Don't expect first-class Bordeaux, but do expect to be surprised at the reasonably good vintages produced at the *Four Sisters*

(Belvidere, tel. 908/475–3671), *Alba Vineyard* (Milford, tel. 908/995–7800), and *Amwell Valley,* (Ringoes, tel. 908/788–5852). Ask your bed-and-breakfast hosts for other recommendations.

Restaurants

Scanticon-Princeton (tel. 609/452–7800). This somewhat modernistic conference-center hotel serves the region's knockout Sunday brunch. In Lambertville **Hamilton's Grill** (tel. 609/397–4343) offers multinational Mediterranean cuisine enhanced by a view of the Delaware. The **Ship Inn** (tel. 908/995–7007), in Milford, specializes in imported British beers. For German and Continental cuisine try the **Black Forest Inn** (tel. 908/347–3344), in Stanhope.

Tourist Information

Hunterdon County Chamber of Commerce (76 Main St., Flemington 08822, tel. 908/782–5955). **Mercer County Cultural & Heritage Office** (Box 8068, Trenton 08650, tel. 609/989–6701). **Princeton Convention and Visitors Bureau** (20 Nassau St., Princeton 08542, tel. 609/683–1760). **Sussex County Chamber of Commerce** (Box 157, Newton 07860, tel. 908/579–1811). **Warren County Dept. of Economic Development and Tourism** (Dumont Administration Bldg., Rte. 519, Belvidere 07823, tel. 908/475–8000, ext. 580).

Reservation Services

Bed & Breakfast Adventures (103 Godwin Ave., Suite 132, Midland Park 07432, tel. 908/444–7409). **Bed and Breakfast of Princeton** (Box 571, Princeton 08540, tel. 609/924–3189). **Northern New Jersey Bed & Breakfast/Temporary Lodgings** (11 Sunset Trail, Denville 07834, tel. 908/625–5129).

Chimney Hill Farm

Moving about among the hot-air balloons that are launched on the grounds of Chimney Hill Farm is a surreal experience. The approach to the inn will take your breath away. As you climb the road, the Delaware River, which dominates the Lambertville–New Hope area, disappears from sight, and the house and its owners, Fred Root and Ken Turi, welcome you.

The original 1820 fieldstone building was enlarged in 1920 by Margaret Spencer, one of the first female architects to graduate from MIT. Spencer added three wings to the house and crowned them with Colonial Revival gables and dormers. There are also seven staircases—"If you're running away from somebody, you *can* get away," Ken quips.

Bright floral fabrics and Oriental carpets complement the reproduction 18th-century furnishings. The living room's Persian rug previously adorned the corporate boardroom of the Reading Railroad Company in Philadelphia.

Horticulturists can wander the inn's 8½ landscaped acres. The sloping, open fields contain a raspberry and exotic-fruit farm, whose harvests are used in Lambertville's Coryell Crossing preserves, served with pancakes at Chimney Hill breakfasts as well as in many Manhattan restaurants. In the inn's greenhouse Fred and Ken grow the plants that fill the guest rooms and the solarium, and visitors may lose themselves in the 50-year-old boxwood maze or in the sunken English garden.

Fred and Ken have restored 10 properties in this area in the past decade. "We'll probably move on, eventually," Ken says, "but you don't find them much better than this."

Address: *Goat Hill Rd., RD 3, Box 150, Lambertville, NJ 08530, tel. 609/397–1516.*
Accommodations: *7 double rooms with baths.*
Amenities: *Air-conditioning in bedrooms, bathrobes supplied, fireplaces in 2 bedrooms and 3 public areas; complimentary cookies, fruit, and snacks; on-site parking, balloon trips ($135 per person).*
Rates: *$105–$150; full breakfast. AE, MC, V.*
Restrictions: *No smoking indoors, 2-night minimum on weekends, 3-night minimum on holiday weekends.*

Inn at Millrace Pond

Nowadays, the paddlewheel doesn't turn inside the Inn at Millrace Pond, but you can pretend the millrace still flows into this 1769 stone gristmill, which supplied the flour to Washington's troops. Located on 23 acres of forested hills in Hope, a historic Moravian village, the inn is close to the scenic Delaware River Water Gap, Waterloo Village, wineries, ballooning, golf, and winter-sports facilities.

Now in its fourth year of operation the inn complex has a restaurant, a tavern, two other Colonial buildings, the Millrace House and Wheelwright's House, and a small pond. When you enter the imposing four-story gristmill you can look down a story and a half at the skeleton of the old wheel and walk downstairs between stone walls to the tavern, with its huge walk-in fireplace, cage bar, and old prints on the walls. The gristmill's architecture is stunning; on the top floor the cathedral ceilings of the bedrooms reveal the enormous timbers of the roof, and the building's beams and wideboard floors have been preserved throughout.

Innkeepers Gloria Carrigan, a former advertising executive, and Dick Gooding, a developer of historic restorations, are serious about the furnishings: The gristmill bedrooms have Shaker reproductions; elsewhere there are regional antiques—made in New York, Pennsylvania, and New Jersey. The five-bedroom Millrace House, a frame building that was the miller's dwelling, has more formal furnishings and a parlor with a fireplace. Its bedrooms and the two in the stone Wheelwright's House have collections of Queen Anne, Chippendale, and Sheraton pieces. Each of the Wheelwright House bedrooms (one upstairs and one down) has its own entrance, and they are prized for romantic seclusion.

Active in the fight to preserve Hope's historic atmosphere, Gloria opens the inn to tours of the city's historic sites. In summer, guests often join one of the guided walking tours.

Address: *Rt. 519, Box 359, Hope, NJ 07844, tel. 908/459-4884.*
Accommodations: *17 double rooms with baths, 1 suite.*
Amenities: *Restaurant, tavern, air-conditioning, phones in bedrooms, cable TV in 9 bedrooms and parlor, fireplaces in parlor and tavern; off-street parking.*
Rates: *$80–$110; Continental breakfast. AE, MC, V.*
Restrictions: *No smoking in guest rooms, no pets, 2-night minimum with Sat. reservation.*

Stewart Inn

Six years ago attorney Brian McGarry had a midlife crisis that he thought he could cure with a grand purchase. "Some guys get blondes and Porsches," he explains. "I decided to do an inn."

His wife, Lynne, an antiques and needlework collector, approved, and the couple bought a 1770 fieldstone manor house originally built for the owner of Stewartsville's gristmill, which ground flour to feed George Washington's troops during the Revolutionary War.

Among the property's previous owners was Harry Bannister, a Broadway producer whose friends in the entertainment industry—among them Clark Gable—used the house as a retreat. Although the stars left nothing behind, the inn has retained a dramatic atmosphere that Brian describes as "privacy amid splendor."

About a 25-minute drive from the many fine restaurants of Lambertville, Stewart Inn has 16 acres of lawns; formal perennial gardens; a stocked trout stream; and a meandering pasture that leads to a working farm with ducks, sheep, goats, and peacocks. Eggs served at breakfast are provided by the farm's chickens.

The best times to visit the inn are summer, when the swimming pool offers a respite from the heat, and fall, when the maple and apple trees show off their bright colors.

Inside, off-white walls bring out the richness of the dark cherry and mahogany furnishings and the bright tapestries and rugs. Many rooms have antique jam cupboards, and all have brass oil lamps on night tables beside the beds. Needlework is displayed throughout the house, and Lynne holds needlework seminars and workshops during sheep-shearing season. She also sells kits for those who are inspired.

Address: *Box 571, RD 1, Stewartsville, NJ 08886, tel. 908/479–6060, fax 908/459–5889.*
Accommodations: *6 double rooms with baths, 2 share bath, 1 suite.*
Amenities: *Air-conditioning, color TV, and phones in bedrooms, 7 fireplaces in public areas; swimming pool, badminton court, trout stream, off-street parking.*
Rates: *$75–$95; full breakfast. MC, V.*
Restrictions: *No pets.*

Cabbage Rose Inn

Pam and Al Scott were telephone-company executives when they met, in 1986. Two years later they bought an 1890 Queen Anne house in Flemington, and after working for three months on the restoration they were married in front of the house's hand-carved mahogany fireplace. The Cabbage Rose Inn opened to the public shortly after.

Formerly the French restaurant La Champagne, the inn is set back from Flemington's busy Main Street and is within the city's historic district. Inside, cabbage rose–motif wallpaper and fixtures predominate. Many of the antiques, which Pam describes as "eclectic light Victorian," are family heirlooms.

Address: *162 Main St., Flemington, NJ 08822, tel. 908/788–0247.*
Accommodations: *3 double rooms with baths, 2 share bath.*
Amenities: *Air-conditioning, complimentary chocolates in guest rooms, cable TV in parlor, breakfast served in room on request, baby grand piano in parlor; croquet area, on-site parking.*
Rates: *$55–$85; Continental breakfast, afternoon refreshments. AE, MC, V.*
Restrictions: *Smoking on porch only, no pets, 2-night minimum with Sat. reservation in summer.*

Chestnut Hill

If you can't sleep without a teddy bear, you can choose from 133 bears in Teddy's Place, a room at Chestnut Hill. "When you're in there, it doesn't seem like that many," innkeeper Linda Costanza says. "We didn't know how many we had until someone counted. We're still not sure. There could be more."

Perched on the bank of the Delaware River, Chestnut Hill is near bicycle-, canoe-, and inner tube–rental shops, just 10 minutes from Lambertville and New Hope. Linda and her husband, Rob, are still working on the 1860 frame house. They're aiming for a balance of whimsy and Victorian detailing—slowly returning the outside of the inn, as well as the cottage next door, to the original period colors, while giving the guest rooms a country Victorian look with flowers and tropical hues. A huge black-walnut apothecary unit and an 1872 pump organ dominate the drawing room. The best views are from the wraparound porch.

Address: *63 Church St., Milford, NJ 08848, tel. 908/995–9761.*
Accommodations: *2 double rooms with baths, 3 doubles share 1 bath, 2 suites (1 with full kitchen).*
Amenities: *Air-conditioning, flowers and mints in bedrooms, turndown service, cable TV in 2 rooms, fireplace in parlor; on-site parking, transportation from Frenchtown bus stop.*
Rates: *$70–$160; Continental breakfast. No credit cards.*
Restrictions: *No smoking, no pets, 2-night minimum on weekends.*

Colligan's Stockton Inn

In 1934 Richard Rodgers and Lorenz Hart escaped from Manhattan to this inn, where they wrote "There's a Small Hotel," which was used in the 1936 musical *On Your Toes*. The song made Colligan's Stockton Inn, which has been entertaining guests since 1796, the most famous in New Jersey, and the inn gets frequent calls from people who want to know if the wishing well is still there. It is.

The Colligan family, however, who gave the inn an eccentric air, are not. They sold the inn in 1983 to a corporation that renovated the rooms with Colonial-style reproductions. The historic touches remain—eight bedrooms and the five dining rooms have working fireplaces—but the mood is more that of a small hotel. There are terraced gardens with waterfalls and trout ponds and a good restaurant that serves American and Continental food.

Address: *Rte. 29, Stockton, NJ 08559, tel. 609/397–1250.*
Accommodations: *11 double rooms with baths.*
Amenities: *Restaurant, air-conditioning and TV in bedrooms, minirefrigerators in some rooms; outdoor dining in warm months, off-street parking.*
Rates: *$60–$130; Continental breakfast. AE, MC, V.*
Restrictions: *No pets, 2-night minimum on weekends.*

Jerica Hill

The first bed-and-breakfast established in the small historic town of Flemington, Jerica Hill is a completely restored turn-of-the-century Victorian house set on a tree-lined street in the center of town. It's painted in shades of gray, with burgundy trim. Owner Judith Studer bought the property from her best friend's grandfather in 1984. She has chosen wicker, brass, oak, and mahogany furnishings to decorate what she calls her "Victorian country home." The large, first-floor bedroom is a favorite for its bay window, four-poster bed, and seating area.

Judith is an avid hot-air balloonist who will arrange balloon trips for guests. She also accompanies guests on winery tours that include a picnic in the country.

Address: *96 Broad St., Flemington, NJ 08822, tel. 908/782–8234.*
Accommodations: *2 double rooms with baths, 3 rooms share 1½ baths.*
Amenities: *Air-conditioning in 4 bedrooms, cable TV in living room, free New York Times, fireplace in living room; off-street parking.*
Rates: *$60–$90; Continental breakfast. AE, MC, V.*
Restrictions: *No smoking, no pets, 2-night minimum on weekends.*

Old Hunterdon House

This roomy 1865 Italianate Victorian mansion on Frenchtown's Main Street features high ceilings, a wraparound porch, and a cupola with views of the Delaware (where guests congregate for late afternoon refreshments). Guest rooms are dominated by huge, mixed-wood Victorian bedroom sets and are ornamented with antiques. The inn is a short walk from the river and 10 miles north of Lambertville and New Hope; public transportation is nearby.

Tony and Gloria Capiello bought the bed-and-breakfast in 1989 "as a new adventure." He had his own advertising agency, and Gloria was a bicoastal talent agent. The couple like their inn to feel "spontaneous, whatever the mood calls for. In Hollywood, I became annoyed with rules and regulations," Gloria explains, "so we let things flow here."

Guests staying in the two-room bridal suite are served breakfast in bed, and balloon trips and picnic lunches can be arranged.

Address: *12 Bridge St., Frenchtown, NJ 08825, tel. 908/996–3632.*
Accommodations: *7 double rooms with baths, 1 suite.*
Amenities: *Air-conditioning in bedrooms, fireplaces in 2 guest rooms and in parlor; on-site parking.*
Rates: *$90–$115; full breakfast. MC, V.*
Restrictions: *Smoking on porch only, no pets, 2-night minimum with Sat. reservation.*

Peacock Inn

In the center of Princeton, a two-minute walk from the university campus, the Peacock Inn has hosted visitors for more than a century. Built as a private home in 1770, the structure was moved in 1875 from its original site on the Princeton campus to its current Bayard Lane location. The Peacock Inn is the city's only full-time bed-and-breakfast, so guests should book far in advance for the fall and spring, when visiting educators fill its rooms. Albert Einstein, F. Scott Fitzgerald, and Bertrand Russell are listed among the inn's distinguished guests.

Although the rooms here vary in color scheme and decor, they all feature Victorian antiques and reproductions. The inn is one of few properties in the state that accept pets. Guests get a 50 percent discount on meals at Le Belumet Royal, the inn's restaurant, where dinner for two, without discounts, averages $100.

Address: *20 Bayard La., Princeton, NJ 08540, tel. 609/924–1707.*
Accommodations: *9 double rooms with baths, 6 doubles share 4 baths, one triple room with bath.*
Amenities: *Restaurant and bar with cable TV, air-conditioning in bedrooms, phones in 5 bedrooms, cable TV in lounge; on-site parking.*
Rates: *$80–$125; Continental breakfast. AE, MC, V.*

The Whistling Swan Inn

A late-1900 Victorian house, with a marvelous Queen Anne octagonal tower room and unusual limestone pillars supporting the veranda, the Whistling Swan is Paula Williams's and Joe Mulay's idea of where travelers should stay but rarely have the chance to. "Before doing this we worked for corporations and had to stay in Hiltons and Holiday Inns," Paula says. "When we traveled for ourselves we sought out bed-and-breakfasts and just had to have our own."

Located in a tiny village in New Jersey's highlands, the Whistling Swan is close to winter skiing and ice skating, summer water sports on the lakes, and cultural activities in Waterloo Village. The Delaware River is a 25-minute drive away.

Most of the inn's guest rooms contain country Victorian antiques and reproductions, but three have themes—Art Deco, 1940s, and Oriental.

Address: *Box 791, 110 Main St., Stanhope, NJ 07874, tel. 908/347-6369.*
Accommodations: *9 double rooms with baths, 1 suite.*
Amenities: *Air-conditioning in bedrooms, cable TV in guest parlor, fireplace in foyer and in dining room; off-street parking.*
Rates: *$65–$95; full breakfast. AE, MC, V.*
Restrictions: *Smoking on veranda only, no pets, 2-night minimum on holiday weekends.*

Cape May

Cape May, the southernmost resort town on the New Jersey shore, sits at the end of the Garden State Parkway, 40 minutes south of Atlantic City, at the tip of the Cape May County Peninsula. The town is known for its carefully researched and beautifully restored inns and small hotels, half of which, or about 35, are bed-and-breakfasts.

Believed to be the oldest ocean resort in New Jersey, Cape May was first sighted in 1620 by the Dutch explorer Captain Cornelius Mey, who modestly named the entire peninsula after himself. Early settlers were fishermen and whalers who came by boat from Philadelphia and from villages along Delaware Bay. Today the commercial fishing port is the third largest on the East Coast, providing Cape May's restaurants with fresh seafood.

As early as the 1760s, guest houses began to appear on the cape, and by the early 1800s they had expanded into huge hotels neighboring the summer mansions of people from Philadelphia, Wilmington, and Washington, DC. Fires and storms periodically ravaged the town, but an astonishing variety of structures managed to survive, including the gaudily appointed Italianate Victorian cottages, inns, and mansions that occupy the city's 2-square-mile historic district.

By the 20th century Cape May lost most of its business to Atlantic City and, in the 1950s, to Wildwood, both more easily reached by car or train. A catastrophic 1962 storm forced the city fathers to take stock of what they had. They used America's first Urban Development Action Grant to create an outdoor pedestrian street, the Washington Mall, which inspired the renovation of the Victorian buildings.

At about the same time, Cape May attracted a group of restaurateurs, most of them from Philadelphia, who found the combination of fresh seafood, locally grown vegetables, and low rents an incentive to try their luck in a town that was still too far down the Garden State Parkway for most tourists. When one succeeded, others followed. Now Cape May has a large district of eclectic restaurants, all within walking distance of one another.

The genteel, relaxing blend of architecture and cuisine in a southern, small-town setting is Cape May's prime attraction. Swimming, bicycling, fishing, and birding in the nearby state park are also popular, and the lighthouse is open to visitors. Most inns require a three- or four-night minimum stay from June 15 to the end of September. Victorian Week, usually at the beginning of October, combines whimsy with serious lectures on Victorian history and restoration. Most Cape May restaurants and inns are closed in January, February, and March.

The beach is adequate—a flat stretch of dark sand that is not as dramatic as those farther north. The town has few diversions for children, but the boardwalk amusement rides of Wildwood are a 20-minute drive away.

Places to go, sights to see

Boat Rides. The *Delta Lady* offers sightseeing and sunset voyages in summer, departing from the Miss Chris Fishing Center (3rd St. and Wilson Dr., tel. 609/884–1919). The *Cape May–Lewes Ferry* (tel. 609/886–2718 or 302/645–6313) takes cars, pedestrians, and bicycles to and from the small town of Lewes. The trip lasts approximately 70 minutes, weather permitting.

Cape May Point State Park (tel. 609/884–2159). An eight-minute drive from the historic district, this 300-acre wildlife preserve has nature trails; a small museum; and a wild, rustic beach where swimming is discouraged because of the rough tides. Call the *Cape May Bird Observatory* (tel. 609/884–2626) to learn what migratory and water birds have been seen lately.

Cape May Point, a residential town founded as a Methodist retreat by Philadelphia merchant John Wanamaker, is a pleasant destination for an afternoon bicycle ride.

Carney's (Beach Dr. and Decatur St., tel. 609/884–3504) is the closest thing Cape May has to a loud rock 'n' roll bar.

The Old Shire (Washington Mall, tel. 609/884–4700). This is a genuine jazz-improv club, and the styles of music played vary widely.

Sunset Beach. At the end of Sunset Road, this pebbled Delaware Bay beach contrasts with the fine-grain ocean beaches less than a mile away. Ocean-polished lumps of quartz, called Cape May Diamonds, can be found along the tide line.

The Top of the Marq (tel. 609/884–3431) offers old-style dinner and dancing, in the Marquis De Lafayette Hotel.

Tours. The best way to see Cape May is to take a walking tour run by the Mid-Atlantic Center for the Arts (MAC, tel. 609/884–5404). *The Cape May Carriage Company* (tel. 609/465–9854) provides tours by horse and carriage.

Restaurants

Cape May is famous for its eccentric, informal, café-style restaurants, many of which do not have liquor licenses (no problem—you can usually bring your own). **The Mad Batter** (tel. 609/884–5907) started the trend, with a mixed Oriental, Continental, and American menu. Restaurants offering a similar cuisine include the **Bayberry Inn** (tel. 609/884–8406), **Louisa's** (tel. 609/884–5882), and **Peaches Cafe** (tel. 609/884–0202). For slightly more traditional, Continental dining, try **Alexander's** (tel. 609/884–2555), which serves a five-course brunch that's the best in town; **Maureen's** (tel. 609/884–3774); or **La Toque** (tel. 609/884–1511). You'll find marvelous Cajun, Creole, and Caribbean-style dishes at **410 Bank Street** (tel. 609/884–2127). **Frescoes** (tel. 609/884–0366) serves nouvelle Italian. For seafood try the **Lobster House** (tel. 609/884–8296), on Fisherman's Wharf, a one-minute drive from the historic district; or **A & J's Blue Claw** (tel. 609/884–5878), on Ocean Drive, a five-minute drive from the causeway connecting Cape May to Wildwood Crest. Both get most of their entrées right off the fishing boats. One last, extraordinary feast is the traditional, Southern-style Sunday supper, served in the late afternoon, at the **Chalfonte Hotel** (tel. 609/884–8409).

Tourist Information

Cape May Convention and Visitors Bureau (Box 403, Cape May 08204, tel. 609/898–0280). **Welcome Center** (405 Lafayette St., Cape May 08204, tel. 609/884–9562).

Reservation Services

Cape May Reservation Service (1400 Texas Ave., Cape May 08204, tel. 609/884–5329 or 800/729–7778) handles exclusively Cape May bed-and-breakfasts.

The Abbey

Built in 1869 as a summer home for Philadelphia coal baron John B. McCreary, the Abbey is one of Cape May architect Stephen Button's best works. With its impressive 65-foot tower and airy veranda, it is the finest example of Gothic Revival architecture in town.

There is nothing remotely religious about the property, which crowns the intersection of Columbia Avenue and Gurney Street. Calling it the Abbey was a bit of whimsy on the part of owners Jay and Marianne Schatz. "We always felt the Gothic Revival look had a religious quality to it," Jay says, "and because of my marketing degree I knew that anything that began with an *a* would be at the top of the list."

A lot more than its initial puts the Abbey at the top of many Cape May bed-and-breakfast lists: The quality of its restoration, the elegance of its appearance (the ruby-and-stenciled-glass windows are just one example), and the opulence of its period antiques all play a part. In addition there's the excellent location, one block from the beach and two blocks from the Washington Mall; and the humor of its owners, who can get just as excited over the 1875 secretary desk in the front parlor as over Jay's wacky hat collection hanging beside the mirror in the front hall (Marianne collects antique jewelry and clothing).

Jay and Marianne are most proud of their 1860 walnut-and-chestnut sideboard with its carved wolf's head and of the massive 11½-foot-tall matching bookcases in the back parlor. The couple were both chemists before their love of old houses and antiques brought them to Cape May, where they opened the Abbey in 1977.

In 1986 they bought and renovated the Second Empire house next door; McCreary had built it in 1873 for his son's family. Each house has two parlors, which are open to guests at all times. The rooms are named after cities and furnished appropriately (the San Francisco Room is the most opulent). Late-afternoon refreshments—wine, cheese, snacks, and tea—are served daily at 5:30.

Address: *Columbia Ave. and Gurney St., Cape May, NJ 08204, tel. 609/884–4506.*
Accommodations: *12 double rooms with baths, 2 suites.*
Amenities: *Air-conditioning in 8 bedrooms, minirefrigerators in 4 rooms; croquet, beach tags, towels, and beach chairs, some on-site parking.*
Rates: *$80–$150; Continental breakfast June 15–Sept. 15, full breakfast other times. AE, MC, V.*
Restrictions: *Smoking on veranda only, no pets, no T-shirts or bathing suits at breakfast, 2- 3-, or 4-night minimum on weekends, closed Dec. to Easter.*

The Chalfonte

A hotel like no other in Cape May—old, creaky, spartan, and proud of it—the Chalfonte is one of the city's most significant preserved structures. Built in 1876 by Colonel Henry Sawyer (on the northern side, he was captured and traded for Robert E. Lee's son), the hotel has dramatic wraparound porches on the ground and second floors, intricate gingerbread ornamentation, and a grand cupola from which the ocean can be glimpsed. It is two blocks from the beach and four blocks from the Washington Mall. Although similar wood structures survive in the Spring Lake area of Monmouth County, the Chalfonte and its two cottages are a legend and an institution.

It is not, however, an up-to-date one. Some of the furnishings are simple to the point of being drab, and most guest rooms share bathrooms. The Chalfonte has no room service, no air-conditioning, and no heat (rooms do have louvered doors, and most have ceiling fans). Noise tends to travel through the halls, and signs hanging outside the shower rooms warn of variations in water pressure.

But despite its faults the Chalfonte attracts well-to-do and blue-blooded visitors, many of them the children and grandchildren of families who have summered here in the past, who will stay nowhere else. The hotel caters to a growing contingent of college students and architecture buffs, who take over during spring and fall "work weekends," when, in exchange for eight hours of skilled or unskilled labor, they receive vastly discounted lodging and sumptuous meals.

The Chalfonte's food is renowned. The kitchen is supervised by the late Helen Dickerson's daughters. The menu may include spoon bread, fried chicken, fish, roast turkey, baked ham, sweet-potato pie, and other regional American specialties.

After such meals, guests struggle to stay awake for the free evening concerts, movie classics (shown with an old projector), poetry readings, plays, and comedy performances. The hotel holds many arts-and-crafts workshops and is unusually accommodating to families. Live entertainment, ranging from blues to bluegrass, is featured in the cozy King Edward Bar.

Address: *301 Howard St., Cape May, NJ 08204, tel. 609/884-8409.*
Accommodations: *11 double rooms with baths, 64 doubles and 2 singles share 11 baths.*
Amenities: *Dining room, bar, cable TV in writing room, 2 fireplaces in common areas, writing and reading room, children's dining room, baby-sitting arranged.*
Rates: *$73–$145, MAP. MC, V.*
Restrictions: *No smoking in bedrooms, no pets, 2-night minimum on weekends, closed Nov.–Apr.*

The Mainstay Inn and Cottage

An 1870 men's social club formerly called Jackson's Clubhouse, the Mainstay vies with the Abbey as Cape May's best bed-and-breakfast. Many a gambler whiled away the hours under these 14-foot ceilings, and many a topic was discussed on the lofty veranda, which, more than 100 years later, is the city's most ostentatious spot for doing nothing.

The property was a deteriorating private house when, in 1976, it was purchased by Tom Carroll, who came to Cape May to serve at the nearby Coast Guard Training Academy, and his wife, Sue, an antiques and Victorian-costume collector. The Carrolls renovated the building with an astonishing attention to detail, and the Mainstay became a focal point in the move to revive Victorian Cape May as a resort town. Included in this magnificent restoration are the house's original chandeliers as well as most of the original furniture. Other antiques are of museum quality.

The Carrolls view their role as innkeepers as a beguiling performance. They socialize actively with guests, many of whom have been inspired to open B&Bs of their own.

"We try to inject a little informality into the formality of the surroundings," Tom says. "We like guests to feel as if they're not just staying with us, but that they're part of the Mainstay's atmosphere—that the inn is better because they're with us, even if all they're doing is sleeping here. If that has become the Cape May style, we're proud to have encouraged it."

In addition to being active in Cape May historic preservation and the city's Victorian Week festivities, the Carrolls are enthusiastic fans of Victorian culture and games, the more whimsical the better. Tom races sailboats, so you might see him on the ocean, from the cupola, which has a distant ocean view.

Address: *635 Columbia Ave., Cape May, NJ 08204, tel. 609/884–8690.*
Accommodations: *12 double rooms with baths.*
Amenities: *Gas fireplace in main-house drawing room, piano, game room; off-street parking for 2 rooms.*
Rates: *$80–$150; Continental breakfast June–Sept., full breakfast at other times. No credit cards.*
Restrictions: *Smoking on veranda only, no pets, 3-night minimum June–Sept. and on most weekends, closed mid-Dec.–mid-Mar.*

Barnard Good House

Near the edge of the historic district, on Perry Street, this lavender-trimmed Second Empire cottage is famous for serving Cape May's most filling, fanciful, and altogether outrageous within-an-inn breakfast. Don't even think about losing weight.

Before opening the Barnard Good House, Nan Hawkins was a marketing director for shopping centers and Tom was an engineer in the plastics business. The couple bought the inn in 1980 and totally restored it, adding baths and accommodations.

They scrupulously chose antiques and Oriental rugs that match the Second Empire architecture. In the dining room they created a Victorian style "Turkish corner," with tented draperies, an antique tufted and tasseled sofa and chairs, and a brass elephant table. The bedrooms have Victorian antique furniture, and one bathroom has a copper tub.

Address: *238 Perry St., Cape May, NJ 08204, tel. 609/884-5381.*
Accommodations: *3 double rooms with baths, 2 suites.*
Amenities: *Air-conditioning in bedrooms; beach tags, off-street parking.*
Rates: *$85-$113; full breakfast. AE, MC, V.*
Restrictions: *Smoking on porch only, no pets, 2-night minimum on weekends, 3-night minimum mid-June–mid-Sept., 4-night minimum on holiday weekends. closed mid-Nov.–mid-Mar.*

Captain Mey's Inn

Located in the center of town, close to the Washington Mall and the beach, this 1890 house was built for a physician and named after Cape May's Dutch discoverer. It became an inn in 1979. It is furnished in European antiques with Dutch accents. A collection of Delft pottery is scattered throughout the public areas, and three Tiffany-style stained-glass windows adorn the foyer.

Rooms are furnished with European antiques and Persian carpets exclusively, and guests can enjoy the small courtyard with its tulip garden. Innkeepers Carin Feddermann and Millie LaCanfora started the city's April Tulip Festival and are active in promoting Victorian restoration.

Address: *202 Ocean St., Cape May, NJ 08204, tel. 609/884-7793.*
Accommodations: *6 double rooms with baths, 3 doubles share 1 bath.*
Amenities: *Fireplace in dining room; beach tags, towels, and chairs, off-street parking.*
Rates: *$80-$150; full breakfast, afternoon tea. MC, V.*
Restrictions: *Smoking on veranda only, no pets, 3-night minimum on weekends May–June and Sept.–Oct., 4-night minimum on weekends July–Aug., 2-night minimum on other weekends.*

The Carroll Villa

Those staying at this pleasantly restored Victorian hotel will enjoy breakfast at the Mad Batter Restaurant, one of Cape May's best dining establishments, which takes up most of the Carroll Villa's lower floor.

"Yankee fans may have to beg," jokes innkeeper Mark Kulkowitz, a baseball buff, who also manages the restaurant. "Phillies fans don't have a problem as long as the Phillies are not ahead of the Mets."

Guests have use of a separate living-room area, a garden terrace, and the cupola, from which the beach can be seen. The mostly-19th-century furnishings give the villa a less formal atmosphere than those inns that have museum-quality antiques. The hotel is a half block from the beach and a half block from the Washington Mall. Be warned that aromas coming from the Mad Batter kitchen can be fatal to diets.

Address: *19 Jackson St., Cape May, NJ 08204, tel. 609/884-9619.*
Accommodations: *17 double rooms with baths, 8 doubles share 2 baths.*
Amenities: *Restaurant (closed mid-Dec.-Apr.), air-conditioning in 8 bedrooms, cable TV in lobby; beach tags.*
Rates: *$63-$90; full breakfast when restaurant is open, Continental breakfast other times. MC, V.*
Restrictions: *No pets, 2-night minimum on weekends May-Oct., 3-night minimum on holiday weekends, closed Jan.-Feb.*

9/96 private bath
#84 - #98

Colvmns by the Sea

Built by an eccentric doctor as his very eccentric summer retreat, Colvmns (eccentric spelling, too) is Cape May's get-away-from-it-all bed-and-breakfast, more than a mile from the historic district. It is named for the fluted Italianate columns that support the massive Colonial Revival second floor over its wraparound porch.

Guest rooms at Colvmns are enormous, and one has a superb Renaissance Revival mixed-wood bedroom set. The third floor commands wonderful views of the ocean. Although heavy seas have washed away much of the beach, at low tide there's plenty of shore to walk along. Swimming is prohibited here but allowed one block away.

The inn is a full-time home for innkeeper Barry Rein; his wife, Cathryn, works in Manhattan in the insurance industry and comes to the inn on weekends.

Address: *1513 Beach Dr., Cape May, NJ 08204, tel. 609/884-2228.*
Accommodations: *11 double rooms with baths.*
Amenities: *Cable TV in parlor, 2 fireplaces in public areas, hot tub on veranda; beach tags, bicycles, parking.*
Rates: *$95-$145; full breakfast, afternoon tea and snacks. No credit cards.*
Restrictions: *Smoking on veranda only, 2-night minimum Memorial Day-Sept, 3-night minimum on weekends, closed Jan.-Apr.*

Holly House

This immaculate Jackson Street guest house is one of the Seven Sister properties, seven identical houses built in 1891 on the lot of a former hotel, as summer rentals for well-to-do families. It is notable for its carefully detailed green-and-red exterior and the theatrical personality of its co-owner, Bruce Minnix, who directs television soap operas in New York. Corinne, his wife, runs the house and is often the person greeting visitors. "She's a lady," Bruce says, "casual, easygoing, friendly."

A former mayor of Cape May, Bruce fought for the preservation and restoration of the town and helped create its popular walking tours. Recently, he produced and directed the video *Victorian Cape May.*

Rooms at Holly House each have three windows, high ceilings, and natural-wood furniture. They're modern, decorated in earth tones, and free of clutter.

Address: *20 Jackson St., Cape May, NJ 08204, tel. 609/884-7365.*
Accommodations: *5 double rooms share 2 baths.*
Amenities: *Fireplace in parlor; porch swing with ocean view, beach tags, off-site parking.*
Rates: *$60–$65; no breakfast served. MC, V.*
Restrictions: *Smoking on porch only, no pets.*

The Manor House

This bed-and-breakfast is amusing, thanks to host Tom Snyder's love of barbershop quartets, comedy, and jokes, the older the better.

"Our rooms are named after significant numbers," quips the former marketing executive. Tom and his wife, Mary, prepare five- and six-course gourmet breakfasts, after which Tom recites his "reading of the day," and introduction to, and sendup of, the city's attractions and distractions. In mid-February the Snyders host a five-day cooking school, for which they gather chefs from all over the country to conduct cooking seminars—some at the Manor House and others at various restaurant kitchens in Cape May.

Rooms at the Manor House contain a harmonious mix of antiques and high-quality reproductions and are decorated with colorful handmade quilts. Guests can snooze in the barber's chair in the den or serenade themselves on the player piano.

Address: *612 Hughes St., Cape May, NJ 08204, tel. 609/884-4710.*
Accommodations: *6 double rooms with baths, 2 doubles share a bath, 1 suite.*
Amenities: *Air-conditioning in 3 bedrooms, whirlpool bath in suite, bathrobes, hair dryers, fireplace in den; beach tags, beach towels, parking.*
Rates: *$60–$145; full breakfast, afternoon tea. No credit cards.*
Restrictions: *Smoking on porch only, no pets, closed Jan.*

The Queen Victoria

This 1881 Second Empire villa and Stick-style adjacent cottage are living lectures in Victorian architecture. Dane and Joan Wells have transformed the property, in the center of the historic district, into an inn that feels immediately, genteelly private.

The furnishings in the Queen Victoria are nearly all carefully researched period pieces that create a dignified, privileged, country-Victorian atmosphere. The common rooms of the inn are decorated in the Arts and Crafts style. Dane did much of the work himself. Joan is active in the restoration and preservation of Victoriana nationwide.

Handmade quilts add color to the rooms, whose furnishings vary in style from white wicker to the dark woods of High Victorian.

Address: *102 Ocean St., Cape May, NJ 08204, tel. 609/884-8702.*
Accommodations: *13 double rooms with baths, 4 doubles share 1 bath, 7 suites.*
Amenities: *Air-conditioning in suites and 8 bedrooms, whirlpools in suites and 6 bedrooms, cable TV in parlor and suites, phones in 2 suites, fireplaces in parlors and in cottage suite; bicycles, beach tags, beach towels, on- and off-site parking.*
Rates: *$60–$228; full breakfast, afternoon tea. MC, V.*
Restrictions: *No smoking, no pets, 2- and 3-night minimum on weekends.*

Springside

Like Holly House (*see above*), Springside is a Seven Sister property. It is decorated with bright, modern art and 1930s mahogany furnishings. Innkeepers Bill and Meryl Nelson raised five children in the house. When the children grew up and moved away, they felt a need for company.

"Bill and I really enjoy meeting and being with people who are doing interesting things," Meryl explains. Among their guests are college professors, theater people, and restoration experts.

Bill is the author of *Surfing: A Handbook* and is a boat builder. Meryl teaches computer science and desktop publishing. The couple share an interest in dollhouses and offbeat books. Their many books—"too many, we've only read about half of them," says Bill—are kept throughout the house and on bookcases in each guest room. The dollhouses can be admired in one of the common rooms.

Address: *18 Jackson St., Cape May, NJ 08204, tel. 609/884-2654.*
Accommodations: *4 double rooms share 2 baths.*
Amenities: *Beach tags, off-site parking.*
Rates: *$50–$65; breakfast not served. MC, V.*
Restrictions: *Smoking on porch only, no pets, 2-night minimum on weekends June–Sept.*

The Victorian Rose

Romance and roses go together, and this Gothic Revival house and adjacent cottage are almost engulfed by the aromatic flowers. The property is surrounded by 150 rose bushes, and rose patterns adorn dishes, wallpaper, and bed linens. Roses also show up in much of the Victorian detailing in the romantic guest rooms, which are furnished with antiques and some unobtrusive reproductions.

The bedrooms are carpeted, and all the curtains are patterned in roses; a first-floor suite has its own entrance, and the two rooms on the third floor are ideal for a family.

Innkeeper Bob Mullock, a former mayor of Cape May, leads town walking tours; he likes Mozart and big-band music. His wife, Linda, enjoys gardening and cooking breakfast.

Address: *715 Columbia Ave., Cape May, NJ 08204, tel. 609/884-2497.*
Accommodations: *5 double rooms with baths, 2 doubles share 1 bath, 2 housekeeping suites, adjacent cottage with bath sleeps 5.*
Amenities: *Air-conditioning in 4 bedrooms, cable TV in suites, gas fireplace in parlor; beach tags.*
Rates: *$75-$130; full breakfast, afternoon tea. No credit cards.*
Restrictions: *No pets, 3-night minimum on weekends June-Sept., 2-night minimum on other weekends, closed Dec.-Jan.*

The Virginia Hotel

The porches and balcony of this superbly restored, first-class small hotel are original, but in stepping through the door guests will find a completely modern interior in mild hues of taupe, peach, and green. The rooms' cherry and poplar furnishings are contemporary pieces with Victorian lines, designed by Tom McHugh, a popular furniture designer. Bathrooms have massage shower heads. One sitting area is furnished in 1870s wicker. The Virginia is highly recommended for those who want a full-service hotel on an intimate scale.

The conference room has all the latest equipment and makes this Cape May's best small property for executive retreats. The Ebbit Room Restaurant, on the premises, serves Cape May-eclectic cuisine of grilled seafood and meats, unusual sauces, and rich desserts (dinner is $50 for two). There's live music in the lobby piano bar.

Address: *25 Jackson St., Cape May, NJ 08204, tel. 609/884-5700, fax 609/884-1236.*
Accommodations: *24 double rooms with baths.*
Amenities: *Restaurant, air-conditioning, telephones, cable TV, VCRs, bathrobes, room service, fireplace in lobby, videotape rentals, meeting room, word processor; beach tags, beach chairs, towels, valet parking.*
Rates: *$135-$220, Continental breakfast. AE, DC, MC, V.*
Restrictions: *No pets, 2-night minimum on weekends.*

Wilbraham Mansion and Inn

Perched on the southwestern edge of Cape May, this immense 1840 private house is the city's only bed-and-breakfast with a heated indoor swimming pool. Everything is larger than life at Wilbraham, from the 80-year-old stained-glass windows to the gilded mirrors and king-size beds—even the booming, resounding voice of innkeeper Pat Downs.

Many of the original Victorian furnishings of the house remain; carpeting, wallpapers, carved headboards, and lace curtains, for example. Pat, a former executive, and his wife, Rose, have three organs, and they offer performances on request. Inspired guests can try their hand at playing the old-fashioned Packard

pump organ. A guitar and an accordion are also available.

Address: *133 Myrtle Ave., Cape May, NJ 08204, tel. 609/884-2046.*
Accommodations: *6 double rooms with baths, 2 suites.*
Amenities: *Air-conditioning in bedrooms, turn-down service, phone, wet bar, and VCR in 1 suite, cable TV in game room, fireplaces in 3 common rooms; swimming pool, beach tags, beach towels, bicycles, parking.*
Rates: *$85–$145; full breakfast, afternoon tea. MC, V.*
Restrictions: *Smoking on porch and in pool area only, no pets, 2-night minimum on weekends Memorial Day–Dec., 3-night minimum on holiday weekends.*

The Wooden Rabbit

Children of all ages, and their parents, are welcome at this playful Hughes Street inn, where the storybook characters of Beatrix Potter dwell. Debbie Burow has been a Potter fan from the cradle; and rabbit figurines, dolls, and illustrations run rampant through her house.

"One of our guests counted 40 rabbits in the dining room and living room, and there are others about the house," Greg Burow says. "They tend to multiply."

The Federal house was built in 1838, and the furnishings are country-style: The rooms, in pastel colors and lace have a cozy feeling, with wicker and oak, brass beds, and

some light-wood antiques. Greg stokes a breakfast fire on cool mornings.

Address: *609 Hughes St., Cape May, NJ 08204, tel. 609/884-7293.*
Accommodations: *2 double rooms with baths, 1 suite.*
Amenities: *Air-conditioning and TV in bedrooms, turn-down service, fireplaces in dining room and living room; beach tags, beach chairs, off-street parking.*
Rates: *$90–$145; full breakfast, afternoon tea. No credit cards.*
Restrictions: *No smoking, no pets, 2-night minimum on weekends, 3-night minimum July and Aug.*

Off the Beaten Track

Charlesworth Hotel

Although this tiny hotel lacks just about all the major amenities, its incomparable location and moderately priced seafood restaurant have kept it in business since 1924. The Charlesworth is located on the windswept Delaware Bay, in Fortescue, a tiny fishing village about 14 miles south of Bridgeton and a 20-minute drive from historic Greenwich.

The unadorned rooms have plain furniture, double beds, writing tables, chairs, and desk fans. There is no heat, no air-conditioning, and no parlor, game room, or television. The hotel closes when temperatures are cold enough to freeze the water in its pipes. It reopens when the ice melts.

Numerous sport-fishing charters and party boats leave from the town's docks from spring through early autumn. The Charlesworth is a fine base for exploring this least-traveled region of New Jersey.

Address: *New Jersey Ave., Fortescue, NJ 08321, tel. 609/447-4928.*
Accommodations: *1 double room with bath, 4 doubles share 1 bath.*
Amenities: *Restaurant open Wed.–Sun. for dinner (BYOB), fireplace in dining room; on-site parking.*
Rates: *$35–$50; breakfast not served. No credit cards.*
Restrictions: *No pets, closed Nov.–Feb.*

Jeremiah H. Yereance House

When developers threatened to tear down this 1841 farmhouse in suburban Lyndhurst, next-door neighbors Evelyn and Frank Pezzola bought the property and went to work restoring the former home of Passaic River shipbuilder Jeremiah Yereance. The Pezzolas used Laura Ashley fabrics and placed antiques, reproductions, and white wicker alongside furniture original to the house.

Located a half hour from the Big Apple but far from its hubbub, in a quiet, residential neighborhood, Yereance House is 1 mile from Fairleigh Dickinson University. Guests can enjoy walking, biking, and tennis across the street in Bergen County Park, and the house is within walking distance of restaurants, a health club, a supermarket, and commuter bus stops to New York.

Address: *410 Riverside Ave., Lyndhurst, NJ 07071, tel. 908/438-9457, fax 201/939-5801.*
Accommodations: *2 double rooms and 1 single room share 1 bath, 1 suite.*
Amenities: *Air-conditioning in suite and 2 doubles, cable TV in parlor and in suite, guest phones in parlor, suite, and 1 double room, fireplace in parlor, kitchen and laundry privileges; off-street parking.*
Rates: *$50–$75; Continental buffet breakfast. AE.*
Restrictions: *No smoking indoors, no pets, closed Aug. 1–15.*

Delaware

Delaware

PENNSYLVANIA

Claymont

Greenville

Wilmington

295 95

Newark

New Castle

95

40

FT. DELAWARE
STATE PARK

NEW JERSEY

Delaware
City

Chesapeake
City

Chesapeake & Delaware Canal

Port Penn

301

Vineland

Odessa

Middletown

Delaware River

Bridgeton

Millville

Sassafras R.

Betterton

13

301

Smyrna

BOMBAY HOOK
NATIONAL
WILDLIFE REFUGE

Chestertown

Leipsic

9

MARYLAND

Hartly

Dover

113

13

Delaware
Bay

Wye Mills

Harrington

Milford

TO
CAPE MAY

1

Choptank R.

CAPE
HENLOPEN
STATE PARK

Easton

Milton

Lewes

404

Rehoboth
Beach

18

Dewey
Beach

Seaford

Georgetown

9

DELAWARE
SEASHORE
STATE PARK

13

113

24

Bethel

Bethany
Beach

Laurel

24

1

Cambridge

Vienna

Mason-Dixon
Monument

TRAP POND
STATE PARK

Selbyville

FENWICK
ISLAND STATE
PARK

N

0   6 miles

0   9 km

Wilmington/Northern Delaware

Delaware is all of 96 miles long and 9 to 35 miles wide, but for such a small state, there's a great deal in it. Everyone knows about its long chain of Atlantic beaches, but Delaware's other points of interest are seldom touted on billboards. This is especially true in the industrialized northern section of the state where travelers zooming to Washington or New York on I-95 can easily bypass the sights worth seeing. Wilmington, the state's commercial hub, is trying hard to polish its cosmopolitan image by creating a downtown pedestrian mall and restoring some old buildings, such as the Victorian Grand Opera House, now home of the Delaware Symphony.

It's easy to track down the extraordinary legacy of Delaware's First Family; the name du Pont is printed on smokestacks and street signs, like tattoos on a sailor. The French du Ponts came to northern Delaware around 1800 and by 1920 were the wealthiest clan in the United States. They built estates such as Winterthur in the rolling countryside north of Wilmington, where they could show off their gunpowder fortunes, and today you'd have to travel to the Loire Valley to see such breathtaking châteaux.

To get a taste of Colonial America in the setting of a living village, head southeast from Wilmington to New Castle, on the Delaware River. The Swedes settled here around 1640; the Dutch came next, and in 1664 the British took possession. But the town's glory days came in the 18th century, when it attracted the Colonial world's rich and famous, including Washington and Lafayette. When the boundary between Delaware and Pennsylvania was surveyed, it was drawn as the arc of a circle whose center was the cupola of New Castle's courthouse. Today the cupolaed courthouse, narrow alleyways, hitching posts, mossy graveyards, and emerald-colored town common remain much the same as they were then.

South of Wilmington are other villages redolent of the past; some, like Odessa and Delaware City, on the banks of the Chesapeake and Delaware Canal, are even quieter than New Castle. From Delaware City it's a 10-minute ferry ride aboard the Miss Kathy *to Pea Patch Island, in the Delaware River, site of the largest historic fort in the country. Fort Delaware was built in 1823 and has massive ramparts from which nesting herons can be seen in the marshes below.*

Places to go, sights to see

Bombay Hook Wildlife Refuge (just north of Leipsic on Rte. 9, tel. 302/653–9345). On these 16,000 acres of tidal marsh and timberland, muskrats, otters, white-tailed deer, and opossums make their homes, and as many as 50,000 Canada geese visit in season.

Delaware Museum of Art (tel. 302/571–9590). The English Pre-Raphaelite painters have their own gallery at this Wilmington museum, as does the illustrator Howard Pyle. In 1987 a new wing was added to accommodate sculpture, painting, ceramics, and photographs by American masters of the last 150 years.

Delaware Museum of Natural History (tel. 302/658–9111). On Route 52 between Centreville and Greenville, this museum is famous for its shell collection, which includes specimens of the venomous cone shell, rare volutes, and a 400-pound clam set under a glass floor and surrounded by coral from Australia's Great Barrier Reef.

Fort Delaware State Park (tel. 302/834–7941). Reached by ferry from Delaware City, this impressive Civil War bastion is a fine spot for picnics and bird-watching.

Hagley on the Brandywine (Greenville, tel. 302/658–2400). Here you can see how the du Ponts harnessed the waters of the Brandywine River to run a powder mill nearby. Eleutherian Mills, a modest, 12-room, white Georgian house where the first five generations of American du Ponts lived, is set on Hagley's manicured 200 acres.

Hotel Du Pont (tel. 302/656–8121). At Wilmington's "company hotel," built in 1911, the du Ponts went to extremes to surround guests with the best. Here you'll find coffered ceilings, travertine marble walls, and a million-dollar collection of Andrew Wyeth canvasses, in the Brandywine-Christina dining room.

Nemours (Rockland Rd., off Rte. 141, tel. 302/651–6912). Alfred I. du Pont's 77-room "little Versailles" is a pink Louis XVI château groaning under the weight of its excesses. Along with gold-leaf ceilings, crystal chandeliers, and Aubusson carpets, Alfred loved gadgets, which explains the state-of-the-art 1910 bathrooms, steam cabinet, bowling alley, and spring-water-bottling generator.

Odessa. A Georgian architectural treasure trove is found on the banks of the swampily atmospheric Appoquinimink River. The Brick House Museum here (tel. 302/378–4069) displays the grandfather clocks of Duncan Beard and furniture crafted by John Janvier. Early December is the best time to visit, when Odessa celebrates Christmas by conducting tours through many of its privately owned historic homes.

Wilmington and Western Railroad (tel. 302/998–1930). A steam-power iron horse leaves Greenbank Station (on Rte. 141, west of Wilmington) on Sunday, for trips into Delaware's Red Clay Valley.

Winterthur (Rte. 52 north of Wilmington, tel. 302/888–4600 or 800/448–3883). This 200-room estate in a lush 64-acre garden contains one of the world's prime collections of American decorative arts (1640–1840). An immense repository of over 89,000 artifacts—silver, ceramics, fabrics, furniture, and carved mantels—the museum offers several tours, including some specializing in topics such as Chippendale furniture, Pennsylvania German folk art, and needlework.

Tourist Information

Delaware Tourism Office (99 Kings Hwy., Box 1401, Dover 19903, tel. 800/441–8846; in DE, 800/282–8667). **Greater Wilmington Convention and Visitors Bureau** (1300 Market St., Suite 504, Wilmington 19899, tel. 302/652–4088 or 800/422–1181).

Reservation Services

Bed & Breakfast of Delaware (Box 177, 3650 Silverside Rd., Wilmington 19810, tel. 302/479–9500).

The Janvier-Black House

Most people who stumble upon New Castle, Delaware, fall in love with the town. It's a place to take a brooding walk over the cobblestones of Packet Alley, romp across the town green, and feast gluttonously at the David Finney or at the New Castle Inn, a restaurant where the house specialty is a buttery seafood-and-chicken pie.

Unfortunately, most visitors to the town don't get the chance to stay at the Janvier-Black House, since it has only two suites. Those who do usually don't want to just visit New Castle: They want to settle in for the duration—hopefully in a Federal double row house just like the Janvier-Black, on the Strand.

The house was built in 1825, as a gift from a doting papa, John Janvier, to his daughter, Ann, and features the finely carpentered door frames and moldings you'd expect in a vintage New Castle home. Its first floor holds a parlor and dining room, with detail work painted in airy blues and pinks and wallpaper that picks up colors and patterns from the Oriental carpets. In the rear there's a country kitchen, and a sun deck perched above the backyard boxwood garden offers views of Battery Park and the stone icebreakers in the Delaware River. The guest rooms have similar views of the river, as well as sitting rooms, commodious modern baths, fireplaces, and country-classic decor. (The self-contained third-floor suite is the best.)

Annabelle and Hank Kressman are the innkeepers responsible for this gem among bed-and-breakfasts. The Kressmans leave a decanter of sherry and the makings for coffee and tea in the third-floor hall and have put together a collection of classic movies on videotape. Annabelle is a former executive director of the Girl Scouts who today spends her free time marketing women's clothing. Samples from her stock are stored in closets throughout the house, so, if they'd like, guests can shop in the comfort of their own rooms. The Kressmans will also shower you with brochures on notable sights in old New Castle, such as the glorious George Read II House just down the block and the Old Dutch House Museum on the green. On the third Saturday in May the town celebrates A Day in New Castle, when many of the private homes are opened for touring. If you plan a trip then, remember to book early.

Address: *17 The Strand, New Castle, DE 19720, tel. 302/328–1339.*
Accommodations: *2 suites.*
Amenities: *Air-conditioning, TV with VCR, fireplaces.*
Rates: *$75–$95; Continental breakfast. No credit cards.*
Restrictions: *No smoking, no pets, 2-day minimum on weekends June–Oct.*

The Towers

It's thought that Edgar Allan Poe used to visit his friend and fellow poet John Lofland at the Towers, which was once the Milford home of Lofland's stepfather, Dr. John Wallace. Lofland was an opium addict and Poe an alcoholic, but in their wildest hallucinations neither could have dreamed up a house like the Towers, a steamboat Gothic palace adorned with 10 varieties of gingerbread painted in 12 colors. Here flamboyant Victoriana oozes from the cherry, sycamore, and walnut finishings. Inside, the music room has a coffered ceiling, a glass cabinet housing a collection of Chinese mud figurines, and an 1899 Knabe grand piano. You're likely to find a record—perhaps Gene Autry's rendition of "Rudolph the Red-nosed Reindeer"—spinning on the Victrola. The parlor is decorated with French antiques, and the dining room provides views of the gazebo, pool deck, and rose garden in back.

The custodian of this marvel is Michael Real, a free-lance interior decorator who has always lived in Victorian homes. He happened on the place while looking for a house to renovate in Lewes; the Towers was in shambles at the time, but he couldn't help noticing the carved garlands on the fireplaces and the gold leaf peeking from beneath the plywood walls. Finishing touches in the upstairs bedrooms include design magazines scattered about for browsing and freshly ironed cotton percale sheets. A favorite room is the Tower chamber, on the second floor, with a turret niche and lots of rosy stained glass. The third floor's two suites are a bit more modern in character but are still whimsically wonderful. The Rapunzel Room, with a sitting room and an extra bed positioned cozily in an alcove, is a good choice for families. For early risers, coffee is available in the hallway before breakfast, and there's a laundry room for guest use.

The inn is within reasonable distance of the beaches and right across the street from one of Delaware's premier eating establishments, the Banking House, which is also an 18th-century–inspired bed-and-breakfast. Dinner at the Banking House and a stay at the Towers is a perfect combination when you feel you've earned the right to indulge.

Address: *101 N.W. Front St., Milford, DE 19963, tel. 302/422-3814, or, outside DE, 800/366-3814.*
Accommodations: *2 double rooms with baths, 2 doubles share 1 bath, 2 suites.*
Amenities: *Air-conditioning, 2 cable TVs in sitting room, fireplaces in suites; pool.*
Rates: *$85–$125; full breakfast. MC, V.*
Restrictions: *No smoking in bedrooms, no pets, 2-day minimum on weekends June–Aug. and holiday weekends.*

The Boulevard Bed & Breakfast

It's only been a few years since Charles and Judy Powell said good-bye to suburbia and moved to fashionable Baynard Boulevard to realize their dream of opening a bed-and-breakfast. The attractive house they moved to is in the Triangle section of Wilmington. This B&B is a fancy, citified 6-bedroom dwelling that has a red-tile roof; neo-Georgian elements in the facade; and eccentric, fluted columns with Doric capitals. Inside, a graceful "good morning" staircase (couples descend via separate routes and meet for a kiss at the landing) greets you, as do Judy and Charles, who treat guests like family. The furnishings in the bedrooms are immaculately maintained generic antiques. More noteworthy is the elaborate Mercer tile surrounding the library fireplace, and Judy's mammoth industrial range, where she cooks breakfast. The Powells attract a frequently returning business clientele, though families fare well here, too, because of the proximity of the Brandywine Park and Children's Zoo.

Address: *1909 Baynard Blvd., Wilmington, DE 19802, tel. 302/656–9700.*
Accommodations: *3 double rooms with baths; 1 double and 1 single share a bath, 1 suite with whirlpool.*
Amenities: *Air-conditioning, cable TV, fireplaces in library and parlor; off-street parking.*
Rates: *$55–$70; full breakfast. AE, MC, V.*
Restrictions: *No pets.*

Cantwell House

Odessa is a little-known historic village, a smaller, country version of New Castle. On the Appoquinimink River, surrounded by fertile fields, it fared well as a Colonial cosmopolitan center, but the railroad passed it by, and today it's charmingly frozen in time. The houses are lovingly maintained, and a branch of the Winterthur Museum has opened in town. The Corbit-Sharp House, built by a Quaker tanner in 1774; the Brick Hotel, displaying American crafts; and the Wilson-Warner House are just three of Odessa's architectural gems. The Cantwell House is the only bed-and-breakfast in town because Odessa, site of St. Andrew's prep school (where they filmed *The Dead Poets Society*), is trying to keep a low profile. The inn is a narrow, sea-green Victorian dwelling built about 1840. Of the guest rooms, one has a canopy bed, another a fireplace, and on the third floor is a suite. Proprietress Carole Coleman serves special breakfasts—with goodies like sticky buns, poached peaches, and home-whipped butter—and she can help you master the bidding game at the DeCaro antiques auctions, held in Odessa frequently.

Address: *107 High St., Odessa, DE 19730, tel. 302/378–4179.*
Accommodations: *2 double rooms share bath, 1 suite.*
Amenities: *Air-conditioning in suite and 2nd-floor canopy bedroom, TV in suite, 2 fireplaces.*
Rates: *$45–$65; Continental breakfast. No credit cards.*
Restrictions: *No smoking, no pets.*

The Christina House

One block away from Market Square, Wilmington's shopping-and-entertainment center, this inn is somewhere between the lavish Hotel du Pont and a homey, urban bed-and-breakfast. It's conveniently located for the Grand Opera House and for business travelers. It cannot claim to be historically noteworthy, though it inhabits the gutted shell of what was once Braunstein's Department Store. The King Street entrance leads to a spacious atrium with a central fireplace, bar, bistro restaurant, and glass-wall elevator. Upstairs, hallways snake through four connected buildings, but once you orient yourself to the maze you'll be rewarded with a comfortable guest room. The rooms are all suites, with fold-out sofas in the sitting rooms, fully equipped wet bars, and luxurious bathrooms. Room 306 is the largest and has a skylight and gently sloping ceilings. The management calls the remaining four rooms singles, but each could easily accommodate two. A copy of *The Wall Street Journal* comes with breakfast.

Address: *707 King St., Wilmington, DE 19801, tel. 302/656-9300 or 800/543-9106, fax 302/656-2459.*
Accommodations: *39 suites.*
Amenities: *Restaurant, air-conditioning, 2 cable TVs and 3 phones per suite; fitness center, 3 meeting facilities, computers, courier service, nonsmoking floor.*
Rates: *$125, $75 weekends; Continental breakfast. AE, D, DC, MC, V.*
Restrictions: *No pets.*

The David Finney Inn

Noting the scarcity of lodging in New Castle, circa 1680, and that the rooms were "dear and mean," Renere Vandercoolen opened this inn at the corner of Third and Delaware streets, opposite the green and the courthouse. His place has functioned largely as an inn since then, though considerable improvements have been made over the past 300 years. Today's guests enjoy a warm, wood-panel bar called the Packet Tavern, a restaurant serving some of the best lunches and dinners in town, and 17 guest rooms that have been nicely renovated into marvels of modernity. They're decorated with a few carefully selected antiques, sparely arranged, as befits the Federal style. Perhaps the only disappointment here is that the upstairs lacks the wood floors found downstairs and are thus a mite motelish.

Nonetheless, President Bush, Robert Mitchum, and the governor of Delaware were all satisfied customers here. The inn is within ambling distance of Delaware Street shops and the town's 18th-century showplaces.

Address: *216 Delaware St., New Castle, DE 19720, tel. 302/322-6367 or 800/334-6640.*
Accommodations: *13 double rooms with baths, 4 suites.*
Amenities: *Restaurant, piano bar, air-conditioning, credit-card phones, conference room.*
Rates: *$60-$110; Continental breakfast on weekdays and full breakfast on weekends. AE, D, DC, MC, V.*
Restrictions: *No pets.*

The Beaches

As the first warm weekend in May heralds the arrival of summer, the sun-starved citizens of Washington, Baltimore, and Wilmington pack their water wings and beach umbrellas and head for Delaware's Atlantic coast—a 25-mile strip of sand and surf stretching from the hamlet of Lewes to the Maryland state line. Here they find three splendid state parks, a handful of beach towns, and opportunities aplenty for sailing, fishing, clamming, and biking.

Rehoboth Beach is the undisputed nerve center of the Delaware seashore. It sprang up as a Methodist camp-meeting ground in the 1870s (Rehoboth means "one more sinner,"), and was overrun by sun worshippers when the railroad reached it 10 years later. Although some vintage Victorian structures (such as the Anna Hazzard Museum and the recently restored railroad station) remain, most of Rehoboth's ocean-side motels, downtown shops, and cottages date from the 20th century. The town is beloved above all by families with children. The city's recreation department schedules concerts in the bandstand; waterfront volleyball, football, and softball games; children's arts-and-crafts programs; and teen dance parties. It's all very wholesome: this place is stuck in the early 1960s and is not about to budge. There was even considerable public outcry at the recent opening of a McDonald's. For nightlife you'll have to head south to nearby Dewey Beach, the seashore's hot spot for singles.

Who, besides modern-day Gidgets and Dobie Gillises, gravitates to Rehoboth Beach, you might ask? For an answer you need only climb on a bike and investigate the neighborhoods (such as Henlopen Acres) away from the boardwalk around Lake Gerar and Silver Lake, where wealthy city families have built handsome summer homes. With its variety of upscale specialty shops and restaurants,

*downtown Rehoboth caters to the older, moneyed crowd
that has been coming to the town for generations.*

*If the bustle of Rehoboth and Dewey gets to be too much,
you'll find other, more peaceable, sandy kingdoms to
explore at the nearby Delaware Seashore, Cape Henlopen,
and Fenwick Island state parks. There you can swim, try
surf fishing, or go boating. Bethany Beach, a peaceful
resort where well-kept summer homes far outnumber the
few shops and restaurants, lies about 10 miles south of
Rehoboth. Increasingly, refugees from other, livelier
Delaware beach towns are coming to Bethany. Watch for
Saturday-night fried-chicken and oyster dinners held at the
town's fire hall. To the north is historic Lewes (pronounced
Lewis), a port community at Cape Henlopen, where charter
fishing is a big draw.*

Places to go, sights to see

Bandstands. In summertime both Bethany and Rehoboth beaches hold starlit
concerts at their beachside bandstands.

Bethel. On cloudy days it's worth leaving the seaside to visit this tiny inland
village, a 19th-century shipbuilding center.

Cape May Ferry (tel. 302/645–6313). This fleet of five vessels cruises across
Delaware Bay in a 70-minute trip connecting Colonial Lewes and Victorian
Cape May.

Carey's Camp Meeting Ground (tel. 302/856–7530.). It's on the National
Register for Historic Landmarks by virtue of the fact that Methodists began
coming here for sun and salvation back in 1888. They still follow Route 24
west of Millsboro to the meeting ground, with its open tabernacle and 47
frame tents.

Delaware's beach state parks. *Fenwick Island* (tel. 302/736–4702), at the
south end of Route 1, is bordered by Little Assawoman Bay and the wide
Atlantic; it's one of the few spots along the coast where surfing is permitted.
Delaware Seashore (tel. 302/227–2800), on a largely undeveloped, 7-mile strip
of sand between Dewey Beach and Bethany, has facilities for camping,
boating, fishing, and swimming. Among the shifting sands of *Cape
Henlopen* (tel. 302/645–8983) is the 80-foot Great Dune (thought to be the
largest dune between Capes Cod and Hatteras). The 3,020 acres of shoreline
at this park contain piping plover nests and cranberry bogs.

Fenwick Island Lighthouse (tel. 302/539–8129). Built in 1859, the 1,500-pound light still shines near the strait between Assawoman and Little Assawoman bays. To the south side of the light you'll find the first marker laid in the Mason-Dixon survey of 1751.

Laurel. The historic town of Laurel, which lies across Broad Creek from Bethel on the site of a Nanticoke Indian reservation, contains 800 buildings listed on the National Register. The free Woodland cable ferry carries hikers over the upper Nanticoke River.

Trap Pond State Park (tel. 302/875–5153). This 965-acre park, shaded by bald cypresses and loblolly pines, features wilderness canoe trails, fishing, and a swimming area that provides "wet wheelchairs" for the handicapped.

Zwaanendael Museum (tel. 302/645–9518). In 1631, 32 Dutch settlers began clearing land in Lewes, only to be massacred by the Leni-Lenape tribe. That sadly terminated colony, and Lewes's Dutch heritage, are remembered at this museum, a replica of a fantastically ornamented Dutch town hall found at the center of the town's historic district. Here you'll find a display on local shipwrecks, the Cannonball House Marine Museum, and the historic Fisher-Martin House, built about 1730.

Tourist Information

Bethany–Fenwick Chamber of Commerce (Box 502, Bethany Beach 19930, tel. 302/539–8129 or 800/962–7873). **Delaware Tourism Office** (99 Kings Hwy., Box 1401, Dover 19903, tel. 800/441–8846 or in DE 800/282–8667). **Rehoboth Beach–Dewey Beach Chamber of Commerce** (73 Rehoboth Ave., Rehoboth Beach 19971, tel. 302/227–2233 or 800/441–1329). **Southern Delaware Chamber of Commerce** (204 N.E. Front St., Milford 19963, tel. 800/345–4444 or in DE 800/345–4200).

Reservation Services

Bed & Breakfast of Delware (Box 177, 3650 Silverside Rd., Wilmington 19810, tel. 302/479–9500). **Maryland Reservation Center** (66 Maryland Ave., Annapolis 21401, tel. 301/263–9084).

The Inn at Canal Square

This decidedly upscale inn is a relatively new addition to the lodging scene in Lewes, a small, historic town that serves as both a gateway to the Atlantic beaches and a peaceful retreat for travelers along the Atlantic seaboard. This inn is special because of its waterfront location and unusual accommodations choices. Aside from 19 conventional rooms in the main building, travelers here can also choose from a lavishly appointed private apartment and *The Legend of Lewes*, a houseboat, whose modern galley, two bedrooms, and two baths float peacefully at dockside (this arrangement is not recommended for families with children under 14). The inn is conveniently situated in a meandering complex of shops and a restaurant. Design purists may protest the stylistic mélange; the exterior looks like a developer's reproduction of a Nantucket village, yet the decor in the apartment resembles the interior of a typical Malibu hideaway. You might find it a bit incongruous, but are ceiling fans, bushy potted plants, a canal-front sun deck, and a baby grand piano really so hard to bear?

In the three-story main building, the rooms are large and furnished with Federal reproductions. You'll pay slightly more for those with porch access and water views and considerably more for the honeymoon suite, which has a cathedral ceiling, Palladian windows, and private balcony.

Caswell and Massey toiletries come with the price of the room, as do simple Continental breakfasts, which can be eaten downstairs or taken back to the bedrooms on trays. Gilligan's, the restaurant next door, is open daily in season, from 11–1 AM, though you wouldn't want to visit Lewes without making a trip to the Rose and Crown Pub for at least one meal.

Diversion isn't hard to come by in Lewes. Besides exploring the Zwaanendael Museum and historic district there are the beaches of Cape Henlopen State Park to keep you occupied, or try your hand at hooking a shark, on a chartered fishing boat.

Address: *122 Market St., Lewes, DE 19958, tel. 302/645–8499.*
Accommodations: *17 double rooms with baths, 1 suite, 1 houseboat.*
Amenities: *Air-conditioning, cable TV and phones in bedrooms; conference room.*
Rates: *$120–$150, houseboat $225 ($1,200 per week). AE, MC, V.*
Restrictions: *No pets, 2-day minimum in apartment and houseboat on weekends, and in main building on some holiday weekends.*

Spring Garden Bed & Breakfast Inn

his inn reveals its character slowly and subtly. It's an abundantly lived-in place that is deeply appreciated by its owner, Gwen North. She was raised by her parents in this half-Colonial, half-Victorian farmhouse on the outskirts of Laurel before she flew the coop for New York. During that absence she came to realize that her heart lay back at home. Says Gwen, "When you stay in the same place all your life, you stop seeing what's there."

What's here is a red-shutter country house, almost invisible from the road, by a creek lined with daylilies in spring. As pleasant as its exterior is, the inside is even better. The Colonial section, built between 1760 and 1780 by a Captain Lewis of Bethel, remained in the Lewis family for 100 years. Its front parlor and back kitchen have wood-plank floors and the snug, slightly off-kilter feeling of a boat. Breakfast, highlighted by Scotch eggs and home-grown fruit, is served beside a wood-burning stove.

A steep, narrow staircase takes guests to the inn's two Colonial rooms; one called Naomi (for Gwen's mother) has a fireplace, a lace-canopy double bed, and a walnut rocker. Three bedrooms in the Victorian section, added in the late 1800s, have views of the garden and are filled with a soothing collection of antique furnishings, including a Victorian spool bed and Belgian cathedral chairs.

The Atlantic beaches are about 20 miles from the inn, but Gwen is quick to point out the other diversions to be found in this landlocked region of Delaware, such as canoeing and fishing at Trap Pond State Park and exploring the historic districts of Bethel and Laurel. Gwen is the moving force behind the new Southern Delaware Antiques and Arts Emporium in town and is an antiques dealer herself.

Tops among the activities here is bicycling, a pastime Gwen has encouraged by organizing the Biking Inn to Inn program, a series of four different, 3–5-day Delmarva Peninsula trips with lodgings at carefully selected inns. The routes take bikers along the flat back roads of the Eastern Shore, and offer opportunities for crabbing, bird-watching, and impromptu swims.

Address: *Rte. 1, Box 283A, Delaware Ave. Extended, Laurel, DE 19956, tel. 302/875-7015.*
Accommodations: *2 double rooms with baths, 3 doubles share bath.*
Amenities: *Air-conditioning, TV in sitting room, 3 fireplaces.*
Rates: *$55–$75. No credit cards.*
Restrictions: *Smoking in designated areas, no pets.*

The Addy Sea

Like Rehoboth, delightful little low-profile Bethany Beach got its start as the site of religious camp meetings, and by the turn of the century a beachfront community began to develop here. The summer home built by John M. Addy, a plumber from Pittsburgh, had carbide lamps and indoor bathrooms and in its day was one of the most modern homes in Bethany. The front yard of this capacious Victorian encompasses a splendid stretch of Atlantic beach. The upper half of the house is covered with brown shingles, and the lower portion is painted white and decorated with lace-like gingerbread. Inside there are tin ceilings (made on a press in the basement), Oriental rugs, and round oak tables. Thirteen of the 14 rooms have ocean views, the best being from the two front corner chambers. The inn is occupied by group rentals in May, June, September, and October; but in July and August anyone is welcome; but remember, no wet suits are allowed inside.

Address: *Atlantic Ave., Bethany Beach, DE 19930, tel. 302/539-3707.*
Accommodations: *2 double rooms with baths, 12 doubles share baths.*
Rates: *$85–$95; Continental breakfast. No credit cards.*
Restrictions: *No smoking in dining room, 2-day minimum stay, closed Nov.–Apr.*

The Corner Cupboard Inn

Open for over 50 years, this is the oldest operating inn on the Delaware shore. A peaceful oasis tucked into a residential neighborhood near Rehoboth's Lake Gerar, the main house, dressed in brown clapboard, sits like a mother hen in the midst of a handful of outbuildings. Inside, everything is English-cottage cozy: There's a fireplace in the living room and a lifetime of collectibles gathered by proprietress Elizabeth Gundry Hooper. In the main house, two guest rooms in particular might catch your eye—the Back Porch Room with its two double beds and the Blue Room overlooking the street. For a bit more privacy there are the annex and cottage rooms, two of which accommodate pets.

One of the most appealing features of the inn is its restaurant. From Memorial Day to mid-September the room rates include hearty morning and evening meals, and during the off-season, breakfast is the only meal served, to guests only.

Address: *50 Park Ave., Rehoboth Beach, DE 19971, tel. 302/227-8553.*
Accommodations: *18 double rooms with bath.*
Amenities: *Restaurant (open Memorial Day–mid-Sept., Mon.–Sat. 8 AM–10 AM and 6 PM–10 PM, Sun. 9–1 and 6–10; BYOB), TVs in sitting rooms and some guest rooms.*
Rates: *$75–$210; full breakfast, dinner in season. AE, MC, V.*
Restrictions: *Pets in some rooms only, with $7.50 charge.*

Lord and Hamilton Seaside Inn

This three-story, yellow-and-lavender Victorian is just a half-block from the boardwalk. It's run today by ebullient Marge Hamilton, a Methodist minister's wife. Travelers return to the Lord and Hamilton (and note, the "Lord" part of the inn's title isn't a family name) year after year: The guest roster is so regular that every spring Marge puts out a newsletter. The broad porch, which wraps around three sides of the house, is the center of summer activity; breakfast is served here, there's a swing, and, as night falls, deep conversations evolve. Inside you'll find Marge's antique doll collection and evidence of her fondness for rose-pattern fabrics; it's also quite clear that she has visited more than a few flea markets to furnish the place.

Her favorite pieces are a set of framed Arrow shirt posters from the '20s. Except for the downstairs suite the rooms are on the small side, and bathrooms are shared (count on a line at peak hours), but there's a shower in the yard and, of course, the ocean just beyond.

Address: *20 Brooklyn Ave., Rehoboth Beach, DE 19971, tel. 302/227-6960.*
Accommodations: *3 double rooms with baths, 4 rooms share 2 baths.*
Amenities: *Air-conditioning in 2 rooms.*
Rates: *$30–$80; Continental breakfast. No credit cards.*
Restrictions: *No smoking, no pets, 2-day minimum on weekends, 3-day minimum on holiday weekends, closed mid-Oct.–early May.*

The New Devon Inn

If the Inn at Canal Square has cornered the market along Lewes's waterfront, then the New Devon Inn, opened in 1989, is the city's downtown hotel. Of course, since Lewes is small, the two are only about a block apart, and the biggest disturbance you might experience while occupying a street-front room at the inn is the frequent tinkling of the bell above the door at King's Ice Cream Shop. The hotel, with its striped awnings and lobby-level stores, is in the heart of Lewes's historic district and has fine views of St. Peter's Episcopal Church and historic cemetery. Built in the '30s, the inn received a complete make-over at the hands of its new owner, Dale Jenkins. Little remains of its past except the lustrous heart-of-pine floors. Its lobby is reminiscent of

a Bloomingdale's window, with curious elephant chairs and an old-fashion cage elevator. The guest rooms are furnished in feminine elegance, with antiques and beds swaddled in designer linens. And the inn offers special touches, such as turndown service, candy and cordials in the rooms, and morning coffee served in delicate antique cups.

Address: *2nd and Market Sts., Box 516, Lewes, DE 19958, tel. 302/645-6466.*
Accommodations: *24 double rooms with baths, 2 suites.*
Amenities: *Air-conditioning, TV in lower lobby, phones in bedrooms; 2 conference rooms.*
Rates: *$70–$140; Continental breakfast. AE, MC, V.*
Restrictions: *No pets.*

The Pleasant Inn

In Rehoboth Beach, Peck Pleasanton's place is an anomaly, an inn with an adult air where you can imagine mature couples playing canasta on the porch until late and periodically ambling over to the wet bar to freshen their gin and tonics. Stylish, prettified, or even immaculately maintained it is not, though it does occupy one of central Rehoboth's most coveted properties—the big, foursquare Victorian with its widow's walk was built right on the boardwalk but was moved to its present location (about a five-minute walk from the beach) following the Great Storm of 1918. There are 10 double rooms in the house plus a downstairs kitchen-apartment and studio. The guest rooms are furnished with well-worn items that may be old but are probably not antiques, and have private baths that appear to have been last decorated in the '50s. A carriage-house out back that sleeps four is rented by the week. Peck himself is a no-nonsense, slow-talking man who looks and acts as if he's seen it all. He doesn't provide breakfast for his guests, but he does make several bicycles available free of charge.

Address: *31 Olive Ave., Rehoboth Beach, DE 19971, tel. 302/227-7311.*
Accommodations: *10 double rooms with baths, 3 suites.*
Amenities: *Air-conditioning, TV on porch, wet bar, kitchenette in 2nd-floor hallway.*
Rates: *$75–$95 June 15–Sept. 15. MC, V.*
Restrictions: *No pets, 3-day minimum mid-June–mid-Sept.*

Maryland

Maryland

Oxford/Eastern Shore

*In 1608 Captain John Smith called the Chesapeake "a faire
bay encompassed . . . with fruitful and delightsome lande."
This description was based on findings obtained while
"gunkholing," Eastern Shore jargon for frittering away
your time in a boat on the tidal rivers like the Miles, the
Choptank, Tred Avon, Sassafras, and Nanticoke.
Gunkholing is still a favorite pastime on Maryland's
Eastern Shore, where every spring fleets of boats descend
on sleepy little ports that haven't seen so much action since
the War of 1812—or since last spring.*

*You could say that Baltimore is the reason Eastern Shore
towns such as St. Michael's, Oxford, Cambridge,
Chestertown, Rock Hall, and Vienna have retained their
small-town charm. In the 18th century these were
metropoli-in-the-making, growing fat off of trade with the
British. But after the discovery of Baltimore City's enviable
deep-water port the parade passed them by, and for the last
200 years these waterfront Colonial towns have changed
little. It fell to the wealthy reclusives of this century to
rediscover the Eastern Shore. The du Ponts, Houghtons,
and other wealthy families quietly bought property here
and moved in to get away from it all. Since their digs are
set discreetly off the roads, the best way to see them is by
taking a cruise from St. Michael's up the Miles River.*

*Besides rubbernecking and gunkholing, there are plenty of
other reasons to visit the Eastern Shore. Because the
terrain is flat and traversed by a network of
companionable country roads, bicyclists flock to the area,
inevitably heading toward shorefront seafood restaurants
and marinas. Come November, tens of thousands of
waterfowl fly through on their way south, followed by
hunters and bird-watchers.*

Each Eastern Shore town has a character of its own. Oxford is the quintessential retirement town, and in landlocked Easton you'll find the Chesapeake Bay Yacht Club; numerous quaint shops; and the November Waterfowl Festival (now in its 20th year), which features an art show, decoy displays, retriever- and birdcalling, and an auction. St. Michael's, with its renowned Maritime Museum, is all about boats, as is Tilghman Island, one of the last domains of the Chesapeake Bay watermen.

Most visitors stick to these Talbot County haunts, but there are subtler pleasures and thinner crowds in neighboring Kent and Dorchester counties. Cambridge, across the broad Choptank River (the focus of James Michener's Chesapeake*), is the gateway to 700 square miles of government-protected wetlands. To the north lies Chestertown, a demure Colonial treasure whose brightest moment came in 1774, when a band of Revolutionary firebrands dumped a British brigantine's tea cargo into the Chester River—an event still celebrated every May with fife-and-drum corps, house tours, and craft displays.*

Along Delaware and Maryland's Atlantic coast the marlin, tuna, and piping plovers roam free, but the people flock to the beaches in rigid pecking order. Well-heeled Washingtonians head to Delaware's Bethany and Fenwick beaches, while blue-collar Baltimore goes to Ocean City, Maryland, where the long main drag and motel flats look forever frozen in 1958.

Places to go, sights to see

Betterton Beach. At the mouth of the Sassafras River, about 12 miles north of Chestertown, the bay's only jellyfish-free beach has a new bathhouse, boardwalk, picnic pavilion, and boat ramp.

Blackwater National Wildlife Refuge (tel. 301/228–2677). Occupying 15,000 marshy acres 12 miles south of Cambridge, this preserve is a haven for endangered Delmarva fox squirrels; bald eagles; peregrine falcons; red-cockaded woodpeckers; and, in fall, hordes of Canada geese and ducks. For spectators there's a visitors center, a 5-mile wildlife drive, an observation tower, and myriad bike and walking trails.

Chesapeake Bay Maritime Museum (St. Michael's, tel. 301/745–2916). Here you'll see the bay's historic boats—including bugeyes, skipjacks, and log canoes—as well as the 100-year-old Hooper Strait Lighthouse, a working boat shop, and an assortment of other maritime displays.

Dixon's Auctions (Crumpton, tel. 301/928–3006). The indomitable auctioneer, Norman Dixon, starts the bidding here every Wednesday morning at 9 AM. Goods ranging from rusty tractors to valuable antiques are arranged in rows running across six fields.

The Patriot (tel. 301/745–3100). This 65-foot cruise boat berthed in St. Michael's takes 1½-hour excursions up the Miles River.

Tred Avon Ferry (tel. 301/745–9023). Highway 33 will get you to St. Michael's and Tilghman Island, but the ferry linking Oxford to Bellevue and carrying up to nine cars is a much more picturesque way to go. Begun in 1683 it's the oldest privately operated ferry in the United States.

Trinity Church. In 1675 the Colonists built Trinity near the village of Church Creek in Dorchester County, which makes this brick building the country's oldest Episcopal church in continuous use. It's surrounded by a graveyard, where lie the remains of three Revolutionary War heroes.

Tourist Information

Dorchester County Tourism (Box 307, Cambridge 21613, tel. 301/228–3234). **Kent County Chamber of Commerce** (Box 146, 118 N. Cross St., Chestertown 21620, tel. 301/778–0416). **Talbot County Tourism** (Box 1366, 805 Goldsborough St., Easton 21601, tel. 301/822–4606).

Reservation Services

Amanda's Bed & Breakfast Reservation Service (1428 Park Ave., Baltimore 21217, tel. 301/225–0001). **Inns of the Eastern Shore** (1500 Hambrooks Blvd., Cambridge 21613, tel. 301/228–0575). **Maryland Reservation Center** (66 Maryland Ave., Annapolis 21401, tel. 301/263–9084). **The Traveller in Maryland, Inc.** (Box 2277, Annapolis 21401, tel. 301/269–6232).

Brampton

Brampton's charming character derives from both its house and its grounds. The inn is set in the fields south of Chestertown, framed by two towering, 120-year-old spruce trees, at the end of a long drive. It's a three-story brick building with a white columned porch and 14 front windows, the perfect gentleman-farmer's country seat. The house is listed on the National Register of Historic Places, as are four of its surrounding 35 acres (the site of some famous experiments in crop rotation). Enter the house and pass through the airy foyer into a bookcase-lined living room or climb the solid-walnut staircase. The front section of Brampton was built around 1860 by Henry Ward Carville, as a wedding present to his wife.

Upstairs in the five guest rooms the present owner's excellent taste becomes apparent. Michael Hanscom spent 10 years in San Francisco renovating old homes before moving here. His Swiss wife, Danielle, is responsible for the European atmosphere in the guest rooms. The bed linen and towels look and smell as if they'd been dried on a line in the Alps. Every room except the suite has a working fireplace or a wood-burning stove. The ceilings on the second floor are 12 feet high, and the Yellow Room at the front of the house is a favorite, a sunny paradise with a Swiss cherry armoire and an antique lace canopy above the bed. The two third-floor rooms are tucked under the sloping eaves and are decorated in country style, with locally crafted chairs and trundle beds.

Danielle and Michael can suggest walks on the Brampton grounds to a pond or nearby Langford Creek. There is something Old World about these quiet, unassuming hosts, both of whom are dedicated to perfecting every detail, right down to the fresh-squeezed orange juice and homemade coffee cake at breakfast.

Address: *RR 2, Box 107, Chestertown, MD 21620, tel. 301/778–1860.*
Accommodations: *4 double rooms with baths, 1 suite.*
Amenities: *Air-conditioning, TV in suite.*
Rates: *$90–$95; full breakfast. MC, V.*
Restrictions: *Smoking downstairs only, no pets, 2-day minimum on holiday weekends and on graduation weekend at nearby Washington College.*

The Inn at Perry Cabin

The grand white frame house, much enlarged from the original farmhouse, sits serenely at the edge of the Miles River, as it has since 1810. Much of the decor of the Inn at Perry Cabin is pure Laura Ashley, which is only fitting, since this, the first Ashley Inn, is owned by Sir Bernard Ashley, husband of the late designer.

The reception rooms have been done à la English country-house hotel, and from time to time Sir Bernard and Lady Ashley swoop down on St. Michael's, bringing new furniture and decorations (not really new, of course, but brought from their house in the Bahamas or from the antiques emporiums of the world). Every object has been chosen with care, and most of them are antique—from the Colonial American chests of drawers, highboys, and bedside tables that came with the house to mirrors, lamps, pictures, and Oriental rugs everywhere you look. The kaleidoscope of pattern upon pattern is a bit busy, but everything is worth examining.

Many of the bedrooms are done in antiques, too, but others are completely Laura Ashley—fabrics, wallpapers, sprig-decorated tables, and beds with spiral posts. The age of the house makes for interesting nooks and crannies, but the fireplaces in several bedrooms are just for looks. The bathrooms are up-to-date, and most have towel warmers.

The books on the bedside tables are the kind you'd like to read.

The main dining room, a soaring chamber two stories high, has an ox-roasting fireplace at one end. The food is excellent, and the silent, unobtrusive service almost too formal—perhaps the staff wants to live up to the British tone of the place. Boat owners would find it a welcome change from galley fare. The 55 employees run the inn impeccably under the direction of Peter Bowling. Construction of 22 new rooms and a snooker room is underway.

Address: *308 Watkins Lane, St. Michael's, MD 21663, tel. 301/745-2200 or 800/722-2949, fax 301/745-3348.*
Accommodations: *15 double rooms with baths, 4 suites.*
Amenities: *Restaurant, air-conditioning, cable TV and phones in rooms, room service; croquet, short-term docking facilities.*
Rates: *$195–$310, suites $260–$450; full breakfast, afternoon tea. AE, DC, MC, V.*
Restrictions: *No smoking in dining room, no pets.*

The Robert Morris Inn

Although the town of Oxford and its historic inn came vividly into the public eye, around the time of the American Bicentennial, the Robert Morris has managed to avoid being spoiled by success. Built by Robert Morris, Sr., as a residence in 1710 and run as an inn since the 1940s, it was bought by Ken and Wendy Gibson in 1975 and is just what a country inn should be.

The 18th-century section of the inn is on Oxford's Morris Street, facing the ferry dock, where there's always a line of tourists waiting to board the tiny Tred Avon Ferry, which tools away between Oxford and Bellevue. You might also find a line at the Robert Morris restaurant, which occupies most of the inn's first floor. Its Hitchcock chairs and murals (actually 140-year-old, handprinted wallpaper samples) make it an attractive place to eat; crab cakes and Oxford coolers head the rather predictable menu. The slate-floor tavern beyond the dining room has a working fireplace and is reputedly where James Michener wrote the outline for *Chesapeake.*

Staying at the Robert Morris may prove more difficult than simply supping there. The Gibsons begin taking reservations on January 10 of each year and won't book a room more than a year in advance. Historic-minded souls should be adamant about claiming rooms in the 1710 section, where there's a rare, enclosed Elizabethan staircase and white-pine floors fastened with hand-hewn pegs. Top choices among the four guest rooms here are 2 and 15, the latter with a step-up poster bed and hand-stenciled borders on the walls. You might also request the room once occupied by Robert Morris, Jr., a signer of the Declaration of Independence, or that of his father (who met a lamentable fate being hit by a cannon fired in his honor).

The Gibsons know that some people are willing to dispense with history altogether in favor of luxurious quietude. To that end they've restored a roomy 1875 summer house, surrounded by mimosa and weeping copper-beech trees, just steps from the main house. Almost all the rooms in Sandaway Lodge are suites featuring screened-in porches, pine paneling, and immense claw-foot tubs (ask for 202, with a chandelier over the bath; for 303, with its own staircase; or one of the romantic River Rooms overlooking the Tred Avon).

Address: *Box 70, on the Tred Avon, Oxford, MD 21654, tel. 301/226–5111, fax 301/226–5744.*
Accommodations: *24 double rooms with baths, 6 suites, 3 cottages.*
Amenities: *Restaurant, air-conditioning.*
Rates: *$70–$160, Continental breakfast Mon. and Tues., breakfast extra other days. MC, V.*
Restrictions: *No pets.*

Wades Point Inn

Aside from a chartered yacht, there's no better place from which to appreciate the blue sweep of the Chesapeake than the Wades Point Inn. Halfway between St. Michael's and Tilghman Island, this rambling bed-and-breakfast on 120 acres is surrounded on three sides by the bay.

The oldest section of the inn was built in 1820 by shipwright Thomas Kemp, whose sleek Baltimore clippers were credited with winning the War of 1812. On the land side, this glowing white Georgian house has porches on two floors and chimneys at either end; an observation nook attached to one chimney was Thomas Kemp's lookout and is reached through a trapdoor in one of three rooms in the old portion of the house.

In 1890, later Kemps built an addition to the house on the bay side and opened the place as an inn. The present owners, Betsy and John Feiler, call this addition the Bay Room and have put it to use as a common area; it's large enough to hold a cotillion and is lined with windows and furnished with white wicker. Above the Bay Room is the Summer Wing, which holds six small chambers. These aren't air-conditioned, but given their proximity to the water, porches, and plentiful windows, they don't need it. There are washbasins in some of the Summer Wing rooms, as well as pastel prints and dancing

white curtains that catch the rejuvenating breeze. Maybe that's why Mildred Kemp, the last of the family to occupy Wades Point, looked so hearty at age 90, when Betsy Feiler met her. "If living at Wades Point made her look like that," Betsy says, "I wanted to buy the place."

Building additions seems to be something of a tradition with the owners of Wades Point. There's a four-room summer cottage, and in 1989 Betsy and John completed a 12-room guest house about 200 yards from the main inn. These modern rooms have water views and balconies, and the two double beds and kitchenette in Number 423 make it a good choice for families. If you are looking for bona fide old Chesapeake Bay atmosphere, however, opt for a room in the main house.

Address: *Box 7, St. Michael's, MD 21663, tel. 301/745-2500.*
Accommodations: *15 double rooms with baths, 9 doubles share 5 baths.*
Amenities: *Air-conditioning in new guest house, TV and fireplaces in common rooms; pond, private crabbing and fishing dock, walking/jogging trail, public boat ramp nearby.*
Rates: *$59–$145; Continental breakfast. MC, V.*
Restrictions: *Smoking on porches only, no pets, 2-day minimum with Sat. reservation, summer wing and summer cottage closed in winter.*

Glasgow Inn

The keepers of the Glasgow Inn are two retired teachers who went to college together and share a common interest in quilting and old homes. Louise Lee Roche is the people person, and quiet Martha Ann the one who gets things done—such as breakfast, which, if you ask for it, can feature apple pancakes. Theirs is one of Dorchester County's most historic houses, a beautiful Georgian riverfront mansion with gable-end entry and Palladian windows, built by a refugee of the Stuart Rebellion. Glasgow's high-ceiling, spacious rooms are decorated with Oriental rugs, 18th-century reproductions, and furniture from Martha Ann's family home, in Ocean City. Beyond the Lombardy poplars on the long front lawn lies the Choptank River, home to whistling swans.

From Glasgow, it's an easy walk to the Brannock Maritime Museum, tennis courts, and the town dock, where the Cambridge skipjack fleet ties up. Ask Louise for directions to Blackwater Wildlife Refuge or to the Amish shop in East New Market. In January a week-long internship for innkeepers is held at the inn.

Address: *1500 Hambrooks Blvd., Cambridge, MD 21613, tel. 301/228-0575 or 800/225-0575.*
Accommodations: *1 double room with bath, 6 doubles share 4 baths.*
Amenities: *Air-conditioning, TV in parlor.*
Rates: *$80–$100; full breakfast. MC, V.*
Restrictions: *No smoking, no pets, 3-day minimum during Waterfowl Festival.*

The Inn at Mitchell House

After an unsuccessful skirmish with the Americans near the village of Tolchester during the War of 1812, the British brought their wounded commander to Mitchell House. Sir Peter Parker didn't recover, but modern-day visitors to this country bed-and-breakfast isolated on 10 corn-filled acres, will fare considerably better.

This three-story, brick plantation house was built in 1743 and enlarged in 1825. Two of the five guest bedrooms have working fireplaces, and the top floor's Hermitage, with its low, slanting ceilings and dormer windows, is a great place to tuck in the children. The owners, Jim and Tracy Stone, welcome hunters in season and encourage their guests to stroll a half mile down the road, to

Tolchester Marina, where from November 1 to March 15 they can learn how to dredge for oysters by chartering the classic wooden sailboat *Elsworth*.

Address: *Box 329, RD 2, Tolchester Estates, Chestertown, MD 21620, tel. 301/778-6500.*
Accommodations: *5 double rooms with baths.*
Amenities: *Air-conditioning, TV with VCR in living room.*
Rates: *$75–$90; full breakfast. MC, V.*
Restrictions: *Dogs allowed outside only, 2-night minimum on holiday weekends.*

John S. McDaniel House

This big, turreted Queen Anne in Easton has seven guest rooms, with the turret nook making the Prentiss Ingraham Room particularly desirable. The decor is a mixed bag of family-style collectibles: nothing fancy, but all neat as a pin. Hosts Bill and Genie Kramedas are happy to fill you in on all the local action, including the inside scoop on the best places to eat—try Cecile's and Peachblossom, just a few blocks away. To newly arrived guests, Genie serves sun tea sweetened with orange juice, just the right thing to sip while unwinding on the wide McDaniel House porch, where there's a swing, lots of white wicker furniture, and hanging plants. If you're headed to Easton for the November Waterfowl Festival this is an excellent, homey place to stay.

Address: *14 N. Aurora St., Easton, MD 21601, tel. 301/822-3704.*
Accommodations: *5 double rooms with baths, 2 doubles share bath.*
Amenities: *Air-conditioning.*
Rates: *$65–$75; full breakfast. AE, MC, V.*
Restrictions: *Smoking on porch only, 2-day minimum May–Nov., closed Dec. 25–Jan. 1.*

The Tavern Inn

Vienna, Maryland, is a genuine backwater on the Nanticoke River, and probably quieter now than during the Revolutionary War, when the British made a habit of raiding it. Recently a new bridge was built over the river, and now the view from the inn includes the bulwark of the old bridge and the splendid Nanticoke, bordered by marshes and cattails that shimmer in the breeze.

The inn has been lovingly restored by Elise and Harvey Altergott. Ask Harvey to point out its wood-case door locks; a carving above the entryway featuring palm trees and coconuts; gray, green, and blue wainscoting, and the gracefully curving stair. Upstairs is the River Room, the first choice because of its high four-poster bed, working fireplace, Colonial wall sconces, and Nanticoke views. There are osprey nests in the marshes out front, an owl in the chimney, and peace. Yet you probably won't be spending much time *en chambre*, with the area's back roads calling. Bikes are available, as are such points of interest as Miss Nora's General Store, on Elliott Island, and Old Salty's (for sandwiches), in Fishing Creek.

Address: *111 Water St., Box 98, Vienna, MD 21869, tel. 301/376-3347.*
Accommodations: *4 double rooms share 2 baths.*
Amenities: *Air-conditioning.*
Rates: *$55–$60; full breakfast. MC, V.*
Restrictions: *No smoking in guest rooms, no pets.*

Victoriana

One day in 1987 Janet Bernstein sailed into St. Michael's and saw a FOR SALE sign in front of the old Shannahan place— known locally as Willow Cottage. She'd restored homes in Cape May and could see the building's possibilities immediately. The house overlooks Navy Point (site of the Chesapeake Bay Maritime Museum) and has a mansard roof decorated with fleurs-de-lis, bespeaking the French Second Empire. The rooms are done with Victorian antiques and are feminine in feeling, with large armoires and canopy beds. The patterns of the linens, coverlets, and dust ruffles are changed every month, and on the pillows you'll find sachets filled with herbs grown in Janet's garden. There's a partially glassed-in, columned porch on the cove side of Victoriana, where Janet sets up the breakfast buffet. From there the lawn, graced by a gigantic magnolia tree, slopes gently toward the water, and you're likely to find Janet's golden retriever, Miss Vicky, lying in some soft patch of grass nearby.

Address: *Box 449, 205 Cherry St., St. Michael's, MD 21663, tel. 301/745-3368.*
Accommodations: *1 double room with bath, 4 doubles share 2 baths.*
Amenities: *Air-conditioning, TV with VCR in porch sitting room.*
Rates: *$85–$125; full breakfast. MC, V.*
Restrictions: *Smoking in porch sitting room only, no pets.*

The White Swan Tavern

To Horace Havemeyer, Jr., old-house restoration is a science. He brought in a team of archaeologists when he bought the Colonial White Swan Tavern to help return it to its 18th-century appearance. A dig at the rear of the brick building unearthed clay pipes and mugs and a Pennsylvania-flagstone tavern yard. Today, the room that was the original kitchen, to the right of this patio area and shaded by a giant elm, is the inn's most requested guest room. Its rough ceiling beams, brick floor, and large fireplace attest to its antiquity and make it an eminently cozy place to sleep. The chambers in the tavern's main section are more formal, with stately wing chairs, canopy beds, and paneled walls. In the years since its renovation the White Swan has become a Kent County landmark, popular for its daily tea. Its enviable High Street location puts guests within walking distance of shops, an old-fashion movie theater, the Confederate Monument on the green, a small park on the banks of the Chester River, and at least two good places to eat—the Ironstone Café and the fancy Hotel Imperial Restaurant.

Address: *231 High St., Chestertown, MD 21620, tel. 301/778-2300.*
Accommodations: *4 double rooms with baths, 2 suites.*
Amenities: *Tea room, air-conditioning, cable TV in sitting room.*
Rates: *$75–$125; Continental breakfast, no credit cards.*
Restrictions: *No pets, closed 2 weeks in Jan. and Feb.*

Annapolis/Western Shore

Bounded by 7,325 miles of coast the Chesapeake Bay is not only the nation's largest estuary, but Maryland's defining feature. Its Eastern and Western shores were joined in 1952 by the 4.5 miles of concrete and steel known as the Chesapeake Bay Bridge. Since then, sun worshippers from Baltimore, Philadelphia, and Washington have had easy access to the Atlantic beaches, making the bay a favorite with wealthy retirees, recreational sailors, artists, and many others.

During their easterly migration along Route 50/301 the sun-and-surf crowd was quick to rediscover Annapolis, founded in 1647 near the mouth of the Severn River.

John D. Rockefeller passed it over in favor of Williamsburg while looking for a Colonial capital to restore, but Annapolitans don't care. Their city, the state capital, boasts more pre-Revolutionary brick buildings than any in America, the oldest statehouse in continuous use, the U.S. Naval Academy, a renowned harbor, a huge October boat show, lots of gentrified shops, and a July feast during which 20,000 blue crabs are devoured. The brick-pattern streets radiating from the heights around Church and State circles are a walker's paradise, but summer weekends can be crowded (and parking a challenge), so it's a good idea to steal away to Annapolis on weekdays or in the November-to-March off-season.

South of Annapolis on the Chesapeake's Western Shore lie three Maryland counties that time forgot—Calvert, St. Mary's, and Charles—where broad rivers such as the Potomac and Patuxent flow gently past tobacco fields, and the mood is redolent of the Old South. Around the turn of the century a railroad tycoon named Otto Mears tried to turn several Western Shore communities into a Coney Island on the Chesapeake, but storms blew his boardwalk

away. The region was next "discovered" in the late 1940s,
when legalized slot machines briefly turned southern
Maryland into "Little Nevada."

Today, though Washington's suburban sprawl is beginning
to encroach from the north, the three counties remain
a fine frontier along which travelers can investigate 18th-
century churches; manor houses such as Sotterley; the
bustling marine center at Solomons Island; lonely land's-
end lighthouses; and St. Mary's City, which predates
Annapolis as a capital of Colonial Maryland.

Places to go, sights to see

Calvert Marine Museum (tel. 301/326–2042). This complex of buildings in the
town of Solomons includes the restored J. C. Lore and Sons Oyster House
and the Drum Point Lighthouse, built in 1883 to mark the entrance of the
Patuxent River, and one of the last cottage-type lights remaining on the bay.

City Dock. Here's where to find the Tourist Information Booth (tel. 301/268–
8687), a fleet of spiffy yachts, and sightseeing boats that cruise Annapolis
Harbor and call at Eastern Shore ports. The historic Victualling Warehouse,
Maritime Museum, Middleton Tavern, and seafood-laden Market House are
across the square from the dock.

Eastport. Just over the Spa Creek drawbridge is Eastport, a nautical hub full
of boat yards, marinas, and watering holes such as Marmaduke's (tel.
301/269–5420), a favorite with yacht crews.

Historic Homes of Annapolis. These debonair Georgian and Federal
buildings include the Hammond-Harwood, Chase-Lloyd, Brice, and William
Paca houses, the latter a must-see for its grand Palladian design and formal
gardens. Maps pinpointing their locations (all within walking distance of one
another) are available at the Tourist Information Booth on City Dock, and
tours can be arranged through *Historic Annapolis,* Inc. (tel. 301/267–8149)
or *Three Centuries Tours* (tel. 301/263–5401).

Maryland State House (tel. 301/269–3400). The oldest American statehouse
in continuous legislative use, this Georgian brick building dates from 1772
and served as the nation's capital for nine months, in 1773 and 1774. In its
chambers, which are decorated with hand-carved tobacco-leaf borders,
General George Washington resigned his commission and the Treaty of Paris
was signed, ending the Revolutionary War.

Point Lookout State Park (tel. 301/872–5688). Point Lookout, at the tip of
the tri-counties peninsula, served as an appallingly overcrowded hospital

during the Civil War. Now its character is far more benign, offering campsites, as well as facilities for swimming, crabbing, and fishing.

St. Mary's City (tel. 301/862–0990). Approximately 60 miles south of Annapolis, this restored village is the site of the fourth permanent settlement in Colonial America. Points of interest include the Godiah Spray Tobacco Plantation and a working reconstruction of *The Dove*, a square-rig sailing vessel that brought settlers from England to St. Mary's in 1634.

U.S. Naval Academy (tel. 301/267–3363). Every year 1,000 midshipmen are commissioned at the Academy, which was founded in 1845. The body of John Paul Jones rests beneath its chapel, and the wardroom is so big the entire student body (4,500 strong) can sit down to dine together. Guided tours of the 329-acre campus leave from the information center at Ricketts Hall.

Tourist Information

Calvert County Department of Economic Development (Calvert County Courthouse, Prince Frederick 20678, tel. 301/535–4583). **Charles County Tourism** (Charles County Government Building, Box B, La Plata 20646, tel. 301/645–0556). **St. Mary's County Chamber of Commerce** (6260 Waldorf Leonard Town Rd., Mechanicsville 20659, tel. 301/884–5555). **Tourism Council of Annapolis and Anne Arundel County** (6 Dock St., Annapolis 21401, tel. 301/280–0445).

Reservation Services

Amanda's Bed & Breakfast Reservation Service (1428 Park Ave., Baltimore 21217, tel. 301/225–0001). **Annapolis Association of Licensed Bed & Breakfast Owners** (Box 744, Annapolis 21404). **Maryland Reservation Center** (66 Maryland Ave., Annapolis 21401, tel. 301/263–9084). **The Traveller in Maryland, Inc.** (Box 2277, Annapolis 21401, tel. 301/269–6232).

Potomac View Farm

Says Kate Meatyard, the proprietress of Potomac View Farm, "Hopefully, my children and grandchildren will know Tall Timbers the way it is today." Kate can make this wish for the tiny town optimistically, since much of Tall Timbers, including a bed-and-breakfast inn and a marina, has been in her husband's family for 90 years.

There's not much to see in Tall Timbers, but for boaters the marina, complete with 180 slips, is a favorite layover spot on Potomac River cruises. People who dock here enjoy a restaurant called the Reluctant Navigator, a swimming pool, and a 7-acre private beach. With Rick Meatyard running the marina and Kate at the helm of a catering business, the family has its hands full; but that didn't stop them from snapping up Potomac View, the historic 138-acre farm owned by the Shadrick family since 1725.

You approach Potomac View Farm down a long rutted lane through a grove of pine trees, and as you near the white 1910 farmhouse you'll see straight through the house to the riverside, where there's an aromatic boxwood garden, a patio, and a private cottage. Downstairs in the house there's a roomy country kitchen, dining room, sitting room, and a sun porch where breakfast is served. The second and third floors hold six guest rooms and four baths, equipped with claw-foot tubs or showers. Kate has decorated the place with loot that includes the amiable wooden cow sculptures she's picked up on barn-raiding expeditions, but for the most part she's left the interior uncluttered and unpretentious. For this reason Potomac View Farm is a blissful choice for groups who want to spread out and relax—for, say, a family reunion with children; in fact, Greenpeace has used it as a spot for retreats.

The beach, pool, tackle shop, and charter-fishing boats are down the road at Tall Timbers Marina. On Sunday, instead of breakfast at the farm, the Meatyards provide coupons for brunch at the Reluctant Navigator, where you can linger on the patio to feed several brazen domesticated geese and watch the nautical parade pass by.

Address: *Tall Timbers, MD 20690, tel. 301/994–0418 or 301/994–0419.*
Accommodations: *6 double rooms share 4 baths, 1 cottage with bath, living room, and kitchen.*
Amenities: *Air-conditioning, TV, stereo, CD player in cottage, fireplace in dining room.*
Rates: *$50–125. AE, MC, V.*
Restrictions: *Smoking only on first floor, pets allowed only in barn, closed Dec.–Mar. except by special arrangement.*

State House Inn

When Paul Pearson came to Annapolis in 1966, the city was an eyesore, far from the Chesapeake jewel that it is today. Fortunately he turned his imagination loose, buying and restoring five antique properties in the next two decades—among them, the State House Inn. Unlike its sister property, the Maryland Inn, a landmark flatiron building that has served as a hostelry since 1776, the State House is a quiet, elegant respite from the bustle. Of Pearson's five-inn domain, known as Historic Inns of Annapolis, the State House is the best-kept secret. It's located on State Circle, a quiet street where there's an archaeological dig under way. Built in 1820 its dormer windows and rocking-chair–laden porch overlook Maryland's distinguished capitol. The elegant Hampton House restaurant occupies a niche downstairs on the Main Street side.

Though the inn doesn't have an elevator or common room, the nine guest chambers, all intriguingly varied in shape, easily make up for the lack. They are swathed in matching wallpapers and draperies and furnished with a mixture of antiques and reproductions; their plump beds are covered with ivory candlewick spreads in a traditional pattern. Lovers of luxury should note that three of the nine suites have whirlpool baths, and that breakfast is served on a tray at your door, along with the morning newspaper every day but Sunday.

If you book a room at the State House Inn (or Pearson's nearby Robert Johnson House) when the legislature is in session (January–March), you're likely to run into some of the harried politicians and lobbyists who favor these two properties. And in any of Pearson's inns, if you're lucky, some morning you might run into the cheerful, friendly mistress innkeeper, Peg Bednarsky (called "Mother" by the staff), as she checks unoccupied rooms to make sure they're up to scratch.

Address: *16 Church Circle, Annapolis, MD 21401, tel. 301/263-2641, fax 301/268-3813.*
Accommodations: *6 double rooms with baths, 3 suites.*
Amenities: *Air-conditioning, cable TV and phones in rooms.*
Rates: *$90–$250; Continental breakfast. AE, DC, MC, V.*
Restrictions: *2-day minimum during Commissioning Week and Boat Show.*

The William Page Inn

If your travels take you to Annapolis for Commissioning Week at the Naval Academy, for the December Parade of Lights, or simply to nose around the city's walkable historic district, there's rest for the weary explorer at the William Page Inn, across from the old Water Witch Fire Company.

Built in 1908 this brown-shingle Victorian is a youngster by Annapolis standards, but one with an accommodating style. Its wraparound porch offers deep Adirondack chairs, and the boxwood in the William Paca House gardens perfumes the air. Somewhere over the high white wall at the end of Martin Street you might hear Naval Academy "middies" drilling, and four blocks away at eateries around City Dock crabs are being devoured, but on the William Page porch such distractions seem light-years away.

The genial innkeepers are Bob Zuchelli and Greg Page, a designer of theatrical lighting and a computer programmer. They took very early retirement to refurbish the inn, which had served as the First Ward Democratic Clubhouse for 50 years. They aired out the smoke-filled rooms; stripped 11 coats of paint from the massive staircase, to reveal oak, mahogany, and cherry wood; and filled the inn with Queen Anne and Chippendale reproductions. They also turned the third floor into one smashing suite, with a sleigh bed, skylight, window seats, and balloon shades that lift to reveal views of the Annapolis rooftops. Guests might take the presence of a whirlpool bath in the suite in stride, but they are likely to be surprised by the one attached to the little blue room on the second floor.

There's a wet bar stocked with setups, a working fireplace in the carpeted downstairs common room, and a discreet dog named Rascals who is always happy to accompany guests on walks. Breakfast, served from the sideboard in the common room, consists of freshly baked muffins and breads, fruit-and-cheese trays, and perhaps an egg casserole or crepes—depending on Chef Bob's mood. Greg earns his keep by running a side business, The Traveller in Maryland reservation service, and he can bend your ear describing other choice places to stay.

Address: *8 Martin St., Annapolis, MD 21401, tel. 301/626-1506.*
Accommodations: *2 double rooms with baths, 2 doubles share bath, 1 suite.*
Amenities: *Air-conditioning, cable TV in suite, wet bar, 2 whirlpool baths, robes for guests using shared bath; off-street parking.*
Rates: *$70–$120; full breakfast. AE, MC, V.*
Restrictions: *No smoking, no pets, 2-day minimum on holiday weekends, 5-day minimum during Boat Show and Commissioning Week.*

Back Creek Inn

Seascape painters and beachcombers would do well on Solomons Island, a finger of sand connected to the mainland by a bridge, bounded on the west by the Patuxent River and on the east by Back Creek Bay. They'd do well at Carol Szkotnicki and Lin Cochran's Back Creek Inn, too. Dating from the 1880s, the robin's-egg-blue waterman's house is unprepossessing from the front, but, inside, Carol has used her grandma's quilts and her green thumb to brighten up the guest rooms (the Chamomile room has abundant charm). Lin, a professional caterer, is responsible for the homemade breakfast breads and muffins. The main house and an annex added in 1984 wrap around the heady-smelling herb garden, which in turn surrounds an outdoor whirlpool bath. From the garden and patio it's fun to watch the water traffic on Back Creek. Charter fishing, sailing, and exploring the Calvert Marine Museum are how most guests spend their salt-sprayed Solomons days.

Address: *Calvert and A Sts., Solomons, MD 20688, tel. 301/326-2022.*
Accommodations: *1 double room with bath, 3 doubles share 2 baths, 2 suites, 1 cottage.*
Amenities: *Air-conditioning, cable TV on porch and in cottage and suites; dock with 2 deep-water slips, access to nearby swimming pool.*
Rates: *$65–$85; Continental breakfast. No credit cards.*
Restrictions: *Smoking on porch only, no pets, 2-day minimum on holiday weekends, closed Dec.–Feb.*

Gibson's Lodgings

Two hundred years ago they called Annapolis Harbor's infamous dockside neighborhood Hell's Point. Well, yesterday's Hades is a gentrified haven today, with narrow brick-paved streets, shade trees, and houses with landmark plaques. Two at the bottom of Prince George Street have been converted into a rambling inn by ex-Illinoisans Cary and Ayrol Ann Gibson. The Patterson dwelling, built between 1760 and 1786, is a brick Georgian town house with dormer windows. Next door, the red stucco Berman home dates from the last century. The Gibsons combed the towns along the Intracoastal Waterway for antiques, yet the decoration of these 18th- and 19th-century neighbors is extremely simple, a little like that of a small-town hotel. The annex built out back two years ago is too new to have much atmosphere, but it does have spacious conference rooms. These days Gibson's Lodgings is professionally managed, which gives it a businesslike air. The venerable houses are as close as can be to the Middleton Tavern's raw bar.

Address: *110–114 Prince George St., Annapolis, MD 20401, tel. 301/268-5555.*
Accommodations: *5 double rooms with baths, 13 doubles share 7 baths, 2 suites.*
Amenities: *Air-conditioning, TVs and phones in parlors and rooms with baths, conference room with kitchenette; free parking.*
Rates: *$68–$120; Continental breakfast. AE, MC, V.*
Restrictions: *No pets.*

Prince George Inn

Lined with bookshops, tobacconists, galleries, and antiques dens, Maryland Avenue, off State Circle, is one of Annapolis's prettiest streets. The Prince George Inn lies just around the corner from this little Left Bank, in a three-story 1884 brick town house that's now the province of Norma and Bill Grovermann. Seven years ago it was the first bed-and-breakfast to open in town; today Norma and Bill have thoroughly mastered the art of B&B, down to the canister of umbrellas for guests on rainy days. Norma, a habitué of estate sales and auctions, has toed a proper Victorian line in decorating the house. The floors are a maze of Oriental rugs, the parlor has a fireplace, and in a corner of the long sun porch she displays delicate turn-of-the-century children's clothing (which is for sale). Upstairs, the white-wicker room with a window alcove and the green-and-apricot room, with a Welsh coverlet on the bed, are favorites. But the fanciful decor of the Arabian Nights room might bring you exotic dreams. Norma's breakfasts often feature home-baked apple and lemon-curd tarts.

Address: *232 Prince George St., Annapolis, MD 21401, tel. 301/263-6418.*
Accommodations: *4 double rooms share 2 baths.*
Amenities: *Air-conditioning, TV in parlor.*
Rates: *$75; full breakfast. MC, V.*
Restrictions: *Smoking downstairs only, no pets, closed Jan. and part of Feb.*

St. Michael's Manor

Dusk is a good time to arrive at St. Michael's Manor, when there's a pale blanket of mist hanging over owner Joe Dick's vineyards and over the creek behind the house. Once inside guests might find Nancy Dick playing her antique organ and Joe offering his homemade wine in front of the roaring fire in the parlor hearth. The three bedrooms at the manor are furnished with quilts and seem homey rather than grand. In the morning you'll awake to find yourself on an inlet of the Chesapeake Bay, at the southern tip of Western Shore Maryland. After breakfast, stroll the manor's 10 acres or try the tire swing out front, then perhaps go paddling in the canoe, visit nearby St. Mary's City, or cruise to Point Lookout State Park on a bike. At the state park there are boat excursions to isolated Smith Island and swimming (before jellyfish season starts, in June). Thirty-five hundred Confederate soldiers died in prison at Point Lookout during the Civil War, which explains the monument across from the turn-off for St. Michael's Manor, and the vaguely haunted feeling of the place.

Address: *Scotland, MD 20687, tel. 301/872-4025.*
Accommodations: *1 double room with bath, 2 doubles share bath.*
Amenities: *Air-conditioning, 2 fireplaces in parlor; swimming pool, tire swing, bikes.*
Rates: *$35–$50; full breakfast. No credit cards.*
Restrictions: *Smoking downstairs only, no pets.*

Shaw's Fancy

haw's Fancy is a perfect bed-and-breakfast for midshipmen's drags—that's Naval Academy slang for dates who are invited to the annual Ring Dance or homecoming game. This brown-shingle 1902 Victorian at the heart of Annapolis, has a Greek Revival porch and porch swing (perfect for long good-byes). Inside, proprietors Judith Rem and Jack House, part-time federal workers, have sustained the romantic fantasy by filling the place with a splendid mixture of Art Nouveau and New Age prints and furnishings, which harmonize better than you might expect with the Victorian tiger-oak woodwork and green-tile gas fireplace. The effect is eccentric, airy, and hedonistic, a little like Berkeley come to Annapolis. The three guest rooms feature Victorian brass beds, and if you book the Shaw's special Romance Package, you get satin sheets, candlelight, armloads of fresh flowers, and chilled champagne—Judith says she picked up a lot of tips on such touches from the midshipmen themselves.

Address: *161 Green St., Annapolis, MD 21401, tel. 301/268-9750.*
Accommodations: *1 double room with bath, 1 double with shared bath, 1 suite.*
Amenities: *Air-conditioning, terrycloth robes; hot tub in garden.*
Rates: *$65–$100. No credit cards.*
Restrictions: *No smoking, no pets, 2-day minimum on special Annapolis weekends.*

Frederick and Thereabouts

In Frederick, about an hour's drive west of Baltimore and Washington, DC, Interstates 270 and 70 meet, and although the character of these thoroughfares has changed dramatically in the last 200 years (I–270 has become such a jungle of office parks that it's known as the Technology Corridor) it is historically appropriate to think of the Frederick area as a transportation hub. America's oldest federal turnpike, the National Road, ran through the town, which was founded in 1745 by Daniel Dulaney. Frederick grew up as a way station on the route west. Some settlers— in particular, those of German extraction—cut their journey short, unloaded their Conestoga wagons, and put down roots in town. To encourage settlement here, land speculators donated property for churches, resulting in a downtown of clustered spires, where there is a house of worship on almost every block. These, as well as the immaculately kept Federal and Victorian houses in Frederick's 34-block historic district, are well charted in a walking-tour brochure available at the visitors center, on Church Street.

The land around Frederick is dotted with farms and villages such as Woodsboro, whose single export and claim to fame is Rosebud Salve (good for almost anything that ails you); New Market, a mecca in the world of antiques, with 40 shops selling everything from rare books to baby spoons; Thurmont, just east of Catoctin Mountain National Park, where not revealing the location of nearby Camp David is a matter of civic pride (not to mention national security); and Emmitsburg, the site of a shrine to America's first native-born saint, Elizabeth Ann Seton. This area is ideal for biking and back-road exploring: Narrow lanes lead over covered bridges and past fruit stands and a handful of venerable country restaurants. Everywhere, historic markers tell tales of Civil War action along the Monocacy River, atop Sugarloaf and South mountains, and outside Sharpsburg, at Antietam.

The historic Potomac River forms the southern boundary of Frederick County. Towns such as Brunswick and Point of Rocks, which overlook the river, witnessed the simultaneous construction of the Chesapeake and Ohio canal and railroad. The train company won the race to link the eastern seaboard with the west, arriving at Cumberland, Maryland, in 1842, eight years before the canal. Today the C&O Canal's towpath is a 184-mile-long national park, highlighted by dramatic views of the Shenandoah and Potomac rivers, the Monocacy Aqueduct, and the ghost town of Four Locks.

Places to go, sights to see

Antietam (tel. 301/432–5124). Just outside Sharpsburg, in Washington County, is the Civil War battlefield where 87,000 Union soldiers under General George B. McClellan attacked General Robert E. Lee's 41,000-man army of Northern Virginia. Twenty-three thousand lives later the North had won the day, prompting President Lincoln to deliver the Emancipation Proclamation. But Antietam is remembered not as a Union victory, but as the scene of the ugliest carnage in the history of American warfare. The visitors center shows an orientation film and provides maps.

Catoctin Mountain National Park and Cunningham Falls State Park (tel. 301/271–7574). Franklin Roosevelt established a presidential retreat here in the Catoctin Mountains called Shangri-la, which later came to be known as Camp David. Here you'll also find Cunningham Falls, a man-made lake, miles of hiking trails, two campgrounds, and rewarding fly-fishing on Hunting Creek.

Frederick. Visitors to this pleasant town should not be deterred by the urban sprawl that surrounds it. The city's charm lies downtown, where visitors (April through November) will find the *Old City Hall*, built as a courthouse in 1862 (tel. 301/694–1440); the *Barbara Frietchie House* (tel. 301/698–4070), a reproduction of the Civil War heroine's home; the *Francis Scott Key Museum* (tel. 301/663–8687), built in 1799; the *Frederick Historical Society Museum* (tel. 301/663–1188), with displays of antique dolls, Native American artifacts, and Amelung glass; the *Hessian Barracks* (tel. 301/663–8687), on the grounds of the Maryland School for the Deaf, constructed in 1777 as a prison for British prisoners of war; and the *Brunswick Rail Museum* (tel. 301/834–7100).

Frederick County covered bridges. There are three, all in the Thurmont area, all built in the mid-1800s: Loy's Bridge, on Route 77, which crosses Owens Creek; the Roddy Road Bridge, also over Owens Creek, on Route 15; and, on Utica Road a mile east of Route 15, the Utica Mills Bridge, which once spanned the Monocacy River, before being swept downstream by the Johnstown Flood of 1889.

Lilypons Water Gardens (tel. 301/874–5133; in DC, 202/428–0686). This fascinating hatchery in Buckeystown, named for an opera star, is a prime supplier of exotic fish and aquatic plants. Its landscaped ponds bloom with lotuses and water lilies between Memorial Day and Labor Day. Lilypons catalogues are available in the aquarium shop, and such special events as jousting tournaments and lotus festivals are held regularly.

New Market. No one knows precisely why this immensely friendly village cast its lot with the antiques trade, but today there are some 40 shops peddling aged items, in a town that is only a few streets wide. *Mealey's Restaurant* (tel. 301/865–5488), New Market's other attraction, occupies a Georgian brick building on Main Street and serves Maryland cuisine.

Rose Hill Manor. This Colonial estate dating from the 1790s was home to Maryland's first governor, Thomas Johnson, who nominated his close friend George Washington as commander-in-chief of the Continental Army. Today the estate's 43 acres encompass a county park and a children's museum (tel. 301/694–1648) where youngsters explore hands-on historic displays.

South Mountain and the Washington Monument. At the summit of South Mountain, accessible by car along Alternate Route 40, lies the nation's first monument to George Washington, constructed by the citizens of Boonsboro in a single day. Nearby are the Dahlgren Chapel, built in 1882, and Old South Mountain Inn. Now a restaurant (tel. 301/432–6155), the former stagecoach stop and hostelry was seized by John Brown just before he raided the Harper's Ferry arsenal.

Tourist Information

Frederick Visitors Center (19 E. Church St., Frederick 21701, tel. 301/663–8687). Ask for the brochure "Inns of the Blue Ridge." **Maryland Office of Tourism Development** (217 E. Redwood St., Baltimore 21202, tel. 301/333–6611).

Reservation Services

Bed & Breakfast Accommodations of Frederick and Western Maryland (7945 Worman's Mill Rd., Frederick 21701, tel. 301/694–5926). **Maryland Reservation Center** (66 Maryland Ave., Annapolis 21401, tel. 301/263–9084). **The Traveller in Maryland, Inc.** (Box 2277, Annapolis 21401, tel. 301/269–6232).

The Inn at Antietam

nyone who's ever visited a Civil War battlefield knows how haunting the site is, how the dawns seem to echo with the sound of bugles and gunfire, how at night the voices of soldiers rise like mist from the glades. Antietam, which surrounds the dusty little town of Sharpsburg, is surely one of the most stirring of such places, for it was here on a September day in 1862 that one of the worst battles of the Civil War claimed 23,000 lives in a single bloody day.

Just north of town there's a national cemetery, with a Daniel Chester French statue called "The Private Soldier" serving as headstone for 5,000 Union dead. Adjoining the graveyard on a hillock facing the hazy Blue Ridge is the Inn at Antietam, a 1908 Queen Anne cottage with a wraparound porch, shaded by a giant silver maple and set amid fields where horses graze. Owners Cal and Betty Fairbourn have restored the place in the style of the Civil War period, filling the parlor with Rococo Revival walnut furniture, the porch with white wicker, and guest rooms with Eastlake dressers and beds.

The Fairbourns, who'd restored another house in the area before moving into this one five years ago, enlisted the aid of a decorator here, which resulted in beautifully finished guest rooms. The converted smokehouse, at the rear, has a large stone fireplace, a sitting room lined with beaded paneling, and a loft bed. The master suite, another favorite, has an 1880s four-poster bed; matching spread, curtains, and wallpaper; and Battenberg lace.

After breakfast, served in the formal dining room on Royal Copenhagen china, Cal and Betty can offer tips on how best to see the battlefield— on foot, by bicycle, or even on cross-country skis. The surrounding area is also surprisingly rich in good restaurants, such as the Inn at Blackford's Crossing; the Yellow Brick Bank, in nearby Shepherdstown, West Virginia; and, for German food, the Cafe Berlin, in Boonsboro.

Address: *220 E. Main St., Box 119, Sharpsburg, MD 21782, tel. 301/432-6601.*
Accommodations: *2 double rooms with baths, 3 suites.*
Amenities: *Air-conditioning, TV in smokehouse suite.*
Rates: *$65–$150; Continental breakfast. AE.*
Restrictions: *Smoking in designated areas, no pets, 2-night minimum on weekends and holidays, closed Dec. 22–Jan. 3.*

Spring Bank

When you ask Beverly and Ray Compton why they bought their cavernous, 100-year-old farmhouse just north of Frederick some 10 years ago, Beverly has a disarming answer: "We bought it to live and be happy in." And indeed it seems this warm couple is happy here, though the road to inhabiting the house was paved with hard work interspersed with joyful architectural surprises. While restoring the Italianate and Gothic Revival structure, the Comptons found details that seemed too good to be true: engraved designs in the glass of the front door, random-width hardwood floors, faux-marble mantels, antique William Morris wallpaper, and a wet-plaster fresco on the ceiling of the old billiard room—now a first-floor guest room. Some of these design points had been damaged over the years, but after a thorough cleaning, they stand as witnesses to another time and lifestyle. Ray is the son of a Chadd's Ford, Pennsylvania, antiques dealer, and perhaps his penchant for restoration is in his blood; last year he received an award from the Historical Society of Frederick for the work he's done here. Beverly haunts local auctions and flea markets, and during the week she commutes to a federal job in Rockville.

The brick house is built in textbook-perfect telescoping style, with porches stretching across the front and along two stories on the side. The backyard gives way to farmland planted in alfalfa; the 20th century rarely intrudes at Spring Bank, despite its proximity to Highway 15. Choose your room upon arrival; the converted billiard parlor and the Sleigh Bedroom on the second floor are favorites, both sparely decorated with Eastlake-style antiques. In keeping with the 19th-century ethos the baths have not been extensively modernized—no whirlpool tubs or French magnifying mirrors here.

For breakfast, the Comptons serve homemade breads with local jams and plenty of information on nearby auctions, held almost every day.

Address: *7945 Worman's Mill Rd., Frederick, MD 21701, tel. 301/694-0440.*
Accommodations: *1 double room with bath, 5 doubles share 2 baths.*
Amenities: *Air-conditioning, cable TV in parlor.*
Rates: *$70–$85; Continental breakfast. No credit cards.*
Restrictions: *No smoking, no pets, 2-night minimum on holiday weekends and weekends Apr.–mid-June and mid-Sept.–mid-Nov.*

The Inn at Buckeystown

Buckeystown, on the Monocacy River, is a lovely collection of Federal and Victorian homes; the inn, built in 1897, is the grandest thing in town. It's a white frame building with three stories (one might say layers, since the building looks like a wedding cake) on a 2½-acre lawn with azaleas. Owner Dan Pelz has created a true country inn crammed with eccentric memorabilia, including an American Indian collection, vintage postcards of Harper's Ferry, and Victorian furniture. Every day of the week an evening meal is served family style, with such dishes as consommé Madrilene, London broil in port sauce, and blueberry parfait. Rooms on the third floor are decorated according to themes—including the Far West and the Children's Corner. Just down the road is the annex, a suite with two bedrooms, a fireplace, and a hot tub. Still, for the traditional inn feeling, we suggest the second-floor rooms in the main building, in particular the Fireplace Room and Love Room.

Address: *Buckeystown, MD 21717, tel. 301/874-5755.*
Accommodations: *4 double rooms with baths, 4 doubles share a bath; 1 double suite.*
Amenities: *Air-conditioning, TV with VCR in annex.*
Rates: *$125–$185, annex suite $225–$375; dinner and full breakfast. AE, MC, V.*
Restrictions: *No smoking in common rooms, no pets, 2-night minimum on holiday weekends and Oct. and Dec. weekends.*

The Marameade

Things aren't finely tuned at this inn, and guests must fend for themselves. The elderly innkeeper, Helen Collins, runs the Marameade solo, with a high school breakfast chef. If you arrive in the early evening you may find that Helen has already retired, leaving you to find your own way to a room and root around for fresh towels. Still the inn, with its mansard roof, is an eminently attractive place, begun around 1800, and nestled in 27 acres on a hillside in the Middletown Valley. There are massive trees, a pond in back, and a delightful flagstone porch. Once you've bedded down under a canopy with several old quilts, you'll find the guest rooms comfortable, and in the morning the honking geese will make sure you don't sleep through breakfast. Helen, originally from the Washington, DC, area, is a pleasure to talk to. For amusement she recommends simple local pleasures such as a dip in the pond or a visit to the farmer's stand across Route 40. For those who wish to venture farther afield Helen says, "Everything good is west"—including Antietam; South Mountain; and Shepherdstown, West Virginia.

Address: *2439 Old National Pike, Middletown, MD 21769, tel. 301/371-4214.*
Accommodations: *5 double rooms with baths, 3 doubles share 2 baths.*
Amenities: *Air-conditioning, TV in sun-room.*
Rates: *$45–$80; full breakfast. MC, V.*
Restrictions: *No pets.*

The National Pike

The National Pike lies just up Main Street in New Market from the Strawberry Inn, and right across from Mealey's Restaurant. Built in three sections, between 1796 and 1804, this Federal-style brown-brick building was topped with a tower at the turn of the 20th century. Tom and Terry Rimel are the proprietors; he's a master at slate roofing, which sparked his interest in restoring old homes. The two have done a fine job on the National Pike, whose parlor has Williamsburg-blue paneling, a fireplace, and two armchairs for watching the action on the historic turnpike out front. There is also an organ, played by their son, who became organist for the local Episcopal church at the age of 10. The two snug guest rooms in the rear section have brass-and-oak beds and are decorated in a country style; they can also function as a suite. The long backyard has azalea gardens, a smokehouse, and carriage house from the 1830s.

Address: *9–11 W. Main St., Box 299, New Market, MD 21774, tel. 301/865–5055.*
Accommodations: *2 double rooms with baths, 1 double suite.*
Amenities: *Air-conditioning.*
Rates: *$75–$100; full breakfast. MC, V.*
Restrictions: *No pets, 2-night minimum on New Market Days (Sept.) and first weekend in Dec.*

The Strawberry Inn

New Market is the quintessential Maryland village, with a shady Main Street that was probably busier 200 years ago than it is today. Once, New Market busied itself outfitting wagonloads of settlers headed west on the National Pike. Today the town has taken a new lease on life, dealing in the past, with 40 antiques shops in the 12-block downtown area—making it the self-styled Antiques Capital of Maryland.

Ed and Jane Rossig bought their Victorianized 1850s farmhouse on Main Street as an investment, but when the mayor of the town persuaded them to open the house to overnight guests in 1973 the Strawberry Inn became one of the first bed-and-breakfasts on the eastern seaboard. Though the white frame house looks tiny from the outside, it holds five guest rooms and several shops' worth of Victorian antiques; breakfast is served on the wide deck. The downstairs suite has a private porch, twin beds, and a pullout sofa; and upstairs, the popular Strawberry Room has a brass bed and rose wallpaper. Out back is Ed's art gallery, in a log house transported from another part of New Market.

Address: *17 Main St., Box 237, New Market, MD 21774, tel. 301/865–3318.*
Accommodations: *4 double rooms with baths, 1 suite.*
Amenities: *Air-conditioning.*
Rates: *$70–$85; Continental breakfast. No credit cards.*
Restrictions: *No pets.*

The Turning Point

The Turning Point, occupying a 1910 estate with a sweeping front lawn, is known locally for having one of the area's best restaurants. The hillside would be picture-perfect but for the mini shopping mall that's sprung up like a modern toadstool on its flank. Nonetheless, the grounds are lovely, with sundials, a barbecue, and lawn chairs scattered hither and yon. You enter the inn by way of a white-column porch and cross a carpeted foyer to reach the two dining rooms, the parlor, and the sun deck. The restaurant's menu offers a sophisticated mix, including blackened swordfish, broiled Delmonico steak Espagnole, and sweetbreads Argentine style. The five rooms upstairs were restored by a retired Frederick-area contractor and his wife and are managed by resident innkeepers Suzanne and Charlie Seymour. Decorated with a harmonic blend of antiques and reproduction furniture, the rooms are extremely comfortable. Favorites are the Palladian-windowed Room with a View, the Country Room, and the cozy Victorian Room.

Address: *3406 Urbana Pike, Frederick, MD 21701, tel. 301/874-2421.*
Accommodations: *5 double rooms with baths.*
Amenities: *Restaurant, air-conditioning.*
Rates: *$75–$85; full breakfast. MC, V.*
Restrictions: *Smoking only in living room, no pets, closed Mon.*

Off the Beaten Track

The Admiral Fell Inn

Funky chic is perhaps the best way to describe Fell's Point, a historic waterfront section of Baltimore where hulking warehouses cast long shadows on the narrow cobblestone streets, tramp steamers dock at the old City Pier, and the bars don't close until late. At the center of this Maryland Macao lies the Admiral Fell Inn, an assemblage of four buildings built between 1770 and 1910 that once housed a vinegar-bottling plant. Rest assured the place has since been fumigated; in fact it's been handsomely renovated and ingeniously converted into a 38-room inn with a restaurant and pub in the cellar. The rooms vary in shape, are decorated with Federal-style reproductions and antiques, and offer views of the erratic rooftops of Fell's Point. A suite and three of the rooms have whirlpool baths and 15 have two double beds. Although there are other, more quietly graceful lodgings in town (such as the Shirley Madison Hotel), no place is more convenient to Baltimore's nightlife, and none better evokes this port city's past.

Address: *888 S. Broadway, Baltimore, MD 21231, tel. 301/522-7377 or 800/292-4667; fax 301/522-0707.*
Accommodations: *37 double rooms with baths (5 nonsmoking), 1 suite.*
Amenities: *Restaurant, air-conditioning, TV and phones in rooms, conference room, room service; parking, free van service in city 7 AM–10:30 PM.*
Rates: *$90–$145; Continental breakfast. AE, MC, V.*
Restrictions: *No pets.*

The Atlantic Hotel

The historic district in Berlin, Maryland, got a significant boost when a group of local investors renovated and opened the town's Victorian centerpiece—the Atlantic Hotel, built in 1895. This three-story, bracketed brick inn just 7 miles from Assateague National Seashore offers beachcombers a pleasant alternative to Ocean City's motels. The 16 guest rooms lining a wide central corridor are decorated with Oriental and floral-pattern rugs, tasseled draperies, Tiffany-style lamps, and antique double beds. Rooms 10 and 14, on the north and south ends, are notable for their spaciousness and Main Street views. Downstairs there's a companionable piano bar and a fancy restaurant whose menu features pricey delicacies such as roast duck Chambord. And you won't mind not having TV in your room when you discover the town's most recent addition: a restored, Spanish Mission–style Old Globe movie house, which shows classics exclusively.

Address: *2 N. Main St., Berlin, MD 21811, tel. 301/641-3589.*
Accommodations: *16 double rooms with baths.*
Amenities: *Restaurant, air-conditioning, phones in bedrooms.*
Rates: *$60–$125; Continental breakfast. MC, V.*
Restrictions: *No pets.*

Chanceford Hall

What is a spruce little town like Snow Hill, Maryland, doing in among the chicken farms of the Delmarva Peninsula? For the answer, look to the narrow but deep Pocomoke River, which in the 17th and 18th centuries made Snow Hill a bustling port, frequented by tall-masted schooners sailing in from the Chesapeake. Today, if you like, you can stay at Chanceford Hall, a bed-and-breakfast inn that would have pleased any visiting Colonial dignitary. The mansion was constructed in three stages, beginning with the Georgian front section in 1759. Two hundred and thirty years later a pair of old-house restorers from Milwaukee, Thelma and Mike Driscoll, moved in and turned Chanceford Hall into a showplace. The Federal-style mantels, painted in cool Williamsburg greens and blues, match the moldings; and there are merino-wool mattress pads and down comforters on the lace-canopy beds. The house has seven working fireplaces and reproduction furniture crafted by Mike himself. Thelma welcomes guests with wine and hors d'oeuvres in the sitting room and will lend bikes or explain where to rent canoes for river exploring.

Address: *209 W. Federal St., Snow Hill, MD 21863, tel. 301/632–2231.*
Accommodations: *4 double rooms with baths, 1 suite.*
Amenities: *Air-conditioning, TV with VCR in common room, dinner on request; lap pool.*
Rates: *$90–$115; full breakfast. No credit cards.*
Restrictions: *No pets.*

The Lighthouse Club at Fager's Island

Perhaps none but the brave would endure the crowds here in season, but for guests at the Lighthouse Club on Isle of Wight Bay, a simple, elegant side of Ocean City exists, too.

Probably the most luxurious place to stay in the area, with extremely reasonable off-season prices, the octagonal Lighthouse Club's 23 pie-shape kitchenette suites are decorated à la Florida by Lawrence Peabody, with heart-shape whirlpools, marble baths, wet bars, and access to a nearby swimming pool and health club. Eight of the rooms are Lightkeeper Suites, preferred for their third-floor location, gas fireplaces, private decks, and four-poster beds. Next door are Fager's Restaurant, where every dusk the *1812 Overture* is played, the cannon timed to the moment of sunset; and the baby-blue Coconut Malorie Hotel, also owned by John Fager, who has filled the place with his passion—Haitian art.

Address: *56th St., in the Bay at Fager's Island, Ocean City, MD 21842, tel. 301/524–5400 or 800/767–6060, fax 301/723–2055.*
Accommodations: *23 suites.*
Amenities: *Restaurant, room service, air-conditioning, cable TV/VCR in 8 suites, phones in suites, turn-down service, conference room.*
Rates: *$90–$220; Continental breakfast. AE, DC, MC, V.*
Restrictions: *No pets.*

Vandiver Inn

Begin a trip to the Vandiver Inn by mastering the pronunciation of the town where it lies; it's Havre (rhymes with *cadaver*) de Grace, located where the Susquehanna River enters the Chesapeake Bay. The Marquis de Lafayette named Havre de Grace during the American Revolution; in the War of 1812 the British leveled the town, which explains its post-Colonial architecture. Indeed, on Union Avenue Victoriana prevails— and nowhere so flamboyantly as at the Vandiver Inn, a lime-green Queen Anne cottage built in 1886 by a Havre de Grace mayor. Inside there's a display of memorabilia (including his bride's high-button shoes), a grand piano, and large bedrooms. The Rodgers Room, which opens onto a porch, is a favorite. On weekends a prix-fixe dinner is prepared by innkeeper Charles Rothwell, an honors graduate of Baltimore's International Culinary Arts Institute. And although Havre de Grace is hardly cosmopolitan it has its own eccentric diversions, including a Decoy Museum, a historic lighthouse, and a restored 1840 lock house, built to service the Susquehanna and Tidewater Canal.

Address: *301 S. Union Ave., Havre de Grace, MD 21078, tel. 301/939–5200.*
Accommodations: *6 double rooms with baths, 2 doubles share bath.*
Amenities: *Restaurant, air-conditioning, swimming pool.*
Rates: *$65–$85; full breakfast. AE, MC, V.*
Restrictions: *No pets.*

Virginia

Virginia

MD

WEST VIRGINIA

0 — 30 miles
0 — 45 km

N

Winchester
Berryville
Bluer
Millwood
White Post
Uppervil
Strasburg
Paris
Middlebu
Woodstock
Front Royal
Flint Hill
Mt. Jackson
Washington
New Market
Luray
W.
Sperryville
Stanley
Rawley Springs
SHENANDOAH NATIONAL PARK
Harrisonburg
Culpeper
Syria
250
Rapidan
Churchville
81
Barboursville
Orange
Staunton
Gordonsville
Warm Springs
Waynesboro
Charlottesville
Trevilians
Hot Springs
Rockfish Gap
L A
Millboro
Nellysford
Raphine
Lexington
Scottsville
River
64
Covington
James
60
Bent Creek
Lynchburg
Appomattox
Amelia
Farmville
Roanoke
Burkeville
Blackstone
Blue Ridge Pkwy
Smith Mountain Lake
Altavista
85
Rocky Mount
Brookneal
Chase City
Martinsville
South Boston
58
Danville
Lake Gaston

MASSANUTTEN MTN.

SHENANDOAH VALLEY

Skyline Dr.

BLUE RIDGE MTS.

Northern Virginia

*Think of northern Virginia as the Colonists' prize. Given
the hostile Indians and mosquito-infested swamps they
encountered around Jamestown, it's sometimes hard to
fathom why they bothered to stay on in North America at
all; but wander farther up the rivers into the verdant fields
and rolling hills of northern Virginia, and the reasons
become clear.*

*The region nurtured great numbers of American
revolutionaries, and almost half the battles of the Civil
War were waged in this countryside. Nowadays, though, it's
refugees from Washington's bureaucratic wars who are
claiming their rewards in northern Virginia. With the
District's shiny office parks and shopping malls
encroaching from the east, development is the area's only
enemy, one being tenuously held at bay.*

*The fast track to this Eden west of DC is Route 66 (except
on Friday and Sunday afternoon), but cognoscenti opt for
Route 50, which in an easy hour of driving puts you in
Middleburg, the capital of hunt country. This discreet town
breathes—and caters to—old money, with a collection of
upscale galleries, antiques stores, and gun shops, with
names like Dominion Saddlery, The Chronicle of the Horse,
and Thoroughbreds. Hunt season in Loudoun, Fauquier,
Clarke, and Rappahannock counties begins in late October
with an opening meet, peaks around Thanksgiving, and
continues into March, provided the ground doesn't freeze.
Experienced riders can join in, but most content
themselves by watching the colorful proceedings. A master
of the hunt presides, while tailgate picnickers slosh down
coffee and Bloody Marys; then 20 or 30 hounds explode
across the fields, followed by the handsomely outfitted
riders. To follow the hunt, keeping in sight of the horses,
a map is helpful, available from the Virginia Department
of Highways and Transportation (Information Services*

Division, 1221 E. Broad St., Richmond 23219, tel. 804/786–2838).

Frankly, most hunt country visitors prefer to spend their time window-shopping at Middleburg real-estate offices and driving Loudoun County's back roads. (Route 734 from Aldie to Bluemont is highly recommended, provided you're on the alert for careering Maseratis and BMWs.)

Northeast of Middleburg lies Leesburg, founded about 1760, which remained in Federal hands during the Civil War and thus retains much of its Colonial architecture. Leesburg's spruced-up storefronts and row houses are now functioning as restaurants and shops.

South and west of Leesburg, a 30-mile corridor between the hamlets of Flint Hill and Syria make for peak auto idling, too. Here the Blue Ridge asserts itself on the horizon as the roads wind up into the foothills. Fauquier County offers horseback riding in Shenandoah National Park, with mounts to be claimed at the Marriott Ranch; and all across the countryside, wineries such as Prince Michel and Dominion are flourishing.

At the southern border of the area sits Fredericksburg, boyhood stomping ground of George Washington, and hotly contested during the Civil War. Between 1862 and 1864 four major battles were fought—at Chancellorsville, Wilderness, Spotsylvania Court House, and just south of Fredericksburg itself—resulting in more than 17,000 casualties. On almost any fair weekend costumed Civil War re-enactors loiter on Fredericksburg's streets or down by the Rappahannock River. Tourists are greeted with cool stares—it seems those of us without muskets are the curiosities.

Alexandria, a mere 10-minute drive from Washington, DC, was surveyed in the late 1740s by a lad named George Washington. Tobacco was shipped from here to the smoky coffeehouses of London, and dissident Scots rankling over the Act of Union with England flocked here (which explains Alexandria's continuing fascination with things Scottish). Early in December Old Town holds its Scottish Walk, when clan banners stream from the windows of Federal row houses and the clamor of bagpipes echoes off the cobblestones.

A walk along Alexandria's shady lanes takes you by handsome brick homes built in the late 1700s and offers peeks into mazelike courtyards. Shoppers will find present-day Alexandria as mercantile as ever; there's an arts-and-crafts center on the historic waterfront and restaurants aplenty, including venerable Gadsby's Tavern (tel. 703/548-1288), which has dispensed spirits and victuals since 1795.

Places to go, sights to see

Alexandria Archaeology Museum (tel. 703/383-4399) preserves the Colonial treasures hidden beneath the paving stones of Old Town.

Carlyle House (Alexandria, tel. 703/549-2997), built in 1752 by a Scottish shipowner, is considered by some the true birthplace of the Revolution, because it was here that British General Braddock conceived of a Colonial taxation scheme that resulted in the detested Stamp Act.

Christ Church (Alexandria, tel. 703/549-1450). Its parishioners included George Washington and Robert E. Lee.

Gadsby's Tavern Museum (Alexandria, tel. 703/838-4242), next door to the tavern where five U.S. presidents signed the register. The Metropolitan Museum in New York City made off with the tavern doorway, then returned it in 1949.

Gunston Hall (15 mi south of Alexandria, tel. 703/550-9220), the Georgian mansion of George Mason, author of the first Virginia constitution and Virginia Declaration of Rights, was built around 1755, with a Palladian parlor and Chinese-inspired dining room.

Historic Fredericksburg. Sights include the *Mary Washington House*, bought by a dutiful son for his retired mother, the *Silversmith's* and *Hugh Mercer Apothecary* shops, and *Rising Sun Tavern*.

Kenmore (tel. 703/373-3381). This Colonial mansion near Fredericksburg, famous for its decorative plaster moldings, was the home of George

Washington's sister, Betty. Its drawing room has been called one of the 100 most beautiful rooms in America.

Manassas National Battlefield Park (tel. 703/745–7107) was the scene of the First and Second Battles of Manassas, during which the Confederacy lost 11,456 men and the Union 17,170. This is where General Thomas J. Jackson's nickname was coined, when a soldier cried, "There stands Jackson like a stone wall! Rally behind the Virginians!"

Morven Park (tel. 703/777–2414) is a handsome Greek Revival mansion near Leesburg, built by a governor of Virginia, with a carriage museum and frequent special events, including steeplechase races.

Mount Vernon (tel. 703/780–2000). In its owner's words, "No estate in United America is more pleasantly situated than this." George Washington's Mount Vernon is 10 miles south of Alexandria. The museum holds Jean-Antoine Houdon's bust of Washington, as well as the first president's sunglasses and sword.

Oatlands (near Leesburg, tel. 703/777–3174), a Classical Revival mansion, was built in 1803 by George Carter, grandson of the Williamsburg planter, "King" Carter. Its terraced formal gardens are considered some of the most distinguished in the state.

Trinity Church, west of Middleburg, in the hamlet of Upperville, is one of the most beautiful Episcopal churches in America, the style being adapted from French country stone churches of the 12th and 13th centuries.

Waterford, a village north of Leesburg so reminiscent of rural England that it could tug at the heart of any Anglophile, is, from one end to the other, a National Historic Site.

White's Ferry. The historic ferry across the Potomac at the edge of Leesburg, is the six-car tugboat, *General Jubal Early.* Dickerson, MD, tel. 301/349–5200, fare $4. Runs daily 5 AM–11 PM.

Restaurants

Bleu Rock, on Route 211 between Washington and Sperryville (tel. 703/987–3190), serves nouveau French and American cuisine and has five rooms for rent. **Davis Street Ordinary,** in Culpeper (tel. 703/825–3909), in a former hardware store, has a fireplace and a player piano. At **4 and 20 Blackbirds,** in Flint Hill (tel. 703/675–1111), all the pastry is baked on the premises. **Jordan's,** on Loudoun Street in Lessburg (tel. 703/777–1471), serves contemporary American food.

Tourist Information

Alexandria Tourist Council (221 King St., Alexandria 22314, tel. 703/838–4948). **Fairfax County Tourism and Convention Bureau** (8300 Boone Blvd., Suite 450, Tysons Corner, Vienna 22182, tel. 703/790–3329). **Fredericksburg Visitors Center** (706 Caroline St., Fredericksburg 22401, tel. 703/373–1776). **Loudoun County Tourist Center** (108-D S. St., SE, Market Station, Leesburg 22075, tel. 703/777–0518, 0519). **Virginia Division of Tourism** (202 N. 9th St., Richmond 23219, tel. 804/786–4484). **Winchester Visitors Center** (1360 S. Pleasant Valley Rd., Winchester 22601, tel. 703/662–4118).

Reservation Services

Bed & Breakfast Guild of Rappahannock (Rte. 1, Box 2080, Flint Hill 22627). **Blue Ridge Bed & Breakfast Reservation Service** (Rocks & Rills, Rte. 2, Box 3895, Berryville 22611, tel. 703/955–1246). **Princely Bed & Breakfast Reservation Service** (819 Prince St., Alexandria 22314, tel. 703/683–2159).

The Ashby Inn

West of Middleburg and Upperville along Route 50, the turnoff for minuscule Paris comes upon you suddenly; half the travelers looking for this hamlet in a hollow below the road probably miss it completely and end up crossing Ashby Gap or the Shenandoah River—not bad detours except that they delay your arrival at the Ashby Inn. The inn has the air of a way station in the wilderness where you'd be happy enough for a slab of overcooked prime rib. Instead, armed with reservations and a somewhat loose grip on your billfold, you're treated to some of rural Virginia's most sophisticated food, prepared by chef Paul Shell and masterminded by innkeeper Roma Sherman. The menu is changed nightly, though some Ashby favorites, like sautéed mixed mushrooms, duckling braised with turnips, and profiteroles stuffed with homemade honey vanilla ice cream, routinely reappear. Dinner runs about $70 for two.

Perhaps the only danger in staying at the inn is that dinner will leave you too blissfully comatose to appreciate your room. There are just six of them, furnished with a spareness that is a calming contrast to the rich food. Quilts, blanket chests, rag rugs, and the occasional cannonball bed set the country tone, though in every case, the views are the chief enhancement. As morning light shines through the windows, you'll spy the garden, the Blue Ridge foot-hills, lowing cows, and other pastoral delights. Guests book many months ahead to stay in the Fan Room, which has two skylights and a glorious fan window opening onto a private balcony. Others find contentment in the dormer rooms, tucked under the green tin roof.

Roma and her husband, John, are generally too busy during dinner to chat, but at breakfast—featuring fresh eggs cooked to order and succulent muffins—you might get to know your hosts. Roma left advertising for innkeeping, and John, once a House Ways and Means Committee staffer, still writes speeches for Democratic politicians between stints as the Ashby Inn's maître d'é.

Nearby, there are vineyards to tour, hiking trails, antiques markets, and, of course, the Middleburg hunt scene. Many come to the Ashby Inn only to dine and bed down, returning refreshed to the metropolis next day, tempted to chuck it all and open an inn in some spot as idyllic as this.

Address: *Rte. 1, Box 2A, Paris, VA 22130, tel. 703/592–3900.*
Accommodations: *4 double rooms with baths, 2 doubles with sinks share a bath.*
Amenities: *Restaurant, air-conditioning.*
Rates: *$80–$115; full breakfast. AE, MC, V.*
Restrictions: *No pets.*

The Conyers House

If you want to climb Old Rag, make the scene at the meeting of the Rappahannock Hunt, have a group of companionable dogs lead you to a swimming hole (which a local church also uses for River Jordan–style baptisms), or go hill-hopping on horseback, the Conyers House will suit you like a pair of jodhpurs. No inn in northern Virginia is more remote; it lies on a narrow country road southwest of Sperryville and shouldn't be attempted in the dark without directions. This is part of its charm—but only a part.

The innkeepers, Norman and Sandra Cartwright-Brown, are responsible for the rest, for the Conyers House is a very personal place, stuffed with family mementos and curios the two have collected in their wanderings. In the Bartholomew Conyers guest room, there's a stuffed zebra head and a Texas bed with—since everything's big in Texas—seven-foot posts. Jarring, you might wonder? Surprisingly not. One imagines that Sandra Cartwright-Brown could design a miniature golf course and still have it turn out tasteful.

She and Norman bought the house, which was a general store in 1810 and a hippie commune in the 1970s, as a summer retreat from their Chevy Chase home. The beige frame structure sits on the side of Walden Mountain. There are four porches and eight working fireplaces, seven of which are in the bedrooms. In ad-

dition to the six rooms in the main building, there's Springhouse Cottage and Hill House out back, where pets are allowed, not to mention a stall for your horse.

With prior arrangement, Sandra and Norman serve a six-course dinner in the gigantic dining room with such entreés as trout; medallions of veal with cider, Calvados, and cream; and charcoal-grilled salmon. The $62.50 price per person includes four wines, tax, and service. They can also direct you to wonderful local restaurants.

The Conyers House has an air of un-stuffy, slightly gone-to-seed elegance. It's the kind of place where you can appear for breakfast in jeans, disappear for the day canoeing on the Shenandoah, and return confident of being invited to sip a preprandial sherry.

Address: *Rte. 1, Box 157, Slate Mills Rd., Sperryville, VA 22740, tel. 703/987–8025, fax 703/987–8907.*
Accommodations: *7 double rooms with baths, 1 suite.*
Amenities: *Air-conditioning, TV/ VCR in common areas and suite, VCR in Springhouse and Hill House, double whirlpool bath in Hill House; riding arranged.*
Rates: *$90–$195; full breakfast, afternoon tea. No credit cards.*
Restrictions: *No smoking in bedrooms, 2-night minimum Oct.– mid-Nov. and on holiday weekends.*

The Inn at Little Washington

In 1978 Patrick O'Connell, master chef at the Inn at Little Washington, and his partner, Reinhardt Lynch, opened a restaurant that grew into a legend, in a village of 150 in the eastern foothills of the Blue Ridge.

From the outside the three-story, white frame building looks like any quiet southern hotel; only the Chinese Chippendale balustrade on the second-floor porch suggests the decorative fantasy within. The sumptuous interior is the work of British designer Joyce Evans, who has designed theatrical sets and rooms in English royal houses. The settees in the inn bear as many as 13 elegantly mismatched pillows each; the garden, with crab apple trees, fountain, and fish pond, cries out to be used as a backdrop in *The Importance of Being Earnest.* One bedroom has a bed with a bold plaid spread, shaded by a floral-print half-canopy— and, amazingly, the mélange works. And in the slate-floored dining room with Robert Morris wallpaper, a fabric-swathed ceiling makes guests feel like pashas romantically sequestered in a tent.

Much has been written about Chef O'Connell's food, all of it giddily rhapsodic. The menu, which changes nightly, makes compelling reading itself, and the five course dinner costs $88 per person on weekends, $68 weekdays, not including wine and drinks.

Clearly the inn, with its staff of 40, is a place for indulgence, and anyone unwilling to succumb to it—both psychologically and financially— should opt for humbler digs. But judging from the waiting list, there are many unabashed hedonists out there (among them famous faces, who add juice to the already electric atmosphere in the dining rooms). Be sure to come with a sense of fun, as the star in a real-life theater piece with fantastical trappings, *grâce à* O'Connell and Lynch.

Address: *Middle and Main Sts., Washington, VA 22747, tel. 703/675–3800, fax 703/675–3100.*
Accommodations: *8 double rooms with baths, 2 suites.*
Amenities: *Restaurant, 24-hour room service, air-conditioning and phones in rooms, whirlpool baths and separate double showers in suites.*
Rates: *$210–$410; Continental breakfast. MC, V.*
Restrictions: *No pets, closed Tues.*

The Bailiwick Inn

Anne and Ray Smith named their Greek Revival town house the Bailiwick because it stands across the street from the historic Fairfax County Courthouse, built around 1800 at the intersection of Ox Road and the Little River Turnpike. Today these two busy roads are still major arteries for western DC suburbs, which makes the Bailiwick's location prime for business travelers. The oldest portion of the house was constructed shortly after the courthouse, and the building's red-brick and green-shuttered 18th-century look has been retained. Inside you'll find carefully crafted reproduction furniture and 14 rooms. In the Lee Room, the bedspread's pattern comes from the White House of the Confederacy. Other chambers re-create surround- ings the founding fathers would feel at home in, though they'd marvel at the 1990s bathrooms. Don't miss Ray's Robert E. Lee eggs in mushroom sauce, or the whimsical portraits in the front parlor, depicting Anne and Ray as 18th-century innkeepers.

Address: *4023 Chain Bridge Rd., Fairfax, VA 22030, tel. 703/691–2266.*
Accommodations: *13 double rooms with baths, 1 suite.*
Amenities: *Air-conditioning, whirlpool tubs in 2 rooms, fireplaces in 4 rooms, 1 room accessible to wheelchairs.*
Rates: *$95–$175; full breakfast, afternoon tea. AE, MC, V.*
Restrictions: *No smoking indoors, no pets.*

Brookside

Even if Carol and Gary Konkel weren't such nice people, you would still like Brookside. This intimate bed-and-breakfast, right beside Spout Run and the historic Burwell Morgan Mill, was built in two stages in the 1780s by the grandson of Williamsburg's "King" Carter. It's a frame house, with a bay added in the late 1800s by a Victorian builder who thought an extra touch would improve the classic facade; fortunately he didn't do much damage. The Konkels have an antiques shop in the rear and opened the B&B as a showplace for such treasures as a mid-1800s schoolmaster's desk, Staffordshire foxes, and everywhere horses—Carol's personal passion. The guest rooms have high feather beds, bed hangings, working fireplaces, and, as a special bonus, Carol lays out antique nighties for ladies to wear. There's a housekeeping suite in the toll house that once taxed traffic over Spout Run. Antiquing and biking are occupations of choice here; Millwood's major industry is antiques, and Carol can attest that Jackie Onassis sometimes appears in a nondescript car and clothes to rummage through the village shops.

Address: *Millwood, VA 22646, tel. 703/837–1780.*
Accommodations: *3 double rooms with baths, 1 suite.*
Amenities: *Air-conditioning, turndown service.*
Rates: *$95–$125; full breakfast. MC, V.*
Restrictions: *No smoking indoors, no pets.*

Caledonia Farm

Before opening his Blue Ridge farmhouse to guests, Bill Irwin went to some 250 bed-and-breakfasts. An enthusiastic environmentalist, he has fought to keep a high-voltage cable out of the Fodderstack Valley. Caledonia Farm, built of local fieldstone in 1812, is now a landmark on the National Register. On a clear day, you can see the Skyline Drive from it, and you can walk out the door and be atop The Peak (2,978 feet) in a little over two hours. There are two rooms on the second floor of the main house, and a suite occupies the old summer kitchen. Hessian soldiers who stayed after the Revolutionary War did much of the handsome carpentry, and 32-foot beams run the length of the house. The historic and natural setting are the keynotes here—not luxury (for instance, the bathrooms, while adequate, look to be vintage 1965). Bill is a host full of bonhomie and advice on exploring nearby caves and vineyards, hiking, cross-country skiing, and dining at the excellent local restaurants.

Address: *Rte. 1, Box 2080, Flint Hill, VA 22627, tel. 703/675–3693.*
Accommodations: *2 double rooms share 1 bath, 1 suite.*
Amenities: *Air-conditioning, TV/VCR in common area, fireplaces in rooms, small conference room; bicycles, hayrides.*
Rates: *$70–$100 (50% surcharge Sat.); full breakfast. No credit cards.*
Restrictions: *No smoking indoors, no pets. 2-night minimum in Oct. and on holiday weekends.*

Fountain Hall

Fountain Hall, a baby-blue Colonial Revival mansion, is surrounded by boxwood bushes and reached by a long brick walkway. Steve Walker, the owner, opened it as a bed-and-breakfast out of sympathy for the business traveler; as night manager at a hotel in Niagara Falls he had listened to their tales of loneliness and displacement. So, Steve and his wife, Kathi, their baby, and yellow lab, Oscar, provide business people temporarily stationed in Culpeper with a place to put down their briefcases and feel cared for. Fountain Hall isn't plush—though a few of its bathrooms do have Jacuzzis—but it offers what many travelers deem essential, phones in every room, parlor TV and VCR, and comfortable corners for entertaining guests. Downtown Culpeper is just a few blocks away, with the Davis Street Ordinary, its solitary hot spot, and the Amtrak station (where the Walkers will meet guests).

Address: *609 S. East St., Culpeper, VA 22701, tel. 703/825–8200.*
Accommodations: *5 double rooms with baths.*
Amenities: *Air-conditioning, phones in bedrooms, TVs and VCR in common areas.*
Rates: *$65–$85; Continental breakfast. AE, D, MC, V.*
Restrictions: *No smoking indoors, no pets, 2-night minimum on Oct. weekends.*

L'Auberge Provençale

Along with the Inn at Little Washington, northern Virginia holds yet another culinary shining star—L'Auberge Provençale is owned and operated by a fourth-generation chef from Avignon, who learned his art from his family. Behind the wide industrial stove in his jampacked kitchen, Alain Borel nightly concocts delicacies; he is renowned for his gourmet breakfasts, which have been known to include freshly baked croissants and lobster claws with tarragon maple syrup. The inn occupies a Victorianized 1750s stone house that looks a little like Appomattox Court House. However, the feeling inside is all Provençale, with modern French prints; shelves of wine (only a few of the 200 varieties on the wine list); and carved Spanish carousel animals that are for sale. There are two additions, but we liked the chambers (with fireplaces) in the main house best, reached by a polished staircase lined with curious reed birds. L'Auberge Provençale is a family-run inn, which, even more than the menu and decor, gives it its authentic French character.

Address: *Box 119, White Post, VA 22663, tel. 703/837–1375, fax 703/837–2004.*
Accommodations: *9 doubles with baths, 1 suite.*
Amenities: *Restaurant, air-conditioning, TV in suite.*
Rates: *$110–$165; full breakfast. AE, DC, MC, V.*
Restrictions: *No pets.*

The Morrison House

AScottish flag snaps in the breeze above the white-pillared portico of the Morrison House, bespeaking the Scottish heritage of the owner, a Washington real-estate developer and world traveler. Robert E. Morrison built the five-story Federal-style building in 1985, under the eye of a curator from the Smithsonian. It is constructed of red brick laid in Flemish bond and has arched windows and a small fountained garden at the foot of the entryway. Little luxuries abound, including state-of-the-art marble bathrooms, triple-sheeting on the high, mahogany beds, afternoon tea, and a bag of Virginia peanuts in every room. All 45 guest rooms are different, decorated with camelback sofas, Chippendale-style chairs, swagged draperies, and a few fireplaces (which, alas, don't work). The Morrison House is a short walk from a Metro station: Patrons can park their cars in the lot beneath the hotel and explore the District and Old Town Alexandria unhampered by the area's byzantine parking regulations and one-way streets.

Address: *116 S. Alfred St., Alexandria, VA 22314, tel. 703/838–8000 or 800/367–0800, fax 212/337–7915.*
Accommodations: *42 double rooms with baths, 3 suites.*
Amenities: *Restaurant, room service, air-conditioning, TV/VCR with collection of videotapes, turndown service, phones in rooms.*
Rates: *$99–$385; full breakfast. AE, DC, MC, V.*
Restrictions: *No pets.*

The Norris House

One Norris House regular returns every August to work his way through Brodie's biography of Thomas Jefferson; even after he finishes it he'll no doubt find reason to come back to this Federal-style inn in the center of Leesburg. Two celebrated early-19th-century builders, the Norris brothers, are responsible for the portico with turned spindles, the Adam-style mantel in the ethereal Blue Parlor, and shiny wild-cherry bookcases in the Music Room. Nowadays, two sisters—Amy Marasco and Laura Walton—set the pleasant tone at the Norris House. Their inn is an airy, relaxed, and civilized place, with unpainted wideboard floors, samplers, lace canopies, and fresh flowers.

On Sunday mornings, the *Washington Post* is likely to be strewn across the Music Room sofa while classical music plays in the background. And should you plan a wedding in the rear garden, Laura will plant perennials in your chosen colors (given notification in the fall).

Address: *108 Loudoun St. SW, Leesburg, VA 22075, tel. 703/777–1806.*
Accommodations: *6 double rooms share 3 baths.*
Amenities: *Air-conditioning. Cable TV and guest phones in library and kitchen.*
Rates: *$68–$112; full breakfast. No credit cards.*
Restrictions: *No smoking indoors, no pets.*

The Pink House

The Pink House lies at a crossroads in the wee village of Waterford, founded in 1733 by Quakers. The town resisted embroilment in the Revolution, but joined the Union during the Civil War, when Confederate troops laid to waste their rolling Loudoun County farms. Today the whole 1,400-acre town is a National Historic Landmark, special among such places because modern development hasn't touched its periphery. This Brigadoon is accessible by bike path from Alexandria or by car via Routes 7, 9, and 662. The Pink House is owned by Chuck and Marie Anderson, who love opera, books, theater, and long, cozy chats. The prettiest of its two homey, cluttered guest rooms, called the Opera Suite, features 18th-century antiques, a whirlpool bath, a

TV/VCR, a baby grand piano, and a folk-arty mural depicting Waterford notables attending a gala at the Met. Both suites have fireplaces, private entrances, and open onto the Waterford fields, where walking is encouraged. Marie's breakfasts include Irish soda bread, but for lunch or dinner you'll have to drive to Leesburg (20 minutes away), as the village puts itself out for tourists only during the October Waterford Crafts Fair.

Address: *Waterford, VA 22190, tel. 703/882–3453.*
Accommodations: *2 suites.*
Amenities: *Private outdoor sitting areas.*
Rates: *$90; full breakfast, afternoon tea. No credit cards.*
Restrictions: *No pets.*

The Red Fox Inn

The Red Fox has always been at the center of things in Middleburg. In fact, it predates the town, for the attractive yellow fieldstone structure was built by Joseph Chinn in 1728 at the halfway point on the road from Alexandria to Winchester. During the Civil War it served as the meeting place for General J.E.B. Stuart and Colonel John Mosby, and as a Confederate field hospital (indeed, the Tap Room's bar was an operating table). Today the Red Fox is still an inn, whose busy restaurant packs crowds into five dining rooms on the first and second floors. Given the tourist traffic, we suggest overnighters opt for rooms in annexes called the Stray Fox Inn and McConnell House, which lie about a half block off Route 50. In the Stray Fox, ask for the palatial

Belmont Suite, or the snugger but equally attractive Hulbert Room, which has a fireplace. All the rooms are individually done in 18th-century antiques, with canopy beds and fourposters, and a *Washington Post* is delivered to your door with breakfast. Just across the courtyard is Red Fox Fine Art, owned by the innkeeper, F. Turner Reuter.

Address: *Box 385, Rte. 50, Middleburg, VA 22117, tel. 703/687–6301 or 800/223–1728; in DC, 202/478–1808, fax 703/687–3338.*
Accommodations: *12 double rooms with baths, 7 suites.*
Amenities: *Restaurant, TV and phones in rooms.*
Rates: *$125–$225; Continental breakfast. AE, MC, V.*
Restrictions: *No pets.*

The Richard Johnston Inn

For such a sweet old town so tied up in history, Fredericksburg isn't exactly blessed in the inn department, but of all its choices the Richard Johnston is the best, owing to its prime Caroline Street location, just across the street from the Visitors Center. It's a diminutive-looking 18th-century brick rowhouse with a dormer on the third floor and a pleasant patio adjoining the parking lot in the rear, shaded by magnolia trees. Inside, restoration work has been top drawer. In the common rooms downstairs board floors are polished to an orangey luster and covered with Oriental rugs. The furnishings are Chippendale- and Empire-style antiques, though, sadly, an unlived-in, unloved look prevails. Still, the guest rooms above the kitchen are recommended; Room 8

holds a fireplace, rag rug, and brass double bed. Two commodious suites, with living rooms, wet bars, and wall-to-wall carpeting, open onto the patio.

Address: *711 Caroline St., Fredericksburg, VA 22401, tel. 703/899–7606.*
Accommodations: *5 double rooms with baths, 4 doubles share 2 baths, 2 suites.*
Amenities: *Air-conditioning, TV in suites.*
Rates: *$55–$120; Continental breakfast. AE, MC, V.*
Restrictions: *No smoking, no pets.*

Sycamore Hill

Get out your cameras, please, for the serious photo opportunities at Sycamore Hill, a ranch-style house seemingly dropped from the sky, onto the crest of Menefee Mountain. As you wind up the mile approach from town, you begin to doubt there could possibly be a lodging at the end of the road. Fear not. Eventually the forest gives way to Kerri Wagner's extensive gardens, and finally you arrive at the Virginia fieldstone house wrapped by a 65-foot veranda. The view from this spot is the raison d'être of Sycamore Hill—there's Old Rag to the right, Tiger Valley, and Red Oak Mountain. And the 52-acre lot is a certified wildlife sanctuary. There are two smallish guest rooms on the north side, but to open your eyes to the Blue Ridge in the morn-ing, you must book the downstairs Blue Suite with its picture windows, full kitchen, sitting room, and big stone fireplace. Kerri Wagner is a cheerful hostess who treats her guests like friends, aided by a shaggy white mop of a dog named Molly Bean, and her husband, Steve, an artist whose fascinating magazine covers line the walls.

Address: *Rte. 1, Box 978, Washington, VA 22747, tel. 703/675-3046.*
Accommodations: *3 double rooms with baths.*
Amenities: *Air-conditioning, TV in living room.*
Rates: *$95–$120; full breakfast. No credit cards.*
Restrictions: *No smoking indoors, no pets, 2-night minimum on holiday weekends.*

Welbourne

There are so many stories attached to this 200-year-old mansion that it makes your head spin. Thomas Wolfe visited and later wrote to his host, "Your America is not my America and for that reason I loved it even more." F. Scott Fitzgerald came often and set his short story "The Last Case" here. During the Civil War a Dulany of Welbourne served J.E.B. Stuart breakfast on horseback outside the front door, even as Yankee bullets pelted the house. Beyond the stories, Welbourne is the genuine, blueblooded hunt-country article, a sweeping, yellow stately home fronted by six columns and surrounded by 550 acres where 50 retired horses roam. It's been in the same family for seven generations, though as owner Sally Morison says, "We have the acreage, but not the bank account." Ergo, the bed-and-breakfast. Recognizing that the old homestead isn't in peak condition, Mrs. Morison downplays it. "Look at these bathrooms. They're awful," she says. But for lovers of history, they're not *so* awful—and perhaps the working Louis XIV table clock and 1790s French porcelain downstairs will compensate. Meanwhile, don't ask where she got the antiques; they've been in the family for years.

Address: *Middleburg, VA 22117, tel. 703/687-3201.*
Accommodations: *5 double rooms with baths, 3 cottages.*
Amenities: *Air-conditioning in bedrooms, TV in living room.*
Rates: *$81.55–$93.20; full breakfast. No credit cards.*

The Eastern Shore

*Most people think of the long peninsula east of the
Chesapeake Bay as territory claimed by the states of
Maryland and Delaware. Indeed, the most developed and
touristy parts of Delmarva are; but if you look closely at
a map you'll see a boundary line with the word* Virginia
*printed beneath. The border lies about 75 miles north of the
peninsula's tip, and in between is Virginia's very own
toehold on the Eastern Shore, encompassing two counties—
Northampton and Accomack—with a combined population
close to that of Charlottesville. The area was settled in the
1600s, by English Colonists; visited by vacationers (who
made the trip by ferryboat) in the 19th century; and
surveyed by the railroad, which reached the peninsular
terminus, at Cape Charles, in about 1885. Several decades
ago the peninsula was bisected by a highway, Route 13,
which brought some—but not many—1950s-style motels and
drive-in restaurants. Off Route 13, however, the Eastern
Shore lives and looks the way it did around the turn of the
century—no quaint restored villages or swishy resorts.
True back roaders will like it immensely—providing they
understand in advance a few basic facts.*

*Above all, Virginia's Eastern Shore is not a beach haven,
except for the stellar sandy stretches at its northeast corner
lying within the Chincoteague National Wildlife Refuge.
On the bay side, tidal creeks and marshes predominate.
Seaside, a string of barrier islands has kept beaches from
forming at the shoreline. The islands themselves are either
privately owned, or, like the islands of Cobb, Smith, and
Hog, are provinces of the Nature Conservancy's Virginia
Coast Reserve. To reach them you'll need to charter a boat,
or sign up for one of the VCR's infrequent island trips.
There are spring and fall boat tours and three-day
photography weekends (tel. 804/442-3049), led by trained
naturalists.*

Nor are there any cities of note on Virginia's Eastern Shore, with the possible exceptions of Chincoteague, whose meager population swells in peak summer months but otherwise figures at about 3,500; and Cape Charles, which thrived during ferry and railroad days but now has only a cranking cement factory to keep it from becoming comatose. County maps show many other towns (with colorful names such as Temperanceville, Birds Nest, and Oyster), but these are really only crossroads with, if you're lucky, a general store. East of Route 13, skinny local arteries such as Routes 679 and 600 reach these villages and the architectural contradictions that surround them. The Virginia peninsula has its own unique building style, followed for hundreds of years: "chain" houses made of frame, consisting, when the pattern holds, of big house, little house, colonnade, and kitchen linked in a row. You can glimpse a good example, the privately owned Holly Brook Plantation, on the west side of Route 13, 8 miles south of Nassawadox.

The town of Chincoteague lies on 8-mile-long Chincoteague Island (not to be confused with the island holding the wildlife refuge, Assateague Island, to which it provides access via a bridge) and exists almost wholly to cater to tourists, with motels, restaurants, and shops. It is atmospherically similar to other Atlantic beach resorts in Maryland and Delaware, but its low-lying, marshy location brings septic and mosquito problems. Nonetheless, it has one attraction that will probably never cease drawing crowds, the legendary Pony Penning event, held in late July. The miniature horses swim the channel between Assateague and Chincoteague and are then corraled and auctioned off, usually for about $600 each. This round-up began in 1924, though it was made nationally famous by Marguerite Henry's Misty of Chincoteague, *in 1947. Misty herself was a real pony; her mortal remains are taxidermically preserved at the Chincoteague Miniature Pony Farm (tel. 804/336–3066).*

Places to go, sights to see

Accomac, a particularly pretty town and the seat of Accomack County, is one of two villages on the Eastern Shore (the other is Eastville) with an 18th-century debtors' prison. The Victorian clerk's office on the west side of the courthouse green holds records dating to 1663. Accomac also contains the office of the Eastern Shore Tourism Commission.

Accomack Vineyards (tel. 804/442–2110). This peninsula winery near the town of Painter completed its first pressing in 1986. Wines produced and sold here include chardonnay, riesling, merlot, and cabernet sauvignon. Tours are available by arrangement.

Cape Charles, a place decidedly in the slow lane, was by 1953 abandoned by the passenger railroad and ferry service that made the town boom briefly around the turn of the century, then—to hammer the nails into its coffin— was bypassed by Route 5. Today most of its 136 acres are a historic district, though an unusual one because the houses date from the first quarter of the century. A walking tour takes you past two Sears-catalogue homes built in the mid-1920s, the pleasant bayside boardwalk, and a wonderful Art Deco moviehouse. Some will feel that industrial works to the south mar the townscape, though at these you can watch freight trains being loaded onto barges that take them across the mouth of the bay to Norfolk. In all, it's a funky, beyond-the-pale sort of place that attracts more and more refugees from northern metropolises, who are finding that they can still buy property in Cape Charles for a song.

Chesapeake Bay Bridge-Tunnel. This 17-mile engineering marvel links the peninsula with Norfolk and Virginia Beach. Completed in 1964, after costing taxpayers $400 million in concrete and steel, it has brought the Eastern Shore into the Virginia fold only to a degree, largely due to the hefty $9 toll—which, as some peninsula dwellers see it, keeps the Navy riffraff out. To support its mammoth span, islands were built, where there are scenic stopping places, a fishing area, and a snack bar; and to accommodate Chesapeake Bay ship traffic, the two-lane bridge gives way to two tunnels, one more than a mile long. The trip is either awesome, unsettling, or soporific, depending on the soundness of your stomach and nerves.

Chincoteague National Wildlife Center (tel. 804/336–6577). Despite the surfboarders and sun worshipers headed toward its long stretch of Atlantic beach, the refuge exists first and foremost for the benefit of birds, snakes, ponies, rare Delmarva gray squirrels, and Sika deer. Many of the species preserved in this veritable Noah's Ark are visible from a 6-mile loop drive that winds through forests and marshes. There is, as well, a visitors center, lighthouse (built 1866), crabbing ridge, and fishing area—but no restaurants, camping, or bonfires. In season the refuge sponsors fishing expeditions, evening cruises, and a wildlife safari, which takes nature lovers along back roads where they can observe the intimate habits of the famed Chincoteague feral ponies.

Custis Tombs. The Custises were Eastern Shore gentry who married into the Lee and Washington clans. At this walled gravesite 6 miles north of the Bay Bridge-Tunnel on Route 644 you'll find the grave of John Custis, known chiefly for his legendarily chilly marriage to Frances.

Eyre Hall, the peninsula's handsomest and most historic plantation, was built in 1733, on land granted to the owners in 1662. The brick and frame house near the Bay is open only during Garden Week, but its grounds, with ancient plantings, flowering shrubs, and venerable trees, can be visited year-round. Turn west 1½ miles north of Cheriton.

Hopkins & Bro. General Store (tel. 804/787–8220). This 1842 country store–cum–restaurant at Onancock's town dock is a Virginia Historic landmark, with a companionable bar and a menu featuring shore inevitables such as crab cakes and seafood salad.

Kerr Place (tel. 804/787–3394) is a distinguished brick mansion on the outskirts of Onancock, built in 1799. Housed within are the collections of the Eastern Shore of Virginia Historical Society, including costumes, portraits, and furnishings.

NASA Goddard Flight Center and Wallops Flight Facility Visitor Center (tel. 804/824–2298). The first rocket was launched, in 1945, at this 6,000-acre NASA enclave (encompassing Wallops Island and areas surrounding Chincoteague). The visitors center, which is the only part of the complex open to visitors, displays space suits, moon rocks, and scale models of satellites and space probes. On the first Saturday of every month NASA conducts model-rocket launches on the grounds.

Pear Valley is the peninsula's oldest house, built in 1672. This one-room cottage with a chimney and loft is owned by the Association for the Preservation of Virginia Antiquities, though currently it is unrestored. It can be seen from Route 689, near Johnstown.

Refuge Waterfowl and Oyster Museums (tel. 804/336–5800 and 804/336–6117 respectively). These two tiny museums are neighbors on Piney Island (barely an island really, as it's only tenuously separated from Chincoteague, by skinny Eel Creek). The Waterfowl Museum has a collection of hand-crafted decoys, and the Oyster Museum tells the life story of the bivalve and how generations of watermen have pursued it.

Tangier Island. To reach this tiny island, stuck like a buoy in the middle of Chesapeake Bay, catch the *Captain Eulice*, at Onancock harbor (tel. 804/787–8220), sailing June–September at 10 and returning at 3. A livestock-grazing range before the Revolution, Tangier is now home to approximately 900 souls—most of them named Crockett, Parks, Thomas, and Pruitt—whose speech is Elizabethan cockney, barely changed since the first settlers moved in. It's an insular place, devoted to seafood harvesting and Methodism, with one main street, too narrow for cars, and the Chesapeake House (tel. 804/891–2331), whose reputation for family-style shellfish feasts has spread far and wide. Slightly less renowned is Double-Six (tel. 804/891–

2410), a local haunt once featured in *National Geographic* because it serves hot oyster sandwiches.

Wachapreague. This sleepy village on the Atlantic side of the peninsula once held a 30-room hotel and attracted vacationers from as far away as New York City. But the hotel burned down, leaving only the 340-odd permanent residents, along with a carnival ground that still lights up in late July. It remains a fishing mecca, with charter boats tied up to its dock; flounder is the prized catch.

Restaurants

Chincoteague is the one place for fancy dining on Virginia's Eastern Shore. Its culinary star is the **Channel Bass Inn** (tel. 804/336–6148; *see* below), where an ex-classical guitarist, James Hanretta, serves 20 guests each night, by reservation only (you give your credit-card number at the time you book). Recently a French restaurant opened in the area (in New Church, just south of the Maryland state line), called the **Garden and the Sea** (tel. 804/824–0672). It's a pleasant spot indeed, offering haute and nouvelle French cuisine. It's also a bed-and-breakfast (*see* below).

Seafood is on the menu at local family spots like **E.L. Willis & Co.** (Willis Wharf, tel. 804/442–4225), the **Trawler** (Exmore, tel. 804/442–2092), **Wright's** (north of Atlantic, tel. 804/824–4012), and **Rebecca's** (Cape Charles, tel. 804/331–3879). *See* also Hopkins & Bro. General Store, above. On Friday several churches serve homemade fare: soul food at **Wachapreague's Grace Methodist Church** and ham and chicken salad at **St. James Episcopal** in Accomac.

Tourist Information

Chincoteague Chamber of Commerce (Box 258, Chincoteague 23336, tel. 804/336–6161). **Eastern Shore of Virginia Tourism Commission** (Box 147, Accomac 23301, tel. 804/787–2460). **Virginia Division of Tourism** (202 N. 9th St., Richmond 23219, tel. 804/786–4484).

Reservation Services

Amanda's Bed & Breakfast Reservation Service (1428 Park Ave., Baltimore, MD 21217, tel. 301/225–0001). **Bed & Breakfast of Tidewater Virginia Reservation Service** (Box 3343, Norfolk 23514, tel. 804/627–1983). **Inns of the Eastern Shore** (1500 Hambrooks Blvd., Cambridge, MD 21613, tel. 301/228–0575).

The Channel Bass Inn

The Channel Bass occupies a pale-lemon building, constructed in the 1880s—making it one of Chincoteague's oldest—and added onto in the 1920s, resulting in an untroubled asymmetry and a kind of appealing architectural buxomness. But the inn's design style, history, even its proximity to Chincoteague National Seashore, are all eclipsed by another feature—its restaurant.

Jim Hanretta, who is both innkeeper and chef, opened the Channel Bass 20 years ago, and since then its culinary reputation has spread. The restaurant is known for its unusual recipes, invented on the premises by Jim, who learned his craft in Barcelona. Here you'll find local seafood brightened with Spanish and Basque sauces, beef tenderloin in a Peruvian marinade, and backfin crab medallions with chorizos. Jim cooks every dish all alone in his compact kitchen, which is why only 20 people can be served each night; dining here is a little like hiring yourself a private chef. The dining room is intimate (just seven tables wide), with windows providing views of the romantically lit garden in back. Wedgwood china, silver, and linen table napkins are de rigueur. Of course you will pay dearly for the Channel Bass dining experience, with the average four-course meal ringing in at approximately $75 for one person, not including drinks. A green salad costs $12, and wines can be astronomical (Jim has a private reserve list topped off with an $800 bottle of 1966 Château Lafite Rothschild).

The nine guest rooms, on the second and third floors, are luxurious, with original art on the walls, plump picture books on the coffee tables, triple-sheet beds, Neutrogena toiletries, and Egyptian-cotton towels. But they do not demonstrate the same unique sense of personality the restaurant does; rather, they are immensely comfortable neutral zones.

By arrangement, Jim holds special three-day cooking vacations, which include dinners and rooms, as well as hands-on lessons in the kitchen, during which some of the Channel Bass's secrets are revealed.

Address: *100 Church St., Chincoteague, VA 23336, tel. 804/336–6148.*
Accommodations: *7 double rooms with baths, 2 suites.*
Amenities: *Restaurant, air-conditioning, turn-down service.*
Rates: *$106.50–$213; breakfast extra. AE, DC, MC, V.*
Restrictions: *No pets, 3-night minimum during Pony Penning, 2-night minimum on weekends, closed Dec. 20–Jan. 20.*

Pickett's Harbor

To begin with, you'll need a county map to help you find Pickett's Harbor, which lies 4 miles north of the Bridge-Tunnel and 2 miles west of Route 13—on the bay side of the peninsula, which thins decidedly as it nears land's end. The road to this isolated bed-and-breakfast winds past sweet-potato fields, through a grove of trees, and crunches underneath tires, since it's made of oyster shells. Eventually the house, owned by Sara and Cooke Goffigan, appears on the left, made of beige frame and brick, a free interpretation of the Eastern Shore style, comprising big house, little house, and littler house still—like schoolchildren lined up by height. Though she's a teacher rather than an architect, Sara designed the home in 1976; it wasn't hard, she claims.

Hard or not, the result is temperately graceful. Cedar trees, loblolly pines, dogwood, and sea grass surround it. Its front yard is a 17-acre stretch of private beach, frequented by deer and horseshoe crabs. What about jellyfish, we asked straightaway, knowing that the gelatinous creatures known locally as nettles make most Chesapeake Bay beaches unswimmable. As Sara explains, Pickett's Harbor is so close to the mouth of the bay that the gentle laving action of the waves keeps the nettles away. So here you'll find a rare thing, indeed, at least for this part of Virginia's Eastern Shore—a sandy beach all your own, complete with dunes and the eerie wrecks of several World War II Liberty ships offshore.

Nor is the inside of the house a disappointment. It's furnished with antiques and family items and has blue wainscoting, high ceilings, and flooring made of rafters taken from a 200-year-old barn on the James River. The one downstairs bedroom has a four-poster bed, easy chairs, and an exceptional water view, but the upstairs rooms are pretty too, especially those beneath the dormers.

Before heading off to school on weekdays Sara serves breakfast, which routinely features sweet-potato biscuits, thin-slice Virginia ham, and popovers. Before she goes, though, see if you can get her to talk about her family, an Eastern Shore clan that came to the area shortly after Captain John Smith explored the peninsula, in the early 1600s.

Address: *Box 97AA, Cape Charles, VA 23310, tel. 804/331-2212.*
Accommodations: *2 double rooms with baths, 4 doubles share 2 baths.*
Amenities: *Air-conditioning, TV in common areas.*
Rates: *$65–$85; full breakfast. No credit cards.*
Restrictions: *Smoking only on porch, no pets, 2-night minimum on holiday weekends.*

The Burton House

The business of little Wachapreague, on the Atlantic side of
the peninsula, is fishing. It's always been that way, although
a hundred years ago it attracted
many more sports enthusiasts than
it does today. The pretty village sits
alone like some hopeful wallflower,
though in late July its amusement
park lights up for the annual Fire-
man's Carnival. The Burton House is
just across the street from the carnival grounds, a pale green, surprisingly ungingerbready Victorian built
in 1883. In back there's a gazebo
and deck, and to the side a rack of
bikes, which guests are invited to
borrow. Though the owners, the
Harts, operate an antiques store in
town, the Burton is homespun in
decor. Perhaps the most important
thing to note is that the Harts have

a boat, and for a price will take
guests out to remote Nature Conservancy barrier islands.

Address: *11 Brooklyn St., Wachapreague, VA 23460, tel. 804/787–
4560.*
Accommodations: *1 double room
with bath, 6 doubles with ½ bath
share 2 baths.*
Amenities: *Air-conditioning; bikes,
boat charters.*
Rates: *$60; full breakfast. No credit
cards.*
Restrictions: *No pets.*

Colonial Manor Inn

This exceptionally homey, neat,
and reasonably priced inn has
been owned and operated by the
same family for over 50 years. It lies
on the road to Onancock, a bayside
harbor town that's recently caught
the attention of Chesapeake boat
people, though it was founded 300
years ago. The white frame house
has three stories and 20 rooms, 14 of
which are guest chambers. For families traveling with children, hoping
to spend something less than
a fortune on lodgings, it's a god-
send. Its huge, third-floor dormer
room has a double bed and two singles, and, according to owner June
Evans is intended to remind you of
Grandmother's attic. Other guest
rooms are small, but adequately
equipped; here you'll find no frills—
you will be served coffee but no

breakfast. For that you'll have to
head into town, where there's
a bakery and coffee shop, as well as
three recommendable dinner spots,
Market Street, Hopkins & Bro., and
Armando's. Onancock harbor is the
place to catch the cruise boat to Tangier Island. The town itself, with
a number of 18th-century buildings,
is worth at least a brief nose around.

Address: *84 Market St., Onancock,
VA 23417, tel. 804/787–3521.*
Accommodations: *4 double rooms
with baths, 10 doubles share 3
baths.*
Amenities: *Air-conditioning, TV;
parking for recreational vehicles
and boats.*
Rates: *$42–$50; breakfast extra. No
credit cards.*
Restrictions: *No pets.*

The Garden and the Sea

Victoria Olian and Jack Betz, former Washingtonians, bought old Bloxom's Tavern, built around 1800 in the hamlet of New Church, and straightaway began doing what they like best—cooking French-inspired meals. The menu routinely contains one or two prix-fixe dinners and à la carte specialties such as baked salmon in pastry and grilled duck breast with cassis. The prices are high, but not exorbitant, and the dining room is an airily pretty place. Overnight guests can take their leisure in the downstairs sitting room, furnished with an Edwardian mahogany and satinwood buffet. At present, there are just two guest rooms, decorated nouvelle Victorian style, with ballooning fabrics and French furniture. The one called Chantilly holds a wicker sleigh bed and ceiling fan; both have luxurious baths with bidets. Jack and Victoria's next project is to remodel the oldest house in New Church, which they moved to the garden behind the inn, for more guest rooms.

Address: *Box 275, New Church, VA 23415, tel. 804/824–0672.*
Accommodations: *2 double rooms with baths.*
Amenities: *Restaurant, air-conditioning.*
Rates: *$75–$105; full breakfast. AE, DC, MC, V.*
Restrictions: *Smoking in common rooms only, no pets, 2-night minimum summer weekends, 3-night minimum during Pony Penning Week, closed Nov.–Mar.*

Miss Molly's and the Little Traveller Inn

These lodgings are owned by Bill and Priscilla Stam; both houses were built in the second half of the 19th century, but Miss Molly's is distinguished by Marguerite Henry's having stayed here while writing *Misty.* "One night I brought a tiny live seahorse into the room and set him in front of a window in a glass of water. In the morning when I awoke those pure white curtains were 'appliquéd' all over with . . . baby seahorses which had hatched in the night from the father's pouch." Somehow, that episode describes Miss Molly's to a T; its back faces the channel still plied by fishing boats, and inside, the furnishings are Victorian—including a fascinating John Rogers Civil War statuette. Marguerite Henry's room is perhaps the best, with blue wallpaper and a three-window bay. However, across the street at the Little Traveller the rooms are nice, too, and there's a comfortable sitting porch overlooking a fountained patio.

Address: *112 N. Main St., Chincoteague, VA 23336, tel. 804/336–6686.*
Accommodations: *2 double rooms with baths, 11 doubles share 6 baths.*
Amenities: *Air-conditioning, TV in common rooms of both houses, refrigerator; beach towels.*
Rates: *$59–$105; full breakfast, afternoon tea. No credit cards.*
Restrictions: *Smoking in public areas only, no pets, 2-night minimum on weekends, 3-night minimum on holiday weekends, 4-night minimum during Pony Penning, closed Dec.–Mar.*

Nottingham Ridge

Bonnie Nottingham's sister-in-law, Sara Goffigan (of Pickett's Harbor just up the lane), convinced her that she should open her brick, Williamsburg-style house, built in 1975, to guests. And so she did. It shares the same 17-acre private beach with Pickett's Harbor, the same smashing Chesapeake Bay sunsets, and visitations by herons and egrets. Inside, it is a slightly homier, less composed place than Pickett's Harbor, with two fireplaces in common rooms, a back porch that is a popular picnic spot, and three guest rooms. Bonnie is a lovable host and part-time farmer with an interest in a cucumber grading and packing business. Sample her sweet-potato biscuits, scrapple, and home-made jam at breakfast. She can help you locate a charter boat for trips to Atlantic-side barrier beach islands, direct you to a nearby pond, and map out canoe trips on peaceful tidal creeks.

Address: *Box 97–B, Cape Charles, VA 23310, tel. 804/331–1010 (at night).*
Accommodations: *3 double rooms with baths.*
Amenities: *Air-conditioning; beach.*
Rates: *$50–$75; full breakfast. No credit cards.*
Restrictions: *No smoking, no pets, 2-night minimum on holiday weekends.*

Sea Gate

Jim Wells and Chris Bannon, both formerly of New York City (as are so many recent arrivals to the town), have laughingly taken to calling Cape Charles "the Cape." The Sea Gate was built in 1913; it's a rotund pink frame house a block from the water, on one of the town's prettiest residential streets. There's a wide porch out front and a grand piano in the entryway; the residents are Albert the cat, Chris, Jim, and Chris's elderly mother. The furnishings are comfortable but hardly rare; rather, it's the relaxed tone of the place that's so winning. Generally guests sit up late talking in the living room—about 1930s musicals, Tahitian islands, real estate, anything. The next morning at breakfast the conversation picks up as if it had never ended. Then it's off to explore Cape Charles (which will take you all of an hour), followed by a visit to the beach, afternoon tea, and phenomenal sunset-watching. Then dinner at the only restaurant in town (Rebecca's), more talk . . . . Call it the Cape Charles warp.

Address: *9 Tazewell Ave., Cape Charles, VA 23310, tel. 804/331–2206.*
Accommodations: *1 double room with bath, 2 doubles with half baths and 1 double with sink share 1 hall bath.*
Amenities: *Air-conditioning, TV in rooms.*
Rates: *$60–$70; full breakfast, afternoon tea. No credit cards.*
Restrictions: *Smoking in public areas only, no pets, 2-night minimum on holiday weekends.*

The Year of the Horse

Every year one man comes to the Year of the Horse just to crab, spending his days with a pot and pole on the 50-foot dock overlooking Chincoteague Sound. Not for him the pristine beaches of the refuge; he's got to keep after those crustaceans, so that he can return home with a full ice chest. For those similarly inclined, the Year of the Horse is an excellent retreat, occupying a summer house built in the 1920s, whose garage once stabled Misty's colt, Cloudy. Carl Bond has surrounded it with Florida-style lawn ornaments—pink flamingoes and the like—and filled its sitting rooms with a weird assortment of collectibles, including a rocking camel, fedora-decked hat rack, Buddha, and Victorian fainting couch. Three guest rooms look out on the bay; they have private decks but unhappily are furnished motel style. In addition, there's a two-bedroom apartment. Carl is a tall, lanky man, soft-spoken and just plain nice; when guests don't finish the cinnamon rolls at breakfast, he takes the leftovers out to the school-bus stop and distributes them to the kids.

Address: *600 S. Main St., Chincoteague, VA 23336, tel. 804/336–3221.*
Accommodations: *3 double rooms with baths, 1 suite.*
Amenities: *Air-conditioning, kitchen in 1 double, cable TV; dock.*
Rates: *$50–$95; Continental breakfast. D, MC, V.*
Restrictions: *No pets, 2-night minimum on weekends, 3-night minimum on holidays, closed Dec.–Feb.*

Williamsburg and the Peninsula

*"Down in Virginia there is a little old-fashioned city called
Williamsburg. It stands on the ridge of the peninsula that
separates the James and York Rivers." This is how* The City
of Once Upon a Time, *a children's book written by Gilchrist
Waring in 1946, opens. That book and* The Official Guide to
Colonial Williamsburg, *are two of the best introductions to
the legendary city, which is visited by some one million
people every year.*

*As both books explain, Williamsburg was the capital of
Virginia between 1699 and 1780, when the colony was
immense, extending west to the Mississippi River.
A planned city like Annapolis, Maryland, and a thriving
business center serving the farms and tobacco plantations
between the rivers, it was an unarguably beautiful place
and still is. In 1926 the rector at Williamsburg's Bruton
Parish Church persuaded John D. Rockefeller to restore the
town, and the continuing project has resulted in
a living-history museum of 173 acres, a mile long and half
a mile wide, holding 88 restored and 50 reconstructed
buildings, and surrounded by a 3,000-acre "greenbelt." The
restoration has become a pattern for similar endeavors
nationwide. As a modern city Williamsburg doesn't really
exist, except as suburbs that grew up in the 1930s, when the
restoration crews moved in. There are outlying malls and
commercial strips, which woo travelers with shopping
opportunities at bargain emporiums like the Williamsburg
Pottery Factory and Soap and Candle Company, and
Merchant's Square, adjoining the historic district which
should not be confused with it, despite its look of
authenticity.*

*Once you've located Colonial Williamsburg proper, you can
simply wander in and soak up the atmosphere, perhaps
slaking your thirst on a cup of cider, peddled streetside, or
you can stop at the visitors center (tel. 804/220-7645 daily*

*8:30–5), which lies off the Colonial Parkway (the National
Park artery that connects Jamestown, Williamsburg, and
Yorktown), to view a 35-minute film and buy passes that
entitle you to enter the buildings and ride the fleet of
shuttle buses that link the top sights.*

*Williamsburg is not the oldest English settlement in the
United States. That title is held by nearby Jamestown,
where a sea-weary party of 104 men and boys aboard the*
Sarah Constant, Godspeed, *and* Discovery *landed in 1607
and hung on, despite hostile Indians, disease bred in
nearby swamps, and chaos engendered by the fear that
they'd been forgotten by suppliers across the Atlantic.
Today Jamestown Island, the site of a national park, is
a much more rustic place than civil Williamsburg.*

*It is entirely understandable that visitors to the area
should feel overwhelmed. Besides Jamestown and
Williamsburg there's nearby Yorktown to explore (the scene
of the last battle of the Revolution and the surrender of
General Cornwallis) and scores of plantations along the
James (among them Carter's Grove and the brilliant chain
of privately owned historic houses off Route 5) that should
not be missed. Charles City County, which hugs the river
between Richmond and Williamsburg, is truly a place
apart. The same handful of families have owned and
farmed its plantations since the 17th century and have
stoically kept development out. So a drive along Route 5,
which offers access to all the historic homes, makes a scenic
trip indeed.*

*Finally, the thing to keep in mind about Williamsburg's
bed-and-breakfasts is that none of them lies within the
historic district; indeed, none of them occupies a historic
home, though a number of them are exceedingly fine places
to stay. Those intent on booking accommodations in a bona
fide Colonial structure with a historic pedigree should
contact the Williamsburg Inn (tel. 804/229–1000 or 800/446–*

*8956). It manages 85 rooms located in taverns and houses
in the restored district.*

Places to go, sights to see

Abby Aldrich Rockefeller Folk Art Center (tel. 804/220–7645) has nine
galleries filled with 125 delightful paintings, carvings, and household items
created by talented, but untrained, American artists, including Edward
Hicks's painting *Peaceable Kingdom*. Closed for renovations, it is scheduled
to reopen in mid-1992.

Berkeley (tel. 804/829–6018), the Harrison family home, occupies the spot
where settlers celebrated the first Thanksgiving, in 1619. The house,
perfectly Georgian in style, was built in 1726 and later lived in by President
William Henry Harrison, of Tippecanoe fame. It is surrounded by 10 acres of
formal boxwood gardens, and you can dine in its Coach House Tavern.

Busch Gardens/The Old Country (off Rte. 60, tel. 804/253–3350). This
theme park re-creates things German, French, Italian, and English and offers
rides on such curiosities as the Loch Ness Monster, Roman Rapids, and Big
Bad Wolf.

Carter's Grove (tel. 804/220–7645), an 18th-century plantation 8 miles east of
the historic district, was built in 1750 by a grandson of the Colonial tobacco
tycoon Robert "King" Carter and renovated and enlarged in 1928. Before
Carter Grove was built, the site was the administrative center for
a plantation syndicate called the Society of Martin's Hundred, whose
palisaded fort and company compound were recently discovered by
archaeologists and partially reconstructed.

The College of William and Mary, the second oldest college in the United
States, was founded in 1693 by charter from King William and Queen Mary
of England. Its centerpiece, the Wren Building, begun in 1695, is thought to
have been influenced by Christopher Wren.

Colonial Williamsburg (tel. 800/447–8679). In the restored district, some of
the most interesting historic buildings are the *Capitol*, where Patrick Henry
delivered his famous speech, *Bruton Parish Church*, and the handsome
Governor's Palace, with its stable, kitchen, exquisite gardens, and working
wheelwright's shop. The *Courthouse* in *Market Square*, fronted by pillories
and stocks, and the octagonal *Magazine and Guardhouse*, where Redcoats
parade and muskets are cleaned, loaded, and discharged, are two of the
town's original structures. Along Duke of Gloucester Street are the *Printing
Office, Mary Stith's Music School*, the *James Anderson Blacksmith Shop*,
and *Golden Ball Silversmith's*. Crafts shops in the historic district include
Prentis Store, for pottery, baskets, soaps, pipes, and tools; the *Post Office*,
for books, prints, maps, stationery, and sealing wax; and *Raleigh Tavern
Bake Shop*, for gingerbread and tarts.

DeWitt Wallace Decorative Arts Gallery (tel. 804/220–7724 or 804/220–7645), a modern museum behind the Public Hospital in Williamsburg, contains 8,000 examples of English and American furniture, ceramics, textiles, and costumes primarily from the 17th and 18th centuries.

Jamestown National Historic Site (5 miles west of Williamsburg, tel. 804/893–3400) is an island, which is why the colonists selected it as a settlement site in 1607. It was to prove a bad choice; in one year alone nine-tenths of the settlers died of starvation, violence, or disease, and the capitol there burned four times before it was relocated to Williamsburg. Today Jamestown is an atmospheric ghost town, where you'll find a visitors center, museum, paths leading through the ruins of "James Cittie," a scenic loop drive, and Glasshouse, where craftspeople demonstrate one of Virginia's first industries, glassblowing.

Jamestown Settlement (adjacent to the National Historic Site, tel. 804/229–1607), run by the state of Virginia, is an outdoor re-creation of Jamestown village, with reproductions of James Fort, a Powhatan Indian village, and the 110-foot *Sarah Constant.*

The Mariner's Museum (Newport News, tel. 804/595–0368). Here maritime history is documented, from the Indian dug-out canoe and Chesapeake workboats to modern shipbuilding at Newport News.

NASA Visitors Center (near Hampton, tel. 804/864–6000). Test your knowledge of aerospace on a computer game, see the *Apollo 12* Command Module and a 4-billion-year-old rock collected on the moon. Exhibits at the center document flight from the Wright brothers onward.

Shirley Plantation (tel. 804/829–5121 or 800/232–1613). Surmounted by a hand-carved pineapple finial, once a landmark for river boats, this Georgian plantation house has been owned by 10 generations of Hills and Carters (Anne Carter was the mother of Robert E. Lee). Shirley was founded six years after the settlers arrived in Jamestown, and the house was built in 1723. Especially noteworthy are its three-story "flying" staircase, which appears completely unsupported, and the Queen Anne forecourt.

The War Memorial Museum of Virginia (Newport News, tel. 804/247–8523) displays a collection of 60,000 artifacts from all of America's wars, including the Vietnam conflict.

Water Country, U.S.A. (tel. 804/229–9300) offers 40 acres of water rides, pools, slides, and shows, including sea lions and the U.S. High Diving Team.

Westover (tel. 804/730–2898). Seat of the Byrd family and considered one of the finest Georgian plantations in the United States, Westover lies on the James River (off Rte. 5). Its spectacular grounds are open daily, though the house can be seen only in the spring, during Virginia's Garden Week.

Yorktown Battlefield National Historic Site (tel. 804/896–3400). Here Washington laid siege to Cornwallis's army, and in 1781 the British surrendered in the (restored) Moore House. English, French, and American breastworks still line the battlefield, and it's a good idea to stop first at the visitors center to view the dioramas and rent a taped tour. The Yorktown Victory Monument commemorates the French, who provided decisive help in winning the battle.

Restaurants

When hunger overtakes you, you'll find several Colonial taverns are scattered around Williamsburg's historic district, among them the **King's Arms, Christiana Campbell's, Shields,** and **Chownings** (tel. 804/229–2141). These serve such traditional fare as prime rib, game pie, Sally Lunn (slightly sweet raised bread), and peanut soup. For formal dining there's the award-winning **Regency Room,** at the Williamsburg Inn (tel. 804/229–2141), and the **Trellis** (tel. 804/229–8610), in Merchant's Square. The **Old Chickahominy House** (Jamestown Rd., tel. 804/229–4689) is noted for its Brunswick stew; **Pierce's** (tel. 804/565–2955), just off I–65 has good barbecue, and at **Indian Fields** (Rte. 5, tel. 804/829–5004) the menu includes such Tidewater delicacies as Virginia ham in pineapple-raisin sauce, and scallops in puff pastry.

Tourist Information

Colonial National Historical Park (Jamestown–Yorktown) (Superintendent, Yorktown 23690, tel. 804/898–3400). **Colonial Williamsburg Foundation** (Williamsburg 23187, tel. 804/229–1000). **Jamestown-Yorktown Foundation** (Drawer JF, Williamsburg 23187, tel. 804/252–4138). **Virginia Division of Tourism** (202 N. 9th St., Richmond 23219, tel. 804/786–4484). **Virginia Peninsula Tourism** (8 San Jose Dr., Suite 3B, Newport News 23606, tel. 804/873–0092). **Virginia Plantation Country** (Box 1302, Hopewell 23860, tel. 804/541–2206). **Williamsburg Area Convention & Visitors Bureau** (Box GB, Williamsburg 23187, tel. 804/253–0192 or 800/368–6511).

Reservation Services

Bensonhouse of Williamsburg (Box 15131, Richmond 23227, tel. 804/648–7560). **Travel Tree Reservation Service** (Box 838, Williamsburg 23187, tel. 804/253–1571 6–9 PM weekdays).

Edgewood

Ridgely Copland of North Bend Plantation (*see* below) and Dot Boulware of Edgewood (just down Route 5, and approximately a half hour from Colonial Williamsburg) are dear friends, but they're as different as, well, the Federal and Victorian styles. Says frothy Dot in her liquid southern accent, "I have to tell you, I am a romantic." Nonetheless, before she and her husband, Julian, bought Edgewood Plantation, just over 10 years ago, she didn't care a bit for Victoriana. Fortunately tastes change, and when she became the mistress of an 1850s carpenter Gothic house she began collecting Victorian antiques like a woman possessed.

Dot's 14-room house, visible from Route 5, looks on the inside like Miss Haversham's dining room, minus the cobwebs. It is full to bursting with old dolls, antique corsets and lingerie, lace curtains and pillows, love seats, baby carriages, stuffed steamer trunks, mighty canopied beds, highboys, Confederate caps . . . the list goes on and on. At Christmastime she personally decorates 17 trees and festoons the banister of the graceful three-story staircase with bows. Clearly, more is more at Dot Boulware's Edgewood.

In her hands, Victoriana is thoroughly feminine, even though in one chamber, the Civil War Room, she's tried to cater to the opposite sex, decorating with intimate details of men's 19th-century apparel. Large people of either sex will have a hard time moving freely in this wildly crowded bed-and-breakfast, and the commonest reason men book a room is as a special treat for their mates. Lizzie's Room, the favorite, has a king-size pencil-post canopy bed and a private bath. The room enshrines the memory of a teenager who, Dot says, died of a broken heart when her beau failed to return from the Civil War; her name is scratched on the window.

Breakfast is served in the dining room by candlelight. Outside there's an unrestored mill house dating from 1725, an antiques shop, gazebo, and a swimming pool with a hot tub. Edgewood is centrally located for touring the Charles City County plantations and is down the road from the area's best restaurant, Indian Fields.

Address: *Charles City, VA 23030, tel. 804/829–2962.*
Accommodations: *2 double rooms with baths, 4 doubles share 2 baths.*
Amenities: *Air-conditioning; swimming pool, hot tub.*
Rates: *$95–$135; full breakfast. MC, V.*
Restrictions: *No pets.*

Liberty Rose

Bed-and-breakfast keepers in Williamsburg are in something of a bind. Because all the historic buildings in town are owned by either the Williamsburg Foundation or the College of William and Mary, they can't offer travelers authentic Colonial accommodations. Some have Colonial-style decoration anyway, but others, like Sandy and Brad Hirz, owners of the Liberty Rose, have come up with different, imaginative solutions to the dilemma.

Understand first that Sandy and Brad are a tremendously romantic story. They were just friends when Sandy decided to leave the West Coast to open a B&B in Williamsburg. Brad was helping Sandy house-hunt when they looked at a 1920s white clapboard and brick home a mile west of the restored district (on the road to Jamestown), and Sandy bought it in five minutes. Then Brad started seriously courting her, but it was Sandy, and not the B&B, who inspired him. Now they're a devoted married couple who run Williamsburg's most romantic B&B, decorated à la nouvelle Victorian with turn-of-the-century touches.

Sandy, a former interior designer, has a special talent for fabrics and is responsible for the handsome tie-back curtains, many-layered bed coverings, and plush canopies. The patterns are 19th-century reproductions. Brad has held up his end of the business by managing remodeling de-

tails. The bathrooms are particularly attractive: One has a floor taken from a plantation in Gloucester, a comfortable clawfoot tub, and an amazing free-standing, glass-sided shower. Old black-faced dolls and Noah's Ark carvings are tucked away in corners, and the furnishings are a copacetic mix of 18th- and 19th-century reproductions and antiques. Sandy's next project is to come out with a Liberty Rose catalogue.

Liberty Rose sits on a densely wooded hilltop, and the lake on the William and Mary campus is a pretty walk away. It is definitely not Colonial, but then the Colonial style isn't that romantic—which is, above all, the tone pursued and achieved at Liberty Rose.

Address: *1022 Jamestown Rd., Williamsburg, VA 23185, tel. 804/253–1260.*
Accommodations: *2 double rooms with baths, 2 suites.*
Amenities: *Air-conditioning, TV in suites (one with VCR).*
Rates: *$80–$125; full breakfast. MC, V.*
Restrictions: *No smoking indoors, no pets.*

North Bend Plantation

Routinely, a stay at this Charles City County plantation begins with a tour of the house and grounds conducted by Ridgely Copland, a farmer's wife and a nurse (several years ago named Virginia nurse of the year). Along the way Ridgely points out Union breastworks from 1864, wild asparagus, herds of deer, a swamp, and the wide James River. At some point during the trip she might stop and repeat the question she asks herself just about every day: "What lucky girl lives here?" The answer is Ridgely, of course, and, for a spell, her bed-and-breakfast guests.

Only one other Virginia bed-and-breakfast—Welbourne, near Middleburg—is so strikingly authentic, but North Bend differs from that slightly gone-to-seed mansion in that it's a working farm. The Coplands are salt-of-the-earth people striving to keep their acreage intact in the face of modern agriculture dilemmas. A stay at North Bend leaves visitors with a sense of reawakened admiration for that very American institution—the family farm.

North Bend, on the National Register and also a Virginia Historic Landmark, is a fine example of the Academic Greek Revival style, a wide, white frame structure with a red roof and a slender chimney at each corner. Built in 1819, with a classic two-over-two layout, large center hall, and Federal mantels and stair carvings, it was remodeled in 1853 along Benjamin Asher designs. But beyond its architectural distinctions, North Bend is drenched in history. Its premier guest bedroom contains a walnut desk used by the Union general Philip Sheridan, complete with his labels on the pigeonholes. His map was found in one of its drawers, a copy of which is framed on the wall of the billiard room. Above all, though, at North Bend history means family. George Copland is the great-great-great-nephew of William Henry Harrison, who, Ridgely laughingly reminds guests, served as president for just 30 days. Family heirlooms are everywhere, as is Ridgely's collection of Civil War first editions, which make fascinating bedtime reading.

As you might expect, North Bend is not a luxurious place. Only the suite has a private bath; there are no quaint touches in evidence—no down comforters, bubble bath, or sachets. There's just North Bend, its history, and the extraordinarily kind owners.

Address: *Rte. 1, Box 13A, Charles City, VA 23030, tel. 804/829-5176 (after 5:30).*
Accommodations: *2 double rooms share 1 bath, 1 suite.*
Amenities: *Air-conditioning; swimming pool.*
Rates: *$75–$85; full breakfast. No credit cards.*
Restrictions: *Smoking only in sunroom, no pets. Closed Dec. 25.*

Applewood

Applewood, so named because its owner collects things with an apple theme, is a spotlessly tidy bed-and-breakfast on Richmond Road, about four blocks from the historic district. It contains ceramic apples, apple prints, and even a copy of John Cheever's *The World of Apples*. Like other houses in the area, it was built in the late 1920s by a Colonial Williamsburg restorer, who added many of the kinds of details he'd been working on in the historic area: The house has a Flemish-bond brick exterior, a handsome 18th century–style portal, and dentil crown moldings in the interior—and the trim is painted in those milky blues and greens that are so common in Williamsburg. Applewood has four bedrooms for travelers; one suite has a canopy bed, fireplace, private breakfast area and entrance, and a convertible sofa bed—a fine choice for families with children. And the Golden Pippin Room sleeps four, one in a trundle bed. Innkeeper Fred Strout serves afternoon tea and breakfast, including, of course, apple muffins.

Address: *605 Richmond Rd., Williamsburg, VA 23185, tel. 804/229–0205 or 800/899–2753.*
Accommodations: *3 double rooms with baths, 1 suite.*
Amenities: *Air-conditioning, TV in parlor.*
Rates: *$65–$95; Continental breakfast, afternoon tea. MC, V.*
Restrictions: *No smoking indoors, no pets, 2-night minimum on holiday weekends and special events.*

Colonial Capital

The Colonial Capital, a frame three-story house painted lime-sherbet green, is within walking distance of the historic district, Merchant's Square, and the College of William and Mary; in fact, it's across the street from both Cary Field and the Alumni House. The exceedingly nice innkeepers, Phil and Barbara Craig, are a retired stockbroker and a university administrator who moved to Williamsburg after 25 years in North Carolina. The Colonial's five rooms are named after Tidewater-area rivers. Second-floor Potomac contains a bed-and-breakfast rarity—a queen-size waterbed, which Phil says makes converts out of travelers who normally wouldn't go near one. Prettiest, though, is Pamlico, with dormer windows and a white-canopied bed. Downstairs, there's a large living room with a fireplace and access to a sun porch, where the Craigs keep games, books, and puzzles. And, perhaps best of all, the Colonial Capital has parking in the rear for guests, which could otherwise prove a serious problem in teeming Williamsburg.

Address: *501 Richmond Rd., Williamsburg, VA 23185, tel. 804/229–0233 or 800/776–0570.*
Accommodations: *4 double rooms with baths, 1 suite.*
Amenities: *Air-conditioning, cable TV/VCR in guest parlor, phones on each floor; bicycles, parking.*
Rates: *$85–$125; full breakfast, welcome drink. MC, V.*
Restrictions: *Smoking only in guest parlor, no pets.*

Newport House

The Newport House takes the prize as the most unusual bed-and-breakfast in Williamsburg, if not all of Tidewater Virginia. The house is a meticulous reproduction of one that once stood in Newport, Rhode Island, designed by the Colonial architect Peter Harrison. Harrison invented "wood rustication" (an exterior wall surface that apes stone), which was used here and also at Mount Vernon. The three-story, dormered house, painted creamy yellow, stands just across the street from the William and Mary Law School on a small lot that contains an herb garden. As if the architectural curiosity of the house weren't enough, the owners, Cathy and John Millar, are practicing Elizabethan country dancers; they hold country-dancing evenings in the ballroom on Tuesday and Thursday, at which they appear in costume. (They also rent costumes.) Finally, this offbeat B&B's pet is a house-trained rabbit named Sassafras, who is let out of its kitchen hutch for floor shows at breakfast.

Address: *710 S. Henry St., Williamsburg, VA 23185, tel. 804/229-1775.*
Accommodations: *2 double rooms with baths.*
Amenities: *Air-conditioning, ballroom.*
Rates: *$90; full breakfast. No credit cards.*
Restrictions: *No smoking indoors, no pets.*

War Hill Inn

The War Hill Inn is three miles north of town; this is a drawback or an attraction, depending on whether you prefer to stay overnight in the thick of Colonial things, or put some space between your lodging and the crowds. The War Hill's feeling of remoteness is stressed by the fact that it's surrounded by pastures where owner Bill Lee's prize-winning Black Angus cows munch on the grass—though a condo development has risen up on one of the property's flanks. Bill is a retired veterinarian who built the house in 1968 to raise a family. It's a copy of the Anderson House in Colonial Williamsburg, and a fine one at that. Inside are architectural features that came from other places— the heart-of-pine floors from a schoolhouse and a staircase from a Lutheran church. The decor in the guest rooms is a mélange of Colonial reproductions and family things; the downstairs chamber is notable for its size and privacy. A good choice for families—thanks to its wide, fenced-in grounds, a small orchard of peaches and plums, and a cottage—two of its rooms sleep four.

Address: *4560 Long Hill Rd., Williamsburg, VA 23185, tel. 804/565-0248.*
Accommodations: *5 double rooms with baths.*
Amenities: *Air-conditioning; cable TV in bedrooms.*
Rates: *$55–$90; full breakfast. AE, MC, V.*
Restrictions: *No smoking, no pets, 2-night minimum on weekends.*

Around Charlottesville

Few cities in this country are so deeply devoted to—one might say, so in love with—a single man as is Virginia's Piedmont capital, Charlottesville. On a farm east of town (in the present-day hamlet of Shadwell) Thomas Jefferson, the third president of the United States, was born; and on a mountaintop overlooking a countryside Jefferson himself considered Edenic, he built his home. We have all seen Monticello, for it appears on one side of the nickel, though its minted image hardly does it justice. The breathtakingly beautiful edifice, constructed on architectural principles that would change the face of America, is a house that reveals volumes about the man who built it and lived there.

For instance, in the terraced vegetable gardens (restored according to Jefferson's Garden Book*) he introduced the tomato to North America and raised 19 types of English peas, his favorite food. (Mr. Jefferson, as he is called around here, attributed his long life—he lived to be 83—to his vegetarian eating habits.) Here he built a glass-enclosed pavilion, where he came to read, write, and watch his garden grow. Most of the 20,000 letters he wrote were penned in his study in a reclining chair with revolving desk (he had rheumatism and worked from a semi-recumbent position). Jefferson was also a collector; the walls of the formal parlor are lined with portraits of friends, like Washington and Monroe, and the east entrance hall displays mastodon bones and a buffalo head brought back from the West by Lewis and Clark.*

"Architecture," wrote Jefferson, "is my delight and putting up and pulling down one of my favorite pastimes." Originally he built Monticello in 1779 as an American Palladian villa, but after seeing the work of Boullée and Ledoux in France, he returned to Monticello with a head full of new ideas, above all, about its dome, and an aversion to grand staircases, which he believed took up too

much room. Today the full effect is best seen from the flower gardens on the west side.

Another reason for Charlottesville's love affair with Jefferson lies at the western end of town—the University of Virginia. If Monticello is a taste of Jeffersonian style, the school's rotunda and colonnade provide the banquet. Jefferson began designing the university buildings at the age of 74; in 1976 the American Institute of Architects voted them the most outstanding achievement in American architecture. The rotunda was inspired by the Pantheon, in Rome, but the dual colonnade that extends from it, intended as both dwelling place and study center for students and faculty, is all Jefferson's own. Students still inhabit the Colonnade rooms, amid fireplaces, porches, and rocking chairs.

Charlottesville today has its shopping malls and fast-food strips, not to mention a serious parking problem. Downtown has been converted into a pedestrian mall where shoppers find intriguing stores, such as Paula Lewis Quilts and the Rubaiyat, for women's clothes.

Charlottesville lies in the piedmont, the Blue Ridge foothills, and the driving here is fun and scenic. Highway 20, called the Constitution Route, takes travelers past Montpelier (James Madison's home) in Orange, 25 miles north of Charlottesville, and south past Michie Tavern, Ash Lawn (where James Monroe lived), and through Scottsville. This village on the James River, once the seat of Albemarle County, is rich in Revolutionary and Civil War history. It's a favorite spot for canoe and inner-tube trips. Twenty miles to the west the Blue Ridge rises, with access to the Skyline Drive or Parkway at Rockfish Gap.

Places to go, sights to see

Ash Lawn (tel. 804/293–9539), just down the road from Monticello, is the restored home of James Monroe, whose mountaintop site (selected by Jefferson) offers views of Monticello's dome. Ash Lawn, which burned in

1840 and was rebuilt in Victorian-farmhouse style 30 years later, is a working, 550-acre farm where sheep and peacocks roam. Summertime brings an opera festival and a Colonial crafts weekend.

Barboursville Vineyards (north of Charlottesville, tel. 703/832-3824), produces pinot noir blanc, chardonnay, merlot, and cabernet sauvignon wines, among others. Tastings are held daily from 10 to 4, and tours on Saturday from 10 to 5. Here you can also explore the ruins of Governor James Barbour's plantation home. The Jefferson Wine Grape Growers Society (tel. 804/296-4188) distributes a brochure on other area vineyards, including Simeon, Chermont, Oakencroft, and Autumn Hill.

Court Square, in downtown Charlottesville, is the locus of Albemarle County government, with a courthouse built between 1803 and 1867. In the 18th century a meetinghouse occupied the site, and it was here that Jefferson worshiped. The square also holds an impressive equestrian statue of Stonewall Jackson.

Michie Tavern (tel. 804/977-1234). This tavern, dating from 1765, was moved to its present location on the road to Monticello in 1920. With its ceaseless crowds and general store, many visitors find it too commercial. The cafeteria-style restaurant serves historic fast food—fried chicken, black-eyed peas, stewed tomatoes, and the like. The adjacent Meadow Run Grist Mill houses the Virginia Wine Museum.

Monticello (tel. 804/295-8181) lies about a mile southeast of the intersection of Routes 64 and 20. The tour, which ascends Mr. Jefferson's "little mountain" by shuttle bus, lasts about half an hour and is extremely rewarding. Afterward visitors are free to roam the gardens, view the hidden dependencies, and make a pilgrimage to the great man's grave. The museum shop is worth a stop, if only for its extensive collection of books by and about Jefferson. Near the shuttle-bus station you'll also find a sandwich shop and the Thomas Jefferson Center for Historic Plants, which sells seedlings of some of the exotic varieties Jefferson cultivated. Note that Monticello is best taken in before the tour buses arrive, around 11 AM. At the visitors center a permanent exhibition displays 400 artifacts and pieces of Jeffersoniana. The film *The Eye of Thomas Jefferson* is shown daily at 11 and 2.

Montpelier (south of Orange, tel. 703/672-1776). James Madison, Jr., served as president after Jefferson and before Monroe. Known as the Father of the Constitution he is credited with seeing America through the War of 1812. He and his wife, Dolley, lived here from 1817 to 1836, followed by William du Pont, Sr., who bought it in 1901. The Montpelier Hunt Race, takes place here on the first weekend in November. The guided tour of the estate leads visitors over the 2,700-acre grounds, through the 55-room house, and past Madison's grave.

Rapidan. This village about 5 miles northeast of Orange is bisected by the Rapidan River and holds the Waddell Memorial Presbyterian Church, an architectural hymn in Carpenter Gothic. Nearby you'll also find the Riverside

Winery (tel. 703/672–4673) and Marmont Orchards (tel. 703/672–2730), where, in season, you can pick your own peaches, plums, and nectarines.

Scottsville sits on the James River and is where Lafayette made a successful stand against General Cornwallis in 1781. The village holds 32 Federal-style buildings and the locks of the James River Kanawha Canal, which were a target for 10,000 bluecoats under General Sheridan during the Civil War. Nearby you'll find the James River Runners (tel. 804/286–2338), where you can rent tubes, rafts, and canoes.

1740 House (tel. 804/977–1740), an antiques store located near Ivy, west of Charlottesville on Route 250, is known for its museum-quality 18th- and 19th-century furniture.

University of Virginia (tel. 804/924–1019). Tours leave the rotunda several times daily (except during holidays and exams). It's just as enjoyable to wander the grounds on your own. Inside the rotunda stands Alexander Galt's statue of Jefferson, which students saved from the fire of 1895.

Restaurants

Charlottesville's restaurant scene is surprisingly cosmopolitan. **Duner's** (tel. 804/293–8352) and **The Gallerie** (804/823–5883) are favored for French and nouvelle American cuisine, and the **Blue Ridge Brewing Company** (tel. 804/977–0017), owned by a nephew of William Faulkner, for its riotous atmosphere. At any of these and other city eateries you may find a celebrity at a table nearby. Among those who've relocated to the lush countryside around Charlottesville are Sissy Spacek and Jessica Lange. Gordonsville has a pleasant restaurant, the **Toliver House** (tel. 703/832–3485).

Tourist Information

Charlottesville/Albemarle Visitors Bureau (Box 161, Charlottesville 22902, tel. 804/293–6789). **Orange County Visitors Bureau** (Box 133, Orange 22960, tel. 703/672–1653). **Virginia Division of Tourism** (202 N. 9th St., Richmond 23219, tel. 804/786–4484).

Reservation Services

Guesthouses Bed & Breakfast, Inc. (Box 5737, Charlottesville 22905, tel. 804/979–7264) is a reservation service run by Mary Hill Caperton, which can arrange entrée to private houses otherwise closed to the public. The oldest service of its kind, Guesthouses handles such properties as an estate that was the home of Thomas Jefferson's nephew and ward, a Japanese house with a tennis court and a sunken tub, a Blue Ridge farm with a spring-fed pond, a 200-year-old log cabin, and an antebellum cottage that was part of the original Jefferson plantation.

High Meadows

High Meadows, in Scottsville, is above all a bed-and-breakfast inn done by hand. The hands in question are those of Peter Shushka, a retired submariner, and his wife, Mary Jae Abbitt, an analyst for the Securities and Exchange Commission. In this unique B&B Federal and late-Victorian architecture exist side by side, now happily joined by a longitudinal hall.

However, it wasn't always so. The Italianate front section was built in 1882 by Peter White, who intended to level the older house several paces behind it. But bearing in mind her growing family, his wife refused to give up the old place, built in 1830, and for a time a plank between the two was the tenuous connector that kept the marriage intact. Today High Meadows is on the National Register and Virginia Trust.

Peter and Mary Jae have decorated the place with great originality, keeping intact the stylistic integrity of each section. They've also used fabrics imaginatively on the bed hangings and windows. Of the three guest rooms in the Federal section and five in the Victorian, who can say which you'd prefer? Fairview, in the 1880s portion, is the quintessential bride's room, with a fireplace, flowing bed drapery, a three-window alcove, and claw-foot tub. The Virginia suite, upstairs in the Federal section has stenciled walls lined with antique stuffed animals, a fireplace, and rafters across the ceiling. In the Patrick Henry common sitting room, there's an ornate gold-leaf mirror in front of which the Revolutionary leader said, "Give me liberty or give me death."

Breakfast, served in the downstairs dining room, consists of Shushka specialties like cranberry-almond muffins and ham-and-egg cups laced with tomatoes and Gruyère cheese. Peter also takes a novel approach to the afternoon and evening meals. By arrangement he'll provide you with reasonably priced gourmet baskets stuffed with wine and ramekins of hot food, to eat in your room or on the terrace. How did a former submarine officer learn to cook? During stints underwater, of course, when there was nothing else to do.

Address: *Rte. 4, Box 6, Scottsville, VA 24590, tel. 804/286-2218.*
Accommodations: *5 double rooms with baths, 2 suites.*
Amenities: *Restaurant, air-conditioning in 5 rooms, fireplaces in 3 rooms and 2 common areas.*
Rates: *$85–$110; full breakfast, evening wine and hors d'oeuvres. AE, MC, V.*
Restrictions: *No smoking, pets permitted in ground-level rooms by arrangement.*

Prospect Hill

For elegance and luxury, Prospect Hill runs second only to the famous Inn at Little Washington. That, added to its architecturally noteworthy setting, makes staying here something worth filling your piggy bank for. Prospect Hill lies east of Charlottesville, in the 14-square-mile Greensprings National Historic District. This one is the oldest continuously occupied frame manor house in Virginia. But except for the obligatory dependencies and impressive boxwood hedges, Prospect Hill doesn't look like a plantation, because it was rebuilt in the Victorian era, when a columned facade and decorative cornices were added. The innkeepers have painted it lemony yellow.

There are four nicely furnished rooms in the main house, but the big treat is to stay in one of the six refurbished dependencies. Sanco Pansy's cottage, about 100 feet away from the manor, is special. It has a sitting room and whirlpool tub for two. The Carriage House, lit by two Palladian windows provides views of ponies in the meadow nibbling the green Virginia turf. Surrounded by such *luxe, calme, et volupté*, it's strange to consider that in the last century, the dependencies were filled with hams, ice blocks, and livestock.

Dinner at the inn is a marvelous production, not so much because of the cuisine (French-inspired and well above average), as the ceremony. You begin with complimentary wine and cider served a half hour before supper—outdoors in good weather. Next, the dinner bell rings, and in you file to hear the menu recited by innkeeper Bill Sheehan or his son, Michael. (Michael looks like a college halfback, but thanks to his delightful mama, Mireille, his French is impeccable.) Then comes grace, delivered so earnestly that it could bring an atheist to God, and five courses.

Breakfast is hot and brought to your dependency on a tray. You could take it in the dining room, but why spoil the fun? In your dependency, you can eat in a whirlpool tub. This really splendid inn is a class-act that hasn't become too smoothly professional. You're bound to meet the gregarious innkeepers and appreciate the way they have put their stamp on Prospect Hill.

Address: *Rte. 3, Box 430, Trevilians, VA 23093, tel. 703/967–0844 or 800/277–0844, fax 703/967–0102.*
Accommodations: *4 double rooms with baths in main house, 5 doubles with baths and 3 suites in dependencies.*
Amenities: *Restaurant, air-conditioning, fireplaces in 12 guest rooms, Jacuzzis in 5 rooms; pool, 1 meeting room.*
Rates: *$120–$180; full breakfast and afternoon tea. MC, V.*
Restrictions: *No pets.*

Chester

A number of years ago, Gordon Anderson and Dick Shaffer, a legal administrator and investment banker, retired from the New York rat race and bought an 1847 Greek Revival mansion in Scottsville. They brought their antiques along, their sophisticatedly urban lifestyle, their Russian wolfhounds, VCR tapes of the Met's Leontyne Price singing *Aida*, and details we saw nowhere else in Virginia—like cigarettes laid out in dishes on coffee tables. The two of them are relaxed hosts who run their bed-and-breakfast like a Noel Coward house party. Take dinner, which they serve by arrangement, cook themselves, and eat along with guests: It's a four-course affair for $18 per person, including California wine, with Gordon and Dick chatting about movies, art, and the Chester's brush with the Civil War until the wee hours of the night. They also know interesting, but unpublicized, facts about the area; for instance, where the celebrities and the richest man in America live. There are five bedrooms, a total of eight working fireplaces, and a laundry room, which guests are free to use.

Address: *Rte. 4, Box 57, Scottsville, VA 24590, tel. 804/286–3960.*
Accommodations: *1 double room with bath, 4 doubles share 2 baths.*
Amenities: *Fireplaces in 4 bedrooms; bicycles, kennel for pets.*
Rates: *$65–$90; full breakfast, complimentary beverages. AE.*
Restrictions: *2-night minimum on graduation weekends.*

Clifton

T homas Randolph, the builder of Clifton and a governor of Virginia, didn't have it easy. Would you want Thomas Jefferson for a father-in-law? Sue Putalik, the current live-in manager, says that Jefferson didn't much care for his son-in-law, which may explain why Randolph didn't adopt Jeffersonian neoclassicism for his house. This white frame, six-columned manse is handsome, nevertheless. It's owned by a Washington lawyer who seems to prefer the lived-in look to a museum ambience (with grounds that aren't quite up to Garden Club standards), but here the bathrooms win the prize; one holds a full-scale wood sculpture of an erotically reclining nude, and all have windows and shining white tiles. In the main house, rooms 2, 4, and 6 are especially attractive. Two dependencies on the back lawn contain three more suites, which have been renovated Malibu style. At Clifton guests are left pretty much to their own devices, which might include a swim in the lap pool, an inner-tube float on the secluded lake, tennis, or bike rides along the back roads.

Address: *Rte. 9, Box 412, Charlottesville, VA 22901, tel. 804/971–1800.*
Accommodations: *5 double rooms with baths, 3 suites.*
Amenities: *Air-conditioning and fireplaces in guest rooms; lap pool, tennis court, pets permitted.*
Rates: *$115–$165; full breakfast. MC, V.*
Restrictions: *No smoking in public rooms.*

The Inn at Monticello

Carol and Larry Engel forsook the plains of the upper Midwest because they were enchanted with Virginia, especially Colonial Williamsburg. When we visited, they were still renovating the Inn at Monticello, an 1850s farmhouse with a two-story front gallery and a brook trickling over the long front lawn. Their bed-and-breakfast has the distinction of being so close to Monticello, Michie Tavern, Ash Lawn, and the Thomas Jefferson Visitors Center that you can walk to several of these attractions. It holds five guest rooms, many of whose mantels and matching moldings are painted in cool Williamsburg blues and greens. Downstairs there's a parlor, a twin-bedded room, and a honeymoon room, which is nicely furnished but too close to the condo development that rises in back. Of the three upstairs bedrooms, we liked the Yellow Room best because of its white cotton balloon shades and plump rope bed. The Engels take special care with the bed linen, which is downy soft and complemented by European coverlets.

Address: *Rte. 20 S, RR 19, Box 112, Charlottesville, VA 22901, tel. 804/979-3593.*
Accommodations: *5 double rooms with baths.*
Amenities: *Air-conditioning; lake for swimming.*
Rates: *$95–$130; full breakfast. No credit cards.*
Restrictions: *No smoking, no pets.*

Mayhurst

The first glimpse of Mayhurst is as heady as a sip of champagne. You wind up a little hillock south of Orange (leaving behind distractions like shopping centers) and there she lies, for this extravagantly playful, white Italianate villa built in 1860 is surely female. Mayhurst's roofline is bracketed and gabled, her four faces beautified with arched windows, porticoes, and bays; above the architectural fantasy is perched a gazebo, making her look for all the world like a Victorian lady in lacy undies and a hat. The interior, which doesn't quite live up to the facade, does have an unusual oval staircase, with radial treads that squeak resistantly as you climb. Of the six guest chambers in the main house, we liked the Victorian Room best, for its floor-to-12-foot-ceiling window bank, bedstead with 10-foot posts, marble mantel, and clawfoot tub. Mayhurst is surrounded by 36 acres on which lie an antiques shop, pond, and cottage (which we found oppressively dark). It could use a touch of restoration, but it is a remarkable house; some will find it the Victorian mansion of their dreams.

Address: *Box 707, Orange, VA 22960, tel. 703/672-5597.*
Accommodations: *5 double rooms with baths, 1 suite, 1 cottage suite.*
Amenities: *Air-conditioning, fireplaces in 4 guest rooms, suite, and cottage suite.*
Rates: *$125–$145; full breakfast. MC, V.*
Restrictions: *Smoking in cottage only, 2-night minimum on Oct. weekends.*

The Shadows

Though it's surrounded by cedars and adjoining a cemetery, the Shadows is anything but melancholy. Pat and Barbara Loffredo, have filled their 1913 farmhouse just up the road from Montpelier with a cheerful collection of country Victorian antiques. Prize pieces are a wryly funny hunt board carved with a brace of dead birds; an old pump organ; numerous clawfoot tubs; and Maxfield Parrish prints wherever the eye rests. The house is what Barbara calls Gustav Stickley Craftsman style, a modified bungalow built of wood and local fieldstone. It has dark oak floors and windowsills around which lace curtains flutter. The four guest rooms upstairs all have standard Victorian trappings (kept spotlessly neat). All the tangibles here are pleasant enough, but Pat and Barbara put the Shadows over the mark. They're refugees from New York, where Pat was a policeman, and their joy in their newfound home is infectious. The two of them delight in coddling guests, overwhelming them at breakfast, laying open their library, and sending them on their way with a hug. Who ever said New Yorkers are unfriendly?

Address: *Rte. 1, Box 535, Orange, VA 22960, tel. 703/672-5057.*
Accommodations: *4 double rooms with baths, 2 cottage suites.*
Amenities: *Air-conditioning.*
Rates: *$70–$100; full breakfast. No credit cards.*
Restrictions: *No smoking, no pets, 2-night minimum May and Oct. and Montpelier race weekends.*

The Silver Thatch Inn

The Silver Thatch, north of Charlottesville off Route 29, was formerly called the Hollymead. The oldest part of its semicircle of connected buildings is log, built by Hessian prisoners during the Revolution. The whole compound has been renovated by owners Joe and Mickey Geller, and it has a new, immaculately kept look. The Gellers also pay close and imaginative attention to the restaurant. Mickey and her chef, Janet Henry, have brought a savvy kind of cuisine to Charlottesville; entrées like grilled veal chops bear tangily vibrant vegetable sauces. In the summer they serve an antipasto plate, cappuccino is available at breakfast, and their wine list recently received an award of excellence from the *Wine Spectator*. The Gellers have done a nice job with the guest rooms, too, which all have quilts, down comforters, and antiques; some have fireplaces. The four cottage rooms surpass those in the main house because of their sparkling new bathrooms. Silver Thatch guests may use a pool and tennis courts nearby.

Address: *3001 Hollymead Dr., Charlottesville, VA 22901, tel. 804/978-4686.*
Accommodations: *7 double rooms with baths.*
Amenities: *Restaurant, air-conditioning, cable TV.*
Rates: *$105–$125; full breakfast. MC, V.*
Restrictions: *No smoking, no pets, closed Dec. 23–26, first 2 weeks in Jan. and Aug., 2-night minimum on weekends Apr.–June, Sept.–Nov.*

Sleepy Hollow Farm

North of Charlottesville, as you roller-coaster past horse farms and vineyards on Route 231, you'll also pass the bright red roof of the barn at Sleepy Hollow Farm. This two-story brick house, begun in the 18th century (though 20th-century renovations keep it from looking historic), is surrounded by fields grazed by Black Angus and Tarentais bulls. It is eminently suited to families with children: There's a play set on the grounds, bunnies in the hedgerows, and a spring-fed pond for swimming. The main house has four rooms, and there are two suites in the chestnut-wood cottage. Sleepy Hollow's owner, Beverley Allison, came to the house as a bride, raised a family, produced the ABC News, served as an Episcopal missionary in Central America, then returned to open her bed-and-breakfast. Thus, she has stories to tell, if you can persuade her; ask for the one about a ghost who frequented one of the guest rooms and then found peace after the room was blessed.

Address: *16280 Blue Ridge Turnpike, Gordonsville, VA 22942, tel. 703/832–5555.*
Accommodations: *4 double rooms with baths, 2 suites.*
Amenities: *Air-conditioning, TV in 2 rooms, TV/VCR in sitting room, 3 fireplaces and 2 stoves in common rooms and suites; stable, kennel, riding arranged.*
Rates: *$55–$100; full breakfast. MC, V with surcharge.*
Restrictions: *No smoking in dining room.*

200 South Street

This popular small hotel in downtown Charlottesville is across the street from and next door to two trendy eateries, Memory and Company and South Street, the latter known for its seafood. The complex consists of two Victorian homes built between 1850 and 1900, which were restored by a team of Charlottesville businessmen. It was a good idea to paint them yellow, which cheers up South Street considerably, and to fill them with English and Belgian antiques including capacious armoires and lace-canopied four-posters. The walls are lined with displays of contemporary art and a much more interesting collection of historic Holsinger photographs. We preferred the 10 rooms and suite in No. 200 to those in the neighboring cottage, because there's a parlor there, and train tracks in back make a front room desirable. But all the rooms are inviting and immaculately renovated, and some of them contain such luxuries as whirlpool baths and fireplaces. Breakfast is brought to your door on a tray, and in the afternoon, tea and wine are served in the sitting room.

Address: *200 South St., Charlottesville, VA 22901, tel. 804/979–0200.*
Accommodations: *17 double rooms with baths, 3 suites.*
Amenities: *Air-conditioning, TV in 3rd-floor lounge, phones in rooms, turn-down service.*
Rates: *$85–$160; Continental breakfast. AE, MC, V.*
Restrictions: *No pets, 2-night minimum on weekends Apr.–May and Sept.–Oct.*

Willow Grove Plantation

Angela Mulloy, who runs Willow Grove, is a little like one of the lady innkeepers in Shakespeare—a Mistress Quickly, for instance, not because of her morals, but because of her style, which is friendly, but no-nonsense. She adamantly insists that Willow Grove is not one of those country inns where they force camaraderie with social hours and hors d'oeuvres. Instead, she offers good food and plenty of it, rooms that are clean and antiques laden, but perhaps a tad ragged around the edges (we noted rust stains in bathtubs). She is also extremely proud of Willow Grove's architectural distinctiveness. This grand plantation house with a Greek Revival facade was built in numerous stages beginning in the 1770s and lived in by just a handful of families who didn't remodel during its long history. As a result, the curator of the Philadelphia Museum commented that "Willow Grove is a unique example of the picturesqueness of growth." Dinners are served in the dining rooms and the tavern; guest rooms occupy the second floor. Continental breakfasts are delivered to your room, accompanied by the morning newspaper, and a full breakfast is served downstairs.

Address: *Rte. 1, Box 30, Orange, VA 22960, tel. 703/672-5982; in DC, 703/256-1976.*
Accommodations: *3 double rooms with baths, 2 suites.*
Amenities: *Restaurant, air-conditioning.*
Rates: *$95–$135; full breakfast. MC, V.*

Woodstock Hall

This Colonial way station has two distinctions. It's one of the least altered historic structures in the area, and owners Clarence and Mary Ann Elder also own the 1740 House antiques shop in Ivy. This explains the fine period furnishings and the careful renovation. The Woodstock stands on a hill near Charlottesville, a prim, mustard yellow beacon in excellent biking country. Inside you'll find a case full of artifacts unearthed during the restoration, fireplaces in all rooms, burnished wood floors, case locks on the doors, much of the original window glass, and a copy of Poe's *The Tale of the Ragged Mountains*—because the poet's stay here inspired him to write it. In the main house, one snug and particularly pleasant room is called the Duc Liancourt Room, and a suite in the old detached kitchen contains two fireplaces and a rather short antique canopy bed. The resident innkeepers keep the place shining and serve breakfast, but they don't assert a sense of personality. It is still a good choice for those who want to visit Charlottesville, but stay in the country.

Address: *RR 637, Ivy (Rte. 3, Box 40, Charlottesville 22901), VA, tel. 804/293-8977.*
Accommodations: *3 double rooms with baths, 1 suite.*
Amenities: *Air-conditioning, TV in rooms.*
Rates: *$95–$130; full breakfast, afternoon tea. No credit cards.*
Restrictions: *No smoking, no pets, 3-night minimum on graduation and parents' weekends.*

The Blue Ridge/ Shenandoah Valley

The standard way to see the Blue Ridge Mountains is to pile into a car on a weekend in October and drive south from Front Royal along the Skyline Drive. If you do this, bumper-to-bumper traffic could keep you from covering the full 105-mile course, your feet may only touch ground at rest stops and scenic overlooks, and you probably won't get past Rockfish Gap (just east of Waynesboro), where the drive becomes the equally (some would claim more) splendid Blue Ridge Parkway. Above all, you'll have only the foggiest idea of the landscape at Virginia's western border, markedly different from the rest of the state, a kind of continental precursor to the West.

In geographical terms the Blue Ridge is the eastern wall of the wide Shenandoah Valley, which is retained at the other side by the Allegheny Mountains. Down the middle of the valley, bisecting it for some 50 miles, rises another mini-mountain range called Massanutten Mountain, even though, cuplike, it holds a pretty valley of its own. The Shenandoah River, which runs through the valley, divides north of Massanutten—to further confuse the issue—into a North and South Fork, which in reality lie east and west of Massanutten.

Once you've got the geography down you can plot a more informed assault on the mountains and valley by crossing the ridge along such strategic and scenic routes as Highways 211, 33, and especially 56, an untrammeled two-laner that's a favorite even of view-jaded locals. These paths lead into the central and southern sections of the Shenandoah Valley, bypassing the tourist traps (or have you a yen to visit petting zoos and reptile parks?) clustered around Front Royal.

This is not to say you should skip the national park. It holds the heights of the Blue Ridge in a 100-mile strip from Front Royal to Waynesboro and provides nonpareil views of the Virginia piedmont to the east and splendid Shenandoah Valley to the west. To the park come fishermen to catch the crafty brook trout, and hikers, who find meanders aplenty, including a 95-mile stretch of the Appalachian Trail and 500 miles of park-maintained paths. The unanimous favorite among walkers is the route up Old Rag Mountain, at 3,268 feet, but even a short stroll from a trailhead on the Skyline Drive brings visitors within viewing range of the park's wildlife: 200 species of birds, chipmunks, salamanders, timber rattlesnakes, white-tailed deer, bobcats, and black bears. Spring and fall are peak seasons for nature lovers. In May the green of new foliage moves up the ridge at a rate of 100 feet a day, with clouds of wild pink azaleas providing contrast. Fall colors are at their most vivid between October 10 and 25, when migrating hawks join the human leaf-gazers to take in the display.

Once over the ridge and in the valley (Shenandoah means "daughter of the stars" in the Indian language), there are better ways to take in the countryside than by zooming north or south along I–81. Route 11 parallels the superhighway in a delightfully labyrinthine fashion, providing access to big-name sights such as the New Market Battlefield and Luray Caverns, and running through small towns, including Woodstock, Edinburg, Mt. Jackson, and Steele's Tavern, where roadside produce stands, flea markets, and local-history museums further delay your progress.

The towns of Staunton and Lexington are Shenandoah gems that will interest lovers of famous men. Staunton, as hilly as Rome, was Woodrow Wilson's home, though it also boasts the pretty campus of the Mary Baldwin College, the Virginia Institute for the Deaf and Blind, and the Museum of American Frontier Culture. Lexington lives and

*breathes for Stonewall Jackson and Robert E. Lee, who was
named president of Washington and Lee University after
the Civil War ended. Next door to the Washington and Lee
campus is the Virginia Military Institute, founded in 1839,
where Jackson taught natural philosophy before bedeviling
Union armies as a Confederate general.*

*West along winding country roads from Staunton and
Lexington lies a countryside often neglected by valley
visitors. Routes 33, 250, and 39 lead to the Appalachian
plateau and West Virginia, bordered by the thick foliage of
the George Washington National Forest. Every 10 miles or
so the roads cross rocky waterways—such as that lovely
trio of rivers, the Bullpasture, Cowpasture, and
Calfpasture—providing excellent spots for wading and
picnicking. Most of the towns in this area are no more
than crossroads, with the exception of Hot Springs, site of
The Homestead, a 15,000-acre resort that's a Virginia
institution. The town at the gates of The Homestead has
a pleasant collection of arts-and-crafts shops, gourmet
delis, and restaurants.*

Places to go, sights to see

Belle Grove (1 mi south of Middletown, tel. 703/869–2028), one of the few
stately homes in the Shenandoah Valley, was built of local limestone in 1794,
with four chimneys and Tuscan porticoes thought to have been added at the
urging of Thomas Jefferson. It suffered greatly in 1864, when Confederate
forces launched an attack on a Union Army headquartered at the mansion.

Blue Ridge Parkway (tel. 704/627–3419). President Franklin Roosevelt was
so taken with the Shenandoah National Park when he visited it in 1933 that
he authorized a national parkway to connect it to the Great Smoky
Mountains, nearly 500 miles away. The resulting scenic highway was finally
completed in 1987. Favorite stopping points are the James River Wayside;
Peaks of Otter (a valley with a 24-acre lake tucked between Sharp and Flat
Top mountains), and photogenic Mabry Mill.

The Chessie Natural Trail is a hiking and walking path linking Lexington
with the nearby town of Buena Vista.

Goshen Pass is a 3-mile gap in the mountains carved by the Maury River, off
Route 39 about 20 miles northwest of Lexington. When the wild

rhododendrons bloom in May, this is one of the loveliest spots in Virginia, with facilities for tubing, swimming, canoeing, fishing, and hiking.

Luray Caverns (tel. 703/743–6551) are famed for the "stalacpipe organ," which gets played on hour-long cave tours. The place is kitschy but fun, though cave aficionados prefer Skyline Caverns, near Front Royal (tel. 703/635–4545 or 800/635–4599), by virtue of their flowerlike mineral encrustations known as anthrodites. Further reaches of the valley's underground world can be surveyed at Grand, Shenandoah, Endless, and Dixie caverns.

Massanutten (tel. 703/289–9441) offers downhill skiing on 11 slopes, one with a 1,150-foot vertical drop. The Massanutten ski resort also has facilities for golf, tennis, and indoor swimming.

Museum of American Frontier Culture (Staunton, tel. 703/332–7850). This museum compound includes three farmsteads (reminiscent of those that early Shenandoah Valley settlers left behind in England, Ireland, and Germany), where costumed staff members demonstrate the ways in which 18th- and 19th-century farmers planted their fields, harvested, and tended to domestic chores.

Natural Bridge (Natural Bridge, tel. 800/336–5727; in VA, 800/533–1410). Thomas Jefferson was so impressed by this 215-foot-high, 90-foot-long rock span that he bought it, in 1774. Before the discovery of vaster natural bridges in Utah, it was high on America's great-sights list. In recent decades it's been degraded by commercialism and is now the focus of a hokey light show and the site of a wax museum.

Natural Chimneys (tel. 703/350–2510). These 120-foot rock formations just south of Harrisonburg are the backdrop for a jousting tournament held every August since 1821. There's a campground, pool, picnic area, and nature trails.

New Market Battlefield (tel. 703/740–3101). Of all Civil War memorials, this is one of the most affecting, for in the last year of the Civil War 247 cadets from the Virginia Military Institute were sent here to a "baptism of fire." Though some in the battalion were just 15, the VMI boys became heroes that day. The Hall of Valor museum commemorates them.

The Shenandoah National Park (Luray, tel. 703/999–2266), 302 square miles in area, holding 60 peaks ranging from 3,000 to 4,000 feet high, offers hope to anyone who cares about the wilderness. By 1900 the thin-soiled land that now comprises much of the park had been farmed out, the forest denuded, the animals gone to happier hunting grounds. In 1926 the Congress and the State of Virginia united in the formation of the park, which in following decades gradually blossomed once again. A movie shown at the Byrd Visitors Center at Big Meadows tells the story of the park's regeneration. Brochures that will guide you to its more than 70 scenic overlooks, hiking trails, and lodges are available here and at the Dickey Ridge Visitors Center, just south of Luray.

Shenandoah River Floating. The lazily meandering river offers opportunities for mostly gentle canoe and raft rides, with a little fishing, swimming, and inner-tubing thrown in. One good outfitter is the *Downriver Canoe Company* (Bentonville, tel. 703/635–5526), which will put you in for sallies on the South Fork, provide equipment, and pick you up, most likely waterlogged, afterward.

Skyline Drive, the park's 105-mile crown jewel, built in the 1930s by the Civilian Conservation Corps, runs past Marys Rock Tunnel, the Pinnacles, Little Stony Man Cliffs, and other landmarks. There are two busy restaurants along the way, at Skyland and Big Meadows, the former remaining open after November 1. The Park Service keeps the drive open all year, though you should check before attempting the trip in snow and other adverse conditions.

Statler Brothers Complex (tel. 703/885–7297). Staunton loves the Statlers, because the four country musicians are local boys who defied Nashville by cutting their records in their hometown. A converted elementary school showcases artifacts from their career, and every fourth of July they give a wildly popular "Happy Birthday, America" concert in Gypsy Hill Park.

Stonewall Jackson House (tel. 703/463–2552). In the heart of Lexington (and just up the street from the visitors center), this trim brick two-story is where Major Thomas Jackson, a philosophy professor at VMI, lived with his wife before he rode away to lead the men in gray. General Jackson died at the Battle of Chancellorsville at the age of 39.

Strasburg Emporium (tel. 703/465–3712) is a 60-square-foot grab bag for antiques collectors, who reach in and generally come up with fun junk and occasionally a treasure. Auctions are held on the first and third Sundays of each month.

Theater at Lime Kiln (Lexington, tel. 703/463–3074). Set in an abandoned lime quarry, this stage for a professional company of actors has been called the most unusual theater setting in the United States. The Memorial Day–Labor Day schedule includes concerts on Sunday and Wednesday.

Virginia Horse Center (tel. 703/463–7060) is a multimillion-dollar equestrian complex on 400 acres just northwest of Lexington, with 480 stalls, a 1,000-seat grandstand, regulation dressage areas, horse trails, and cross-country courses. Its calendar includes such events as the Bonnie Blue National, U.S. Pony Club Regional Rally, and the Virginia Horse Trials.

Virginia Military Institute (Lexington, tel. 703/464–7207) was founded in 1839 as the nation's first state-supported military school. Uniformed cadets conduct tours of the campus, which, except for the anomalous Stick Victorian admissions building, is an austere and blocky Gothic Revival fortress. With any luck you'll catch the cadets drilling on the parade grounds and at the George C. Marshall Museum steal a peek at the Nobel Prize of this VMI alumnus and at the Academy Award won by the producer of the movie *Patton.*

Virginia School for the Deaf and Blind. A walk down Staunton's graceful
Beverley Street leads past the VSDB's handsome main building, whose Greek
Revival facade and columned portico were inspired by the architectural
principles of Thomas Jefferson.

Washington and Lee University (Lexington, tel. 703/463–8768) was founded
in 1749, subsidized by George Washington when the institution was near
bankruptcy in 1796, and presided over by Robert E. Lee in the late 1860s. An
extraordinary front Colonnade and the Lee Museum and Chapel, beneath
which the general is buried, are its most noteworthy sights.

Wintergreen (tel. 804/325–2200 or 800/325–3300). This 11,000-acre, privately
owned resort lies on the eastern flanks of the Blue Ridge, 45 miles
southwest of Charlottesville. It has an 18-hole golf course, 10 ski slopes, an
equestrian center, one indoor and five outdoor swimming pools, restaurants,
lounges, shopping centers, condos perched mountainside, and an acclaimed
nature program. Wintergreen's annual Spring Wildflower Symposium is a big
event.

Woodrow Wilson Birthplace (tel. 703/885–0897), an imposing, white Greek
Revival home in the prettiest residential section of Staunton, offers lots of
Wilson memorabilia, a film on his presidency narrated by E. G. Marshall, and
Wilson's spiffy Pierce Arrow limousine.

Tourist Information

Front Royal Chamber of Commerce (Box 568, Front Royal 22630, tel.
703/635–3185). **Harrisonburg–Rockingham Chamber of Commerce** (191 S.
Main St., Box 1, Harrisonburg 22801, tel. 703/434–3862). **Jefferson National
Forest Information Center** (Box 10, Natural Bridge Station 24579, tel.
703/291–2188). **Lexington Visitors Center** (102 E. Washington St., Lexington
24450, tel. 703/463–3777). **Rockfish Gap Regional Information Center** (301
W. Main St., Waynesboro 22980, tel. 703/943–5187). **Shenandoah Valley
Travel Association** (Box 1040, New Market 22844, tel. 703/740–3132).
Staunton Tourism (Box 58, Staunton 24401, tel. 703/441–5266). **Virginia
Division of Tourism** (202 N. 9th St., Richmond 23219, tel. 804/786–4484).

Reservation Services

Bed & Breakfasts of the Historic Shenandoah Valley (402 N. Main St.,
Woodstock 22664). **Blue Ridge Bed & Breakfast Reservation Service** (Rock
& Rills, Rte. 2, Box 3895, Berryville 22611, tel. 703/955–1246). **Historic
Country Inns of Lexington** handles the 43 rooms of three Lexington houses
(11 N. Main St., tel. 703/463–2044).

Boxwood

oxwood, built as a summer house in 1925, wasn't designed by Frank Lloyd Wright, but it brings to mind the architect's famous Pennsylvania home, Falling Water, because of the wonderful way it's integrated with the setting. It lies on the Allegheny side of the Shenandoah Valley, on a winding country road 10 miles west of Harrisonburg, so close to the Dry River that it's been damaged by floods in recent springs. The two-story house, made of river rock and wood, is surrounded by patios where a Japanese kite shimmers in the breeze, and bordered on at least two sides by the river. Untreated pine paneling lines the walls in the big living room, there's a yawning stone fireplace at one end and a staircase placed oddly—though not unattractively—in the middle.

Climb the stairs and you're confronted with owner Nancy Jones's collection of quilts and books on the American West. There are three homey guest rooms, all of them prettily decorated and veritably singing with the sound of rushing water. One of the upstairs rooms is called the Fiction Room for its shelves of novels, short stories, and poetry. This is as it should be, since besides heading the English department at the local high school, Nancy is a writer with a number of biographies to her credit. She also does a column on local history for the Harrisonburg newspaper, and has uncovered a good deal of information on the area's past. Around 1800 therapeutic springs were discovered just up the road from Boxwood, and by 1870 the hill beyond Nancy's home was the site of a resort, with a 150-room hotel, bathhouses, and gardens. Today a walk into the woods will take you to the ruins, a picturesque spot on nearby Black Run called the Old Bathtub, or to a swimming hole on Dry River, complete with a diving rock. In season there is trout fishing, wild blackberry bushes to pillage, and 10 miles west lies West Virginia with its airy mountaintops and idyllic valleys.

Continental breakfasts are served in the riverside dining room, featuring breads from a local Mennonite bakery, and Nancy's conversation. After that, it's off for a wade in the river or to a rocker on the porch to do nothing all the blissful day long.

Address: *Rte. 847, Rawley Springs, RR 1, Box 130, Hinton, VA 22831, tel. 703/867–5772.*
Accommodations: *1 double room with bath, 2 doubles share a bath.*
Amenities: *TV/VCR in living room; swimming holes.*
Rates: *$50; Continental breakfast. No credit cards.*
Restrictions: *No smoking, no pets, 2-night minimum on Oct. weekends.*

Jordan Hollow Farm

As anyone who's traveled much in rural America knows, farms aren't always the idyllic-looking places city folk fantasize about. However, Jordan Hollow, a working horse farm set in its own little valley beneath Hawksbill Mountain (on the western side of the Blue Ridge), comes as close to the ideal as possible. It's surrounded by 45 acres of fields and meadows where some 25 Norwegian fjord and Holsteiner horses graze, one can only assume in deep contentment. The passel of cats who have the run of the place also have it good—they sleep on the porch on top of an electric blanket!

Marly and Jetze (pronounced Yetsuh) Beers are the proprietors, and they're a handsome, outdoorsy couple; Marly's blond, and Jetze strikingly tall and dramatically bearded. They met in Liberia, where she was working for AID and he represented a Dutch marine-engineering firm. When they opened Jordan Hollow as an inn about 10 years ago, their first customers were Peace Corps volunteers in training. Today though, 80 percent of the visitors are family groups with a passion for horseback riding. Every day, several equestrian groups leave the farm to wander over the foothills; youngsters go on pony rides. And when Marly gets a break from her cooking duties, she might be prevailed upon to hitch up the pony cart. Jetze's forte is keeping things jovial at the Watering

Trough, a lounge and game room several paces from the barn.

The main section of the inn is in a white clapboard farmhouse fronted by a galleried porch. Portions of this structure were built of log around 1790, and in two dining rooms the rough wood and chinking is still visible. Breakfast and dinner are served here and in two other dining rooms. No meals are included in the room.

There are two low-ceilinged and slightly dark guest rooms in the main house, 16 more in the motel-like lodge, and four upscale rooms in a new log building called Mare Meadow Lodge. These are carpeted and have fireplaces, quilts and matching curtains, cedar furniture, and Jacuzzi tubs.

Address: *Rte. 626 (RR 2, Box 375), Stanley, VA 22851, tel. 703/778-2209 or 703/778-2285.*
Accommodations: *21 double rooms with baths, 1 suite.*
Amenities: *Restaurant, air-conditioning, TV in suite, Mare Meadow Lodge, and lounge, fireplace in lounge, phones in rooms; horseback riding, 1 large or 2 small conference rooms.*
Rates: *$75–$125; breakfast extra. D, DC, MC, V.*
Restrictions: *No pets.*

Trillium House

You've got to hand it to Ed and Betty Dinwiddie. To them, building a bed-and-breakfast on the grounds of Wintergreen resort may have seemed the most natural thing in the world; after all, their family had vacationed there for years. But to skiers, refugees from the Blue Ridge Parkway, wildflower enthusiasts, and all-round mountain devotees, the idea was a stroke of genius. The simple fact that Trillium House lies across the road from the gargantuan sports complex, with its indoor pool, tennis courts, ski slopes, hiking trails, golf course, and stables should give you a clue as to the kinds of activities available.

From Wintergreen's gate, a roller-coasterish road brings you 2½ miles to the doorstep of Trillium House. The beige frame building fronted by a porch and a Palladian window, surrounded by trees and stylish condominiums owned by Wintergreen residents, was built in 1983. You enter the Great Room, which is two stories high, near a staircase at the side leading to a loft library. The front sitting area has a wood-burning stove, above which hang several organ pipes; by the front door, a canister holds a collection of walking sticks. Breakfast is served in the dining rooms, with views of the backyard gazebo, and on Friday and Saturday, dinners are cooked by chef Ellen, who formerly worked in one of Wintergreen's restaurants.

The 12 guest rooms at Trillium House lie in two wings off the Great Room. Their architectural tone is slightly motelish, but decorative touches add some personality—here a quilt or a framed picture that could only have been created by one of the Dinwiddie brood, there a writing desk from The Homestead or a bed with a lace canopy.

The odds are that you'll spend most of your stay here pursuing varieties of R&R on the resort or ensconced in the Great Room, chatting with other guests or Ed and Betty, who manage to seem amazingly relaxed, despite their demanding housekeeping duties. The single disappointment is that Trillium House doesn't have mountain views; if that's what you're after, you'll have to grab a stick and walk.

Address: *Box 280, Nellysford, VA 22958, tel. 804/325-9126 or 800/325-9126.*
Accommodations: *10 double rooms with baths, 2 suites.*
Amenities: *Dinner served Fri. and Sat. by reservation, air-conditioning, TV/VCR in sitting room with videotape-movie collection; stables.*
Rates: *$80-$140; full buffet breakfast. MC, V.*
Restrictions: *No smoking in dining room, no pets.*

Belle Grae Inn

The Belle Grae is a classic small-town hotel occupying an old Victorian house and several surrounding buildings five minutes from Staunton's downtown. On your arrival, you'll be met by Bellboy, a sanguine boxer, who, according to owner Michael Organ, works for biscuits. The Old Inn, built circa 1870, has a wide porch offering views of Bessie Belle and Mary Grae, two of the town's many hillocks. Its eight bedrooms have high ceilings and are decorated with amiable Victorian antiques, and downstairs there are two restaurants—one fancy, in Staunton terms, and the other a bistro bar lined with windows. The suites in the Townhouse, adjoining the bistro, are Belle Grae's top-of-the-line, for their upscale decor and such amenities as fireplaces, phones, and cable TV.

Varied accommodations are also available in Jefferson House, in a bungalow near the hotel's terrace garden, and in the Bishop's Study. But best of all is the earnest tone at the Belle Grae, a place that's trying hard to be the best Staunton has to offer, and succeeding, if quirkily.

Address: *515 W. Frederick St., Staunton, VA 24401, tel. 703/886-5151.*
Accommodations: *10 double rooms with baths, 8 suites, 1 apartment.*
Amenities: *Restaurant, bistro, fireplaces in 10 rooms and 3 common areas, air-conditioning, cable TV and phones in 11 rooms.*
Rates: *$55–$135; full breakfast. AE, DC, MC, V.*
Restrictions: *No smoking in Jefferson House, no pets.*

Buckhorn Inn

The Buckhorn is primarily a restaurant, a historic one, opened in about 1811 for travelers heading to Warm Springs. It later served as a Civil War hospital and catered to shaggy-haired mountain men. Today, with the George Washington National State Forest bordering it on all sides and black bears occasionally putting in appearances, it's a good, rustic spot for hunters, though dedicated eaters passing through the area should be aware of it, too. Roger Lee, the current owner, has always hired good cooks, who have contributed such dishes as peanut-butter pie, tenderloin in gravy, fried oysters, and scalloped potatoes. Reasonably priced meals are served buffet and family style in a series of dining rooms that seat a total of 250. And glory be,

there isn't a word of French on the menu! In terms of decor and amenities, the guest rooms above, with ancient linoleum and garish wallpaper, can't hold a candle to the food, although the Stonewall Jackson Suite *does* have a Jacuzzi tub. Still, rates are low, particularly in the loft, which sleeps 10 to 12 for just $12 a head—a good choice for groups.

Address: *Rte. 250 W (HCR 33, Box 139), Churchville, VA 24421, tel. 703/337-6900.*
Accommodations: *6 double rooms with baths, 1 suite.*
Amenities: *Restaurant, air-conditioning, TV in bedrooms.*
Rates: *$45–$65; full breakfast. MC, V.*
Restrictions: *No pets.*

Fassifern

Think of it. There are 96,000
horses in Virginia. If you want
to buy or show one of them, the
place to do it is at the Virginia
Horse Center, just north of Lexington. And if you make the trip, you'll
be glad to know there's one of the
Shenandoah Valley's prettiest bed-
and-breakfasts just a trot down the
road. The place is called Fassifern,
after the Scottish ancestral home of
its builder, who erected this three-
story, beige brick farmhouse in 1867.
It's owned by Francis Whitsel Smith
and managed by her animated
daughter, Ann Carol Perry, who
keeps two horses of her own, named
Sinner and Pi, in the pasture.
There's no particular history connected to Fassifern; it's just a lovely
country place with a pond, towering
maple trees, and an old icehouse

that's been converted into two extra
guest rooms. We liked the Colonel's
Quarters best because of its wide
plank floors and pasture views. In
the main house, three more guest
rooms are furnished with Victorian
armoires, Oriental rugs, and crystal
chandeliers. Ann Carol is fun; she
likes to gab and can help you plan
your Lexington sightseeing.

Address: *Rte. 39 W. (RR 5, Box 87),
Lexington, VA 24450, tel. 703/463-
1013.*
Accommodations: *5 double rooms
with baths.*
Amenities: *Air-conditioning.*
Rates: *$65–$75; Continental breakfast. AE, MC, V.*
Restrictions: *No smoking, no pets,
closed Thanksgiving, Christmas,
and New Year's Day.*

Hotel Strasburg

This white frame landmark at the
northern end of the Shenandoah
Valley is a showcase for the
most baroque form of Victoriana,
much of it for sale—a statue of
a nymph riding a stallion;
a mock-heroic painting of Daniel in
the lion's den; antique lace curtains;
dark, clunky beds with soft mattresses; and mirrors so elaborately
ornamented that they seem ready to
grab you if you admire yourself too
long. Some people dote on this kind
of thing; others despise it. If you're
of the former class, it's certainly
a place to stop, especially if you're
headed for the antiques emporium in
Strasburg. The hotel has
a restaurant, reasonably priced but
not noted for its cuisine, and
a convivial Depot Lounge. Among
the hotel's annexes is the recently

added neighboring Taylor House,
which is perhaps the best choice,
since it's somewhat secluded and has
four suites with whirlpool tubs.

Address: *201 Holliday St., Strasburg, VA 22657, tel. 703/465-9191.*
Accommodations: *13 double rooms
with baths, 14 suites.*
Amenities: *Restaurant, air-
conditioning, cable TV in 11 suites
and 7 rooms, phones in rooms,
whirlpools in 7 suites.*
Rates: *$69–$149; Continental breakfast Mon.–Fri., breakfast extra on
weekend. AE, DC, MC, V.*
Restrictions: *No pets.*

The Inn at Narrow Passage

Pack your inner tubes, gang, and your swimming togs and fishing rods; they will all prove useful at the Inn at Narrow Passage, which sits right above the North Fork of the Shenandoah River. Ed Markel, owner of the Inn, will kindly put you in about a mile south, and from there it's a 3½ hour float to reach home. Most likely when you return there will be a fire crackling away in the log sitting room in the oldest section of the inn. It was built as a way station on the Wilderness Trail (now Route 11) around 1740, and the Markels meticulously restored it, but guests still claim that you can see daylight through the chinks. There are three guest rooms on the second floor of this section, and nine more in wings built in 1985. The latter are nice, but

motelish; we preferred the old rooms by a long shot. They have handmade hinges, tongue-and-groove pine walls, and a lovely hammer dulcimer at the top of the steps. When the valley is blanketed in snow, the inn is a cozy place with a total of 10 working fireplaces. There's skiing at Bryce Mountain a half hour away, and plenty of hiking, too.

Address: *Rte. 11 S, Woodstock, VA 22664, tel. 703/459–8000.*
Accommodations: *10 double rooms with baths, 2 doubles share a bath.*
Amenities: *Air-conditioning, TV in sitting room, 1 conference room.*
Rates: *$55–$85; full breakfast. MC, V.*
Restrictions: *No smoking in guest rooms, no pets, 2-night minimum Oct. and holiday weekends.*

Joshua Wilton House

Harrisonburg, a commercial center and the site of James Madison University, is not a markedly handsome town. In it, the Joshua Wilton House strikes the highest note—it's a lovingly renovated and luxuriously equipped mauve, lavender, and pink Queen Anne cottage with triple-decker bays and a turret. It is said that it was the first house in the valley to get electricity, and when the lights went on people came from outlying farms to witness the miracle. You enter by way of a front door surrounded by leaded glass and through a foyer with gleaming parquet floor, a chandelier, and bushy potted ferns. Throughout the four downstairs dining rooms you'll find painted mantels and pictures displayed by the Shenandoah Valley Watercolor Associa-

tion. The guest chambers are really lovely, particularly Room 5, with its four-poster bed and white wing chairs, and Room 4, which has a three-window alcove in the turret. The owners are Roberta and Craig Moore, who live on the premises. Fancy dinners and breakfasts, perhaps with crab-and-cheese omelettes, are available.

Address: *412 S. Main St., Harrisonburg, VA 22801, tel. 703/434–4464.*
Accommodations: *5 double rooms with baths.*
Amenities: *Restaurant, bar, air-conditioning, phones in rooms, fireplace in 1 room.*
Rates: *$85; full breakfast. AE, MC, V.*
Restrictions: *Smoking in bar only, no pets.*

Oak Spring Farm and Vineyard

We saw Oak Spring Farm while it was still being renovated, but even then all signs were good. To begin with, the proprietors, Jim and Pat Tichenor, restored and operated nearby Fassifern before selling it to its present owners—clearly, they have an eye for properties that fix up well. Oak Spring is a two-story farmhouse whose sections were built in 1826 and 1840. While deep in plaster and paint, the Tichenors discovered walls in the ell made of oak planks stacked up like pancakes—an architectural point that will make Oak Spring a shoo-in for the National Register of Historic Places. The three guest rooms are on the second floor, and are filled with fine antiques; we liked the Regency Room best, because a window by its claw-foot tub provides pastoral views while you soak. The farm is surrounded by 40 acres planted in hay and alfalfa, a meadow where 20 burros graze, and 5 acres of grapes. Oak Spring Farm is a good out-of-town headquarters for exploring nearby Lexington, and an excellent spot to lay over during trips on the Blue Ridge Parkway.

Address: *RR 1, Box 356, Raphine, VA 24472, tel. 703/377-2398.*
Accommodations: *3 double rooms with baths.*
Amenities: *Air-conditioning, fireplace in guest living room.*
Rates: *$55–$65; Continental breakfast. MC, V.*
Restrictions: *No smoking, no pets, 2-night minimum on parents' and graduation weekends.*

Thornrose House

Proprietors Ray and Carolyn Hoaster are admirers of English bed-and-breakfasts and have fashioned Thornrose along those lines, offering strong English tea and grilled tomatoes at breakfast, cramming the place with heavy Victorian antiques, and presiding over it all with true British conviviality. The house is pretty enough, with upstairs bedrooms named Canterbury, Windemere, and Yorkshire; but Ray and Carolyn are far and away its most attractive features. He was with the Air Force band; she's an ex-chanteuse—and occasionally the two of them still hold forth at Staunton's Belle Grae Inn. They're full of quirky ideas, like Victorian Sampler weekends, when Thornrose House rings with music-hall songs and guests play whist. Ray's collection of VCR tapes includes episodes from British comedies like *Fawlty Towers* and *Good Neighbors*. The house is across the street from bucolic Gypsy Hill Park, where there are a swimming pool, tennis courts, a golf course, and the July Fourth Statler Brothers concerts.

Address: *531 Thornrose Ave., Staunton, VA 24401, tel. 703/885-7026.*
Accommodations: *3 double rooms with baths.*
Amenities: *Air-conditioning, cable TV/VCR in guest sitting room.*
Rates: *$45–$60; full breakfast. No credit cards.*
Restrictions: *No smoking, no pets, 2- and 3-night minimum Oct., July 4th, and graduation weekends.*

Off the Beaten Track

Fort Lewis Lodge

On a 3,200-acre farm in the Allegheny foothills, John and Caryl Cowden
raise Angus cattle, soybeans, and
corn. The beautiful Cowpasture
River deepens into a swimming hole
nearby, and Tower Hill Mountain
looms above, traversed by paths and
logging roads. Below the manor
house there's a dining hall in an old
mill, and a lodge. The Cowdens
began by catering to bow hunters in
pursuit of deer, wild turkey, and the
occasional black bear, then opened
their lodge to summertime rustica-
tors. They arrange camping trips for
guests, with dinner delivered to
a shelter, where bedding is laid out.
The common rooms contain stuffed
bears, raccoons, and red fox—all Allegheny Highland species. The lodge
rooms are exceptionally comfortable,
with locally made headboards and
spreads and curtains from the Sears
and Spiegel catalogues. There's
a laundry room, and a stone hearth
in the gathering room. A tower in
a converted silo provides views of
a countryside and nothing else. All
you'll find at Fort Lewis Lodge are
fields, rivers, mountains, forests, and
Cowden hospitality.

Address: *HCR3, Box 21A, Millboro,
VA 24460, tel. 703/925-2314.*
Accommodations: *4 double rooms
with baths, 6 doubles share 3 baths,
1 suite.*
Amenities: *TV with VCR in game
room; guided hunting,*
Rates: *$110–$125. MC, V.*
Restrictions: *Smoking in gathering
room only, no pets, closed Jan.–
Mar.*

The Inn at Gristmill Square

Bath County in western Virginia covers 540 bumpy square miles inhabited by just 5,000 souls, and it hasn't
got a single stoplight. Warm
Springs, the county seat, has a post
office, courthouse, and inn—and
that's about all. Still, the Inn at
Gristmill Square, occupying
a restored mill, miller's house, and
hardware store, is reason enough to
visit this quintessentially peaceful
spot. Its Waterwheel Restaurant is
one of the area's best places to sup,
with a chef trained at the Virginia
Culinary Institute and a cool subter-
ranean wine cellar. A pebbled courtyard separates the restaurant and
country store from one bank of
rooms, and across the lane there's
an inn annex, called the Steel House,
a small swimming pool, and tennis
courts. The Miller House, up the
road, has rooms named Oat, Barley,
Rye, and Wheat, which we liked best.
Janice McWilliams and her son,
Bruce, are the able proprietors, former owners of an inn in Maine. They
serve breakfast and the *Richmond
Times Dispatch* in a picnic basket at
your door.

Address: *Box 359, Warm Springs,
VA 24484, tel. 703/839-2231.*
Accommodations: *12 double rooms
with baths, 2 apartments.*
Amenities: *Restaurant, air-
conditioning in Miller House, fireplaces in 7 guest rooms, cable TV
and phones in rooms; swimming
pool, sauna, 3 tennis courts, store.*
Rates: *$90–$125; Continental breakfast. MC, V.*
Restrictions: *No pets.*

West Virginia

West Virginia

The Eastern Panhandle

Like so much of West Virginia, the three eastern counties that make up the panhandle region are mountainous, reaching elevations of 2,300 feet. Long a wild, uninhabitable part of the west, it was not until George Washington surveyed the area in the mid-1700s that a number of villages sprang up along the Potomac River, among them Shepherdstown, Harpers Ferry, Charles Town, and Martinsburg.

Today, the state is still relatively untamed and is a wonderland for explorers, who can drive for miles along surprisingly well-maintained highways without tripping over condo developments or fast-food restaurants. In the last few decades the state government, based in Charleston, has turned its attention to nurturing the wildest portions of the Allegheny Front and Plateau, once devastated by lumbering and strip mining, by creating a first-rate network of parks. Six thousand–acre Cacapon State Park— with its skiing facilities, trails, and Robert Trent Jones golf course—is among these, as is Berkeley Springs State Park, a funky spot equipped with tiled Roman baths, steam cabinets, and some of the best spring water in the world (beloved by George Washington, in fact).

The most popular tourist attraction in West Virginia lies in the Eastern Panhandle—Harpers Ferry, site of a national park. Thomas Jefferson described it best, writing: "On your right comes up the Shenandoah, having ranged along the foot of the mountains a hundred miles to seek a vent. On your left approaches the Potomac, in quest of a passage also. In the moment of their junction they rush together against the mountain, rend it asunder, and pass off to the sea . . . This scene is worth a voyage across the Atlantic." The spot where these rivers converge so dramatically is also where, on October 16, 1859, the abolitionist zealot John Brown led his 21-man assault on the Harpers Ferry arsenal. Today, strips of Harpers Ferry national parklands line the rivers like a glove, and historic markers tell the story of John Brown's raid and of the town's tumultuous involvement in the Civil War.

Shepherdstown, sitting high above the Potomac, across from Sharpsburg, Maryland, was founded in 1762 and is the oldest town in West Virginia. Visitors can browse the pleasant collection of shops along the main drag here, and, since all the Panhandle's main towns are close together, can make a short trip to the Charles Town track to take in the horse races in the afternoon before heading back to one of the area's many fine inns.

Potomac and Shenandoah river rafting abounds, and there are numerous bicycling routes (among them Route 230 between Harpers Ferry and Shepherdstown and the Tuscarora Pike near Martinsburg) and a huge collection of outlet stores in Martinsburg where you can snap up designer clothing for a fraction of the department-store price. If you have more time to explore, head west to Berkeley Springs and Cacapon State Park, where you'll discover the real West Virginia—that of logging trucks, black bear, wild turkey, and mountains that don't let up until the Ohio River.

Places to go, sights to see

Berkeley Springs State Park (tel. 304/258–2711 or 800/225–5982). Located within the city limits of the town of Bath, this state park has a museum and a pool. In the bathhouse you can sample the therapeutic waters, which rush out of the springs at an unvarying temperature of 74.3 degrees and a volume of 2,000 gallons a day. The bathhouse itself has seen better days; still, where else but here can you have a massage and get wrinkled in a Roman tub for a slim $20? The water's the same at other places, where the surroundings are swisher and the price tag higher. In fact, the water's the same everywhere in funny little Berkeley Springs (a.k.a. Bath); it comes out of every tap.

Cacapon State Park (tel. 304/258–1022 or 800/225–5982). Cacapon lies 10 miles south of Berkeley Springs, off Route 522, and encompasses a narrow strip of mountains that reaches almost to the Maryland and Virginia borders.

A paved road leads to the summit of Cacapon Mountain, and the park has 27 miles of hiking trails, as well as a 50-room lodge, 18-hole golf course (for which reservations are encouraged), and a man-made lake with a sandy beach.

Charles Town Races (tel. 304/725–7001). The thoroughbreds pound the turf from January to December at this track just outside Charles Town (about 5 miles southwest of Harpers Ferry).

Harpers Ferry National Historic Park (tel. 304/535–6371). This is the site of the arsenal that John Brown held for two days before it was stormed by marines under Robert E. Lee. A network of hiking routes originate at Harpers Ferry, including the Appalachian Trail.

O'Hurley's General Store (tel. 304/876–6907). This Shepherdstown emporium is crammed with "the most extensive variety of time-tested products available in this modern age," including boxes, barrels, baskets, anvils, harnesses, coffins, guns, books, and dinner bells.

Pack Horse Ford. Just east of Shepherdstown, this historic Potomac River crossing was first used by German settlers heading south into the Shenandoah Valley, by both Southern and Northern forces during the Civil War, and as an escape route for Lee's troops after the Battle of Antietam.

Panorama Point. Follow Route 9 4 miles west of Berkeley Springs to the shoulder of Prospect Peak for a view of the Great Cacapon Valley, where three states—Maryland, West Virginia, and Pennsylvania—converge. This panorama is one of the finest sights in America.

Tourist Information

Jefferson County Convention and Visitors Bureau (Box A, Harpers Ferry, 25425, tel. 304/535–2627). **Travel Berkeley Springs** (304 Fairfax St., Berkeley Springs 25411, tel. 304/258–3738). **West Virginia Department of Commerce** (2101 Washington St. E, Charleston 24305, tel. 800/225–5982).

Reservation Services

Blue Ridge B&B Reservation Service (Rocks & Rills, Rte. 2, Box 3895, Berryville 22611, tel. 703/955–1246).

Boydville

The story always told about Boydville, Martinsburg's grandest house, concerns its near destruction by Union troops during the Civil War. One often hears how some pretty Southern belle pleaded with roughshod Federals to spare her family manse, but in the case of Boydville, the tale is documented. Mary Faulkner, of the clan that has resided in Boydville for 150 years, wired Abraham Lincoln, whose decision to let Boydville stand arrived just before Northerners lit the torch.

A later Faulkner served as U.S. senator, commuting to the nation's capital by train (just as present part-owner, Ripley Hotch, does today). When the six o'clock train from the District hooted over nearby Bull's Eye Bridge, the Boydville servants began crushing ice for the senator's mint julep. And when he arrived on the wide front porch and reclined in a green rocker (the very one there today), his drink was waiting.

Boydville, a white-stucco, shuttered mansion surrounded by 10 green acres, was built in 1812 by Elisha Boyd, a friend of Martinsburg's founder, Adam Stephen. Obviously, it's a historic place, and perhaps also the northernmost outcropping of the old South, gracefully moldering, vaguely decadent, but still lovely. Its present owners, Owen Sullivan and Ripley Hotch, have done Martinsburg and West Virginia a good turn in taking Boydville to

their hearts and allowing bed-and-breakfast guests to enjoy it. The owners begin a visitor's introduction to the inn by mentioning its 70 places to sit and by pointing out the case locks, stamped with the imprimatur of the locksmith to King George IV, and the English molding in the downstairs parlors. The rooms are enormous, the most desirable being the Adam Stephen Room; it has hand-painted mural wallpaper imported around 1800 from France and the first tiled bathroom in Martinsburg. Fine, too, is the Adirondack Room, with a private entrance and working fireplace.

Ripley and Owen are collectors of art, bringing to Boydville paintings by American Impressionists, Oriental soapstone carvings, and Imari pottery. Happily, however, the place is no museum; those 70 reclining spots and the accommodating veranda are still good places for mint juleps.

Address: *601 S. Queen St., Martinsburg, WV 25401, tel. 304/263-1448.*
Accommodations: *6 double rooms with baths.*
Amenities: *Air-conditioning in bedrooms, cable TV/VCR in garden room.*
Rates: *$95–$115; breakfast. AE, MC, V.*
Restrictions: *No smoking, no pets, 2-night minimum Memorial Day weekend and on Oct. weekends.*

Hillbrook

Would Hillbrook, hidden along a country lane outside Charles Town, be such a special place without its innkeeper, Gretchen Carroll? One tends to think not, although the house itself is spectacularly eccentric, splayed in six stages along a hill, never more than one room wide or one room deep. The house has 13 sharply peaked gables, half-timbered white-stucco walls, and mullioned windows—the one in the living room has 360 panes. Ann Hathaway would feel right at home. Gretchen calls the style "Norman Tudor" and explains that during World War I a civil engineer by the name of Bamford fell in love with an inn in Normandy and determined to re-create it in the wilds of West Virginia. Erratically, he chose to start with two ancient log cabins, the logs and mortises of one of these are still apparent in the sun porch.

Gretchen was a foreign-service brat who grew up in the far corners of the world, including Turkey, Vietnam, and the Ivory Coast; and Hillbrook is full of exotic curios and objets d'art. The living room holds pottery and a Senegalese fertility statue; in bedrooms you'll find Oriental rugs, an antique Vuitton steamer trunk, and a Thai spirit house. Richly patterned wallpaper, upholstery, and pillows; randomly angled ceilings; potted plants; and architectural cubbyholes complete the Hillbrook picture. The Cottage guest room,

with its private entry leading to an ancient springhouse (from which Hillbrook gets its water), has paisley-pattern wallpaper, a high cannonball rope bed, and a wood-burning stove lined with Italian tile. Locke's Nest overlooks the 20-foot-high living room and has brass double and single beds and a lavender bathtub.

Besides decorating, Gretchen cooks. Her seven-course dinners have been known to include grilled swordfish with jasmine rice; feta-cheese-and-pomegranate salad; and chocolate fudge cake. Her breakfast specialty is French toast Tatiana, dripping in cranberry-orange syrup and sour cream.

Bullskin Run Creek trickles away at the bottom of the Hillbrook lawn, the haunt of ducks and inn guests. There are, of course, attractions to visit in the surrounding area but nothing that would keep one away from idyllic Hillbrook for long.

Address: *Rte. 2, Box 152, Charles Town, WV 24514, tel. 304/725-4223.*
Accommodations: *5 double rooms with baths.*
Amenities: *Dinner served on request ($50, including drinks and wine), air-conditioning in bedrooms.*
Rates: *$100–$175; full breakfast. AE, MC, V.*
Restrictions: *No pets.*

Aspen Hall

Aspen Hall, in Martinsburg, is a native-limestone Georgian manor house with a very long history. It was begun sometime around 1754, as the fortified residence of a settler named John Mendenhall and by 1761 was a grand enough place for a wedding, which was attended by George Washington. Today, the approach to the hall is not as auspicious as its history; it's reached by a long street of erratically kept houses of 1930s vintage. Still, Aspen Hall itself is handsome, occupying a hollow alongside Tuscarora Creek, shaded by giant locusts that were probably saplings in Washington's time. Its blond-floor foyer is a space suitable for presidential entrances, and its twin parlors have 12-foot ceilings, 19th-century antique furniture, and swag draperies. In those parlors Gordon and LouAnne Claucherty hold tea dances and on Wednesday afternoon serve high English tea, a Martinsburg event. The nicest of the three guest bedrooms is the front one, with lace curtains, a four-poster canopy bed, and a claw-foot tub. There's a two-bedroom apartment in the old carriage house, though it isn't as elegant and airy as the rooms in the main house.

Address: *405 Boyd Ave., Martinsburg, WV 25401, tel. 304/263-4385.*
Accommodations: *3 double rooms with baths, 2-bedroom apartment.*
Amenities: *TV in common room.*
Rates: *$95; full breakfast. No credit cards.*
Restrictions: *No smoking, no pets, closed Dec. 24–25.*

The Carriage Inn

When generals Ulysses S. Grant and Philip Sheridan met at what is now the Carriage Inn to map out the Union Army's Shenandoah Valley campaign, there was a picket fence around the house and a Greek Revival portico. Otherwise, things haven't changed much at the old Rutherford place in Charles Town—anyway, guests don't mind the addition of a broad front porch and modern plumbing. The owner of this shady, blue Colonial-style house is Robert Kaetzel, who helped restore Shepherdstown's Thomas Shepherd Inn before deciding to fix up a bed-and-breakfast of his own. He not only made every canopy bed at the Carriage Inn, he cut down the wood to make them. And he has a strong aversion to the ubiquitous "Continental" breakfast. "Either it's breakfast or it's not," he says. Besides hearty morning meals, the Carriage Inn offers big bedrooms (four with fireplaces), two sitting rooms, polished floors, solid brick walls, and a bookful of Civil War stories to tell—like the one about Stonewall Jackson's flag, which was buried behind the house when the Federals came.

Address: *417 E. Washington St., Charles Town, WV 25414, tel. 304/728-8003.*
Accommodations: *5 double rooms with baths.*
Amenities: *Air-conditioning.*
Rates: *$65–$95; full breakfast. MC, V.*
Restrictions: *No smoking in bedrooms, no pets.*

The Cottonwood Inn

About 6 miles south of Charles Town along Kabletown Road, a trio of silos rises, marking the winding road to the Cottonwood Inn. This yellow frame farmhouse has occupied a hollow alongside Bullskin Run Creek for almost 200 years—as its uneven pine floors and big brick dining-room hearth attest. To it came Colin and Eleanor Simpson and their nine children in 1976; after the kids left this lovely nest, Colin and Eleanor began taking in bed-and-breakfast guests. Days at the Cottonwood are spent communing with cows amid farmy scents, fishing for trout in the creek, pitching horseshoes, or snoozing in a hammock out back. And when night falls the guest rooms are exceptionally cozy places to rest: in particular, the fireplace suite and four-postered double room in the rear. Several years ago the Simpsons added a wing to the farmhouse, holding two guest rooms that are spacious and handsomely decorated but are not as atmospheric as the rooms in the old section. The Cottonwood is close to the Blue Ridge, which beckons on the horizon; and to the north lie the Charles Town Race Track and Harpers Ferry.

Address: *Rte. 2, Box 61–S, Charles Town, WV 25414, tel. 304/725-3371.*
Accommodations: *6 double rooms with baths, 1 suite with fireplace.*
Amenities: *Air-conditioning, TV in rooms.*
Rates: *$65–$85; full breakfast. AE, MC, V.*
Restrictions: *No smoking in dining room, no pets, closed Dec. 23–29.*

The Country Inn

From the outside the Country Inn, in Berkeley Springs, looks a little grander than the image the name summons up; it's a four-story brick building, with a columned front porch, that was built in 1932. First came a set of wings in 1937, and then, after Jack and Adele Barker bought the place, a conference center, motel annex, and spa out back. The additions haven't damaged the integrity of the old inn much, for its rooms are still old-timey, with mismatched quasi-antiques; a long, carpeted central corridor; and a country store downstairs. The inn is next door to Berkeley Springs State Park, but the spa facilities at the inn come with a view of the town and the ridge. The inn has two dining rooms, one a garden affair with a dance floor, where there's live music on weekends. Jack Barker, a former teacher, disliked retirement and came to Berkeley Springs in the early 1970s.

Address: *Berkeley Springs, WV 25411, tel. 304/258-2210 or 800/822-6630, fax 304/258-3986.*
Accommodations: *58 double rooms with baths, 12 doubles share 4 baths, 1 suite.*
Amenities: *Restaurant, pub, room service, air-conditioning, cable TV in rooms, phones in hall and in annex rooms, spa, 2 conference rooms.*
Rates: *$35–$130; breakfast extra except in suite. AE, DC, MC, V.*
Restrictions: *No smoking in suite or annex, no pets, 2-night minimum on major holiday weekends.*

Dunn Country Inn

The busy kitchen at the Dunn Country Inn, with its easy chairs and stone hearth, is the nerve center for activities at this homey bed-and-breakfast. This is as it should be, since the building, begun in 1805, is a cozy farmhouse. Around 1870 the resident farmer felt able to expand, adding a grand front addition (like the back, of native limestone), with Romanesque windows, elaborate molding, and 12-foot ceilings. Dianna Dunn is responsible for the inn's decoration, which includes folk-arty stenciling and teddy bears, wreaths, and a pleasant assortment of country antiques—all of which make the place very much like one of the painter Carl Larsen's Scandinavian interiors. That, too, is as it should be, because Dianna is half Norwegian. Her husband,

Prince, grew up in Martinsburg and these days commutes to the Pentagon, where he's a consultant. The newest additions are baby Colin and a pair of exuberantly friendly stray dogs named Jessica and Rose. Two of the three rooms in the 1870s section are notable for Art Nouveau and Art Deco bed sets.

Address: *Rte. 3, Box 33J, Martinsburg, WV 25401, tel. 304/263–8646.*
Accommodations: *1 double room with hall bath, 4 doubles share 2 baths.*
Amenities: *Air-conditioning, picnic lunches prepared.*
Rates: *$65–$95; full breakfast. No credit cards.*
Restrictions: *No smoking, no pets, 2-night minimum late-Sept.–early Nov. and holiday weekends.*

Highlawn

The house Algernon R. Unger built for his bride, Chaffie Ziler, is just the sort of place for an Algie and Chaffie to summer in, a white Queen Anne cottage with 21 rooms, a wide front porch, and a tin roof that vibrates musically when it rains. The present owner, Sandra Kauffman, who bought the Unger place just a few years ago, is a true believer in the therapeutic qualities of the Berkeley Springs waters. She takes a Roman bath at the state park about once a week and cheerfully reminds guests that every tap in her house dispenses the miracle cure. The private suite has its own tin-roofed porch and hand-painted Victorian furniture. All the bedrooms have lace curtained windows, plump pillows, and turn-of-the-century furnishings like brass beds and rockers.

Sandra serves dinner at Highlawn (with advance reservations) on special occasions such as the gala October Applebutter Festival. Her breakfasts, which include such delicacies as lemon bread with lemon butter, buttermilk biscuits, and chocolate-chip coffee cake, provide the sustenance required for the hard work of spa-going.

Address: *304 Market St., Berkeley Springs, WV 25411, tel. 304/258–1788.*
Accommodations: *5 double rooms with baths, 1 suite.*
Amenities: *Air-conditioning, TV in bedrooms.*
Rates: *$70–$90; full breakfast. AE, MC, V.*
Restrictions: *No pets, 2-night minimum on weekends June–Oct.*

Hilltop House Hotel and Restaurant

Some things, like Hilltop House, never change; when dilapidation strikes, someone grabs a two-by-four and props it up, a salvage operation we noticed beneath a cliffside corner of the landmark Harpers Ferry hotel. If that doesn't give you pause, the food at the hotel restaurant will, being of the overcooked variety that lends country fare a bad name. That said, you simply haven't seen Harpers Ferry unless you make the pilgrimage to this hotel, which opened in the 1880s and has hosted the likes of Mark Twain and Pearl Buck—possibly in the same beds and bottomed-out easy chairs in use now. Despite its infirmities, it's a marvel, all on account of the view; and unless you stay overnight you may miss the sunrise show: Dawn pulls the curtain and the rivers make their entrance, thinly veiled in mist, roaring away below like disinherited kings. Pay the extra cost for a room with a view, and don't be persuaded to book in the new lodge, which hasn't got the vistas.

Address: *Box 930, Ridge St., Harpers Ferry, WV 25425, tel. 304/535-2132 or 800/338-8319; fax 304/535-6322.*
Accommodations: *52 double and 6 single rooms with baths, 4 suites.*
Amenities: *Restaurant, air-conditioning, TV in living rooom and some bedrooms, phones in bedrooms, 8 conference rooms.*
Rates: *$54–$85, breakfast extra. AE, MC, V.*
Restrictions: *No pets, 2-night minimum with Sat. reservation.*

Prospect Hill

This handsome Georgian house, built of brick in 1804, is surrounded by a 225-acre farm that stretches to the top of North Mountain and lies along what was once the Pack Horse Trail, a main road to the West. Its old dependencies—including Flemish-bond brick slave quarters, now converted into an apartment—are in particularly good condition, with a stream wandering beside them. Owners Charles and Hazel Hudock restored the place and are proud of its unusual details, like the several working Franklin fireplaces dating from the 1790s and a mural depicting Prospect Hill and scenes from American life. Charles is an inveterate collector who, during his years as a Navy meteorologist, combed the world for a surprising variety of items, including Yugoslavian chairs, Shanghai rugs, several original Currier and Ives prints, and early photos of Yellowstone Park. The Hudocks are also gardeners, and the fruits of their labors—homemade grape juice, fresh raspberries, and peaches—often appear on the breakfast table.

Address: *Box 135, Gerrardstown, WV 25420, tel. 304/229-3346.*
Accommodations: *2 double rooms with baths, 1 apartment.*
Amenities: *Air-conditioning in bedrooms, TV in apartment and living room, phones and fireplaces in rooms.*
Rates: *$75–$85; full breakfast. MC, V.*
Restrictions: *Smoking in living room only, no pets.*

The Thomas Shepherd Inn

Shepherdstown is easily the prettiest village in Panhandle West Virginia, built in the mid-1800s, and thus a showplace for late-Federal architecture. Its shop-lined business district lies along German Street, where, up a ways, you'll find the Thomas Shepherd Inn, named for the town's founder, whose grist mill still stands, with a huge cast-iron wheel. The inn was built in 1868 as a Lutheran parsonage and expanded in 1937. It's a gracious place that would look at home in Colonial Williamsburg, with green molding, inset shutters, and a spacious courtyard garden in the rear. Though it's been an inn since 1981, Margaret Perry, a former homemaker who loves to sew and cook, took over in 1989. Her breakfasts can be elaborate, featuring eggs Benedict with caviar and French toast made from brioches. All guest rooms have polished floors, Oriental rugs, and handsomely coordinated upholstery and spreads; but the favorite is Room 6, because of its garden view, claw-foot tub, and four-poster bed. The inn has become a prime way station for bike-trippers on back roads and for people heading for Maryland's Antietam Battlefield, 5 miles north.

Address: *Box 1162, Shepherdstown, WV 25443, tel. 304/876–3715.*
Accommodations: *4 double rooms with baths, 2 doubles share bath.*
Amenities: *Air-conditioning in bedrooms, TV in library.*
Rates: *$75–$95; full breakfast. MC, V.*
Restrictions: *No smoking, no pets.*

The View

Why, one might wonder, aren't there more bed-and-breakfasts in Harpers Ferry, which has all the earmarks of a perfect B&B town? The answer is simple. There's an ordinance against B&Bs with more than two rooms, which puts a distinct damper on the ardor of potential innkeepers. One of the nicest two-roomers around, however, is the View, though it's decidedly unassuming from the front. Behind a small, carefully manicured lawn is a small brown frame house built in 1983 as a vacation cottage. Its principal charm is only apparent inside—though the place's name should clue you in; the Big Sur–style construction affords plenty of window space on two levels, below which the Potomac River pounds over rapids in pursuit of the Shenandoah. Etta Mae and Bill Hannon, formerly of Vienna, Virginia, have decorated with deep couches, softly colored area rugs, and contemporary art, giving an air of suburban California. On the lower level there's an indoor hot tub right next to windows opening onto the gorge of the Potomac and within viewing range of the cable TV/VCR. Both guest rooms, one a suite, are equipped with coffee-making paraphernalia and a stocked refrigerator.

Address: *Box 286, Harpers Ferry, WV 25425, tel. 304/535–2688.*
Accommodations: *1 double room with bath, 1 suite.*
Amenities: *Air-conditioning, cable TV with VCR in downstairs gathering room, hot tub.*
Rates: *$75; full breakfast. MC, V.*

The Mountains

The *Allegheny Mountains of West Virginia* are a substantial range, reaching from around Davis in the north to the Greenbrier Valley in the south. They are wide, too—it takes a hard day of driving to cross them east to west—and it's easy to sympathize with the early pioneers, who struggled over the same hills without the convenience of automobiles. Not all of the settlers made it to the west, though: some, particularly Scotch-Irish immigrants, gave up before reaching the fertile Ohio Valley and settled in this high, wild territory that would become West Virginia. They were harried by the Shawnee Indians in the late 1700s, but they managed to hang on to the land that would later prove a valuable, if limited, source of timber and coal.

Long overlooked by the rest of the country, West Virginia has recently been rediscovered. Tourism, especially skiing, has begun to replace mining and lumbering as an Allegheny Mountain cash crop. The four finest ski resorts in the region, Canaan Valley State Park, Timberline Four Seasons Resort, Silver Creek on Cheat Mountain, and Snowshoe, have one of the longest skiing seasons in the east. Hikers, naturalists, hunters, anglers, and cyclists will also find a paradise in the Allegheny Mountains, one million acres of which are part of the Monongahela National Forest. There are plenty of state parks, too, including Watoga, Cranberry Glades, and the remote Dolly Sods Wilderness. The Seneca Rocks/Spruce Knob Recreation Area is at the top of the mountain chain, with Spruce Knob, at 4,860 feet, officially the highest point in the state.

As you journey south the mountains relax into hills, sloping down to the idyllic Greenbrier Valley and the historic town of Lewisburg. This former frontier fort was the site of battles in both the Revolutionary and Civil wars. Today it's a peaceful town of fine Federal and Victorian *homes. To the east the famed Greenbrier resort, where the Vanderbilts and Astors took the waters in the early part of the century, is still as grand as ever.*

Visitors who want to see America in all its variety and eccentricity couldn't do better than to drive into the mountains of West Virginia, where they can attend ramp festivals (ramps are a potent mountain onion that make the eater a social outcast for a week); spend some time with a snake-handling religious cult (hard to find but still active in the Allegheny wilds); or hike the 200-mile Allegheny Trail and ponder how anyone could ever have forgotten about West Virginia.

Places to go, sights to see

Canaan Valley State Park (tel. 800/225–5982). Long known for downhill skiing, this 21-trail park is particularly good for families because of its low prices.

Cass Scenic Railroad (tel. 304/456–4300 or 800/225–5982). Near the intersection of routes 250 and 28, Cass is the base for the logging line that once carried lumberjacks up Bald Knob Mountain and now carries sightseers on a four-hour trip to the Allegheny plateau. Pack a lunch and warm clothes; you'll reach an altitude of almost 5,000 feet.

Dolly Sods Wilderness (tel. 304/636–1800 or 304/567–2827). Near the town of Davis and the Canaan Valley, this remote refuge is overrun with sphagnum bogs, stands of wind blown spruce, heath barrens, and patches of wild onions.

Droop Mountain (tel. 800/225–5982). This restored Civil War battlefield offers a small museum, observation tower, and hiking trails.

National Radio Astronomy Observatory (Green Bank, tel. 304/456–2011). If there is intelligent life out there, the people manning the wires at this federal installation are likely to be the first to know. The observatory has a 300-foot movable radio telescope, the largest of its kind in the world.

New River Bridge. The world's biggest single-arch span (3,000 feet long) is situated on Route 19 between Hico and Fayetteville.

New River Gorge. Rangers conduct guided tours of this 52-mile-long gorge known as the Grand Canyon of the East. For information about river running, contact *New/Gauley Expeditions* (tel. 304/574–3679 or 800/472–7238), *Class VI River Runners* (tel. 304/574–0704), *Mountain River Tours* (tel. 304/658–5266 or 800/822–1386), or *Whitewater Songer* (tel. 304/574–0133 or 800/356–7238).

Pearl Buck Home (tel. 800/225–5982). Pearl Buck, the Pulitzer- and Nobel Prize–winning author of *The Good Earth*, came from Hillsboro, West Virginia, and her home is now preserved as a museum.

Seneca Rocks (tel. 800/225–5982). These twin Tuscarora-sandstone promontories rise 1,000 feet above the North Fork River; the visitors center provides telescopes for watching the precarious progress of rock climbers. Should you be tempted by the heights, contact the *Seneca Rocks Climbing School* (tel. 304/567–2600), *Seneca Rocks and Transmontane Outfitters* in Davis (tel. 304/259–5117), or the *Seneca School of Survival Arts* (tel. 304/567–2624).

Snowshoe (tel. 304/572–522). This is considered the most challenging ski facility in West Virginia, with 33 trails, a 1,500-foot drop, and full snowmaking capability.

Watoga State Park (tel. 800/225–5982). Seventeen miles south of Marlinton, this is West Virginia's first and largest state park, bordered by the beautiful Greenbrier River. Recreational facilities, including a pool, cabins, commissary, lake, and lookout tower, are open in the summertime.

Tourist Information

Lewisburg Convention and Visitors Bureau (105 Church St., Lewisburg 24901, tel. 304/645–1000). **Pocahontas County Tourism** (Box 275, Marlinton 24954, tel. 304/799–4636). **Pocahontas Highlands Convention and Visitors Bureau** (Box 1459, Elkins 26241, tel. 304/636–8400). **West Virginia Department of Commerce** (2101 Washington St., E, Charleston 24305, tel. 800/225–5982).

Reservation Services

Martindale B&B Reservation Service (Box 1308, Lewisburg 24901, tel. 304/647–4777).

Cheat Mountain Club

Standing 3,800 feet above sea level, on the shoulder of the colossal Cheat Mountain and surrounded by nine of West Virginia's 10 highest precipices and the 70,000-acre Monongahela National Forest, the Cheat Mountain Club has a setting that will always be enough to make it special among inns. Lovers of the outdoors are sure to appreciate the changing seasons here, whether the lodge is buried in snow, blanketed with wild rhododendrons, or enveloped in a fog so thick that no one bothers to step outside the front door. The grounds include 180 acres, across which the trout-rich Shavers Fork River flows. From it a tracery of old logging roads spirals away into the mountains—one route leading 18 miles south to Bald Knob. Five miles of trails within the club's boundaries, along which shy black bears are often spied, are groomed for hiking, mountain biking, and cross-country skiing.

Until 1988 this Elysium was privately owned, used as a retreat for the executives of a logging company. Later it was sold to a group of five West Virginia families, who brought in resident managers Deb and Norm Strouse, and opened it to the public. Norm is a graduate of the Forestry School of West Virginia, a latter-day mountain man who knows everything there is to know about the area. Deb is a trained hotelier who cooks and serves the three excellent meals included in the club's daily rate.

The pine-paneled guest rooms on the lodge's second floor are functionally decorated and immaculately kept. Only one has a private bath, but the large, multiple shared bathrooms (one for women, another for men) are extremely comfortable and outfitted with tubs, showers, and piles of fresh linen; there's also a sink in each guest room. The third floor holds a dormitory-style room. Downstairs is a gigantic gathering hall, and there is almost always a crackling fire in the stone hearth. The room is full of topo maps, magazines, and books, and is a meeting place where guests enjoy predinner drinks.

Address: *Box 28, Durbin, WV 26264, tel. 304/456-4627.*
Accommodations: *1 double room with bath; 7 doubles, 1 single, and dormitory (sleeps 6) share 2 multiple baths.*
Amenities: *Box lunches available; fishing, mountain biking, cross-country skiing, canoeing, horseshoes, 2 meeting rooms.*
Rates: *$118–$198; full breakfast, lunch, and dinner and use of recreational gear. No credit cards.*
Restrictions: *No smoking in bedrooms, no pets in lodge, 2-night minimum on weekends, closed Christmas Day.*

The General Lewis Inn

This is a country hostel of perfect proportions (just 25 rooms), run by the Hock family since 1928. It lies in a shady residential section of Lewisburg, a National Register town with a historic academy, stone church, and Confederate cemetery. Down the street from the inn are pleasant shops selling West Virginia quilts, ladies' dresses, and antiques. You can see everything Lewisburg has to offer in an easy afternoon, leaving you lots of time to sit on the veranda at the General Lewis. Out front there's a restored stagecoach, which used to rumble over the James River and Kanawha Turnpike (now Route 60), and in the back garden is owner Mary Hock Morgan's large old dollhouse.

Mary's parents started the General Lewis in the original house, built in the early 1800s; the architect who designed the West Virginia governor's mansion in Charleston later supervised an addition to the building, which blends flawlessly with the older section. The Hocks were great antiques collectors, and the inn is full of their prizes, including farming implements and a nickelodeon that still plays "The Man in the Moon Has His Eyes on You." The front desk came from the Sweet Chalybeate Springs Hotel, and was reputedly leaned on by Patrick Henry and Thomas Jefferson. In fact, the only nonantiques you'll come across are the chairs in the dining room.

Though the inn is ably managed by young Rodney Fisher, Mary Hock Morgan is usually around to show children where to find the checkers. She lived in the General Lewis until the age of 15 and is dedicated to keeping it retrogressive. Rodney is trying to talk her into putting in newfangled contraptions such as touch-tone phones, and he may just succeed. But Mary won't let him refinish the furniture; she wants guests to see where generations of hands have rubbed and polished the cannonball beds.

All the rooms on the first and second floors are different, and when unoccupied, the doors are left open so that guests can nose around. The favorites are in the old section and include Rooms 208 (the master bedroom), 206, and 202 (a two-bedroom suite). Because the same rate can apply to rooms of radically varying size, guests might want to ask for the largest in any given category. But even if you wind up in a cozy chamber, you won't be disappointed.

Address: *301 E. Washington St., Lewisburg, WV 24901, tel. 304/645–2600.*
Accommodations: *23 double rooms with baths, 2 suites.*
Amenities: *Restaurant, room service during restaurant hours, air-conditioning, cable TV, phones in rooms.*
Rates: *$55–$80. AE, MC, V.*
Restrictions: *Pets $5 charge.*

The Cardinal Inn

Eunice Kwasniewski has single-handedly worked miracles at this inn, a yellow-brick Queen Anne Victorian overlooking the Tygart River Valley. She restored this cavernous place all by herself (it took a full year and 438 gallons of stripper to remove the paint from the oak woodwork, claims Eunice) and runs it solo as well, cooking lunches and dinners for groups by arrangement, tending an herb garden, and cleaning the nine guest rooms. As if that weren't enough, she still intends to restore a 19th-century log cabin out back. The turreted main house was built by Elihu Hutton in 1901 and is surrounded by a big white wraparound porch, providing views of the valley and the Cheat Mountain range beyond. Two of the most desirable guest rooms are the five-window Paisley Room and the rather eerie third-floor Turret Room, complete with a mounted deer head. The inn is 25 miles north of Snowshoe, making it perfect for those who love to ski but don't care for the resort's condo-style accommodations.

Address: *Rte. 1, Box 1–Rte. 219, Huttonsville, WV 26273, tel. 304/335–6149.*
Accommodations: *9 double rooms share 3 baths.*
Amenities: *TV with VCR in sitting room, phones on each floor. MC, V.*
Rates: *$35–$40; full breakfast.*
Restrictions: *No smoking, no pets.*

The Current

The Current, a 1904 white frame farmhouse with only a modest touch of gingerbread, is found along a winding country lane outside the town of Hillsboro, once the home of writer Pearl Buck (and site of a fine eatery called the Rosewood Café). To reach the house you'll have to pass fields inhabited by buffalo, peacocks, and llamas (part of a rich weekend farmer's private zoo), the huge Denmar State Hospital, and a one-room Presbyterian Church. The bed-and-breakfast is owned by Leslee McCarty, who came to this part of her home state to work in rural community development and married a farmer while she was here. Her house is full of oak woodwork, quilts, Victorian clothing, and airy white curtains. Its only drawback is the lack of baths; there are just two on the first floor serving all four bedrooms upstairs. Still, Leslee's guests don't seem to mind much—most of them arrive on foot or bike from the nearby Greenbrier River Trail and are quite satisfied with a soak in the hot tub and a quiet afternoon snooze on the porch.

Address: *Box 135, Hillsboro, WV 24946, tel. 304/653–4722.*
Accommodations: *4 double rooms share 2 baths.*
Amenities: *TV in sitting room, hot tub.*
Rates: *$45; full breakfast. MC, V.*
Restrictions: *No smoking.*

Hampshire House 1884

Route 50, the main route across the state in the north, passes through the town of Romney at the South Branch of the Potomac River. Here you'll find Hampshire House, a perfectly kept red-brick Victorian, on a street behind the courthouse. The house and its garden are owned by Scott Simmons and his wife, Jane, who manage the property with the help of three local women, Delcie Patterson and her daughters. Though the dining room is only occasionally open to guests, breakfast is always included in the room rate—and a substantial breakfast it is, including steak and eggs.

Scott is a collector of antique lamps, which occupy tables all over the inn. The four guest rooms are lovely, decorated almost exclusively with Victo-

rian antiques, including Eastlake beds, Rococo Revival chairs and settees, and quilts. In addition to the formal parlor downstairs, you'll also find a kitchenette, laundry facilities, and a big music room with a wide-screen TV and piano.

Address: *165 N. Grafton St., Romney, WV 26757, tel. 304/822-7171.*
Accommodations: *4 double rooms with baths.*
Amenities: *Air-conditioning, TV with VCR in music room.*
Rates: *$60–$65; full breakfast. AE, DC, MC, V.*
Restrictions: *No smoking, no pets.*

The Inn at Elk River

Also known as the Willis Farm, this lodging complex, sitting on the banks of the Elk River, is also an outdoor recreation center. Owner Gil Willis came to the area in 1977 for the downhill skiing; today he outfits Nordic skiing expeditions on a 50-kilometer trail system, guides spelunkers into some of the 1,000 wild caves in the area, and has organized a self-directed Greenbrier River Trail trip, with lodgings in bed-and-breakfasts along the way. The 100-year-old sheep farm now offers five guest rooms in the old farmhouse, a two-bedroom cottage, and a new lodge holding five more guest rooms, a restaurant, and a store. The lodge is best for couples, since all its hardwood-lined rooms have private baths. But the old farmhouse, with its many-bedded

rooms, common space with woodburning stove, and hot tub, is perfect for families and groups. You wouldn't call any of the accommodations luxurious (though they do sport auction- and flea-market-quality antiques), but that doesn't matter: At Elk River no one spends much time indoors.

Address: *Elk River Touring Center, Slatyfork, WV 26291, tel. 304/572-3771.*
Accommodations: *5 double rooms with baths, 5 suites share 3 baths, 2-bedroom cottage.*
Amenities: *Restaurant, hot tub; swimming hole, Nordic ski trails.*
Rates: *$30–$90; full breakfast. MC, V.*
Restrictions: *No pets, 2-night minimum on weekends in ski season.*

James Wylie House

The James Wylie House may not be the biggest or poshest lodgings in White Sulphur Springs, but it is the only true bed-and-breakfast in this resort town. On the National Register, this historic house was built in 1819 by a local surveyor whose 1794 log cabin still stands out back. The main house was Victorianized at a later date, giving it its single-gable brick facade and broad, white front porch. The lawn stretches down to Route 60, just south of the business district. On the second floor are three high-ceiling bedrooms decorated in country style by owners Cheryl and Joe Griffith. Up on the third floor is a special two-bedroom suite, with green floors and woodwork, lots of windows, and exposed wood beams. The Wylie House is a convenient headquarters for excursions into the mountains to the north or to the wet and wild New River, about an hour's drive west.

Address: *208 E. Main St., White Sulphur Springs, WV 24986, tel. 304/536-9444.*
Accommodations: *3 double rooms with baths, 1 suite.*
Amenities: *Air-conditioning on 3rd floor, TV in rooms.*
Rates: *$55; breakfast. MC, V.*
Restrictions: *No smoking, no pets.*

Lynn's Inn

This 50-year-old white-columned farmhouse, on 16 acres just north of the Lewisburg town line, has a long history as an inn. Owner Richard McLaughlin is no stranger to innkeeping either; his parents ran McLaughlin's Tourist Home in this house for many years, while he was growing up. A fire two years ago resulted in extensive renovation, and today the comfortable white frame house is open once again. There are four guest rooms on the first and second floors, upstairs and downstairs sitting rooms, and a peaceful front porch from which you can see the McLaughlins' Hereford and Angus cows and watch Lynn McLaughlin gathering eggs. The guest rooms feature many pleasant touches, including locally handmade quilts, Fenton glass lamps, white wicker and golden oak furniture, walnut bedsteads that have been in the family for years, and rocking chairs, which Lynn feels are important to have in every room. Her breakfasts include those fresh eggs, homemade jellies and jams, and country ham.

Address: *Rte. 4, Box 40, Lewisburg, WV 24901, tel. 304/645-2003.*
Accommodations: *4 double rooms with baths.*
Amenities: *Ceiling fans in rooms, cable TV and phones in the two sitting rooms.*
Rates: *$40-$50; full breakfast. No credit cards.*
Restrictions: *No smoking, no pets.*

The Wayside Inn

For five weeks every July and August the town of Elkins hosts the popular Augusta Festival, at which visitors can sign up for courses in blacksmithing, Appalachian literature, autoharp playing, weaving, herb gardening, and loghouse construction, among other topics. For accommodations while visiting the festival there's no better place than the Wayside Inn, which sits close to the grounds of the local college, where the festival takes place. The white Queen Anne cottage was built in 1886 and is presently operated by two families: Linda Barry and her daughter and Brooke Rodgers and her two girls. Though the house is not in peak condition, it wears its years reasonably well, with the help of glowing stained glass, an intricately detailed terra-cotta fire-place, and a grand old front porch. There are four guest bedrooms in all (two with private baths), a sun porch, two parlors, and a formal dining room.

Across the street there's an inviting park with a playground and picnic tables. The college has tennis courts, and downtown the Starr Café and Augusta Books are good idling spots.

Address: *318 Buffalo St., Elkins, WV 26241, tel. 304/636–1618.*
Accommodations: *2 double rooms with baths, 2 doubles share a bath.*
Rates: *$45; full breakfast. AE, DC, MC, V.*
Restrictions: *No smoking, no pets.*

Directory 1:
Alphabetical

Directory 2:
Geographical

Delaware

Bethany Beach
The Addy Sea *169*
Laurel
Spring Garden Bed &
Breakfast Inn *168*
Lewes
The Inn at Canal
Square *167*
The New Devon Inn
170
Milford
The Towers *161*
New Castle
The David Finney Inn
163
The Janvier-Black
House *160*
Odessa
Cantwell House *162*
Rehoboth Beach
The Corner Cupboard
Inn *169*
Lord and Hamilton
Seaside Inn *170*
The Pleasant Inn *171*
Wilmington
The Boulevard Bed &
Breakfast *162*
The Christina House
163

Maryland

Annapolis
Gibson's Lodgings *191*
Prince George Inn *192*
Shaw's Fancy *193*
State House Inn *189*
The William Page Inn
190
Baltimore
The Admiral Fell Inn
202

Berlin
The Atlantic Hotel *202*
Buckeystown
The Inn at
Buckeystown *199*
Cambridge
Glasgow Inn *182*
Chestertown
Brampton *178*
The Inn at Mitchell
House *182*
The White Swan
Tavern *184*
Easton
John S. McDaniel
House *183*
Frederick
Spring Bank *198*
The Turning Point *201*
Havre de Grace
Vandiver Inn *204*
Middletown
The Marameade *199*
New Market
The National Pike *200*
The Strawberry Inn
200
Ocean City
The Lighthouse Club
at Fager's Island
203
Oxford
The Robert Morris Inn
180
St. Michael's
The Inn at Perry
Cabin *179*
Victoriana *184*
Wades Point Inn *181*
Scotland
St. Michael's Manor
192
Sharpsburg
The Inn at Antietam
197

Snow Hill
Chanceford Hall *203*
Solomons
Back Creek Inn *191*
Tall Timbers
Potomac View Farm
188
Vienna
The Tavern Inn *183*

New Jersey

Atlantic City
Inn at the Ocean *128*
Avon-by-the-Sea
Cashelmara Inn *125*
Bay Head
Conover's Bay Head
Inn *126*
Beach Haven
Bayberry Barque *124*
Pierrot by the Sea *122*
Victoria Guest House
130
Belmar
The Seaflower *129*
Cape May
The Abbey *144*
Barnard Good House
147
Captain Mey's Inn *147*
The Carroll Villa *148*
The Chalfonte *145*
Colvmns by the Sea
148
Holly House *149*
The Mainstay Inn and
Cottage *146*
The Manor House *149*
The Queen Victoria
150
Springside *150*
The Victorian Rose
151
The Virginia Hotel *151*

Milford
Cliff Park Inn *66*
Mount Joy
The Cameron Estate
   Inn *98*
Narvon
Churchtown Inn *94*
New Hope
Inn at Phillips Mill *75*
The Logan Inn *80*
Pineapple Hill *81*
The Wedgwood Inn *76*
The Whitehall Inn *77*
Pomeroy
Stottsville Inn *90*
Scenery Hill
Century Inn *112*
Schwenksville
Highpoint Victoriana
   89
South Sterling
The French Manor *63*
Starlight
The Inn at Starlight
   Lake *65*
Strasburg
Limestone Inn *96*
Stroudsburg
The Inn at
   Meadowbrook *64*
Thornton
Pace One *90*
Unionville
The Whitethorne *87*
Upper Black Eddy
Bridgeton House *78*
West Chester
The Bankhouse Bed
   and Breakfast *88*

Virginia

Alexandria
The Morrison House
   218

Cape Charles
Nottingham Ridge *231*
Pickett's Harbor *228*
Sea Gate *231*
Charles City
Edgewood *238*
North Bend Plantation
   240
Charlottesville
Clifton *249*
The Inn at Monticello
   250
The Silver Thatch Inn
   251
200 South Street *252*
Woodstock Hall *253*
Chincoteague
The Channel Bass Inn
   227
Miss Molly's and the
   Little Traveller Inn
   230
The Year of the Horse
   234
Churchville
Buckhorn Inn *263*
Culpeper
Fountain Hall *217*
Fairfax
The Bailiwick Inn *216*
Flint Hill
Caledonia Farm *217*
Fredericksburg
The Richard Johnston
   Inn *220*
Gordonsville
Sleepy Hollow Farm
   252
Harrisonburg
Joshua Wilton House
   265
Leesburg
The Norris House *219*
Lexington
Fassifern *264*

Middleburg
The Red Fox Inn *220*
Welbourne *223*
Millboro
Fort Lewis Lodge *267*
Millwood
Brookside *216*
Nellysford
Trillium House *262*
New Church
The Garden and the
   Sea *230*
Onancock
Colonial Manor Inn
   229
Orange
Mayhurst *250*
The Shadows *251*
Willow Grove
   Plantation *253*
Paris
The Ashby Inn *213*
Raphine
Oak Spring Farm and
   Vineyard *266*
Rawley Springs
Boxwood *260*
Scottsville
Chester *249*
High Meadows *247*
Sperryville
The Conyers House
   214
Stanley
Jordan Hollow Farm
   261
Staunton
Belle Grae Inn *263*
Thornrose House *266*
Strasburg
Hotel Strasburg *264*
Trevilians
Prospect Hill *248*
Wachapreague
The Burton House *229*

Please help us evaluate B&Bs and country inns for the next edition of this guide. Mail your response to Fodor's Travel Publications, Inc., 201 E. 50th St., New York, NY 10022.

B&B or Inn

City/State

Comments

B&B or Inn

City/state

Comments

General Comments

Your Name *(Optional)*

Number/Street

City/State/Zip

Fodor's Travel Guides

U.S. Guides

Alaska
Arizona
Boston
California
Cape Cod, Martha's
 Vineyard, Nantucket
The Carolinas & the
 Georgia Coast
The Chesapeake
 Region
Chicago
Colorado
Disney World & the
 Orlando Area
Florida
Hawaii

Las Vegas, Reno,
 Tahoe
Los Angeles
Maine, Vermont,
 New Hampshire
Maui
Miami & the
 Keys
National Parks
 of the West
New England
New Mexico
New Orleans
New York City
New York City
 (Pocket Guide)

Pacific North Coast
Philadelphia & the
 Pennsylvania
 Dutch Country
Puerto Rico
 (Pocket Guide)
The Rockies
San Diego
San Francisco
San Francisco
 (Pocket Guide)
The South
Santa Fe, Taos,
 Albuquerque
Seattle &
 Vancouver

Texas
USA
The U. S. & British
 Virgin Islands
The Upper Great
 Lakes Region
Vacations in
 New York State
Vacations on the
 Jersey Shore
Virginia & Maryland
Waikiki
Washington, D.C.
Washington, D.C.
 (Pocket Guide)

Foreign Guides

Acapulco
Amsterdam
Australia
Austria
The Bahamas
The Bahamas
 (Pocket Guide)
Baja & Mexico's Pacific
 Coast Resorts
Barbados
Barcelona, Madrid,
 Seville
Belgium &
 Luxembourg
Berlin
Bermuda
Brazil
Budapest
Budget Europe
Canada
Canada's Atlantic
 Provinces

Cancun, Cozumel,
 Yucatan Peninsula
Caribbean
Central America
China
Czechoslovakia
Eastern Europe
Egypt
Europe
Europe's Great Cities
France
Germany
Great Britain
Greece
The Himalayan
 Countries
Holland
Hong Kong
India
Ireland
Israel
Italy

Italy 's Great Cities
Jamaica
Japan
Kenya, Tanzania,
 Seychelles
Korea
London
London
 (Pocket Guide)
London Companion
Mexico
Mexico City
Montreal &
 Quebec City
Morocco
New Zealand
Norway
Nova Scotia,
 New Brunswick,
 Prince Edward
 Island
Paris

Paris (Pocket Guide)
Portugal
Rome
Scandinavia
Scandinavian Cities
Scotland
Singapore
South America
South Pacific
Southeast Asia
Soviet Union
Spain
Sweden
Switzerland
Sydney
Thailand
Tokyo
Toronto
Turkey
Vienna & the Danube
 Valley
Yugoslavia

Wall Street Journal Guides to Business Travel

Europe

International Cities

Pacific Rim

USA & Canada

Special-Interest Guides

Bed & Breakfast and
 Country Inn Guides:
Mid-Atlantic Region
 England
 outh
 'est

Cruises and Ports
 of Call
Healthy Escapes
Fodor's Flashmaps
 New York

Fodor's Flashmaps
 Washington, D.C.
Shopping in Europe
Skiing in the USA &
 Canada

Smart Shopper's
 Guide to London
Sunday in New York
Touring Europe
Touring USA